Essentials of Pentecostal Theology

Essentials of Pentecostal Theology

An Eternal and Unchanging Lord
Powerfully Present & Active by the Holy Spirit

TONY RICHIE

foreword by Steven Jack Land

RESOURCE *Publications* · Eugene, Oregon

ESSENTIALS OF PENTECOSTAL THEOLOGY
An Eternal and Unchanging Lord Powerfully Present & Active by the Holy Spirit

Copyright © 2020 Tony Richie. All rights reserved. Except for brief quotations in critical publications or reviews, no part of this book may be reproduced in any manner without prior written permission from the publisher. Write: Permissions, Wipf and Stock Publishers, 199 W. 8th Ave., Suite 3, Eugene, OR 97401.

Resource Publications
An Imprint of Wipf and Stock Publishers
199 W. 8th Ave., Suite 3
Eugene, OR 97401

www.wipfandstock.com

PAPERBACK ISBN: 978-1-5326-3881-7
HARDCOVER ISBN: 978-1-5326-3882-4
EBOOK ISBN: 978-1-5326-3883-1

Manufactured in the U.S.A.   02/25/20

To
Carolyn Louise Richie
&
Carolyn Sue Richie
~ Astute Pentecostal "theologians" in their own right ~

It is our purpose to encourage both men and women, young and old; to undertake great things for God and expect great things from God.

—A. J. Tomlinson, "Preface," *The Last Great Conflict* (1913)

Contents

Foreword by Steven Jack Land		ix
Acknowledgements		xi
Introduction		1

Part One: Various Accents and Conflicts

1	Representative Perspectives	19
2	A Major Controversy over Sanctification	39
3	A Major Controversy over the Godhead	52

Part Two: A Description Not a Definition

4	An Unchanging Christ	69
5	Experiencing God's Presence in Worship	83
6	Experiencing God's Presence in Prayer	109
7	A Full Gospel Biblical and Classical Framework	132
8	A Full Gospel Theological and Pastoral Paradigm	147

Part Three: Crucial Commitments

9	The Doctrine of Subsequence	169
10	Purpose of Spirit Baptism	182
11	Examining Initial Evidence	197
12	Significance of Glossolalia	208
Bibliography		221

Foreword

I have known Tony Richie since he came to Pentecostal Theological Seminary (as it is now known) as a student pastor over thirty years ago. We continue at PTS now as colleagues, and at times as team-teachers in Pentecostal spirituality and theology. I have observed firsthand his passion for theology, a passion which I can best describe as "Pentecostal." So, I am especially pleased for an opportunity to speak here to the publication of the present volume. The richness of this important work is reflected in and grows out of the multidimensional character of its author. Husband, parent, grandparent, pastor, and educator—all these characteristics combine in this insightful and understandable resource for laity and pastors.

This volume arises from an orientation of various streams of thought resources which flow into modern Pentecostalism as well as an insistence that the roots of the movement are still to be respected. Dr. Richie is conversant with the various strands of the Pentecostal movement itself, with other Christian groups, and indeed with other world religions. Always before him is the people to be discipled into Christ and into the most powerful and extensive move of the Holy Spirit in history. This is a book for lay people, professional ministers, teachers, and for anyone wishing to be faithful to the original call of Christ which Pentecostals strive to represent.

In this regard you will learn why it is important to state carefully but forcefully the nature of an underlying Wesleyan-Pentecostal approach. This perspective represents the essential core of the movement. Indeed, the Pentecostal movement from the beginning showed its Wesleyan-Pentecostal roots. Concern for power upon the sanctified life combined to produce a militant missionary force and commitment to holiness of heart and life. In this way, Richie demonstrates the efficacy and integrity of Pentecostalism. Although aware of its faults and failures, he nevertheless sees the

FOREWORD

crucial nature of this theological and spiritual formulation for the future of the church in general and for Pentecostalism in particular.

If taken seriously, this book will become essential reading for all those who are interested in the heart and soul of the movement. You are going to enjoy reading this book! It is not a boring treatise but a call for continual renewal of the church for its increasingly important role in church and society. I recommend reading this book straight through and returning to those questions that emerge. We are privileged to have such a work from such a committed servant of the Lord!

Steven Jack Land
Pentecost 2019

Acknowledgements

I am beyond grateful to those who have sacrificially helped in the production of this manuscript. The following colleagues and friends have been helpful partners for reading and responding to all or parts of an earlier draft of this manuscript: Sandra Inman, Jackie David Johns, Lee Roy Martin, Dan Tomberlin (all from Pentecostal Theological Seminary); Coleman Bailey (Missions Pastor at Mercy Ridge Church, Rossville, GA), Jeff Brickle (Urshan Graduate School of Theology), Marcia Clarke (Fuller Theological Seminary), Bill Oliverio (SUM Bible College and Theological Seminary), Lisa Stephenson (Lee University School of Religion), Larry Sterling (Lead Pastor at Eastpointe, Florida Church of God), and Ben Wiles (Lee University/Pentecostal Theological Seminary). I am indescribably indebted to them for their comments and insights.

Further, Cheryl Bridges Johns (Pentecostal Theological Seminary) provided helpful verbal feedback in various conversations over the book as it developed. In addition to our numerous—and intense—conversations regarding the development of this manuscript, I am deeply grateful to Steven Jack Land (Pentecostal Theological Seminary) for writing the Preface to this volume. Of course, only I can own its obvious limitations.

Wipf and Stock has been a great publishing partner. I particularly appreciate the professional guidance—and patient encouragement—of Matthew Wimer. Without you, Matt, it would not have happened!

This book is dedicated to my mother, Carolyn Louise Richie, and my wife, Carolyn Sue Richie. Although neither of them received academic training as professional theologians, I consider both of them astute theologians in their own right. Without question my dad was the Bible authority in our home. However, it was often at my mom's knee that I felt free to wrestle openly with deeper issues of Christian doctrine as a Pentecostal believer. I will be ever grateful for her patience and understanding.

Sue profoundly loves God's Word and is naturally inquisitive about any and all of its theological implications and, most especially, practical applications. Her thinking is usually concrete, straightforward; and yet, it is precisely our conversations in this mode that often help uncover exquisite nuances of thought. I am ever grateful for her keen insight and quick wit which more often than not provide her with an uncanny ability to penetrate beyond the veil of professional theologians' standard assumptions.

Introduction

THE BOOK YOU NOW hold in your hand began with an odd feeling. Let me explain. Early in 2017 Klaus Vellguth, editor of *Theology of the One World*, requested I contribute an article for the series. He suggested the (English) title "The Essential Features of Pentecostal Theology."[1] I happily agreed. But as I went to work, I began to experience an unusual sensation that I could not quite place. After a while, it occurred to me that there was something oddly familiar about what I was writing although it was a completely new piece. Finally, I realized what was happening. In my efforts to "boil down" Pentecostal theology to its essential features I was reconnecting with the Pentecostal belief and practice in which I had been raised, in which I had begun my ministry, and which I still affirm as central to Pentecostal identity and ethos. Much of Pentecostal theology today is dedicated to developing complex implications of numerous nuances of the tradition. I agree that this is an important and needful process. Yet the fundamentals of the faith are critical not only to that process but to the practice of ministry. However, I was discovering that this "old time religion" has incredibly fresh and rich implications that I had not previously plumbed. It was then that I realized I had a book on my hands. I am pleased that Wipf and Stock agreed. The present volume is the result.

Hispanic theologian Justo González helps put the significance and scope of contemporary Pentecostalism into perspective. The following lengthy quote is worthy of inclusion.

> [One] of the most significant developments in the history of Christianity in the twentieth century was the Pentecostal movement. While in many ways Pentecostalism has almost become a new confessional family, its impact is seen

---

1. See Richie, "Grundzüge der Pfingsttheologie, 101–112, for the German language edition.

in every other Christian confession. Part of this impact is resulting in renewed attention to the doctrine of the Holy Spirit and to eschatology. Significantly, although many see a distance and even enmity between the Pentecostal awakening and the various theologies advocating social and political liberation, the two coincide in their emphasis on hope as central to the Christian faith. Thus, it would appear in the near future theology will be much concerned with eschatology, the doctrine of the Holy Spirit, and the relationship between the two.[2]

Since the Pentecostal movement is dramatically impacting Christianity and Christian theology, then it seems relevant to ask, "What is Pentecostalism?" More specifically, "What do Pentecostal Christians believe and practice?"

Simply put, Pentecostal Christians wholeheartedly believe in the possibility of receiving the same experience of the Holy Spirit today as did the disciples on the Day of Pentecost.

> When the Day of Pentecost had fully come, they were all with one accord in one place. And suddenly there came a sound from heaven, as of a rushing mighty wind, and it filled the whole house where they were sitting. Then there appeared to them divided tongues, as of fire, and *one* sat upon each of them. And they were all filled with the Holy Spirit and began to speak with other tongues, as the Spirit gave them utterance. (Acts 2:1–4)[3]

Pentecostals see the attendant phenomena of wind and fire in audible and visible forms as dramatic manifestations symbolic of the Holy Spirit which are not normatively repeatable on an individual level. However, Pentecostals consider the personal infilling with the Spirit and Spirit-inspired speech consisting of unlearned languages, or speaking in tongues, paradigmatic for Christians and for the church then and now.

Traditional Pentecostal interpretation of Acts 2:1–4, and of Scripture in general, is driven by a rather straightforward, literal approach to the Bible. Hermeneutics (discipline of biblical interpretation) has recently become a topic of major interest for Pentecostal theologians.[4] Probably most Pentecostals prefer uniting a high view of Scripture (verbal inspiration) and its authority with spiritual discernment and spiritual experience. Along with inspiration by the Holy Spirit of the biblical text itself, Pentecostal communities emphasize the Spirit's illumination, or continuing guidance in interpreting and understanding the truths of the Bible.

---

2. González, *Christian History*, 348.

3. Unless otherwise noted, Scripture quotes in this volume are from the New King James Version (NKJV) (Nashville, TN: Thomas Nelson, 1982).

4. Representative hermeneutical works include Fee, *Gospel and Spirit*; Yong, *Spirit, Word, Community* and *The Hermeneutical Spirit*; Archer, *A Pentecostal Hermeneutic*; Martin, *Biblical Hermeneutics* and *Pentecostal Hermeneutics*; Oliverio, *Theological Hermeneutics in the Classical Pentecostal Tradition*; and Keener, *Spirit Hermeneutics*.

Introduction

A basic Pentecostal hermeneutic can be (and has been) described as a "This is that!" hermeneutic.[5] Appropriately enough, taking their cue from Peter's Pentecost Day sermon (Acts 2:16; KJV), Pentecostals discern a rather direct correspondence between life and Scripture. Clarity is discovered for the life of faith in a straightforward reading of Scripture. While subtler nuances, for example, appreciation for the various literary genres employed in Scripture, is becoming more common, the general approach remains relatively consistent. In spite of some tendency toward naiveté it has served well. Under fire for a simplistic hermeneutic, a Pentecostal might well retort, "At least 'this is that' is better than 'that was then'!" Of course, all Pentecostal hermeneutics share aversion for hypercritical (hypocritical?) approaches which relegate so much of the Bible's message to a bygone era. Pentecostals believe it is essential to maintain the "dynamic and transforming capacity" of God's Word (Heb 4:12).[6] The present volume affirms a high view of Scripture as divine revelation and, consequently, its preeminent importance for the task of doing theology.[7]

Pentecostalism is dramatically diverse. There is no monolithic definition of Pentecostal identity broad enough to encompass all adherents.[8] Even within the same Pentecostal denomination a great deal of diversity frequently exists, if not in doctrine at least in applications thereof. For example, Lance Colkmire, editor of the *Church of God Evangel*, notes that he has encountered several different ways his own denomination practices water baptism in various international settings.[9] In some places children cannot be baptized in water before going through a confirmation process but in others children are ineligible to be baptized at all. Nevertheless, in many places there are no age restrictions for recipients of water baptism other than being mature enough to make a personal confession of faith. In other places all baptismal candidates must wear white robes during the rite's performance but in others there is no prescribed dress other than what is practical for the setting of the rite itself. None of this diversity is a problem in the Church of God so long as its basic commitment to the mode of water baptism (Trinitarian, immersion) and the obligation of all who repent (converts)

---

5. Although Yong admits in his Preface to *Pentecostal Theology and N. T. Wright*, that a "this is that" hermeneutic may run the risk of collapsing the horizons of Scripture and the present, he nevertheless argues that it serves well to testify that "what happened back then continues to happen today," xiii.

6. Martin, *Pentecostal Hermeneutics*, viii. Rickie Moore's academic testimony, "Deuteronomy and the Fire of God," 110–20, exemplifies the ill effects of harshly imposing historical critical hermeneutical paradigms upon Pentecostals.

7. Most Pentecostals theologically embrace the Protestant principle of *Sola Scriptura* (Scripture alone). However, functionally they operate (arguably) more in terms of *Prima Scriptura* (Scripture primarily). Pentecostals clearly affirm Scripture as the inspired and authoritative Word of God. Yet the traditional distinction is not really phrased well for Pentecostals since they do not sharply segregate the Spirit's scriptural inspiration from the Spirit's scriptural illumination.

8. Harold Hunter, *Spirit Baptism*, 15. Nichols, *The Pentecostals*, asserts that beyond a few basic agreements on Spirit baptism, speaking in tongues and spiritual gifts, and divine healing, many "Pentecostals are *not* alike," 17 (original italics).

9. Colkmire, "Young, Significant, Diverse, and Needy," 7.

to be baptized are scripturally observed. For our purposes, this is an instance of a commonly encountered "flexibility with boundaries," as I call it, extending into many areas of Pentecostal beliefs and practices.

Before going any farther with diversity, it may be necessary to express my strong commitment to discerning doctrine. Justo González is certainly correct to maintain that not all doctrines are equally valid.[10] Accordingly, it behooves believers to exercise sound judgment about the teaching they absorb and/or espouse. Yet, as González further explains, "Doctrines are human words with which the church seeks to bear witness to the Word of God."[11] I am firmly convinced that we must never equate (or confuse) our human words about God with God's Word itself. Some theologians remind me of Aaron's lame claim that the Israelites' gave him gold, he "cast it into the fire, and this calf came out" (Ex 32:24). Doctrines do not appear out of nowhere. Neither are they worthy of worship. Established doctrines are "forged through long years of theological reflection, from established practices of worship, within the context of spirituality, in opposition to opinions that seem to attack the very center of faith, and even as a result of political intrigues."[12] This painstaking process of discerning development has, for the most part, served Christian theology well. Hopefully, it can also teach theologians a measure of humility and respect for diversity.[13]

Nevertheless, I intend no dilution of doctrine within the pages of this volume. I wholeheartedly agree with Presbyterian thinker Diogenes Allen that Christian doctrine is important because it is true.[14] Christian doctrine is not judged by an assessment of its pragmatic usefulness or practical utility. Whether we find a doctrine comforting or discomfiting is not the issue. Truth is at stake. Yet I suspect that my methodology will be disconcerting to some, perhaps especially to fellow theologians. Theologians prefer their doctrinal "packages" neatly wrapped and precisely labeled. But Pentecostal theology can be a bit raw and messy at times. I try to bear in mind that "A theologian's vocation is to understand the self-revelation of God so that it casts light on all areas of thought and life, including those matters that challenge the vocation itself."[15] Accordingly, I will consider a level of angst among theological colleagues a not (necessarily) unhealthy response.

To return to diversity. Pentecostal diversity may be attributable to numerous factors. Historical roots and geographical settings, denominational emphases, exceptional leadership influences, and racial and gender identities, as well as numerous other

---

10. González, *Christian Thought*, viii.
11. González, *Christian Thought*, viii.
12. González, *Christian Thought*, viii.
13. Carly Simon's 1971 pop song "You're So Vain" could have been written about some theologians. See Carly Simon, *Boys in the Trees: A Memoir* (NY: Flatiron Books, 2015), 254.
14. Allen, *Spiritual Theology*, 159.
15. Allen, *Spiritual Theology*, 158.

Introduction

factors, have all contributed to today's diverse constituencies.[16] As shall be shown, theological differences exist also. But—although it does not "dodge" or "duck" real disagreements—this book is more about similarities than differences. Deep affinities are especially evident across the spectrum of grassroots Pentecostal theology.[17] Here a broad range of varied but related ideas tend to overlap. These commonly shared commitments exhibit features formed by identifiable continuities. Accordingly, at a certain level I think of this volume as a kind of grassroots Pentecostal theology.[18]

A phenomenological (i.e. how it appears in experience) way of describing Pentecostalism would perhaps identify it as an expression of popular religion.[19] Popular religion may be defined both by a negation (not necessarily a negative) and by an affirmation. In the former vein, popular religion does not focus on the abstract, conceptual, dogmatic side of religion. In the latter vein, popular religion does focus on the lived faith of people—their relationship with God, their faith community, family, and on their real needs—in more direct fashion.[20] Popular religion tends to be holistic and practical with an integration of everyday life and spirituality. It is driven by eschatology both in the sense of personal destiny and in its passion for ecclesial mission. These core commitments appear amazingly apt for Pentecostal movements.

---

16. Deiros and Wilson, "Hispanic Pentecostalism," describe the movement as "obviously heterogeneous and versatile" with Latin American Pentecostalism, for example, exhibiting an amalgamation of individual with communal experiences, cultural preferences and generic similarities with distinguishable varieties, and economic challenges with deep and rich spiritual resources, 294. Warrington, *Pentecostal Theology*, 1–4, also mentions the wide range of "antecedents and influences" on Pentecostalism. He is correct, as are Deiros and Wilson. However, many contemporary Christian movements can point to diverse background dynamics. What makes Pentecostalism so unique is its creative incorporation and application of diverse streams that feed into it and then its addition of its own quite distinctive content to the pool.

17. For me, "grassroots" describes theology that a common, ordinary Pentecostal believer and pastor can recognize and relate to (and, hopefully, own and embrace) rather than theology intended for an elite audience. From a sociological perspective, Cartledge, *Mediation of the Spirit*, 25–27, refers to "the ordinary theology" of believers and congregations. Chan's *Grassroots Asian Theology* highlights this lived faith aspect of Pentecostalism, e.g., 33, 40–41, and 61. As with any specialized discipline, theology has concepts and terms that can be challenging for lay persons. Nevertheless, efforts to stay in touch with the general Pentecostal movement and the trajectory of its basic beliefs and practices should be apparent throughout this volume.

18. Accordingly, readers will notice a wider range of resources than usual utilized herein, including not only biblical, historical, and theological works but also popular and general church level materials as well.

19. Parker, "Popular Religion," 679–83. The "folk religion" category can be a mixed bag. Pentecostals can affirm a "split-level" contrast between formal (official, institutional) and folk (informal, populist) religion; but, any associations with superstition or syncretism is anathema to Pentecostals. See Shaw, "Folk Religion," 326–28. Much depends on whether one regards folk religion experiences as parallels to Pentecostal experiences or as carryovers from traditional religions, Kärkkäinen, *Holy Spirit and Salvation*, 408–09.

20. Please notice that we are discussing *focus*. Obviously, both the conceptual and practical are essential. Pentecostals would not be the first Christians (or others) to wrestle with appropriate balance between the two. Later I will argue that Pentecostals do not always accept, much less employ, such Aristotelian categories.

Accordingly, whether we call it "grassroots theology" or "popular religion" the present volume strives to stay in touch with the pastor in the pulpit and the people in his or her pews while aiming no less at maintaining a valid level of academic credibility and intellectual coherence. I am reminded of a frequent statement by my former professor and now colleague and friend, Steve Land, that having pastors who are theologians is not a bad thing (more on this topic below).

Here might be an appropriate place to mention yet another phenomenon of contemporary Pentecostalism: its' not-so-subtle influence beyond itself. For example, many officially non-Pentecostal congregations increasingly incorporate Pentecostal worship into their services to an extent that they are aptly described as having been "Pentecostalized."[21] A well-known Anglican theologian, Tom Wright, who does not self-identify as "Pentecostal" per se, nevertheless talks freely about his Pentecostal-type encounters, including frequently praying in tongues.[22] While this volume endeavors to address Pentecostals it understands that the label can be a bit elastic at times. And it joyfully welcomes the reality that the experience of the Holy Spirit as on the Day of Pentecost is not restricted to sectarian boundaries.

David Barrett argues that what appears at first glance to be several different types of Pentecostals and others nevertheless constitutes a single renewal movement because "they share a single basic experience."[23] For all its diversity there exists an underlying, and unifying, spiritual theology among participants in the Pentecostal movement.[24] Further, there is a shared worldview among Pentecostals which has been well described as God-centered, systematic or unified, and trans-rational.[25] True enough, only in recent decades have Pentecostals begun to intentionally develop and cogently articulate anything like sophisticated theological formulations for their movement. Nevertheless, the profundity of the basic theological categories of early Pentecostals should not be overlooked or underestimated. Likely all Pentecostals would agree that the biblical book of Acts in some sense provides a model for Christian life and service today, that Spirit baptism is a gracious empowerment subsequent to (or following) conversion promised to every believer, and that speaking in tongues (glossolalia) is

21. See Armstrong, "Embrace Your Inner Pentecostal." In all fairness, there is often cross fertilization between Pentecostals and others, particularly Evangelicals, and then combined impact on global Christianity. Thus Yong, *Future of Evangelical Theology*, describes the "evangelicalization" and "pentecostalization" of Pentecostals and Evangelicals, 43, 125.

22. Wright, "The Word and the Wind," 143–44. According to Synan, "Streams of Renewal," an ongoing "Evangelicalization/Pentecostalization" back and forth has both negative and positive consequences: on one hand, Pentecostals are in danger of compromising their original theology; on the other, charismatic worship is becoming more acceptable among Evangelicals, 350–51.

23. Barrett, Worldwide Holy Spirit Renewal," 393.

24. Menzies, *Pentecost*, acknowledges the movement's increasing theological diversity yet argues against ideological and sociological minimizations of Pentecostalism's relatively clear and straightforward nature, 9–18.

25. Johns and Johns, "Life in the New Creation," 174. Cp. Jackie Johns, "Pentecostalism and the Postmodern Worldview," 92.

INTRODUCTION

somehow linked to the experience of Spirit baptism.[26] Ardently convinced of the immense potential of such fundamental theological agreement and its implications, I focus in this volume on these kinds of shared essentials (but not on *the* essentials as if my discussion is exhaustive).

The term "essentials" is particularly apropos—and pregnant, deriving from "essence." Generally speaking, essence signifies the basic nature of a thing, or more precisely, the quality or qualities which make it distinctive. More philosophically, essence is the property or set of properties which constitute an entity's fundamental identity and reality without which it ceases to be what it is. In short, the essence of an entity is that which is necessary to its authentic existence. Therefore, "essentials" of Pentecostal theology describes characteristic features necessarily congruent with its intrinsic nature.[27]

Colloquially, an "essential" feature can describe simplifying a discussion by avoiding (at least temporarily) advanced complexities unnecessary for addressing a specific purpose through focusing on its most fundamental meaning. Comparative simplification is also in mind in this volume. There are numerous wonderful works, some referenced herein, about the developmental maturation of Pentecostal theology. These address intricacies of, for a few examples, Christology or pneumatology or eschatology, and so on. I applaud, and sometimes participate, in these more complex endeavors.[28] However, explicit efforts to name the touchstones of original and authentic Pentecostal ethos are necessary as well.[29] Arguably, providing a model or standard by which to measure the movement's ongoing theological development requires apt attention to these essential features. Hence this study of theology, in so far as it is a human endeavor to know and understand God's self-revelation, has a specific focus.[30]

Although the concept of essentials may suggest something of a "bare bones" approach, we will not hesitate to investigate profound, and perhaps at times, provocative, inferences of fundamental Pentecostal belief. I suggest these "bones" may be best thought of in terms of anatomical skeletal imagery describing a framework supplying firm support for fleshing out the "body" of Pentecostal thought. Yet, to press the image a bit farther, a human skeleton has joints with attached ligaments that enable it to

---

26. Johns and Johns, "Life in the New Creation," 17. Glossolalia signifies speaking in languages unlearned by and/or unknown to the speakers as the Holy Spirit enables.

27. This text does not pretend to address the essentials of Christian theology in general. Similarly, early in his career Steve Land, "Pentecostal Spirituality," 481, 482, 484, 490, 493, began to explore the "inherent logic" or "inner logic" of Pentecostalism.

28. E.g., I have a chapter (#10) in Wariboko and Yong, *Paul Tillich and Pentecostal Theology*. For an individual treatment in monograph form of a particularly difficult developing discipline, see Richie, *Toward a Pentecostal Theology of Religions* or Richie, *Speaking by the Spirit*.

29. A joint effort representing this line of theology would be Howard and Richie, *Pentecostal Explorations of Holiness Today*.

30. Higgins, et al, *Introduction to Theology*, 1–2.

bend and move in carrying out its activities. Accordingly, intellectual inflexibility, that is, dogmatic rigidity, is counterproductive to fertile theological endeavor.

Perhaps at this point readers may ponder the association of our anatomical analogy with the New Testament (NT) metaphor of Paul (Eph 4:6; Col 2:19). There unity and diversity within the body are correlated to a radical dynamic of corporate growth in love which has Christ as both its source and goal.[31] In a word, Pentecostal theology recognizes that vital relationship with Jesus Christ forms the basis of all valid spiritual blessings in Christ.[32] Pentecostal theology affirms that everything authentically "Christian" begins and ends with Jesus Christ, the Alpha and Omega of Christian existence, identity, and understanding (Rev 1:8; 21:6; 22:13).

Yet without the enabling power of the Holy Spirit all our framework and structure are mere "dead, dry bones" (Ezek 37:1–14).[33] The Spirit empowers the dead, dry bones, giving them life and animation, imparting vitality and nourishing health. This pneumatological animating principle is applicable for nations, for churches, and for individuals. For Pentecostal theology the all-too-often dead, dry bones of all-too-much of what passes for Christianity—overly institutionalized and dogmatized but under-energized—can amazingly, and miraculously, receive potential, and even actual, resurrection life and vitality through an impartation of the Holy Spirit (cp. Gen 50:25; Josh 24:32; Heb 11:22; 2 Kgs 13:20–21). Like an ancient Jewish narrator, Pentecostals "confirmed the query of Ezekiel, 'Shall these dry bones live?'" (4 Macc 18:17 NRSV)[34] Pentecostals believe they are part of a "last days" revival sent by the Lord to restore his people, win a world of lost sinners, and prepare for the eschaton in the life-giving, life-changing power of the Holy Spirit.[35]

And yet, for Pentecostals, all resurrection power is inseparable from the dying and rising again of the one whose bones were not broken (John 19:36). The Bride of Jesus Christ, which is his Body, bone of his bone and flesh of his flesh (Eph 5:30), is enlivened and energized by the Holy Spirit. Thus, for Pentecostals there is no contradiction—and certainly no competition—between Christology and pneumatology. Jesus Christ is our Savior and the Holy Spirit is our Helper—all part of God's great redemption plan (Eph 1:3–14). Like the seamless robe which covered the body of the betrayed and beaten Lord, it is all woven together as one (John 19:23). Those

---

31. O'Brien, *Ephesians*, 313.

32. Melick, *Philippians, Colossians, Philemon*, 273.

33. Cooper, *Ezekiel*, 325.

34. After deciding to use this descriptive analogy, popular among early Pentecostals, I was pleasantly surprised to come across Jenson's *Theology in Outline: Can These Bones Live?* Note: I accept the important distinction between canonical and apocryphal literature. I nevertheless occasionally employ apocryphal testimony as helpful for understanding the beliefs and practices of the ancients. 4 Macc 18:17 references Ezek 37:3.

35. Interestingly, Jonathan Edwards suggested a similar scenario. See Richie, "'The Grand Design of God in All Divine Operations.'" That the Pentecostal movement was birthed, in part, out of a rich revivalist tradition especially active in America can hardly be credibly doubted. See Conkin, *Cane Ridge*, 3, 9, 164.

Introduction

who demand whether Pentecostals focus on Christ or the Holy Spirit plainly miss the point. Thus, this volume portrays a Pentecostal perception of *Jesus Christ as the eternal and unchanging Lord powerfully present and active by the Holy Spirit today* without any sense of contradiction or tension.[36]

Admittedly, and unapologetically, a great deal of what I write reflects my own journey as a North American Classical Pentecostal.[37] More specifically, I am a third generation Pentecostal with deep roots in the southeastern United States of America, especially the Appalachian Mountains of Kentucky and Tennessee—a region heavily impacted by the Pentecostal movement.[38] Of course, context always informs perspective. Since the culture and locale of the southeastern United States has been especially prominent in the origin and development of certain streams of contemporary Pentecostalism, perhaps its influence is especially significant. Pentecostalism certainly shares with Appalachian religion an identity as an "authentic counterstream to modern, mainstream Protestantism."[39] Pentecostal insistence on personal salvation and suspicion of social work as a substitute for spiritual work coupled with Pentecostalism's ability to offer strength and reassurance to beleaguered and impoverished people certainly reflects its Appalachia roots as well.[40] Not surprisingly, Pentecostal historian Edith Blumhofer states that southern culture and religion have impacted Pentecostalism and that southern Pentecostalism is distinctive in some ways even from the broader Pentecostal movement.[41] In any case, the context of Appalachia and the American South certainly seasons the flavor of the Pentecostal theology in this study.

Nevertheless, deep appreciation for the broad diversity of Pentecostalism affirms its more inclusive aspects. I have been personally impacted by the strength and wisdom of Pentecostal type movements in the Global South and in Eastern Europe.[42] The special privilege of observing and interacting with Pentecostals on a national and

---

36. This position does not intend to minimize Christology for the sake of pneumatology or vice versa; rather, it affirms the intricate connection between Christology and pneumatology for Pentecostal theology.

37. Pentecostals originated in the early twentieth century revival movement which had as its primary (but not sole) catalyst the Azusa Revival; but, "Classical" was added as a clarifying descriptor in the mid-twentieth century in distinction from the Charismatic Movement, which had associations with historic, traditional (non-Pentecostal/non-Charismatic) denominations. See Synan, "Classical Pentecostalism," 552–55. The present text consciously identifies as Classical Pentecostal but occasionally draws on Charismatic thinkers as well as the broader Christian tradition. Yet it may be safely assumed that unqualified references to Pentecostals and Pentecostalism refer to the classical varieity.

38. Bare's *They Call Me Pentecostal* is an interesting example of a distinctively Appalachian Pentecostal journey. Drawing on personal experience supported by sociology of religion Bare both debunks and exemplifies prevalent stereotypes.

39. Jones, "Appalachian Religion," 21.

40. Jones, "Appalachian Religion," 23–24.

41. Blumhofer, "Pentecostalism," 110.

42. Cp. Kärkkäinen, *Holy Spirit and Salvation*, xxi–xxiii.

international scale has driven home to my mind the breadth and depth of this unique group of Christians. Perhaps an example is in order. In November of 2016 it was my privilege to teach a couple of theology courses at the Pentecostal Theological Institute in Bucharest. I enjoyed preaching in the seminary's chapel services as well as traveling around the nation preaching in several Romanian Pentecostal churches.

I had been informed in advance that Pentecostal worship in Romania does not tend to be as exuberant and expressive as I am accustomed to in the United States. I was given to understand that decades of communist oppression and persecution had necessitated a quieter, more cautious style of congregational gatherings. That is understandable. Years later that imprint is still present. However, I discovered to my joy that though the style of worship was somewhat different the substance was not. I most certainly experienced God's presence and power in a moving and uplifting manner while in our Romanian Pentecostal churches. Neither was it difficult to discern the Spirit of our Lord in the lives of the sisters and brothers.

On the other hand, I have taught theology courses at different times (most recently, September 2017) at the Theological Seminary of the Church of God in Haiti (Port au Prince). If anything, their exuberance and expressiveness is more than I have been accustomed to (at least in recent years) in most Pentecostal churches in the United States (reminding me of my childhood in Appalachia). I found the joyful worship and loving deportment of these blessed saints almost overwhelming but certainly uplifting. There is no doubt in my mind that they have the same Spirit as Romanian Pentecostals—and North American Pentecostals.

In the following pages I invite readers to keep in mind, for example, that when discussing experiencing the presence of God all these settings—and more besides—may be in mind. It will be apparent that I speak most comfortably, and possibly, often unconsciously, out of assumptions shaped by my own upbringing and ministry context. Yet it would be a mistake to forget that, whether I always make it clear or not, Pentecostal theology and spirituality is, as an old spiritual says of the Jordan River, "wide and deep."[43]

Pentecostalism characteristically embodies variegated local and global phenomena; thus, it can be simultaneously bewildering and bewitching.[44] Internal tensions continue to exist, and often are embraced, without easy resolution.[45] For instance, some Pentecostals are adamant pacifists while others are staunch anti-pacifists.[46] Small wonder that adjectives such as boring or dull simply do not apply to Pentecostals! Mark Galli complains that overworked adjectives such as "sensational" and "phenomenal"

---

43. William Francis Allen, Charles Pickard Ward, Lucy McKim Garrison, compilers, *Slave Songs of the United States* (Bedford, Massachusetts: Applewood, 1995 reprint of 1867 original), 23.

44. Vondey, *Pentecostalism: Guide*, 1–8.

45. Vondey, *Pentecostalism: Guide*, 3.

46. Goff, "Peaceniks," 22–23. Bernard, *Practical Holiness*, 275–301, has a quite strong discussion on the sanctity of life in relation to war and other forms of violence, capital punishment, and abortion.

INTRODUCTION

are nevertheless still the best words to describe Pentecostalism—although some use "embarrassment" and "dangerous."[47] Galli (mostly) denies that Pentecostalism is an embarrassment to Christianity but does admit it can be dangerous, although (again, mostly) in a good way. It certainly challenges the status quo.

Perhaps Pentecostalism can best be described as a movement, signifying that which is always in motion, even in transition, and characterized more by elasticity than staticity, more by fluidity than rigidity.[48] Yet the great Pentecostal river has firm banks and clear boundaries. For all their distinctiveness and diversity, contemporary Pentecostal/Charismatic movements are part of a rushing stream of spiritual tradition existing more or less consistently throughout much of Christian history.[49] It is true that Pentecostalism is unprecedented in its specific, sustained embrace and explicit affirmation of spiritual gifts and manifestations such as speaking in tongues, divine healing, and miracles. However, since the earliest days of Christian history there have been those, such as Justin Martyr, Irenaeus, Tertullian, Pseudo-Macarius, Hildegard of Bingen, Simeon the New Theologian, Teresa of Ávila, and John Wesley, who have evidenced Pentecostal-type faith and practices.[50] Some of these women and men were outstanding church leaders in their day who have made significant and enduring contributions to the development of Christian theology across traditional denomination boundaries.

Not surprisingly perhaps, Pentecostals today tend to think of doing theology in terms of the dynamic, enduring tradition of spiritual movements.[51] True enough, early Pentecostals tended to be a-historical, interpreting the early and latter rain prophecy of Joel 2:23 as descriptive of the biblical Pentecost and their own "last days" Pentecostal movement (cp. Acts 2:17) with little to no regard for happenings of intervening centuries. While still clinging, for the most part, to early and latter rain imagery, many Pentecostals today are more aware, and more appreciative, of the refreshing showers of God's Spirit throughout history. Through this integration contemporary Pentecostals can point to these historical precedents as adding increased credibility to their movement even while positing its unique nature in the world today. Especially in terms of sustained focus and scale of influence the argument is impressive.

It is perhaps important to note that Pentecostals, in spite of tendencies toward triumphalism, understandable enough at that after rough beginnings among marginalized people and groups, for the most part do not argue for the distinctiveness of their

---

47. Galli, "One Dangerous Religion," 8.

48. Galli, "One Dangerous Religion," 155–58. Pentecostalism's Wesleyan heritage shows here. Wesley was logical and systematic in a pastoral and practical sense but deplored petty debates about speculative points of doctrine. He was relatively tolerant of diverse opinions within the overall bounds of orthodoxy. See Oden, *Wesley's Scriptural Christianity*, 19–28 and 91–98.

49. Cartledge, *Encountering the Spirit*, 33–50. Cp. Chan, *Pentecostal Theology*, 73–77.

50. Burgess, *Christian Peoples of the Spirit*, has compiled an extensive list of Proto-Pentecostal and Pentecostal believers.

51. Chan, *Pentecostal Theology*, 7–8.

movement solely out of sectarian pride.[52] Pentecostals view speaking in tongues as a sign of Spirit baptism, and signs and wonders generally as indicators of in-breaking of the kingdom of God into the present world order. Additionally, Pentecostals consider the "last days" outpouring of the Holy Spirit an eschatological portent of Christ's coming again (Acts 2:17–21). In a sense we may appropriately refer to the Holy Spirit as the eschatological Spirit or the Spirit of the eschaton. In Pentecostal theology there is a clear link between Spirit baptism, the kingdom of God, and Christ's coming again.[53] Thus the global Pentecostal movement itself may be considered an eschatological sign. It can be especially informative to evaluate Pentecostal self-understanding in terms of semiology (scientific study of signs).[54]

Pentecostal theology as it is done in this volume is not reducible to an abstract science of philosophical speculation and precise argumentation, though these are certainly relevant, even required, in their proper place. Pentecostal theology is a bit like art. It reminds of music and partakes of poetry. In this aspect it resembles the biblical book of Psalms—brimming over with an abundance of rich theology but not so much in an abstract, systematic sense as in a confessional, doxological mode.[55] I often think of Pentecostal theology as a testimony of faith. It bears witness to what God is doing among us in Christ by the Spirit.[56] It tells our story, interprets its meaning, especially its significance, and invites others to understand—and perhaps even experience it for themselves. Yet credibility comes only with accountability. And accountability entails critique. Even artists must contend with the critics. Therefore, the present volume does not shrink from occasional self-criticism as deemed necessary. However, these segments should be understood as constructive and sympathetic rather than antagonistic or polemic.

Most of all, as I learned from the late Hollis Gause who was first my professor, later my colleague, and finally my friend, doing theology is doxological. Theology done appropriately is theology done for God and for God's glory. Ultimately, doing theology is an act of worship. For me, this mode of doing theology implies an evocative offertory. That is, it results in an offering to God of a sacrifice of adoration and reverence with contents that (hopefully and ideally) evoke praise and thanksgiving from readers. As a Pentecostal I love to praise and worship God in one accord with my sisters and brothers; and that includes praise and worship through doing theology together.

---

52. When I make broad, sweeping statements about what Pentecostals believe or think I do not presume that I am speaking for every Pentecostal everywhere. Rather, as a third-generation Pentecostal believer I am giving my general impression regarding currents and trends based on a lifetime of up-close, in depth involvement.

53. E.g., Macchia, *Baptized in the Spirit*, 42, 89.

54. More specifically, I am speaking of the philosophy of semiotics or study of the meaning and significance of—or, in this case, theology of—signs.

55. Cp. Ellington, "Reciprocal Reshaping in the Psalms," 18–31.

56. Richie, "Pentecostal Testimony," (forthcoming).

Introduction

In an effort to bring a measure of clarity to honest inquirers as well as focus to sincere devotees the present text identifies and develops the theological significance of some of the most distinctive elements of traditional Pentecostal beliefs. It does not claim to be exhaustive; but, it does aim to be fairly representative. Along the way it joins the sweet psalmist of Israel in singing a chorus: "Oh, taste and see that the Lord is good" (Ps 34:8 MEV).[57]

Academically, this work demonstrates an often-unexploited theological profundity in the consistent themes within Pentecostal theology in simultaneity with critiquing the tradition and challenging it to move toward greater maturation. Furthermore, as both an academic theologian and a senior pastor my work tends to target a readership encompassing academicians and informed clergy. I often specifically aim at the pastor-scholar or student-pastor. Accordingly, there is a unique integration of theological and pastoral concerns that is (in my opinion) all-too-rare.[58] *Essentials of Pentecostal Theology* aims to be theologically articulate with pastoral attention to spiritual devotion and formation.[59] Yet I do not see this approach as introducing a novelty—rather the reverse. I concur with the lament of Diogenes Allen, a noted American philosopher-theologian, that so much of today's "academic theology has narrowed its focus and neglected the field of spiritual theology."[60] Furthermore, as a Pentecostal I cannot but delight in his scathing description of many seminary and other academic conversations as resembling "the plight of people after the disaster of the tower of Babel rather than the deep communion brought about by the Holy Spirit at Pentecost."[61] Amen!

Readers are invited to keep two guiding principles in mind as points on the theological compass. First, *continuity* with the Classical Pentecostal tradition is of fundamental value. Second, *creativity* in addressing contemporary contexts is a motivating vision. The present text consciously endeavors to be faithful to the heritage of Pentecostalism while striving to meet a critical need in the wider world. In the words

---

57. The Holy Bible, Modern English Version (Lake Mary, Florida: Passio/Charisma, 2015).

58. I heartily affirm Janet Meyer Everts' statement in her Introduction to *Pentecostal Theology and N.T. Wright*, 3, that, "Pentecostal scholars are also practitioners of their faith, not just theoretical theologians." However, I fear that, first, of course that is not quite always the case, and, second, even when it is so the theological method to which most subscribe rather obscures pastoral/practical contributions.

59. In a *Pneuma* editorial Althouse and Waddell note that contemporary Pentecostal theologians wrestle with the appropriate utilization and interrelatedness of academic disciplines, including ethnographic research, and "the logic of God's self-revelation located in the community of the church." See "Christian Theology, the Logic," 425. For me, this is not an either/or proposition. However, appropriate integration calls for skill and sensitivity. I essentially agree with Autero, "Reading the Epistle of James," that, in any case, an "empirical hermeneutic" is necessary for both biblical and theological interpretation, 504. In this manner, theological and practical reflections can benefit churches and practitioners. Thus Estrada, "Is a Contextualized Hermeneutic the Future of Pentecostal Readings?" rightly argues that the theology of the community of faith must (at least) include historical experience and contextual reality, 341–55.

60. Allen, *Spiritual Theology*, 3.

61. Allen, *Spiritual Theology*, 4.

of the late Charismatic Baptist theologian Clark Pinnock, "We are being called to strive for the dynamic equilibrium of continuity and creativity that characterizes great theology."[62] This text aims at that kind of bi-lateral focus. The result is an affirmation of the Pentecostal tradition, and an exploration of, to an extent, innovative avenues. It is my judgment that contemporary Pentecostal theology flourishes best when both values function in tandem.

This work consistently endeavors to utilize the critical thinking and toolset of sound scholarship. However, it is not primarily intended as an academic treatise *per se*.[63] A pastor of over thirty-five years who currently teaches historical and doctrinal theology at Pentecostal Theological Seminary, I write, as my teacher, colleague, and friend French Arrington is fond of saying, "as a churchman for the church." Indeed, I expect well read "people in the pew" may benefit from the better part of it. Of course, it is my hope that students, teachers, administrators, and other members of the academy may well benefit from a careful consideration of these contents. I have taught much of this material in the classroom and, with some adaptation (interpretation of theological tongues!), preached it in the pulpit. I have found that good theology preaches well.

By the way, readers will note that, quite unlike most theology texts, this book includes what some would describe as anecdotal accounts. These stories are not merely illustrative; they arise out of the Pentecostal penchant for testimony combined with a desire to represent the popular theology of rank and file, that is, nonacademic, Pentecostals. Furthermore, a case can be made for the theological value of testimony (within certain parameters). In fact, it will be noted in Chapter One that Hollenweger does just that. As Arrington puts it, through sharing the testimonies of their experiences Pentecostals endeavor to "illuminate, clarify and verify aspects of God's work" in their lives and in the world.[64] Warrington argues that a chief characteristic of Pentecostal theology is the conviction that right belief must work well in the context of concrete praxis.[65] In my view, testimonies flow naturally enough out of a "this is that" hermeneutic relating the life of faith with the truth of Scripture, and are therefore theologically significant and fertile. Accordingly, here and there, as deemed appropriate, I include brief testimonies for the insight and vitality they bring to theological endeavors.[66]

---

62. Pinnock, "A Pilgrim on the Way," 2.

63. Readers will notice that for the most part technical details or ancillary discussions are placed in the footnotes. This is partly to avoid distraction. Those who are not necessarily interested in the technical asides and other information can read the body of the text with minimal consultation. However, when the discussion calls for it, as in the use of a Greek term or phrase, for example, or a certain line of reasoning, for another, it is included in the body for clarity.

64. Arrington, *Encountering the Holy Spirit*, 423.

65. Warrington, *Pentecostal Theology*, 16.

66. Further note, Richie, "Pentecostal Testimony." Also see, Thorsen, *The Wesleyan Quadrilateral*. One might even argue that testimony is part of the communal interpretive nature of Pentecostal hermeneutics.

Introduction

An example may be helpful. One Sunday morning late in 2003 our daughter Kathy came with her husband to the altar for prayer. She had some health problems which had become quite painful. Her physician recommended a hysterectomy but wanted to put it off as long as possible. She was only 23-years-old and unable to have children. But a few months after that prayer she was expecting. However, in the eighth month of pregnancy a problem developed. During a routine prenatal check-up her obstetrician became concerned. The baby was not moving. They spent a long day trying unsuccessfully to stimulate movement. First, she drank a medicinal concoction. Then they applied electrical charges. After incrementally increasing the current to the limit without any response, they began to prepare for the possibility that the baby was no longer alive.

By this time, it was late at night. Kathy called us, and Sue and I headed to the hospital. Already we had been praying furiously. As we made the 20-minute drive to the hospital we were anxious and tense. Suddenly, I felt a peace come over me. I told Sue, "God didn't work a miracle to bring this baby to life to allow the devil to kill him now." Amazingly, after we arrived at the hospital and had been there for only a short while, the baby moved without any further stimulation. A month later, on August 27, 2004, Robby was born. He is a healthy teenager at the time of this writing. This testimony exemplifies a Pentecostal theology of prayer and healing affirming God's miraculous intervention today (Jas 5:13–18).

The following consists of twelve chapters organized into three parts. Part One: Various Accents and Conflicts, addresses the specific background of nuance and difference among Pentecostals. To that end, Chapter One: Representative Perspectives selectively presents various viewpoints on Pentecostal theology while Chapters Two and Three on Major Controversies outline the major breaks within the movement. This section provides important background for understanding the Pentecostal movement theologically. Further, as I interact a bit with each group or individual along the way it provides a sampling of what is to come.

Part Two: A Description Not a Definition describes the theological landscape, as it were, of Pentecostalism. Accordingly, Chapter Four: An Unchanging Christ looks at Christology, Chapters Five and Six, on Experiencing God's Presence in worship and in prayer, explicate the role of experience and its actual focus, and Chapters Seven and Eight explore the Full Gospel as major paradigm for doing Pentecostal theology. This section provides a foundation for the distinctive features of Pentecostal theology, particularly pneumatology.

Part Three: Crucial Commitments examines what may be considered nonnegotiable doctrines for retaining original Pentecostal theology and further developing it legitimately. Therefore, Chapter Nine: The Doctrine of Subsequence and Chapter Ten: Purpose of Spirit Baptism discuss the role of Spirit baptism in relations to soteriology (or conversion and/or sanctification) and vocation (service). Chapter Eleven: Examining Initial Evidence and Chapter Twelve: Significance of Glossolalia take up the daunting task of articulating the role of speaking in tongues in Christian faith and life. This section provides a theological rationale for, on one hand, some of the most controversial and, on the other hand, some of the most creative aspects of traditional Pentecostal theology. An undergirding concern for ecclesiology and missiology will be evident. These three parts are followed by a brief Conclusion offering some assessment on the fruits of this volume's contents and their significance moving forward.

Before continuing, I would draw a lesson from Jesus' sending out of his disciples in Mark 6:12–13. "So they went out and preached that *people* should repent. And they cast out many demons, and anointed with oil many who were sick, and healed *them*." At this point in their ministerial career, the disciples were at best reluctant and timorous, perhaps even uncomprehending and ill-prepared. The following statement seems particularly apropos: "No matter how much exegesis, theology, and counseling one has studied, one is never 'prepared for ministry'"—to which may well be added, "It is only in awareness of such that the Christian experiences the presence and promise of Jesus Christ, and learns to depend not on human capabilities but on the one who calls and in the power of the proclamation to authenticate itself."[67] I consider it a special privilege (and serious responsibility) to have the opportunity to teach and write theology, that is, to be a "theologian." I am keenly aware of my inadequacies and limitations. Yet I am convinced that my confidence in the Gospel of Jesus Christ is not misplaced. With these few words and a prayer for the glory of God's name and the help of God's grace let us proceed.

---

67. Edwards, *Gospel according to Mark*, 182–83.

PART ONE

Various Accents and Conflicts

1

Representative Perspectives

ONE CAN COMPARE PENTECOSTAL theology to the phenomenon of pronunciation in which the same language exhibits different accents. Out of many possible candidates, as it were, I have selected a few particularly significant representatives of nuanced perspectives from across the Pentecostal tradition. These include, among others who could (and should) well be named, Walter Hollenweger, French Arrington, Hollis Gause, Steve Land, Frank Macchia, Estrelda Alexander, Leonard Lovett, Cheryl Bridges Johns, Lisa Stephenson, Samuel Solivan, Eldin Villafañe, Cecil M. Robeck, Amos Yong, and Veli-Matti Kärkkäinen. Taken together, the range of their interests and approaches reflects important theological trends in the movement along with a bit of assessment and interaction on my part. Please note that I attempt to present the thought of each representative in the best possible light from their perspective. I ask readers not to assume that I agree uncritically with everything each espouses. For that matter, I do not assume that they would agree uncritically with everything I espouse or with each other. However, I certainly consider these thinkers to represent some of the best and most productive Pentecostal theology being done today.

Before proceeding, please bear in mind two realistic features of the development of contemporary Pentecostal theology. First, doing Pentecostal theology as a specific, sustained discipline, is a relatively new endeavor. For the most part, early Pentecostals were content to draw on their understanding of the Scriptures in the context of their formative traditions in light of their experience of the Holy Spirit without professional, academic theological support or direction. Second, recent Pentecostal theology has made incredible strides in an amazingly short time. The surging growth of global Pentecostalism has generated a widespread interest, extending even beyond the movement, which, coupled with the increasing affluence and influence of at least large sectors of the movement itself, has contributed to a proliferation of scholarship, in almost all fields of religious inquiry, which together have made the last several decades a period of unparalleled theological development and maturation.

WALTER HOLLENWEGER: PENTECOSTAL THEOLOGY AS AFFECTIVE ORALITY

A Swiss historian and theologian from a Pentecostal background but with Reformed commitments, Walter Hollenweger stressed the orality of Pentecostal worship and thought as processed and expressed primarily in songs, testimonies, preaching, worship, and prayer.[1] In this view Pentecostal theology is not so much discursive as it is affective and intuitive. Early Pentecostal thought certainly did not present itself through analytical, logical argumentation. Rather, it embraced the potential epistemological richness of attitudes, dispositions, emotions, immediate apprehension or insight—in other words, the ability to attain knowledge apart from evident rational thought. In this regard Pentecostal theology is an art rather than a science. Thus, Pentecostalism represents a dramatic (pun intended) alternative to how much of Christian theology is done.

Admittedly, overemphasis on this affective-emotional-intuitive dimension can become anti-intellectual and anti-educational. It can degenerate into fanaticism. Most negative stereotypes of Pentecostals are probably traceable to unpleasant encounters with some form of this unfortunate phenomenon.[2] In actual practice Pentecostal appreciation for the supra-rational or non-rational (not irrational) usually facilitates a more holistic life of faith offering a much-needed corrective to reductionist extremes of post-Enlightenment rationalism and modernity's disenchantment of ontological reality. I am reminded of two sides of C. S. Lewis. An ever-popular apologist and theologian, Lewis complemented brilliant intellectual, cognitively-oriented works such as *Mere Christianity* and *The Abolition of Man* with sublime intuitive, en-spiritedly imaginative works such as *The Chronicles of Narnia* and *The Space Trilogy*.[3] For him

---

1. Hollenweger, "After Twenty Years," 3–12. Hollenweger's *The Pentecostals*, a classic in Pentecostal studies, was followed by *Pentecostalism: Origins and Developments*.

2. Admittedly, a decline in commitment to traditional Pentecostal beliefs and practices appears to be occurring among some Pentecostal clergy. Increased graduate level religious education has been suggested as a possible culprit instigating this devolutionary process. However, the influence of generic Evangelicalism on susceptible Pentecostals has been identified in long term, in depth studies as more likely the chief culprit. See Stewart, et al, "Changes in Clergy Belief and Practice," 481.

3. Perhaps not surprisingly, C. S. Lewis affirmed the value of glossolalia. See Richie, "Transposition and Tongues," 117–37.

theology was not either/or when it comes to analytical logic and spiritual insight; it was both/and.

An abundance of reputable Pentecostal scholars and theologians over the last several decades indicate that Pentecostals are coming to terms with the life of the mind. Along with other followers of Jesus, Pentecostals love God not only with their heart and soul but with their mind as well (Matt 22:37). And yet Pentecostal theologians must not forget the rare and precious jewel of spiritual insight and revelatory understanding as an intrinsic and essential element of knowing the things of God (1 Cor 2:10–16). The great American theologian and philosopher Jonathan Edwards well said, "*holy affections* not only necessarily belong to *true religion*, but are a very great part of such religion."[4] We do well to hear him further: "As there is no true religion where there is nothing else but affection, so there is no true religion where there is no *religious affection*."[5] Or as Welch well observes, although education is becoming increasingly important among Pentecostal clergy, spiritual anointing and charisma are still essential.[6] Doing Pentecostal theology should be both an art and a science.

FRENCH ARRINGTON: PENTECOSTAL THEOLOGY WITH AN EVANGELICAL IDENTITY

French Arrington presents a Classical Pentecostal theology similar in many ways to that of typical Evangelical theologies—but with distinctive and pronounced pneumatological and charismatic emphases.[7] Thinking on God, Christ, the Holy Spirit, the church and its mission, and even eschatology, although more intense and with numerous variations, are almost identical with many non-Pentecostal conservative Christians. Notable exceptions are extensive and affirmative treatments of Spirit baptism and spiritual gifts, especially speaking in tongues and divine healing. I have found this approach largely representative of a majority of Pentecostals in the United States and in Latin America as well as significant groups of global Pentecostals with ties to the same.[8] Some, though not all (certainly not Arrington) incline toward a more rigid, even Fundamentalist worldview, than many Evangelicals per se.[9] Unfortunately,

---

4. Edwards, *Treatise Concerning Religions Affections*, 1:238. Italics are original. "Holy" affections are founded in the moral excellence of divine love as "the spring" of all, 1:278.

5. Edwards, *Treatise Concerning Religions Affections*, 1:243.

6. Welch, 'Women with the Good News', 69.

7. Arrington, *Christian Doctrine*. Stephenson, *Types of Pentecostal Theology*, places older Pentecostal writers Myer Pearlman and E. S. Williams in this same category with Arrington as representatives of doing theology as an organized exposition of "Bible doctrines," 11–27.

8. Cp. Anderson, *An Introduction to Global Pentecostalism*, and Smith, *Pentecostal Power*.

9. Evangelicalism is a broad term but generally identifies those who emphasize such doctrines as biblical inspiration and authority, conversionary evangelism, and cruciform soteriology. Fundamentalism agrees doctrinally but is stricter and more rigid in its application. See Bebbington, *Dominance of Evangelicalism*.

some Pentecostals, as well as others, do not appear to distinguish drastic differences between Evangelicalism and its angry counterpart, Fundamentalism.[10] Fortunately, a close reading of Arrington's corpus can hardly help but open the horizons for any Pentecostals unsure of the theological scope of their movement's orientation.

The question of the nature of the relationship between Pentecostals and Evangelicals is significant. Pentecostals have long enjoyed a close and mutually enriching relationship with Evangelicals.[11] In certain contexts some even refer to "pent-evangelical theology."[12] Perhaps most Pentecostals, including myself, are quite comfortable with an Evangelical label. Some even think of Pentecostals as a subset of Evangelicalism, "Evangelicals with a plus" so to speak. With the phenomenal global growth of Pentecostalism this disproportionate mathematical equivalency is becoming increasingly difficult to defend.[13] Yet, although at first glance a superficial assessment might conclude that the debate is mostly about size and numbers, with whatever influence and prestige that may entail, comparable to an offspring outgrowing his or her parents, or older siblings, this would be premature—and mistaken. More than familial status or sibling rivalry is at stake.[14]

There are important distinctions, even differences, in theology and spirituality between Evangelicals and Pentecostals. On the one hand, few, if any, appear to doubt the generally evangelical nature of the (especially Classical) Pentecostal movement. On the other hand, some wonder whether the full reservoir of Pentecostalism really is reducible to Evangelicalism with speaking in tongues as a fringe benefit or more or less optional add-on.[15] Certainly, the contemporary global Pentecostal movement appears to be something other than "Evangelicalism with tongues tacked on." Pentecostal openness to the Holy Spirit has far-reaching effects.

Perhaps most importantly, Pentecostalism, which is of course newer and younger than Evangelicalism, as movements go, is attempting to hammer out its own inner ethos and sense of identity. This process is essential for Pentecostal theology's

---

10. Cox, *Future of Faith*, 200, argues that emphasis on a direct experience of the Holy Spirit sharply divides Pentecostals from Fundamentalists, especially, and even to an extent, distinguishes them from Evangelicals, with whom they have a better but still "touchy" relationship, 201.

11. Synan, "Evangelicalism," 613–16.

12. E.g., Yong, *Future of Evangelical Theology*, 36, 125.

13. Pew Forum research on "Global Christianity: A Report on the Size and Distribution of the World's Christian Population (Dec 2011), http://www.pewforum.org/files/2011/12/Christianity-full-report-web.pdf, concluded that Pentecostalism by itself is roughly as large as all Evangelicalism put together with the Charismatic movement slightly larger than either. Pentecostals and Charismatics together are more than double the size of Evangelicalism. Over 600 million Christians today identify as Pentecostal/Charismatic.

14. Although if we were to continue the analogy it might be framed in terms of parents/older siblings (Evangelicals) releasing their young (Pentecostals) into maturity with their blessings and the young (Pentecostals) remaining ever grateful for the wisdom and strength of their parents/older sibling (Evangelicals) from which they have benefited—and will continue to benefit—greatly. And the entire family grows together for the glory of God.

15. E.g., Cross, "'A Proposal to Break the Ice,'" 44–73.

maturation and development.[16] I for one am sure that Pentecostalism as a movement will continue to be Evangelical, including continuing partnership and rapport with Evangelicalism per se. I also celebrate the "coming of age," as it were, of Pentecostal theology, and the implications, opportunities—and responsibilities—appropriate for a measure of intellectual and spiritual adulthood.[17] It is an exciting time to be a Pentecostal theologian.

HOLLIS GAUSE AND STEVE LAND: PENTECOSTAL THEOLOGY AS WESLEYAN-HOLINESS ORIENTATION

Hollis Gause and Steve Land explicate Pentecostal theology within a Wesleyan-Holiness model highlighting crisis-process soteriological schemas. Gause focuses on salvation in Christ as an ongoing journey, or *via salutis*, marked by distinct but unitary redemptive, and transformative, experiences in the Holy Spirit.[18] Land offers an integrative dispositional framework of orthodoxy, orthopathy, and orthopraxy with an emphasis on eschatological missiology via Trinitarian revisioning—or the integration of holiness and power in a Spirit-filled life of witness and worship with a passion for the coming of Christ's kingdom with God as all in all.[19] This perspective interprets Pentecostalism's origins in the nineteenth century American Holiness movement as not only historical but paradigmatic. Accordingly, the inherited Wesleyan-Arminian spirituality and theology so formative for the earliest Pentecostals continues to be central to the development of Pentecostal theology today.[20]

For me, it makes sense that Pentecostals' deep roots in the Wesleyan-Arminian-Holiness tradition should bring forth good fruit in contemporary Pentecostalism.[21] Today different Pentecostal organizations continue to claim their Holiness heritage with varying degrees of commitment, and, as stated already, global Pentecostals are

---

16. A colleague has wondered aloud to me whether Pentecostalism needed Evangelicalism as kind of an "umbilical cord" but has now been birthed into its own movement. This analogy suggests the intimate and interdependent relationship of the two movements but may not give due credence to their distinct identities.

17. Thomas, "Pentecostal Theology in the Twenty-First Century," 3–19.

18. Gause, *Living in the Spirit*. Pentecostals are almost universally Wesleyan-Arminian rather than Calvinist/Reformed, with rare exceptions among denominational Charismatics.

19. Land, *Pentecostal Spirituality*. Stephenson, *Types of Pentecostal Theology*, places Asian Pentecostal theologian Simon Chan in the same category with Land in the sense that they both focus on Pentecostal theology as spirituality, 28–58. Likewise, Warrington, *Pentecostal Theology*, and Kärkkäinen, *Pneumatology*, highlight divine encounter and dynamic charismatic spirituality overflowing in worship and in witness as the essential, distinctive thrust of Pentecostal theology.

20. James Arminius (1560–1609), a Dutch theologian and pastor, argued that predestination was based on God's foreknowledge of those who would freely accept or reject Christ. John Wesley (1703–91), an English evangelist, pastor, reformer, and theologian, essentially agreed, particularly stressing the universal availability of grace. Those who adopt similar views are "Wesleyan-Arminian."

21. Richie, "Pentecostalism's Wesleyan Roots and Fruits," http://seedbed.com/feed/pentecostalisms-wesleyan-roots-fruit/.

certainly diverse.[22] Nevertheless, this significant historical and theological—and foundational—trajectory is widely acknowledged. Additionally, the Wesleyan-Arminian tradition constitutes an overall approach to doing Christian theology remarkably consistent with existing Pentecostal thought and practice—and conducive for its further theological development.

However, Pentecostal appropriation of its Wesleyan heritage has tended to be, if I may say so, sporadic and spotty. Often even Wesleyan-Pentecostals consult and cite Wesley and his interpreters mostly when it comes to sanctification, usually when embroiled in controversies over the nature and experience of holiness.[23] But the Wesleyan doctrinal tradition is broad and deep. I suggest Pentecostals need to expand our appreciation and appropriation. Wesleyan theology emphasizes God as holy love, the primacy of Scripture, the prior agency of God's grace, the image of God and salvation as the restoration of God's image, the gospel for the poor, God's wisdom in creation, the renewal of the church, and the restoration of all creation.[24] The enduring relevance of Wesley's theology includes implications of his doctrine of prevenient grace for missiology, and, yes, his pneumatology in light of contemporary Pentecostal and Charismatic movements, therapeutic view of salvation (healing from sin's disease), and applications of his doctrine of creation to ecotheology and environmental ethics. Finally, Wesley's theology of ministry transcends clergy-laity dichotomies and confronts restrictive gender stereotypes. Perhaps we would do well to widen our theological loop?

FRANK MACCHIA: PENTECOSTAL THEOLOGY IN CONVERSATION WITH CLASSICAL THEOLOGIANS

Frank Macchia outlines parameters of contemporary developing Pentecostal theology via a more encompassing conversation with the broader Christian theological tradition while lifting up Spirit baptism as the distinctive theological contribution of Pentecostalism.[25] This approach places Pentecostals in conversation with significant Church Fathers such as Augustine, with the Magisterial Reformers (Martin Luther, John Calvin), and more recent continental (European) theologians such as Karl Barth,

---

22. Yet certainly all Pentecostals would affirm the imperative to worship the Lord in "the beauty of holiness" (Ps 29:2). Cox, *Future of Faith,* 210–11, suggests Pentecostal commitments to conversion and holiness may play a decisive role in the "revolution in Christianity" apparently ushering in a fresh "Age of the Spirit."

23. My complaint is not at all intended to deny or minimize the incredible richness of Wesley's theology for the renewing of holiness in the Christian life. For an affirmative and integrative effort in this regard, see Kärkkäinen, *Spirit and Salvation,* 352–60.

24. Snyder, "Wesleyanism, Wesleyan Theology," 932–36.

25. Macchia, *Baptized in the Spirit.* Cp. Macchia, "Theology, Pentecostal," 1120–41. Stephenson, *Types of Pentecostal Theology,* observes that Macchia utilizes an overarching rubric of the Kingdom of God, 59–81. For Vondey, *Pentecostal Theology,* Pentecostal theology addresses the renewal of the Christian life identified by the transforming work of the Holy Spirit and directed toward the Kingdom of God.

Emil Brunner, Wolfhart Pannenberg, and Jürgen Moltmann. This process represents a traditional approach to doing theology; but, with Pentecostal theology serving as a valid, significant, and constructive contributor which is in turn informed and/or critiqued, if and when necessary, by the larger theological community.

Of course, the potential takeaway of reciprocal productivity is a chief asset of these kinds of open-ended theological conversations. For Pentecostals, it is both challenging and rewarding. On the one hand, Pentecostal theology does not "start from scratch" or "reinvent the wheel." It is compelled to grapple with the complex but incredibly rich and vast reservoir of theological categories and concepts across the centuries and across the traditions of multiple communions through Christianity's best and brightest representatives. Only after reaching a reasonable level of understanding, perhaps even appreciation, for the best thought of others, are we adequately equipped to enter the kind of conversations that can produce the most enriching results all around.

On the other hand, Pentecostals can bring fresh wind and new wine into what can, and has, at times, become stale, somber myopic theologizing all-too-easily losing sight of the Spirit's innovative nature and constructive agency. For example, the classic Protestant doctrine of justification by faith tends to be inordinately forensic and transactional; but, with the perspective of the Spirit's involvement theological, and yes, spiritual, revivifying influences flow forth in surprising abundance.[26] Participatory and experiential aspects are elucidated. Setting the discussion within a larger framework of the Spirit of Life as the realm of God's favor sustains a pneumatological theology of justification by faith that is Trinitarian, ecclesiological, and eschatological in orientation (1 Cor 6:11; 1 Tim 3:16).

Compromise is a prevalent and, in my opinion, a legitimate concern for Pentecostals (and doubtless for about everyone else too). Compromises might occur in various ways. Compromise may mean sacrificing our own commitments for that which is less demanding or more popular. It may occur as gradual, subtle dilution of those commitments through assimilation with others. A colleague recently said (perhaps only half-jokingly) that it does not benefit anyone for us to become "a Pentecostal version of Robert Jenson" (a popular American Lutheran and ecumenical theologian). I consider his consternation quite understandable. Yet compromise is not an inevitable outcome from ecumenical interaction.[27] Often quite the opposite occurs. In the critical case of Spirit baptism interaction with the broader tradition can reaffirm Pentecostals' association of Spirit baptism and empowerment, including spiritual gifts like glossolalia, while expanding the metaphor to include God's eschatological goal of filling all creation and every creature as the temple of the divine presence (Eph 4:10; 1 Cor 15:28; Rev 21:3).[28] Affirmation *and* expansion of Pentecostal theology can be a definite plus.

26. See Macchia, *Justified in the Spirit*.

27. MacGregor, *Contemporary Theology*, 147–48, points out that Latin American Pentecostals have been especially adept at integrating ecumenism and multiculturality.

28. Macchia, *Baptized in the Spirit*, 105 and 117.

ESTRELDA ALEXANDER AND LEONARD LOVETT: PENTECOSTAL THEOLOGY AND RACIAL EGALITARIANISM

Estrelda Alexander applies Pentecostal theology to social ethics, particularly in regard to race and gender, often through theological observations on the African American Pentecostal journey through history.[29] Alexander has been particularly adept at helping the Pentecostal movement today reclaim important contributions of this important segment of the Pentecostal movement to its worship styles and to the shaping of its theological conversations.[30] Unfortunately, although Black Pentecostals shared the Christian faith and Spirit empowerment of their white Pentecostal sisters and brothers, they were nevertheless unable "to overcome the social realities of American politics in the first half of the twenty-first century" and therefore frequently suffered "the double indignity of racial discrimination and religious persecution."[31] Nevertheless, since the middle of the twenty-first century the rise and growth of middle class Black Pentecostals and their impact on the wider civil and political society continues to affect other Pentecostals as well.[32]

Leonard Lovett traces the development of Black theology, with its enduring stress on freedom or liberation, by pointing out varying emphases along with internal as well as external tensions which have contributed to its continuing formation.[33] Significantly, for Black Pentecostals the Holy Spirit is not only a dove but also wind and fire; not only Comforter, but also Strengthener. Social justice as well as personal peace and joy are evidences of the Holy Spirit's presence and power. Indeed, "Authentic Pentecostal encounter cannot occur unless liberation becomes the consequence."[34] Arguably the Spirit of Pentecost is certainly egalitarian (Acts 2:17–18). Thus, the global Pentecostal revival came to an African American congregation "whose pastor had a vision for multiracial and multiethnic worship."[35] Here Pentecostal scholar David Daniels encourages us that although the dream of racial harmony broke down early, for many Pentecostals, both black and white, the hope still lives on and is advancing be it ever so slowly.[36] One can pray he is right.

Growing up during the civil rights movement, I had some painful experiences . . . literally.[37] While walking home from school in Owensboro, Kentucky, my brother

---

29. See Alexander, *Black Fire*. See also Alexander, *Limited Liberty*.
30. Alexander, *Afro-Pentecostalism*, 1–20.
31. Alexander, *Afro-Pentecostalism*, 4–5.
32. Alexander, *Afro-Pentecostalism*, 6–7.
33. Lovett, "Black Theology," 428–31.
34. Lovett, "Black Theology," 430.
35. Robeck, *Azusa Street Mission & Revival*, 314.
36. Daniels, "They Had a Dream," 19–21.

37. To be clear, I heartily affirm the many positive accomplishments of the civil rights movement. Here I draw attention to an unfortunate incident that the devil used to plant a stronghold of sin in my life. While a frightening experience, in no way do I wish to depict Black males as inevitably dangerous.

and I were attacked by a gang of older boys—Black boys. I was a second grader and Tim a first grader. There were about half a dozen of them. Most were probably sixth or seventh graders. One was my classmate, and another was Tim's. The four of us had been recess playmates previously—but never again. A neighbor seeing the "fight" ran out of his house to chase the older boys away. Fortunately, Tim and I were not seriously hurt. We only had bloody noses and black eyes, and a few scrapes and scratches. Our dad was upset enough to stir up such a ruckus that Tim and I enjoyed an early dismissal with a police escort coming home from school for the rest of the year.[38]

The upshot of our Owensboro incident was that Tim and I nursed a malignant hatred for Black people. Throughout our youth and into adulthood we regarded all African Americans as implacable enemies. We were racists. However, when I became a Christian, I mean, when I was born again or converted, the hatred and resentment simply, miraculously, vanished. That is when I knew it for what it was—sin. An incident with some boys after school was no excuse for hating an entire race of human beings. Sin had taken hold in my heart to incite unreasonable anger toward a whole people. When I allowed the Lord to take away my sins then my racism went away. That is probably why to this day I cannot comprehend how anyone who claims be Christian can hang on to racist attitudes.[39] My life has been immeasurably enriched by deep relationships with brothers and sisters in Christ of different races. I am glad that Christ shed his blood for all people of every race (Rev 5:9; 7:9).[40]

I realize that throughout America's tumultuous history there have been Black people who, often with justification—or at least, provocation—have viewed whites as their "natural enemies" as well.[41] But our shared redemption in Christ is also our shared hope for reconciliation not only with our Creator but with one another as well. Therefore, Pannenberg urges Black theologians to specifically include "God's affirmation of the life of black *and* white human beings with their common calling in

---

Further, a disturbing question is whether if the situation had been reversed would Black children have been given a police escort? That is, even in this unfortunate childhood incident was white privilege on display?

38. I now wonder how the parents of the Black children involved felt or what, if any, recourse they had in the situation?

39. Tim Wise, *White Like Me*, and Robin DiAngelo, *White Fragility*, probe the difficult question of how some Christians continue to be racist. This is no minor matter. It is of ultimate importance. Theologically speaking, racism can be a form of idolatry or polytheism in its elevation of one race to a place of practical deification at the expense of demonizing others and marring the manifestation of true Christianity. See Fields, *Black Theology*, 57–63. Cp. Gause, *Revelation*, 133–34.

40. Oddly, it is necessary to insist that "reverse discrimination" or "reverse prejudice" (discrimination/prejudice against members of a dominant or majority group, in favor of members of a minority or historically disadvantaged group) is sinfully unchristian too. Although it may seek to correct existing inequalities, it nevertheless perpetuates inequality and potentially fosters further resentment. E.g., twice in my academic career I have been told the basis of denying me appointments was because as a white male I did not meet desired diversity goals. As my grandmother used to say, "Two wrongs don't equal one right!"

41. Jackson, *Reclaiming Our Heritage*, 87.

one church out of all nations and races."[42] Yet he adds, this "would not preclude the concern for a special calling of black people today, but within the framework of the universal church and not in terms of hostility against others."[43] Furthermore, I cannot but insist that it does not release white Christians from the weight of responsibility for renouncing racial injustice and oppression in all forms. Unfortunately, tragically, even sinfully, all-too-often churches have been unwilling to be a fully prophetic voice, unwilling to act as God's conscience regarding racial prejudice and oppression.[44] But that can change. It should change. It must change.[45]

CHERYL BRIDGES JOHNS AND LISA STEPHENSON: PENTECOSTAL THEOLOGY AND GENDER EGALITARIANISM

Cheryl Bridges Johns and Lisa Stephenson apply the egalitarian and evocative insights of Pentecostal theology, spirituality, liturgy, catechesis, and praxis to current issues of gender (as well as other topics). Johns argues that Pentecostals employ a powerful process of formational catechesis, which has enabled believers among the marginalized of society to own and articulate the Christian story, as she moves beyond the rationalism found in a praxis epistemology into a distinctively Pentecostal worldview.[46] For her, patriarchy is a dark power, the oldest form of oppression, a curse from which the daughters of Eve have been freed through redemption in Christ. She challenges the church to actively implement redemptive liberty for women in the face of persistent resistance.[47] Stephenson translates the pneumatological language of Acts 2 into a fully liberating praxis for Pentecostal women in ministry. Stephenson proposes a feminist-pneumatological anthropology and ecclesiology addressing problematic dualisms that perpetuate ecclesial restrictions on Pentecostal women in ministry.[48] In the view of these theologians, theology is not merely theory; it is activist-oriented and gender inclusive.

As already noted, the Spirit of Pentecost is egalitarian (Acts 2:17–18). The Azusa Revival was birthed and flourished in a congregation that recognized "the ministry of women as legitimate and equal with that of men."[49] Historian David Roebuck points out that in the early years of Pentecostalism it was not out of the ordinary for women

---

42. Pannenberg, *Christian Spirituality*, 67. Italics are original.

43. Pannenberg, *Christian Spirituality*, 67.

44. Jackson, *Reclaiming Our Heritage*, 89.

45. Although in a different context, Michael Baker's, *You and Your Church*, 109–10, compelling call for change so long as it is the right kind of change appears applicable here.

46. Johns, *Pentecostal Formation*.

47. Johns, "Letter to Young Christian Feminists," https://juniaproject.com/letter-young-christian-feminists/.

48. Stephenson, *Dismantling the Dualisms for American Pentecostal Women*.

49. Robeck, *Azusa Street Mission & Revival*, 15. While many Protestants have finally affirmed women in ministry in response to criticism from secular feminism, early Pentecostals based their openness to women in ministry on the Acts 2:17–18 fulfillment of the promise of Joel 2:28–32.

to serve as preachers, pastors, and denominational leaders.[50] Constructive theologizing utilizing the concept of the egalitarian Spirit has potential to evoke profound applications in a carnal and sinful world of bias, prejudice, and oppression. If God shows "no partiality" (Acts 10:34), then why would any of us ever exalt ourselves up above anyone else who has received "the same gift" of Christ's Holy Spirit as we have received (Acts 11:17)?

Aspects of egalitarian theology, Pentecostal or otherwise, can often be controversial. For an apt example, feminist theology is an explosive field. This (to an extent) well-deserved notoriety is probably because much of modern feminist theology per se is liberal and pluralist, even secular, in many of its presuppositions and, not surprisingly, its conclusions.[51] Radically revisioning not only female and male human roles but the person and being of God seems to be the primary objective. And that is problematic in a huge way. Therefore, the very term "feminism" is now a negative. Even women affirming the Christian roots of authentic feminism may avoid it out of fear over misidentification with "very vocal leftist views."[52] However, there are solid biblical, theological, historical, and practical studies which supply surprising results well worth consulting.[53] Christian egalitarianism is self-consciously biblical, building on Pauline egalitarianism (Gal 3:28) in affirming the equal worth and value of women and men as well as racial minorities or the economically oppressed as equally created in God's image (*Imago Dei*) (Gen 1:26–27) and therefore equal in redemption and in vocation.[54]

In the early days of the Pentecostal movement egalitarian relationships and ministries were the norm.[55] Over time, that situation changed, and not for the better.[56] Unbiblical and unchristian power broking, that is, abusive and exploitative leadership patterns (contra Mark 10:42), forced the almost universal subjugation of Spirit-filled and Spirit-called women (and other minorities). Largely, Christian egalitarians seek

50. Roebuck, "Loose the Women," 38–39. Most Pentecostals readily accept women in ministry, that is, as preachers, teachers, and as pastors and evangelists, some question their role regarding authority, that is, as bishops or overseers/superintendents in denominational leadership. Alexander argues that this bifurcation is the result of a desire for acceptance leading to acquiescence to Evangelicals but contrary to early Pentecostals examples—although she admits cultural limitations on women among Pentecostals even early on, *Limited Liberty*, vii–xiv, 147–49.

51. E.g., Clack, "Theaology and Theology," 21–38.

52. Welch, *'Women with the Good News'*, 10–11. Welch points out later, 105–06, that aversion to extreme feminist views does not excuse accusations and attacks against women in ministry.

53. E.g., see Grenz and Kjesbo, *Women in the Church*.

54. Pentecostals understand the divine image (צֶלֶם אֱלֹהִים/*tzelem Elohim*) to include humanity's moral-intellectual-spiritual nature, Munyon, "Creation," 252.

55. From the outset Pastor Seymour was firmly committed "to a policy of non-sectarianism, the equality of the races, and the equality of women and men," Robeck, *Azusa Street Mission & Revival*, 30–31.

56. Reed, *"In Jesus' Name"*, 363, laments that Pentecostals have repeatedly and ignominiously failed at early and idealistic efforts for racial and doctrinal unity; but, he continues to be hopeful for the future.

to reclaim an original vision of Pentecostal ministry, spirituality, and theology as discerned in the Scriptures. It would be a categorical mistake and a practical tragedy to reject Christian egalitarianism because of the overwrought radicalism of a few feminist theologians.[57]

Moreover, a move from individual Pentecostal experience to social applications is quite appropriate. The original Pentecost itself was *both* an individual *and* a corporate experience occurring, after all, in a quite public and even social setting.[58] In Acts 2:1–4, when "each" and "all" experienced the Spirit's infilling and speaking in tongues then immediately "the multitude came together." Perhaps the well-known global appeal of Pentecostalism to the disenfranchised and marginalized of society would be even more remarkable if more Pentecostal theologians (and others) intentionally embrace and extend its inherent egalitarian emphases. The Azusa Street Mission Revival made history with its racial and gender breakthroughs.[59] However, the heirs of Azusa have not kept up the pace set by their courageous ancestors. Arguably, they have fallen far behind.[60] Is it not high time the Pentecostal movement as a whole lived up to its illustrious heritage?

SAMUEL SOLIVAN, ELDIN VILLAFAÑE, AND DANIEL ÁLVAREZ: LATIN/HISPANIC-AMERICAN PENTECOSTAL THEOLOGY

The growth of the Pentecostal movement has been remarkable among the Hispanic-American community. Solivan presents an overview of Hispanic diversity, with its common roots and struggles. It reveals the influence of liberation theology with a Hispanic Pentecostal context and pneumatological insistence.[61] Critical issues include religious experience, suffering, the work of the Holy Spirit, the importance of language and culture, and acculturation and assimilation. He shows how a community's

---

57. Significantly, Alexander, *Limited Liberty*, describes early Pentecostal women leaders not as fostering radical feminist activism, which they too "deemed sinful," but as representatives of "lived feminism" and "practical feminism," 150, 159.

58. Kuhlin, "'I Do Not Think I Could be a Christian on My Own,'" thinks contemporary Pentecostals are moving away from an early emphasis on individual piety toward a more "relational piety," 482. I tend to think that an early inclusion of both individual and communal piety is presently being recovered. Nevertheless, her work among Swedish Pentecostal women is quite intriguing as we await investigative research for broader implications.

59. Sometimes called "silent Pentecostals" because their story is rarely told, many Hispanic Americans were heavily involved in and influenced by the Azusa Revival. See Gaston Espinosa as included in Deiros and Wilson, "Hispanic Pentecostalism," 304 (cp. 296–97).

60. International Pentecostal Holiness Church Presiding Bishop (at the time, 2009) James Leggett states flatly that Pentecostals have some catching up to do regarding women in leadership; but he expresses confidence that the leadership role of women in IPHC will increase, Welch, *Women with the Good News*, 58.

61. Solivan, *Spirit, Pathos and Liberation*. 147–49.

suffering and oppression can be transformed by the Holy Spirit into a liberating life, full of hope and promise.

Eldin Villafañe has captured the attention of theologians, ethicists, and members of the Hispanic community alike with his construction of a social ethic for the Hispanic Pentecostal Church in America that coheres with the Hispanic American socio-cultural experience and yet remains consistent with Hispanic Pentecostalism's self-understanding of ethics emerging from its experience of the Spirit.[62] Villafañe insists that if the Hispanic-American Pentecostal church is to survive with authenticity and relevance "*then* it must see itself not just as the community of the Spirit *in* the world, but rather as the community of the Spirit *for* the world, but not *of* the world—a sign of the promise and the presence of the Spirit's historical project, the Reign of God" (Gal 5:25).[63] Doesn't that sound like good advice for us all?

Daniel Álvarez draws upon pastoral experience and academic training to develop a Pentecostal theology of immigration. He places the concepts of *mestizaje* ("intermixture") and *hibridez* ("racial and cultural intermixture") into conversation in constructing a pneumatological approach to immigration.[64] He speaks about undocumented immigration in ways that point to its reasons and causes, nuancing this condition and examining the work of the Spirit of God among these people. Mirroring the tension between divine immanence and transcendence in Pentecostal praxis, Álvarez highlights tension between *identidad* ("identity") and *otredad* ("otherness"), identifying a back-and-forth process that shapes these people through *hibridez*.[65] Focus on the perspective of pneumatic peoples enriches the broader theological conversations about immigration.[66]

In travels through Central and South America I have been blessed by the freshness and vitality (and, frequently, hospitality) of Pentecostal Christians in that part of the world. As a local church pastor and seminary professor in the United States it has been a special blessing to work with and worship alongside many wonderful Hispanic-American Pentecostals. I have often appreciated the energy and sincerity of their spirituality. The work of Solivan, Villafañe, Álvarez (and others) clearly demonstrate the depth of the theological contribution of Hispanic Pentecostals as well. They are thinking through some tough topics that we all need to be thinking about.

Growing up Pentecostal in Southeastern Appalachia, I instinctively knew that many of our churches and their congregants were among the less affluent, the less educated, and the less influential. But we knew that although the world might look at us as "less" that with the Holy Spirit's fullness we were actually among the "more"—if you will. That was reassuring. But Hispanic-American Pentecostal theologians are moving

---

62. Villafañe, *The Liberating Spirit*, 222.
63. Villafañe, *The Liberating Spirit*, 222. Italics are original.
64. Álvarez, *Mestizaje and Hibridez*, 83–102.
65. Álvarez, *Mestizaje and Hibridez*, 79–80.
66. Álvarez, *Mestizaje and Hibridez*, 103–04, 148.

far beyond anything like sociological deprivation theory to articulate and promote a theology which provides a firm basis for the liberation of oppressed peoples. The grace of God in Jesus Christ and the power of the Holy Spirit save and set free from. That sin—and therefore salvation from it—includes not only individual evil but social evil as well. As Hispanic Pentecostals theologize about their experience with systemic oppression and suffering, especially about the liberating impact of the gospel on their marginalization, they are also theologizing about what it plain means to be Pentecostal. And that is helpful to all of us.

CECIL M. ROBECK: PENTECOSTAL THEOLOGY AS ECUMENICAL ENGAGEMENT

More than a theorist, Mel Robeck has built on the work of Donald Gee and David du Plessis to become "the century's leading pentecostal ecumenist."[67] He maintains that early Pentecostalism clearly exhibited a true ecumenical vision that is currently in dire need of reclamation in spite of challenges.[68] Ecumenism refers to efforts by Christians of different traditions to develop closer relationships and better understandings.[69] Sometimes but not always it may refer to efforts towards some form of visible, organic unity. More often it refers to various degrees of interdenominational dialogue and cooperation. Ecumenical efforts usually arise out of interpretations of the Lord's words in John 17:21–23 implying that Christian unity is God's will and purpose for all the churches (cp. Eph 4:3). Convinced that "the scandal of division" is a major stumbling block to Christian mission and witness, ecumenists are committed to overcoming hindrances to progress, belief, and understanding that result from public perception of internal Christian animosity.

Pentecostal ecumenists do not claim that early Pentecostals were involved with formal ecumenical organizations or efforts. Rather, Pentecostals initially saw themselves as transcending denominational boundaries and traditional sectarianism.[70] For example, Carrie Judd Montgomery advertised her revival meetings as opportunities for salvation of the lost, Spirit baptism or Pentecostal fullness, divine healing, and greater unity in Christ.[71] Sensing the significance of an environment of

---

67. Spittler, "Robeck, Cecil Melvin, Jr." 1023.

68. Robeck, "Pentecostals and the Apostolic Faith," 61–84. Cp. Robeck, "Pentecostals and Christian Unity," 307–38. Similarly, Hocken, *Pentecost and Parousia*, 1, affirmed that the Charismatic renewal movement was/is inherently ecumenical.

69. Unfortunately, too many Pentecostals appear unable, or unwilling, to distinguish between ecumenism (positive relations between various Christian bodies) and relativist religious pluralism (equation of different world religions). See Bare, *They Call Me Pentecostal*, 45–50.

70. Sectarianism, or excessive devotion to a certain religious group coupled with discrimination toward others, has long been challenging for the international Church. Proliferation of denominations has taken on unprecedented complexities in America. See Richey, ed., *Denominationalism*.

71. Miskov, *Life on Wings*, 127 (Cp. 290–92).

corporate unity prominent in the Pentecost narrative (Acts 2:1) early Pentecostals extended offers of fellowship and partnership. However, mainstream elitism coupled with counterproductive Pentecostal inclinations toward extremism led to mutual disapproval and, often, to antagonistic rejection. After Pentecostalism continued to grow, numerically and in maturity and stability, other branches of the Christian family began to pay serious notice (especially in the United States). But by that time Pentecostals had become almost universally and incurably suspicious of their former detractors and, at times, persecutors.

Unfortunately, Pentecostals have exhibited self-defeating, debilitating tendencies toward divisiveness with one another as well as with non-Pentecostals. Harvey Cox, a long-time sympathetic observer of global Pentecostalism, admits continuing concerns over the impact of internal fragmentation among adherents of the movement. "I knew that arguments over theology, personality clashes, racial and ethnic divisions, regional differences, and denominational labels still prevented pentecostals from being the united people the promise of the first Pentecost held out."[72] Appropriately enough the several concerns enumerated are sandwiched between divisions over theology and denominationalism. Also appropriate is Cox's chiding reminder to Pentecostals about the unifying promise of the paradigmatic Pentecost in the NT Book of Acts. His challenge still rings in our ears.

The question of Pentecostal ecumenism is at heart a theological one. It is also historical. First note the historical. As noted, early Pentecostals resisted sectarianism stridently. For example, the original name of the denomination with which I am affiliated, the Church of God, was actually "The Christian Union," an appellation signifying a self-understanding transcending sectarian divisiveness.[73] Our early founders and pioneers were opposed to adding yet another sect to an already-too-large list. Eventually, for the Church of God as well as for many other Pentecostals, the necessity of cooperative missional efforts and enforceable standards of accountability required organizational and institutional formation and development. Yet a significant wing of the Pentecostal movement continues to identify as nondenominational or "Independents."[74] Even denominational Pentecostals are uncomfortable with denominational nomenclature. Many prefer to identify as a "movement."[75] Movement indicates dynamism and flexibility and feels more comfortable for those accustomed to the blowing winds of the Spirit than formal denominational conceptualizations and terminology (Acts 2:2; cp. Gen 1:2; John 3:8).

---

72. Cox, *Fire from Heaven*, 264. Warrington, *Pentecostal Theology*, 324, an astute insider, says "The fragmentation of Pentecostalism is an ongoing concern."

73. Richie, "The Church of God Today," 29–31.

74. My own maternal and paternal family background was largely shaped by a nondenominational/Independent influence.

75. Popular also, especially among Charismatics, are networks or fellowships, Strang, "Nondenominational Pentecostal and Charismatic Churches," 934.

One could conjecture that Pentecostals aware of their history would be motivated to reclaim an ecumenical or unifying impulse.[76] An ongoing discomfort with denominational status, perhaps not altogether realistic, nevertheless testifies to remnants of early commitments to overcome sectarianism that may still be exploited for a more realistic, though hopefully not less optimistic, ecumenical enterprise. Nevertheless, the theological rationale for ecumenism, while receiving impetus from Pentecostalism's early history, provides a better basis for Pentecostal ecumenism. Historical incidents may be attributed to the idealistic naivety of new movements in general are one thing. An inherent theological impulse toward unity is quite another. And that impulse still exists. If only Pentecostals will more fully learn the hard but happy lesson that Joshua and John finally grasped: God's will is not to exclude others from participating in the Holy Spirit or in Christ's work but to include them (Num 11:24–29; Luke 9:49–50).

At the heart of ecumenical theology is the critical concept of κοινωνία (*koinōnia*).[77] *Koinōnia* is usually translated "fellowship," "communion," "sharing," or "participation." In general, it signifies commonality, solidarity, and shared responsibility.[78] For our present purposes it is important to note that *koinōnia* specifically describes the apostolic church in the immediate aftermath of Pentecost (Acts 2:42). Not surprisingly, *koinōnia* is closely associated with the agency of the Holy Spirit (2 Cor 13:14; Phil 2:1). As such it describes "a dynamic experience that is inextricably related to receiving the love of the Father and the grace of the Lord Jesus Christ, the Son."[79] Here ecumenical theology appears close to Pentecostal appreciation for participation with the Spirit in the person and work of Jesus Christ.

Ecumenical theology employs the concept *koinōnia* to describe and promote trans-denominational fellowship and unity of all believers in Christ. Highlighting its significant placement in the Pentecost Day narrative enables Pentecostals to agree, and, arguably, to frame unifying fellowship among believers as an authentic work of the Holy Spirit essential for the integrity of their movement's identity. In short, *koinōnia* ought to be manifested in Spirit-filled living through ecumenical engagement. Like the *charismata*, the spiritual harmony and unity of *koinōnia* ought to be an uncompromising commitment for Pentecostals. Not surprisingly, as Syan notes, Pentecostals have become

---

76. I had an eye-opening experience in Cuba in 2008. Our team attended a local church for Sunday worship. The Baptist pastor conducted the service with some obvious incorporation of Episcopal liturgy although he preached a quite Baptist sermon. Furthermore, we enjoyed some Pentecostal singing, testifying, and praying. Later I inquired regarding the (to me) strange mix. I learned that communist persecution under Fidel Castro had taught the Christians how to worship together! That single congregation was indeed made up of Baptists, Episcopalians, Pentecostals, and, actually, a few more "brand names." They survived by banding together.

77. R. Saarinen, "Ecumenism," 267–68.

78. Davis, "Assembly, Religious."

79. Toon, "Fellowship," 256. Cp. 1 John 1:3–6.

"the largest and most dynamic grassroots ecumenical force in the Christian world"—although not everyone approves.[80]

AMOS YONG: PENTECOSTAL THEOLOGY AS PNEUMATOLOGICAL IMAGINATION

Via pneumatological imagination Malaysian-American Amos Yong explores hermeneutics, epistemology, philosophical presuppositions, Trinitarian theology, theology of religions, ecumenical and interfaith relations, theology of disability, engagement with contemporary culture, and the religion and science conversation.[81] This approach is guided and unified by a way of theologizing informed by the Pentecostal experience of and orientation toward the Holy Spirit. Arising out of the conviction that pneumatological experiences and insights offer important inferences far beyond traditional categories of soteriology (theology of salvation) and charismology (theology of spiritual gifts), indeed, even beyond pneumatology proper as it were (theology of the Holy Spirit), it is ambitious and systematic in its commitment to explore all of Christian life and thought in light of these pneumatological nuances. The results are often dramatic and surprising—even provocative and occasionally controversial—but undeniably productive.

In many ways focusing on pneumatological nuances for the overall theological enterprise is a long overdue corrective. The history of Christian theology is characterized by a serious lacuna regarding pneumatology. Aside from formal articulations of Trinitarian theology or an occasional nod here and there to the Holy Spirit's role in the Christian life, pneumatology has too often been subsumed under Christology, or even ecclesiology, if not neglected altogether. Investigating pneumatological contributions to the broad range of theological categories can produce incredibly fertile and versatile contributions to existing Christian thought and practice.[82] To name only a few, Christian theologies of creation, soteriology, and ecclesiology are opened up and extended significantly by exploring even the standard, classical teaching with the additional consideration of the pneumatological element.

I am confident that a concern that is occasionally expressed need not be fatal to the endeavor. The concern is that emphasizing pneumatology will result in minimizing other important areas, namely Christology. I offer two observations. First, to put it frankly, this concern is, in my opinion, often expressed out of a mindset that has become so accustomed to minimizing pneumatology that almost any pneumatological attention appears overdone. In other words, some theologians, like too many others,

---

80. Synan, "Streams of Renewal," 361, 363.

81. Vondey and Mittelstadt, *The Theology of Amos Yong*, serves well as an introduction to and interaction with Yong's theology. Stephenson, *Types of Pentecostal Theology*, points out that Yong is much more philosophically-oriented that has been typical of Pentecostal theology, 82–110.

82. Cp. Pinnock, *Flame of Love*.

are just flat out uncomfortable with the Holy Spirit. To me, such inordinate pneumatological discomfort only affirms the dire need for a corrective.

Second, a robust Trinitarian theology is an effective safeguard against any abuse or imbalance, real or imagined, regarding a consistent and dynamic integration of pneumatology into the overall theological enterprise. The Persons of the Trinity are co-eternal, co-existent, and co-equal—there is no competition or rivalry in the Godhead. The unity of the Divine Essence exists perfectly in the plurality of the Divine Persons (Matt 28:19). Correcting the lacuna in pneumatology, therefore, is not only theologically accurate, it is doxologically essential (2 Cor 13:14). Worshiping God aright requires adequate attention to the Holy Spirit as well as to the Father and the Son—indeed to the Triune God; despite or neglect of any Person of the Trinity in effect insults the entire Trinity (Heb 10:29). Notably, Jesus particularly cautioned against misunderstanding and misusing—or just plain missing—the Holy Spirit (Matt 12:31). Accordingly, I heartily applaud any revival of focused, sustained interest in pneumatology, especially, although not only, in Pentecostal theology.

VELI-MATTI KÄRKKÄINEN: PENTECOSTAL THEOLOGY FOR THE PLURALISTIC WORLD

Many Pentecostals typically view the world's religious systems as essentially false substitutes destined for eschatological judgment.[83] Finnish/American and Lutheran/Pentecostal theologian Veli-Matti Kärkkäinen has undertaken the ambitious task of a constructive systematic theology engaging the realities of cultural and religious pluralism in today's world.[84] This approach is indebted to the relatively new discipline of "comparative theology."[85] In this case, comparative theology includes Pentecostalism in a constructive theological proposal rooted in the Christian tradition but taking into serious consideration the insights of other traditions. Kärkkäinen's work is integrative and hospitable toward others but is nevertheless oriented toward "a coherent, balanced understanding of Christian truth and faith in light of Christian tradition" with its definitive role in the current climate of diversity.[86]

---

83. E.g. Gause, *Revelation*, 133–34. Pentecostals adhere to an eschatological schema suggesting corrupt religion will serve as a diabolical instrument of Antichrist, 221–22. Likely the primary proof text (Rev 17) refers to corrupt, perverse religion's historic culmination eschatologically via Antichrist's exploitation rather than to specific organized world religions per se.

84. Most notably, see Veli-Matti Kärkkäinen's five volume series on *Constructive Christian Theology for the Pluralistic World*.

85. Comparative theology is not to be confused with the older discipline of Comparative Religions, an analytical comparison of the world's major religions with guiding emphases on generality and objectivity.

86. Kärkkäinen, *Hope and Community*, 1. In this five-volume series, Kärkkäinen's direct appropriation of Pentecostal theology is somewhat uneven. E.g., *Spirit and Salvation* includes Pentecostals more so than *Hope and Community*.

Representative Perspectives

Why should Pentecostals do—or not do—comparative theology? To address the negative first, one might wonder if this is the proverbial "slippery slope" toward compromise of Christian doctrine and eventual embrace of relativism. Pentecostals certainly would not be in favor of any concessions altering the essential makeup of biblical Christianity. Neither would they be amiable to any process denying the existence of absolute truth or claiming that the truths that any individual or culture happen to believe are equally valid with myriad other such truth claims.[87]

But compromise and relativism are not inherent to doing comparative theology. Of course, the exception would be whenever a given comparative theologian held to those kinds of presuppositions him/herself. But that is the fault of the respective theologian, not of the discipline per se. The work of the discipline can be carried out from the perspective of biblical, historic, and, yes, Pentecostal commitments—as Kärkkäinen ably demonstrates. Caution is nonetheless advisable for circumspect theological engagement with religious diversity.

Now for the positive. Pentecostals can—and ought to—engage in comparative theology for several reasons.[88] First, Pentecostalism's explosive global growth means that many Pentecostals are now more than ever before in close, and perhaps constant, contact with adherents of other faiths. Second, the increasing migration of people of diverse faiths all over the world due to modern globalization means that many of the people among whom Pentecostals live and minister, perhaps even family, friends, or neighbors, are more than ever before in close, and likely constant, contact with adherents of other faiths. Third, Pentecostals' own theological identity requires them to be open to understanding the working of God's Spirit in the world, including in the world of religions. All of these reasons, and others which could be offered easily enough as well, indicate that if Pentecostal theology is to rise to the occasion to meet the demands of today's pluralistic world, it needs not merely to have some facile infatuation with exotic belief systems but to do intentional engagement with other religions in such a way as to demonstrate the distinctive validity of the Christian faith in its Pentecostal form.[89]

Perhaps an example will be helpful. Even a cursory study of cultures and religions confirms that eschatology is omnipresent in society and pan-religious.[90] For Kärkkäinen, an investigation into Jewish and Islamic eschatologies along with Hindu and Buddhist perspectives sets up a discussion of Christian eschatology.[91] There are significant similarities between the Abrahamic/monotheistic faiths (for example, on resurrection, final judgment, Heaven, Hell) but drastic differences between these,

---

87. Smith, *Who's Afraid of Relativism?* offers an intriguing discussion by a Pentecostal/Charismatic philosopher on the subtleties involved with an in-depth discussion on the nature of truth.

88. For detailed treatment, see Richie, *Speaking by the Spirit*.

89. Newbigin's *Gospel in a Pluralist Society* is great for this topic.

90. Kärkkäinen, *Hope and Community*, 7–23. Even scientific theories utilize the category, 24–39.

91. Kärkkäinen, *Hope and Community*, 40–74.

including Christianity, and the Eastern/pluralist religions (for example, on reincarnation). Of course, Christianity has differences with others all around regarding the role of Jesus Christ (for example, as returning Lord).

What is really distinctive about Christian eschatology? The all-orienting role of hope linked to the nature of the Divine Being is unparalled. Christian eschatology is a Trinitarian theology of hope focusing on creation, providence, and consummation as the joint work of the Triune God.[92] The God of hope restores hope and meaningfulness through confidence in God's promise and faithfulness in assurance of the Son's resurrection and ultimately completed by the Holy Spirit.[93] Specific scenarios aside, which are often speculative anyway, that is a powerful, uplifting summation.

Note that in the above instance comparative theology does not simply lay the different eschatologies side by side in order to finally say, "Oh, look how much better our Christian eschatology is than theirs!" Rather, a comparative analysis helps toward mutual understanding while eventually aiding movement toward enhanced self-understanding. By means of this process deeper insight is acquired into the distinctive nature of nature of our own Christian faith via conversation with the faith of others. Paradoxically, increasing our understanding of others often enhances self-understanding—and sometimes, a level of appreciation and respect all around.

The preceding list of representative Pentecostal theologians is not exhaustive. There are many other important theologians with their particular approaches to doing Pentecostal theology that could, and perhaps should, be named. Time and space simply will not permit it. However, these will suffice as significant samples representing those who are doing Pentecostal theology today. Some of it is fairly traditional, some quite avant-garde. Yet their emphases are not necessarily incompatible. Each has its own accent. Each expresses Pentecostalism in continuity and, usually, in community with the others. But Pentecostals have had their share of internal debates. A few of these debates has brought sharp division—as the next two chapters clearly indicate.

---

92. Kärkkäinen, *Hope and Community*, 75.
93. Kärkkäinen, *Hope and Community*, 75–89.

2

A Major Controversy over Sanctification

Pentecostals debate, at times heatedly, several topics. Wesleyan-Pentecostals, harking back to Holiness roots, emphasize sanctification as definitive crisis experience within a growth process. Baptistic Pentecostals view sanctification as an ongoing growth process definitively unattainable in this life. Ecclesial polity and practice often reflects the specific branch of Christianity out of which a particular Pentecostal group originated. A prominent wing of Pentecostalism (Independents) stresses non-denominationalism. Certainly, Pentecostals are far from unanimous regarding the role of women in ministry, political activism, social responsibilities, environmentalism, ecumenical relations, or dialogue with non-Christian faiths. However, although it is important to understand these theological differences, and the stories behind them, it is advisable to remember that there exists a remarkably consistent unity of spirituality.[1]

Further, Pentecostals stridently debate the nature of the Divine Being. A large majority of Pentecostals is Trinitarian, while a strong minority is Unitarian.[2] Many North American Pentecostals and their affiliates affirm the doctrine of initial evidence—speaking in tongues as the first observable sign of Spirit baptism. Denominational Charismatics and global Pentecostals are less likely to emphasize initial evidence.

1. Archer, 'I Was in the Spirit on the Lord's Day', 333.

2. It is critically important to distinguish between liberal Unitarianism, which affirms monotheism through denying the deity of Jesus Christ, and Pentecostal Unitarianism, which affirms monotheism through affirming the deity of Jesus Christ. Trinitarian Pentecostals affirm one God who eternally exists in three persons, namely, the Father, the Son, and the Holy Spirit.

Pentecostals are becoming increasingly diverse regarding eschatology. Many traditional Pentecostals are classic dispensationalists while others argue that dispensationalism's embrace of cessationism is inherently averse to Pentecostalism.[3] The latter tend to adopt an inaugurated, already/not yet eschatology in conjunction with more conventional approaches to Christ's second coming and the consummation of history.

Out of the preceding list of several debated topics, two clearly stand out as having had dramatic impact on the development of Pentecostal theology. Sanctification and the Godhead are so prominent that they have become distinctive labels for different wings of the Pentecostal movement. Holiness Pentecostals or non-Holiness Pentecostals are also known as Wesleyan or Baptistic/Reformed Pentecostals, respectively. Although a predominant majority of Pentecostals are Trinitarian, a significant number are Oneness or Unitarian. This chapter and the next focus on theological aspects of these two internal debates that erupted into major, long lasting controversies.[4] In each case, after some background orientation and developmental preparation, I offer a creative proposal for moving beyond the tradition of impasse through specific, distinctive, and consistent application of inherent Pentecostal motifs.

NATURE AND ROLE OF SANCTIFICATION

Pentecostals virulently debate the nature and role of sanctification in the Christian life. Wesleyan-Pentecostals emphasize sanctification as definitive crisis experience within a growth process, but Baptistic Pentecostals view sanctification as an ongoing growth process definitively unattainable in this present life.[5] The stage was set for this disagreement in the origins of the Pentecostal movement. Pentecostalism originated in the nineteenth century Holiness movement in the United States, especially influenced by members of the National Holiness Association, which arose as a radical reaction to a perceived cooling of Methodist commitment to the doctrine and practice of the Wesleyan touchstones of entire sanctification and Christian perfection. However, the broader Holiness movement was also influenced by the Keswick Convention for the Promotion of Practical Holiness, which arose in northeast England and which was non-Wesleyan. Although initially the Pentecostal movement was unanimously

---

3. Cessationism claims spiritual gifts (*charismata*) esp. speaking in tongues, divine healing, and miraculous signs and wonders ceased after the Early Church age, rejecting the authenticity and credibility of Pentecostalism, Horton, "Spirit Baptism," 82–83. Synan gives a helpful overview of cessationism's historical rise and fall with the reappearance of spiritual gifts, "Pentecostal Roots," 15–38, in *The Century of the Holy Spirit*.

4. Chapter 11 will discuss the doctrine of initial evidence, so incredibly important in Pentecostal theology, and also controversial, though more so for non-Pentecostals.

5. Jones, "Holiness Movement," 726–29. Synan, *Holiness-Pentecostal Movement in the United States* and Dayton, *Theological Roots of Pentecostalism* offer in depth information on the historical and theological origins and developments of the sanctification debate in Pentecostalism.

Wesleyan, it eventually felt the influence of the Keswick stream and struggled to come to terms with it.[6]

Early Pentecostals did not so much disagree on the premium place of holiness in Christian life as on the nature of its inception and extent of its actualization. In other words, Pentecostals continue to agree that holiness of heart and life is God's standard of living for believers (per Heb 12:14) but do not agree regarding its implementation. In a sense, their Holiness heritage was destined "both to unite and divide them."[7] The division side of that conjunction came to the fore in a fast and furious fashion with the head-on collision of William J. Seymour with William H. Durham. Their no-holds-barred fight over the future direction of Pentecostal theologies of sanctification almost singlehandedly assured that rapprochement would be out of reach any time soon.

Interestingly, Durham, an Anglo pastor from Chicago, had nothing but praise for Seymour, the African American pastor of the Azusa Street Mission in Los Angeles, when they first met. For his part, Seymour repeatedly invited Durham to preach at Azusa (where, after all, Durham had experienced Spirit baptism).[8] All that fine fellowship forever changed a few years later when Durham started promoting a "finished work" theology of sanctification.[9] In a word, it insisted that one is granted positional sanctification in Christ at conversion as the beginning of a lifelong pursuit of actual sanctification.[10] An intense, often bitter struggle ensued between the two men and their followers that spilled over into the entire movement. When Durham died the following year, "he left as his legacy a movement divided over the issue of sanctification."[11]

The Seymour-Durham conflict served as the catalyst for the movement's division over sanctification, but more than that was in play. Methodist and Baptist Christians who came into Pentecostalism brought with them many of their previous beliefs and practices. It was only a matter of time before clashes occurred. Almost inevitably sanctification became a flashpoint. For nearly four decades the division resulted, functionally at least, in two adamantly opposed Pentecostal movements. Finally, after World

---

6. I.e., some Pentecostals opted for a progressive view of sanctification holding that entire sanctification is not attainable until or after death.

7. Jones, "Holiness Movement," 728.

8. Robeck, *Azusa Street Mission & Revival*, 91, 115.

9. Robeck, *Azusa Street Mission & Revival*, 173. In the so-called "finished work" theology there is no definite work of sanctifying grace which occurs subsequent to conversion. Oddly enough, given the moniker, sanctification is *not* finished in this life but gradually progresses until eventual completion occurs at/after death. However, there is evidence that Durham's original vision, apparently abandoned and restructured by later followers, while indeed denying subsequence, may have been a kind of "radicalized Wesleyanism" which claimed instantaneous and entire sanctification at conversion. See Knight, *Anticipating Heaven Below*, 94–95. If so, it was not the attainability or entirety of sanctification which bothered Durham but the timing of its experience.

10. Robeck, *Azusa Street Mission & Revival*, 315–17.

11. Robeck, *Azusa Street Mission & Revival*, 317. Cp. Riss, "Finished Work Controversy," 638–39. Durham's untimely death meant he never succeeded in developing his theology and its implications further. More than anything else, it offered followers a "rejection of sanctification as a second definite experience of grace," Clayton, "Significance of William H. Durham," 39.

War II Pentecostals began to (re)unite in fellowship, worship, and missional partnership.[12] However, the divisive theological issue has never been resolved.[13] Rather, Pentecostals from both Wesleyan-Holiness and Baptistic/Reformed camps have learned to minimize the invective animosity of their historic theological disagreement at least enough to allow more positive, less vindictive interaction.

RESOURCES FOR PROGRESS

Which is right, the Holiness Pentecostals or the Baptistic Pentecostals? Obviously, I cannot here resolve that hard, old question to everyone's (or perhaps even, to anyone's) satisfaction. In the interest of full disclosure, my own background has been largely in the Holiness wing. The Church of God with International Offices in Cleveland, Tennessee, of which I am a member and with whom I am an ordained bishop, has a marked Holiness heritage. Further, Pentecostal Theological Seminary, where I teach theology, is well known for its distinctive Wesleyan-Pentecostal approach. Furthermore, my own theological orientation is staunchly Wesleyan-Holiness Pentecostal. Therefore, it will perhaps be surprising to some that I am not going to come down on the Wesleyan-Holiness side. Neither am I going to come down on the Baptistic/Reformed side. Rather, I aim to identify an already-existing avenue between the two before offering an alternative.

Leonard Lovett points out that Black Holiness Pentecostalism, a movement encompassing several denominations, has "historic roots embracing, but not always restricted to" both Wesleyan-Arminian and finished work orientation.[14] Amazingly, Black Holiness Pentecostalism is able to hold several potentially tense positions in tandem. How? It can offer a widely welcoming embrace because of leadership commitment to what Lovett calls "double discernment"—or discovering "how to say no to loyalties that divide and yes to the moving of the Spirit that heals and restores persons and institutions torn asunder by idolatrous loyalties."[15] Notably, only idolatry adequately describes any loyalty that is placed before God—including before God the Holy Spirit (Ex 20:3). That puts all partisanship into perspective. Ultimate allegiance belongs only to God.

How might "double discernment" help me regarding respective Holiness and Baptistic stances on sanctification? It inspires me to make three concomitant commitments. First, I refuse to be divided from my precious Baptistic Pentecostal sisters and

12. Riss, "Finished Work," 639.

13. In her fascinating and suggestive recent study, Holley, "Johannine Theology of Sanctification," 255, concludes that Wesleyan-Pentecostals relied more heavily on the explicitly Trinitarian portrait of sanctification in the Johannine corpus (esp. John's Gospel and 1 John) in developing their doctrine of sanctification than did Baptistic Pentecostals.

14. Lovett, "Black Holiness Pentecostalism," 419. Of course, it would be naïve not to acknowledge that partisanship can affect any group. Yet the principle seems sound.

15. Lovett, "Black Holiness Pentecostalism,," 427.

brothers over our differences regarding sanctification. John Wesley said that if we cannot believe alike we ought at least to love alike.[16] Sometimes we have lost sight of that all-important principle. Let us reclaim a holy love that refuses to entertain evil against one another (1 Cor 13). Second, I affirm the valuable contribution that the Baptistic or progressive perspective brings to the doctrine of sanctification. There is no automatic, instant holiness. Ongoing growth in grace is essential (2 Pet 3:18). Philemon Roberts, a Holiness-Pentecostal, once put it this way: "Purity is instantaneous but maturity takes time."[17] Accordingly, holiness is an area where humility is undoubtedly a most important virtue. Thirdly, I remain convinced along with Holiness sisters and brothers that holiness of heart and life is neither a peripheral command nor an empty promise. The Apostle's injunction, "but as He who called you *is* holy, you also be holy in all *your* conduct, because it is written, *'Be holy, for I am holy.'*" (1 Pet 1:15–16; cp. Lev 11:44–45; 19:2; 20:7), implies that actual holiness is both essential and attainable. But how do I consistently hold these three commitments together theologically?

Here I take advantage of an assist from Myer Pearlman, an early Pentecostal scholar who is counted in the Baptistic camp.[18] Pearlman insisted that sanctification is positional and progressive, arguing against views such as eradication of the sinful nature as erroneous.[19] Nonetheless, he made a number of interesting acknowledgements. For one, he suggested that a kind of "awakening to one's position in Christ" constitutes what some experience as a second definite work of grace.[20] For another, he affirmed the truth of entire sanctification or Christian perfection (carefully defined), arguing that John Wesley's view and John Calvin's view are both scriptural and therefore compatible.[21] Finally, citing Isaiah chapter six for support, Pearlman says: "It must be acknowledged that progress in sanctification often involves a crisis experience almost as definite as that of conversion," adding that "this experience has been called a second work of grace."[22]

Pearlman appears to have been operating in a conciliatory mode trying to bridge the gap with the Holiness wing of Pentecostalism without conceding his own Baptistic commitments. I have long thought his effort worthy of emulation. However, a facile

---

16. John Wesley, "A Catholic Spirit," Wesley Center Online: http://wesley.nnu.edu/john-wesley/the-sermons-of-john-wesley-1872-edition/sermon-39-catholic-spirit/.

17. Roberts, *God's Will for God's People*.

18. Interestingly, Pearlman was from a Jewish family background in Scotland. After migrating to the United States, he converted to Christianity and received the baptism of the Holy Spirit, G. H. Gohr, "Pearlman, Myer," *New International Dictionary of Pentecostal Charismatic Movements* (*NIDPCM*), 959.

19. Pearlman, *Knowing the Doctrines of the Bible*: 252–54 and 257.

20. Pearlman, *Knowing the Doctrines of the Bible*, 261.

21. Pearlman, *Knowing the Doctrines of the Bible*, 263–67. "Sanctification for Calvin is the process of our advance in piety through the course of our life and in the pursuit of our vocation," "Introduction," xxix–lxxi, Calvin, *Institutes*, lx.

22. Pearlman, *Knowing the Doctrines of the Bible*, 266.

attempt will not suffice. Thus, I do not suggest that Holiness and Baptistic Pentecostals have really been saying the same thing after all. Yet neither is there an impassable barrier between Baptistic and Holiness Pentecostals.

Theologically speaking, a crisis-development model of sanctification has much to offer. In this context "crisis" signifies a moment or stage in a sequence of events or experiences at which the direction or trend of future events or experiences, either for better or for worse, is set or determined. In other words, it is a turning point. "Development" signifies an act or process of growth and progress. Development certainly implies more dynamism than crisis but there is no reason to assume that it cannot include punctiliar aspects, that is, actions or experiences occurring at a definite point in time—or that one might be especially significant. In short, the experience of sanctification and its expression in the Christian life may involve both distinct experience and extended progress without any contradiction. Thus, spiritual growth is a process of ongoing crisis (Ps 139:23–24), an ontological and existential journey of encounter (Isa 6:6–7). For biblical support, note that 1 Thessalonians 4:1–7 and Titus 3:4–7 certainly include crisis-development themes with clear soteriological and pneumatological implications. In this sense, purity indicates moral integration as believers grow in and toward God's goal for his people—that is, going on to perfection (Heb 6:1). Therefore, "the goal of salvation is not forgiveness but holiness, not justification but sanctification; salvation is to be restored to the image of God in this life."[23]

Probably the theological "wrench in the works," as they say, is entire sanctification or Christian perfection. The doctrine that believers may be made holy in their complete being is scriptural (1 Thess 5:23) but controversial. Much of the problem probably stems from entire sanctification having been misrepresented by some of its advocates as well as misunderstood by some opponents. And the very word "perfect" (Matt 5:48) is, if anything, even more disturbing and suspicious for many. Yet Pearlman affirms the doctrine of entire sanctification or Christian perfection—in a carefully qualified sense.[24] Only God is perfect in an absolute sense, but human beings can be perfect in a relative sense. Old Testament perfection entails wholehearted desire and determination to do God's will, while NT perfection is more variegated, including positional and progressive perfection, spiritual maturity and understanding, perfection in certain particulars, such as perfect love (love as the integrating center of all life), and ultimate perfection in Heaven.[25]

23. Knight, *John Wesley*, Kindle location, 1205. Cp. 1231 and 1301–02. In a word, "The goal of Christian perfection is to be restored to the image of God; perfection is reached when that goal is attained," Knight, *John Wesley*, 1318. But even its attaining is not a static state but a relational dynamic characterized by continual increase and progress, Knight, *John Wesley*, 1361–86.

24. Wesley and Wesleyans follow a similar strategy. Cp. Oden, *Wesley's Scriptural Christianity*, 319–27.

25. Pearlman, *Knowing the Doctrines of the Bible*, 263–64. Oddly, although many have problems with terms like "perfect love," world history portrays the nature of "perfect hatred" quite graphically. Ought not redemption history portray perfect love?

In my opinion, entire sanctification or Christian perfection without any restriction, exception, or qualification is not descriptive of realistic human expectations for attainment in this present—or for that matter, in any—age. Christian perfection is and always will be derivative and relative. It has its origin and end in the infinite God commensurate with finite creaturely existence and identity (Rom 11:36). Put another way, Christian perfection can only ever exist via connection, that is, in union, with God, through necessary dependence upon God. And yet it is of course completely reasonable to conclude that relative perfection or entire sanctification will manifest itself in ethical, holy living, living not characterized by sinful thoughts, words, or deeds but rather by consistent demonstration of God's "good, acceptable, and perfect will" (Rom 12:2).[26] Here is the counterpart for the all-too-common malady of Christians living conflicted, frustrated lives. In purity of heart and singleness of intention believers wholly or entirely commitment themselves and their lives to God's grace, that is, God's favor and power.

Of course, there have been (and are) extremists. Calvin rightly railed against fanatical versions of perfectionism which denied obvious realities of temptation and human weakness.[27] Calvin concluded, "Thus it comes about that, far removed from perfection, we must steadily move forward, and though entangled in vices, daily fight against them."[28] His candid description rings true with the real-life experiences of many of even the most devout believers. That being said, Christian perfection and entire sanctification in the best Wesleyan tradition does not deny the realities of temptation and human weakness. It admits that perfecting grace is a moment-by-moment relationship capable of either progress or regress.[29] Yet Wesley refuses to call temptations, infirmities, or errors in judgment *sin*. For him, they are mistakes. Only willful disobedience is sin.[30] Interestingly, on this topic Calvin disagrees with Augustine, considered the greatest of the Early Church Fathers and his primary theological mentor, whose position appears to be, oddly enough, closer to Wesley.[31]

PROPOSAL FROM A PENTECOSTAL PRESUPPOSITION

To bring this discussion to the point, what does the traditional sanctification debate mean for Pentecostal theology today? I argue that Pentecostals may have been inadvertently sucked into the whirlpool of a debate that really did not belong to us. At

26. Bernard, *In Search of Holiness,* thus distinguishes between absolute and relative perfection, 24.
27. Calvin, *Institutes,* 606–07.
28. Calvin, *Institutes,* 607.
29. As Kärkkäinen observes, the "the perfecting work of the Spirit" is ultimately eschatological with an ever-present view toward "the total redemption of humanity," *Hope and Community,* 88–89 (88).
30. Wesley's essay "A Plain Account of Christian Perfection," *Wesley's Works,* 11:366–445, most thoroughly presents his views and debunks false stereotypes.
31. Calvin, *Institutes,* 602–03. Calvin thinks Augustine is inconsistent on this point.

the least, we do not have to continue owning it and, consequently, agonizing over it. Above I affirmed the value of Black Holiness Pentecostalism's principle of "double discernment" for facing divisive theological issues that so often arise out of partisan loyalties. I still do. Yet I think it may be possible to move along a bit farther, theologically speaking, as well. Certainly, it is desirable to move beyond the traditional Wesleyan/Reformed debate over sanctification into a more specifically, that is, a more consistently and distinctively, Pentecostal theology of sanctification transcending, as it were, both models. The demands of time and space prevent more than a bare beginning; but, I humbly attempt at least a fresh start.[32]

What I propose is utilization of two threads consistently running throughout Pentecostal theology: commitments to *unlimited possibilities* and to a *pragmatic outlook*. Pentecostals are known for resisting any and all attempts to limit spiritual gifts to the first century or to deny the reality of the miraculous. The movement was birthed in the midst of a burst of such activities; it cannot deny them without acquiescing its identity. Against all odds, Pentecostals insisted that such things as speaking in tongues, divine healing, and miraculous responses to believing prayer do indeed legitimately occur today. They still insist that mindboggling experiences and events defying comprehension are possible—and reasonable, in view of God's inexhaustible ability.

As a boy growing up in Pentecostal churches one of the Bible quotes I heard quite frequently was, "If thou canst believe, all things *are* possible to him that believeth." (Mark 9:23 KJV)[33] It was often backed up with, "For with God nothing shall be impossible." (Luke 1:37) The Pentecostal relatives and friends of my childhood were endeavoring to follow the example of Abraham, who "being fully persuaded that, what [God] had promised, he was able also to perform." (Rom 4:21 KJV) To this day, Pentecostals are inclined to interpret such texts as literal expressions of unlimited possibilities through faith in an all-powerful God. Pentecostals instinctively resist placing restrictions on possibilities which have their origin in the affirmative agency of God according to God's express will or purpose.

Although Pentecostal affirmation of unlimited possibilities is best known in regard to spiritual gifts, divine healing, and other miraculous occurrences, it is not restricted to these few points. It is a core value, an essential aspect of a broader worldview. Harvey Cox's highly regarded work on Pentecostalism says as much too. Analyzing the incredible growth and vitality of the movement in Latin America, Cox picks up on the theme of doing even "greater works" than Jesus (John 14:12–13). He repeatedly heard this phrase quoted via a Pentecostal woman's striking testimony and conversation.[34]

---

32. Van de Walle, *Rethinking Holiness*, 147–50, well says that above all holiness is a way of being in the world derivative of and dependent on the divine nature which is humanly attainable only in union with Christ by the power of the Holy Spirit.

33. It also appears to be a favorite refrain for Jesus. In addition to Mark 9:23 and Luke 1:37 see Mark 10:27 and Matt 9:26.

34. Cox, *Fire from Heaven*: 166 and 184.

Inferences of the amazing possibilities involved were not confined to conversions, spiritual gifts, and healings but included cultural and political transformation. Cox was so impressed that he decided to use the "greater works" theme as the definitive descriptor for his chapter on Latin American Pentecostalism.[35] The chapter discusses several academic theories about the phenomenal impact of Pentecostalism in Latin America, most of which in Cox's telling end up sounding passé. Cox takes the unlimited possibilities of grassroots Pentecostals' faith as the definitive, and multifaceted, qualifier.

Pentecostals as a whole are people who believe in the actualization of amazing, unlimited possibilities in God. To say that complete victory over sin is impossible—that it *cannot* happen for *anyone*—goes against the grain of the Pentecostal gestalt. God can and does save the lost, heal the sick, set the captive free, grant victory over sin, and answer a host of other prayers in accordance with God's revealed will. And there is no question but that the Bible reveals that God's will for his people is sanctification/holiness (1 Thess 4:3, 7). Neither is there any question but that God is able. As Johns summarily declares, "Such is the power of the gospel."[36]

As an adult convert, my Pentecostal preacher father sat me down and talked with me about holiness and sanctification.[37] He did not mention Calvin or Wesley. He did not use any of their terminology. Years later when I learned about Calvin and Wesley, I discovered that my father was aware of them and of the sanctification debate, and that he personally identified as Holiness Pentecostal; but, he did not feel compelled to follow that angle slavishly. What he stressed was living an overcoming life and enjoying complete victory over sin (1 Cor 15:57; 1 John 3:7–10; 5:4).[38] According to him God has commanded holiness and is able to accomplish it (1 Pet 1:15–16). Since then I have often encountered other Pentecostals in congregational or pastoral settings who exclaim that "God is able!" God is able to save. God is able to heal and deliver. God is able to sanctify and give victory over sin. A Pentecostal theology of sanctification arising out of divine omnipotence can be quite appealing, even compelling.

Pentecostal pragmatism is well known too.[39] Think of the same examples as above: speaking in tongues, divine healing, and miracles. Many early Pentecostals initially held to a theology of xenolalia, or missionaries' unlearned ability to speak in the languages of indigenous cultures for the purposes of evangelism and witnessing (hence

---

35. Cox, *Fire from Heaven*, 161.

36. Johns, "Cultivating a Heart for Holiness," 33. Johns asks, "But, in a sinful world, how is it possible to live a life of personal holiness?" She answers with "the journey into holiness is not easy. It calls for the reshaping of our affections." (33) Johns explains that, "Such lives are possible if we are willing to pay the price. We pay that price in the fires of death to self." (37)

37. My father is not seminary trained. As of this writing 59 of his 84 years have been spent actively preaching the gospel.

38. This "overcoming life" and "victorious life" language, with its strong emphasis on power over sin, has roots in certain elements of the non-Wesleyan/Keswickian wing of the Holiness movement. See Waldvogel, "The 'Overcoming Life,'" 7–19.

39. This is a major point of Wacker's *Heaven Below*.

"missionary tongues"). Although a few such cases were reported by missionaries from the field it soon became evident that they were at best rare and certainly not a viable model for missions.[40] Pentecostals did not give up on tongues. Without denying occasional occurrences of xenolalia, most shifted their focus to the role of tongues as initial evidence and in prayer and worship. This historical reassessment is typical of contemporary Pentecostals as well.

Pentecostals have had a long and abiding, though sometimes controversial, commitment to the doctrine of divine healing. Many early Pentecostals, and a few since the early days, have been known to refuse medical care out of their faith in divine healing. However, most Pentecostals today combine appreciation for medical science and belief in miraculous healings.[41] Recently, my wife Sue had surgery for colon cancer. Prior to her surgery my State Administrative Bishop told me that he believes God heals in one of three ways: (1) By taking us to himself where there is no sickness; (2) In conjunction with medical science; and, (3) Apart from human agency through direct intervention. In Sue's case it was number two. We had a great team of physicians and a surgeon who prayed with us and did his job very well. Yet our surgeon gladly affirms that several rather remarkable developments in her care were best attributed to God's mercy and power. These remarkable developments extended to her recovery so that she never had to undergo chemotherapy or radiation as previously expected.

Again, Pentecostals are known for enthusiastic attestations to miracles.[42] Pastor Dean Pickens began his ministry after he was saved and delivered from alcoholism in a tent revival in the Midwest conducted by my evangelist father in the early 1960s. Pastor Dean soon planted a church in the Great Lakes region. On the podium in the sanctuary he inscribed large the words "Expect a Miracle" as the optimistic descriptive theme of his ministry.[43] Years after his passing, that church is still going strong and abounds in miracle testimonies—not the least of which is his formerly recalcitrant son now serving as pastor. Yet for years its founder worked hard and long in a local factory as a bi-vocational pastor to help finance the ministry of his fledgling congregation. Belief in miracles, in God's supernatural power, as he put it, did not negate the hard realities of daily life; but then, neither did the hard realities of daily life contradict belief in God's miraculous power.[44]

---

40. Nevertheless, documented testimonies exist of people speaking languages they did not know which were understood by native speakers. E.g., see Arrington, *Encountering the Holy Spirit,* 431–34.

41 Theron, "Practical Theological Theory for the Healing Ministry," 49–64.

42. See Richie, "Affirmative Pentecostal Theology of the Miraculous."

43. Optimism may be rooted deeply in the American psyche, Cole, *Northern Evangelists,* 11; but, Pentecostal faith transcends national traits in its affirmative and positive view of God's activity in the world today.

44. One of this pastor's favorite stories was of a time when they did not have enough money in the offering to pay the church's bills. They counted it again and had a little more. They counted it again until it was enough and stopped. He considered this a miraculous provision. But he did not quit his "day job" as they say. By the way, this is a not unknown occurrence in struggling Pentecostal congregations. I experienced it myself once in my first pastorate at a little country church in Tennessee.

If it is inconsistent with the Pentecostal theological gestalt to approach the doctrine of sanctification with presumptions limiting the infinite God, then it is equally contradictory to deny or ignore the realities of finite human existence.[45] Human beings are by nature limited. Often human frailties and infirmities are all too apparent. And this realism applies no less to sanctification than other anthropological considerations. Realistically speaking, even deeply devout Christians are frequently tempted and sometimes cave into temptation's pressure. Who can imagine Jesus, sinless Son of God though he most certainly was, struggling so intensely in the Garden of Gethsemane with God's purpose and will for his life—or, more correctly, for his death—without wondering that the rest of us mere mortals often waver or are overcome?[46]

In my opinion, any theology of sanctification which does not adequately account for the shortcomings of real people itself comes up way short. Jesus certainly understood, for he taught us to pray each day both for daily bread and for forgiveness (Matt 6:11–12). In all honesty, I suspect that the vast majority of Christians do not in this life experience a level of living that they would themselves call "entire" or "perfect." If it is not impossible it may nevertheless be unlikely. Probably the most many hope for is a fairly consistent life not characterized by regularly committing actual sin. One reason for this near universal lack of complete victory may be traceable to common teaching that all they may reasonably expect is a comparable level of godliness. If people are not taught that holiness is attainable, then they likely will not strive for it as zealously—and they are probably not too surprised when they do not achieve it either. But, that being said, the realities of finite human existence, and day-to-day human limitations, should not be casually dismissed.

Nevertheless, I am committed to a theological anthropology.[47] In short, our theology should assess humanity from the perspective of divine creation, redemption, and provision. Theologians talk about doing theology "from above" or doing theology "from below." The former starts with God and moves toward humans. The latter approach starts with human beings and moves toward God. If we start with God's unlimited power, then I do not think we will so readily dismiss the very *possibility* of *anyone* experiencing complete and lasting victory over sin in this life. If we start with human finitude and frailty, then likely we will find the possibility of complete victory too credulous to entertain even for a moment.

The Bible starts with God (Gen 1:1). I think Pentecostal theology should start with God too. For me, that means my understanding of sanctification starts with the unlimited power of God. Thus, I affirm an attainable, sustainable victory over sin in the Christian life. But starting with God does not mean ignoring human beings. After

---

45. One of the greatest theologians among the Church Fathers, Gregory of Nyssa, puts it thus: "For this is truly perfection never to stop growing toward what is better and never placing any limit on perfection." See *ACCS,* "1–2 Corinthians," 226.

46. Luke's account (22:40–46) is particularly descriptive in depicting Jesus' very real anguish.

47. Cortez, *Theological Anthropology*, is a helpful introduction to this topic.

all, the Bible ends with God's people (Rev 22:21). Thus, I acknowledge the limitations of human finitude. In short, Pentecostal theology can encourage a victorious, overcoming life, made possible by the grace of God through faith in Christ and in the power of the Holy Spirit, with authentic pastoral sensitivity to the struggles and temptations that sisters and brothers in the pews (and pulpits) encounter in their life journey.

I suggest that Pentecostal theology of holiness and sanctification is not primarily about Calvinism versus Wesleyanism or Holiness Pentecostals versus Baptistic Pentecostals. It is more about who God is and who we are.[48] Yes, we struggle; but, God gives the victory. Interestingly, Bernard's study of the role of the Holy Spirit in justification concludes that "justification involves not only a change of standing but also victory over sin and the beginning of a new life."[49] He sums up nicely:

> While justification is by grace through faith and not of works, it is not merely an extrinsic, forensic transaction. Rather, it is the dynamic work of the Holy Spirit in the human heart that enables believers to enter the new covenant and participate in the resurrection life of Jesus Christ.[50]

I agree heartily with Robeck's timely advice, which I think is representative of Pentecostals across the board:

> When we speak of revival, we often speak about the purifying fire of the Lord that accompanies it. This fire burns away non-essentials—attitudes, worries, even sin. The revival at the Azusa Street Mission fell upon those who took personal holiness seriously. We may not all agree about how our sanctification is accomplished through Jesus Christ, but there's no debating that holiness is critical to a truly transformed life! When relativism seems to be winning the day, Pentecostals must once again reevaluate their commitment to matters of personal holiness.[51]

Bernard similarly suggests that "The most important thing is to be willing to grow and learn and to sincerely do the will of God" and thus "develop holiness in the sight of God."[52]

Finally, recent Pentecostal NT scholarship supports an optimistic and realistic approach to holiness in the life of believers that overcomes the traditional impasse.

---

48. Basil the Great, the 4th century Cappadocian theologian, asserted that God the Father is the original cause of all that is, the Son is the creative cause, and the Holy Spirit the perfecting cause, *On the Holy Spirit*, 16.38. Of course, "perfecting" here is not meant in the restricted sense of sanctification. If we understand Christian perfection as being made conformable to God's purpose for us in Christ (Rom 8:29), then the connection becomes apparent.

49. Bernard, *Justification and the Holy Spirit*, 121.

50. Bernard, *Justification and the Holy Spirit*, 121.

51. Robeck, *Azusa Street Mission & Revival*, 321–22.

52. Bernard, *In Search of Holiness*, 276.

For instance, the comprehensive work of Ayodeji Adewuja on holiness in the Pauline corpus insists on the multifaceted nature of holiness, warning against reductionism, and emphasizes both purity standards and relational holiness in the context of pastoral and hortatory concerns rather than regulatory.[53] Perhaps even more significantly, the holiness theology which Adewuja discerns in Paul integrates a perspective of God as "both the Source and Enabler of holiness" with the demand for "a divine-human partnership."[54] Thus believers attain unto biblical holiness through expectant prayer and daily striving.[55] Cannot all Pentecostals agree to this much?

---

53. Adewuja, *Holiness in the Letters of Paul*, 17–19.
54. Adewuja, *Holiness in the Letters of Paul*, 162.
55. Adewuja, *Holiness in the Letters of Paul*, 162–64.

3

A Major Controversy over the Godhead

THE PREVIOUS CHAPTER FOCUSED on one of the most divisive theological issues among Pentecostals: sanctification. The present chapter addresses another: The Godhead.[1] Pentecostals stridently debate the nature of the Divine Being. The majority of Pentecostals is Trinitarian, while a strong minority is Unitarian. How this difference came about, what it means, and suggestions for how Pentecostals today might approach their dilemmas surrounding the doctrine of God is the subject of the present chapter.

HISTORICAL RUPTURE

Initially all the early Pentecostals were classical Trinitarians. Seymour and his Azusa Street Mission, along with most other Pentecostals, remained so.[2] However in 1914, soon after William Durham's death in 1912, some of his disciples further radicalized his mission. Attempts to focus ever more exclusively on the finished work of Christ eventually led to replacing traditional Trinitarian doctrine with a Christocentric modalistic view of God, preoccupation with the name of Jesus, and insistence on water baptism in

---

1. In Col 1:9 the KJV translates θειότης (*theótes*), meaning the Deity or Divine Being, as in the quality of being divine, as "Godhead." Godhead (cp. variants in Acts 17:29 and Rom 1:20) has become a much-used term in the Trinitarian/Unitarian Pentecostal debate.

2. Robeck, *Azusa Street Mission & Revival*, 318.

Jesus' name.[3] Frank Ewart, Garfield T. Haywood, R. E. McAlister, Franklin Small, and Andrew Urshan were early leaders of what has been variously called the "New Issue," "Jesus Only" or "Jesus Name" movement, "Apostolic," or "Oneness Pentecostalism." The initial impetus of the movement came in a 1913 international camp meeting in Los Angeles. John G. Scheppe, after meditating on a McAlister sermon on the topic the night before, ran through the camp in the early morning hours shouting that he had received a new revelation about the truth of water baptism in the name of the Lord Jesus Christ. It functionally equated Jesus with the fullness of the Godhead (cp. Col 2:9).[4]

The controversial new movement spread rapidly among Baptistic Pentecostals, especially the Assemblies of God, until, after all mediating efforts failed, a decisive rupture finally occurred. In 1916 the Assemblies of God General Council drafted a "Statement of Fundamental Truths" including clear and uncompromising affirmation of the historic doctrine of the Trinity. The split was instant. Later that same year Oneness adherents started their own organizations, or revised preexisting ones, most notably the Pentecostal Assemblies of the World, although they soon (1920s) bitterly divided along racial lines.[5] In 1945 a series of mergers eventuated in what eventually became by far the largest Oneness organization, the United Pentecostal Church Incorporated.[6] Theological disagreement plagued its membership, particularly on the manner of relating water baptism in Jesus' name and Spirit baptism with the new birth. The Pentecostal Assemblies of the World, although officially racially integrated, has been a predominately black organization since 1931 (retaining Haywood's early influence). The Apostolic World Christian Fellowship represents something of an umbrella organization, but a large nondenominational or Independent segment still exists.[7]

THEOLOGICAL DEVELOPMENT

In defensive fashion, early Oneness Pentecostal theology first redefined the classic doctrine of the Trinity in terms of tritheism (belief in three Gods), and then forthrightly

---

3. Reed, "Oneness Pentecostalism," 936. Further, Oneness advocates can appeal to historic Evangelical tendencies toward Jesus-centric piety. Cp. Small, *Living Waters*, 85; Patterson, *The Real Truth*, 19.

4. Not to be overlooked is that anti-institutional and anti-creedal emphases of early Pentecostals certainly set up openness to possibilities of challenging aspects of historic orthodoxy such as Trinitarian theology, Reed, *In Jesus' Name*, 105. To be fair, Pentecostal attitudes were preceded by and resonated with the revival theology of Dwight L. Moody in minimizing theological statements and emphasizing a personal relationship of saving faith in Jesus Christ. MacGregor, *Contemporary Theology*, 101–02.

5. For more on racial relations within the movement see French, *Early Interracial Oneness Pentecostalism*.

6. Later changed to United Pentecostal Church International (UPCI).

7. Reed, "Oneness Pentecostalism," 938–40. My own maternal and paternal family background felt the influence of nondenominational Jesus' Name churches. My overall family constituency was almost evenly divided between Oneness and Trinitarian Pentecostalism.

rejected it as a dangerous distortion of biblical monotheism.[8] At times the caricature of Trinitarian teaching appears due to a lack of theological precision and sophistication; but, apparently deliberate distortion of the Trinitarian position for apologetic and catechetical purposes also occurs. For example, Oneness advocates repeatedly charged that Trinitarians view God as existing in three "separate" and "distinct" persons despite Trinitarians' well known and explicit rejection of any idea of separate persons in the Godhead.[9] (Admittedly, when Trinitarians accuse Oneness advocates of not believing in the Father or the Holy Spirit the same tendency in reverse is evident.)

In either case, as Oneness Pentecostalism continues to grow as part of the expanding global Pentecostal movement, more will be required from it. If in its infancy it was able to exist with "little knowledge of and only antipathy toward the classical formulations of the Christian faith" it will not be able to do so in maturity.[10] Fortunately, insightful and skillful Oneness theologians such as David Bernard are increasingly demonstrating serious desire to wrestle authentically with the complexities of the historical development and articulation of Trinitarian doctrine.[11] One can hope that in the process Oneness Pentecostal theology may actually evolve into something more than merely "an *anti*-Trinitarian movement."[12]

As for its more positive development, Oneness Pentecostal theology focuses on the significance of the name of the Lord for the nature of God. In short, it argues for an equivalency of YHWH and Jesus (in name and in nature).[13] Further, it argues that Father, Son, and Holy Spirit are three modes or manifestations in the revelation of the one God (historically the heterodox position of modalism). It might be described as reclamation of Jewish monotheism except for the radical difference that it is Christocentric in its Unitarianism.[14] Notably, Reed describes Oneness Pentecostalism as "a non-historical sectarian expression of Jewish Christian theology."[15] Along this line note that Oneness advocates have long suspected that the traditional doctrine of the Trinity developed as a tragic compromising synthesis of polytheistic, pagan (Greek) philosophy and monotheistic Judaism.[16] Therefore, as Reed says, "The most distinctive aspect of Oneness Christology, and fundamental to it, is its understanding of the name of Jesus."[17] Not only the Oneness doctrine of God but also its doctrine of

---

8. Reed, *In Jesus' Name*, 179–80.

9. Fauss, *Buy the Truth, and Sell it Not*, 22; Urshan, *Almighty God*, 91; Haywood, *Victim of the Flaming Sword*, 56. 58.

10. Reed, *In Jesus' Name*, 223.

11. E.g., see Bernard, *Oneness and Trinity* and *The Trinitarian Controversy* as well as *The Glory of God in the Face of Jesus*.

12. Reed, *In Jesus' Name*, 273.

13. YHWH is the Hebrew (יְהֹוָה) name for Israel's covenant Lord (Ex 3:14).

14. Reed, "Oneness Pentecostalism," 940–443.

15. Reed, *In Jesus' Name*, 306.

16. Miller, *Is God a Trinity?* 13, and Weeks, *Jehovah-Jesus—the Supreme God*, 107.

17. Reed, "Oneness Pentecostalism," 942.

salvation hinges upon its understanding of the meaning of the name of Jesus and its implications for all of Christian thought and practice.

Acts 2:38 is of paradigmatic importance both in Oneness theology of the Godhead and in Oneness theology's three stage soteriology of repentance, water baptism, and the gift of the Holy Spirit: "Then Peter said unto them, Repent, and be baptized every one of you in the name of Jesus Christ for the remission of sins, and ye shall receive the gift of the Holy Ghost." (KJV) Oneness interpretations of Acts 2:38 blend its conversionist theology, Pentecostal doctrine of Spirit baptism, and Unitarian teaching of the name of Jesus. However, there has been disagreement among various wings of the Oneness movement regarding whether the new birth occurs at water baptism or at Spirit baptism. To an extent these internal differences are attributable to diverse appropriation of Reformed or Wesleyan soteriological emphases in Oneness efforts to integrate one or the other into its schema of water baptism and Spirit baptism (or vice versa, as the case may be).[18]

The simple appeal of Oneness Pentecostalism is evident in its global growth. True enough, to an extent it shares in the benefits of association with the overall success of the broader (Trinitarian) Pentecostal movement. However, Reed is no doubt right that "People hear only the story of the *one* God who is revealed in Jesus, and they enter gladly into those acts of faith set forth in Acts 2:38." Clearly, "For them, the message is simple and the tools are adequate for the journey."[19] Conversely, the classical doctrine of the Trinity is notoriously complex, even confusing. It is not surprising that many conclude they can well do without it. Yet, as is often the case, the resolution of one problem often is the foundation of another, even greater, problem—or problems.[20]

SPECIFIC PROBLEMS

For our purposes, two problems in the soteriological schema (Trinitarian debate aside, just for a moment) of Oneness Pentecostals call for consideration. First, it appears to result in the doctrine of baptismal regeneration. Second, it excludes those who have received water baptism in its Trinitarian formula or who have not experienced Spirit baptism accompanied by speaking in tongues from the new birth. The first problem is denied by Oneness theologians by placing emphasis on the critical role of active faith in the experience of water baptism and the new birth. It is uncertain as to whether this reply effectively answers the charge because it still ties saving faith to water baptism executed in Jesus' name. That insistence distinguishes Oneness baptism from paedobaptism (infant baptism) but not necessarily from baptismal regeneration. The second problem is nuanced by proposing various hierarchical scenarios in which non-initiates are comparable

---

18. Reed, "Oneness Pentecostalism," 943. For an in-depth insider's view on Oneness Pentecostalism see Talmadge French, *Our God is One: The Story of the Oneness Pentecostals*.

19. Reed, *In Jesus' Name*, 223.

20. Reed, *In Jesus' Name*, argues that Oneness Pentecostals today are facing greater doctrinal challenges than ever in their history, 337 (cp. 360).

to Old Testament saints or relegated to embryonic status. In either case, only those baptized in water in the name of Jesus and baptized in the Spirit accompanied by speaking in tongues are viewed as partakers of full salvation.[21] This is a further radicalization of the traditional Pentecostal position that only those baptized in the Spirit experience the full blessings of the gospel (i.e., the full gospel); but, it goes beyond it by withholding salvation from them as well, something Trinitarian Pentecostalism does not do.[22]

The prevalent attitude of Oneness Pentecostal theology toward other Christians may be viewed both as an "ecumenical offense" and as "the fragile threads" of "ecumenical intersections."[23] On the first take, it is insulting and offensive that Oneness Pentecostals deny (at least) the full salvation of other Christians, including other (Trinitarian) Pentecostals.[24] On a second take, it is (somewhat) reassuring that Oneness Pentecostals appear determined to find a place for other Christians, including other Pentecostals, within their soteriological schema that does not totally discount their salvific identity and journey. In this light, Reed suggests that "the fragile strands of respect" "if nurtured" could "grow strong bonds of fellowship."[25] In spite of past problems, he continues to be hopeful for the future.[26] So am I.

Optimism for future relations between Oneness and Trinitarian Pentecostals (and others) may be more than mere wishful thinking. For example, under the leadership of UPCI General Superintendent David Bernard, a prolific author and articulate theologian,[27] the UPCI homepage asserts that,

> Our experience and doctrine should conform to the complete biblical pattern. As we respond to the gospel and believe on Jesus Christ, we will repent of our sins, be baptized in the name of Jesus Christ, and receive the gift of the Holy Spirit (Acts chapters 2, 8, 10, 19). We do not reject those who have not received the complete New Testament experience, but we encourage them to receive everything God has for them.

---

21. Reed, "Oneness Pentecostalism," 943–44. Nevertheless, Reed suggests that it was the very exclusivity of Oneness Pentecostalism which probably provided the energy that made a break with Trinitarian Pentecostals inevitable, *In Jesus' Name*, 166.

22. I cannot count the times someone has argued with me that Pentecostals deny salvation to anyone who has not spoken in tongues. I usually discover that they were either influenced by Oneness encounters or making ungrounded assumptions based on non-Pentecostal interpretations of Spirit baptism as synonymous with conversion.

23. Cp. Reed, "Oneness Pentecostalism," 944, with Reed, *In Jesus' Name*, 6.

24. A rumble worked its way through our family at the funeral of my paternal grandmother. An Oneness cousin lamented to an uncle that he would not see her in Heaven because "She had not been baptized in Jesus' Name." Our Trinitarian uncle did not receive well a condemnatory assessment of his deeply pious and godly mother.

25. Reed, *In Jesus' Name*, 6.

26. Reed, *In Jesus' Name*, 105.

27. E.g., see, Bernard: *The Oneness of God,*; *The Oneness View of Jesus Christ*; and, *Understanding the Articles of Faith: An Examination of United Pentecostal Beliefs*. I have met Bernard a couple of times and heard him speak several times. Frankly, I am impressed with his intelligence and openness.

> Ultimately, each of us is accountable to God for our response of faith. The Bible is the sole authority for salvation; the basis of salvation is Christ's death, burial, and resurrection; salvation comes only by grace through faith in Jesus Christ; and the application of grace and the expression of faith come as a person obeys Acts 2:38, thereby receiving the new birth promised by Jesus.[28]

This appears to me as an admirable effort to be faithful to their own convictions in conjunction with a certain civility and respectfulness toward others. Significantly, the UPCI also acknowledges its historical indebtedness to the earlier Pentecostal movement associated with the initial (1901) outpouring at Topeka, Kansas and the birth (1906) of the global revival at Azusa Street Mission.[29] However, a denominational website may not be best source for understanding the details or depths of Oneness theology. For example, its stated beliefs on "About God" and "Appreciation for God's Identity," while well written, appear deliberately vague.[30]

Furthermore, rank and file membership and academic scholarship may not always be on the same page regarding theological engagement with others and its associative consequences. For example, at the academic level Oneness and Trinitarian scholars of Society for Pentecostal Studies (SPS) joined to participated in a six-year dialogue focusing on specific issues, namely, the historic division between Oneness and Trinitarian Pentecostals, water baptism, Christology and the Godhead, salvation, and holiness.[31] It was a fruitful conversation. However, in 2017 when the Oneness Urshan College/Graduate School of Theology in St Louis volunteered to host SPS for its annual meeting, predominately including Trinitarians, some UPCI clergy and congregations objected so vociferously that the meeting had to be relocated at literally the last instant.[32] This unfortunate incident occurred despite the affirmative leadership of UPCI General Superintendent, and SPS member, David Bernard as well as the active cooperation and participation of UC/GST. Bernard, Urshan faculty, and many UPCI members (including a glorious choir!) nevertheless (graciously, and bravely, I might add) continued to participate in an off-site St Louis convention facility.[33] This incident illustrates the height of hurdles with which Pentecostals are confronted when attempting rapprochement between Oneness and Trinitarian sisters and brothers.

---

28. See https://www.upci.org/about/about-oneness-pentecostalism (accessed 12/23/2017).

29. See https://www.upci.org/about/about-the-upci (accessed 12/23/2017).

30. See https://www.upci.org/about/our-beliefs and https://www.upci.org/about/about-oneness-pentecostalism (accessed 12/23/2017).

31. See "Oneness-Trinitarian Pentecostal Final Report, 2002–2007" *Pneuma* 30:2 (2008): 203–24.

32. In fairness, a controversial paper presented by Felipe Angredano, "A Royal Priesthood: LGBT Apostolic Oneness in the Political, Ethnic and Historical Context," was an explosive and much politicized issue.

33. The reader may note that I was present and involved in this SPS meeting.

THEOLOGY PROPER

Getting back to the theology of God, properly speaking, in discussing Oneness Pentecostals the issue of modalism is daunting but especially intriguing. Not surprisingly, Oneness Pentecostals do not quite fit the mold—but are too close for comfort, that is, close enough to raise serious questions. Modalism is the unorthodox belief that God is one person who has revealed God's Self in three forms or *modes*. However, Trinitarian doctrine teaches that God is one being eternally existing in three persons. According to modalism, during the Incarnation, Jesus was simply God acting in one mode or role, and the Holy Spirit at Pentecost was God acting in a different mode. Thus, God does not exist as the Father, Son, and Holy Spirit at the same time. Rather, God is one person who has merely manifested himself in these three modes at various times. Therefore, modalism denies the basic distinctiveness and coexistence of the three persons of the Trinity. Modalism may be the most common theological error concerning the nature of God. Oneness Pentecostals are often identified by Trinitarians as modalists.[34] But I have discovered they do not necessarily self-identify as modalists.

I well remember facilitating at a SPS meeting for an Ecumenical Studies Interest Group dialogue session with Trinitarians and Oneness Pentecostals some years ago in which Oneness participants flatly denied the modalist label.[35] I was surprised. I expected a defense of modalism rather than a rejection of the label itself. It is interesting that while Reed describes Oneness Pentecostals as modalists he offers qualifications on two counts: "its radical christocentric orientation, and its theology of the Name which particularizes and personalizes the revelation of God in the name of Jesus as God's 'proper' name."[36] Yet Oneness theologians prefer to speak of the Father, Son, and Holy Spirit, traditionally "persons" of the Trinity, as "manifestations" of God—explicit modalist terminology.[37] Bernard explains that as "manifestations" Father, Son, and Holy Spirit cannot refer to separate (noted above as improper charge against Trinitarians) persons or personalities but "only different aspects or roles of the one Spirit-being."[38]

Are Oneness Pentecostals "closet" modalists, or perhaps, semi-modalists? This would be a superficial and problematic assertion. Rather than asking whether Oneness Pentecostals are modalists or not would it be better to ask in what sense they are or are not modalists—and, of course, what difference does it make? Or perhaps the modalist category just does not work for describing Oneness Pentecostals? Or, even

---

34. See "Modalism," https://www.theopedia.com/modalism (accessed 12/23/2017).

35. Earlier, Oneness and Trinitarian scholars of SPS participated in a six year dialogue focusing on specific issues, namely, historic division between Oneness and Trinitarian Pentecostals, water baptism, Christology and the Godhead, Salvation, and Holiness. See "Oneness-Trinitarian Pentecostal Final Report, 2002–2007" *Pneuma* 30:2 (2008): 203–24.

36. Reed, *In Jesus' Name*, 272.

37. I well recall my mother explaining to me (as a questioning teenager) that God exists as different manifestations at different times but it is always Jesus.

38. Bernard, *Oneness of God*, 134.

more startling, is there something misleading about the whole modalist controversy? Along this line, it is interesting to recall that leading twentieth century Trinitarian theologians have struggled with changing and problematic conceptions of personhood and personality since the original classical Trinitarian formulations. For instance, Karl Barth went so far as to explore utilization of terminology such as "modes of being" for describing the Father, Son, and Holy Spirit.[39] Is it not interesting that a theologian who led a revival of interest in the doctrine of the Trinity had problems with aspects of its traditional statement? At the least, these developments suggest that the conversation is not finished once and for all.

For the most part, Pentecostal theology of the Trinity tends to be straightforward. True, several Pentecostal theologians are developing advanced implications of the doctrine of the Trinity from a Pentecostal perspective. Steve Studebaker is a good example. His *From Pentecost to the Triune God* is a distinctly Pentecostal work in its approach and methodology.[40] Studebaker relates Trinitarian theology to pneumatology in an in-depth fashion before exploring Eastern and Western, Reformed Evangelical, Charismatic theological emphases, and finally plunging ahead even further with implications of Trinitarian theology for a Christian theology of the religions and for a contemporary theology of creation. It is a rich and rewarding effort—even if at times its avant-garde nature makes it (potentially) controversial.

Yet, as I said, for the most part Pentecostal theology of the Trinity tends to be straightforward, accenting the devotional and practical rather than the speculative or philosophical. An example is French Arrington's treatment in his series on Christian doctrine.[41] Perhaps somewhat surprisingly, or uncharacteristically, given Pentecostalism's non-creedal nature, but nevertheless refreshingly, given its significance, Arrington quotes the Athanasian Creed as a short summary of the doctrine of the Trinity: "So the Father is God; the Son is God; and the Holy Ghost is God. And yet there are not three gods but one God."[42] Yet he immediately delves into a scriptural presentation of the importance of the affirmation of the deity and personhood of the Holy Spirit in Trinitarian doctrine for Pentecostal experience and worship. Then he affirms the biblical doctrine that God is one, or the unity of God, before explaining that the one God exists in three persons, namely, the Father, Son, and Holy Spirit, according to the witness of the Old and New Testaments (as usual, replete with numerous biblical references).

Arrington carefully details that the three persons of the Blessed Trinity are distinct without being divided (that is, without being separated). He explains that the Trinitarian understanding of God arose out of the experiential reality of the early

---

39. See Barth, *Church Dogmatics*, I:1, 355. Of course, it is quite possible to talk about God existing *simultaneously* in different modes of being without falling into the modalist heresy of *successive* modes of being which deny real distinctions in the Triune Godhead.

40. Studebaker, *From Pentecost to the Triune God*.

41. Arrington, *Christian Doctrine*, 1:27–41. See also Higgins, et al, *Introduction to Theology*, 19–20.

42. Arrington, *Christian Doctrine*, 1:27.

Christians as they encountered God in Christ and in the Holy Spirit; but, he insists that God is a unified being. It is clear throughout that Arrington sees the doctrine of the Trinity as not only biblically based but also as established on believers' experience of God. Arrington's bifocal approach is true to the historic Christian tradition. Thus, I find it ironic that Pentecostals, often lambasted for using experience as a basis for theology, are following a pattern faithful to the formulation of the most distinctive Christian doctrine of all—the Holy Trinity.

Arrington next briefly describes some interpretations which have "proved to be inadequate in light of Scripture."[43] Among these are views which fail to recognize the full deity and/or full humanity of Christ or deny the deity and personality of the Holy Spirit. Further, he takes special care to refute two errors, or false views of God, which regrettably continue to have great influence: modalism and tritheism.[44] According to Arrington modalism emphasizes the unity of God to the exclusion of the Trinity while tritheism emphasizes the distinctions of the Father, Son, and Holy Spirit to the point of denying God's essential unity. In tritheism the Godhead is thought of as something like a team with separate persons playing on it together. Basically, tritheism depicts three gods. Arrington assesses both modalism and tritheism as out of accord with the teaching of Scripture.

For Arrington, the teaching on the Trinity is more than a doctrine. It is a way of life. Just as the persons of the Trinity exist in community and enjoy one another's fellowship, so believers are drawn into fellowship with God and with each other as they worship and serve God together. Thus, Arrington asserts that "The foundation of our life in Christ and our Pentecostal experience is the blessed Trinity."[45] Indeed, he concludes with "praise to the Father, the Son, and the Holy Spirit—one God, blessed forever."[46] Here a Pentecostal approach to the doctrine of the Trinity is ultimately doxological as well as devotional.

IMPORT OF SPIRIT BAPTISM

Conflict over the nature of the Godhead has been even more intractable and volatile than that on the nature of sanctification. I do not suppose that I have the solution. With British Pentecostal theologian Jonathan Black, I am aware that whenever we speak of the Triune God "we are attempting to speak of the ineffable."[47] God's being is too great to be expressed or described in words. But we must humbly make the attempt. As Augustine so well says, "You are my God, my Life, my holy Delight, but

43. Arrington, *Christian Doctrine*, 1:39.
44. Higgins, et al, *Introduction to Theology*, take a similar approach, 20.
45. Arrington, *Christian Doctrine*, 1:41.
46. Arrington, *Christian Doctrine*, 1:41.
47. Black, *Apostolic Theology*, 78. Black nevertheless insists, 90–91, that the Trinity is the center of the Christian faith and the doctrine out of which all other doctrines flow.

is this enough to say about you? Can any man say enough when he speaks of you? Yet woe betide those who are silent about you!"[48] Accordingly, I do have something to offer out of our shared Pentecostal tradition that I hope and pray will be helpful. First, let's recall the principle of Black Holiness Pentecostalism on "double discernment"—or discovering "how to say no to loyalties that divide and yes to the moving of the Spirit that heals and restores persons and institutions torn asunder by idolatrous loyalties."[49] Personally, my extended family loyalties include both Oneness and Trinitarian relatives. My denominational loyalty is Trinitarian, as is my own theological orientation. I can certainly sympathize with the difficulties in confronting, much less overcoming, divided loyalties between Oneness and Trinitarian Pentecostals.

However, I remain impressed with Black Holiness Pentecostalism's model for rising above rivalries of this kind out of concern that sectarian partisanship itself can become idolatrous. Most definitely issues regarding the nature of the divine being are not minor disputes or peripheral topics. They have to do with the very heart of the Christian faith. Yet would it not be disastrous and tragic if Oneness and Trinitarian Pentecostals made idols out of their belief systems and sectarian loyalties? Charges of blasphemy and idolatry have certainly flown back and forth through the air over the years. What if the greatest danger of committing either is inordinate attachment to our preferred theological constructs at the expense of Christian love for sisters and brothers who differ?

I mentioned earlier the failed attempt of Oneness and Trinitarian Pentecostals to meet at Urshan College and Graduate School of Theology in St Louis in which UPCI General Superintendent David Bernard, members of the Urshan faculty, and many UPCI members nevertheless graciously and bravely continued to participate at an offsite St Louis convention facility. So then, it really was not a failed attempt after all. We met elsewhere but we nevertheless met—and it was phenomenal. I treasure the memory of the opening evening service in which the Urshan Chorale led the gathering in songs of praise and worship. They sang wonderfully; but even greater, the Spirit of the Lord came into our midst in a special manner. All across the assembly hall Oneness and Trinitarian Pentecostals were worshiping together "in Spirit and in truth." Joyful shouts of acclamation, of "Amen!" and "Hallelujah!" and "Praise the Lord!" could be heard everywhere—as well as the sound of many praying and worshiping in a heavenly language. Almost everyone stood with hands raised high, some with tears streaming down glistening cheeks. There was a tangible sense of Divine Presence.[50]

---

48. Augustine, *Confessions*, 23 (I, 4).

49. Lovett, "Black Holiness Pentecostalism," 427.

50. This was an example in action of what Tomberlin has said: "Worship is a joyful and ecstatic experience, because as believers worship, the Spirit of grace is encountered." See *Pentecostal Sacraments*, 72. Like the older revivalist tradition, Pentecostals may describe their experience of joy in worship as "getting happy," Conkin, *Cane Ridge*, 178.

As I recall, the differences between us seemed to melt away as we all felt the same Holy Spirit and responded alike to God's presence. That makes me hopeful. But it also raises an important question: what does it mean that Oneness and Trinitarian Pentecostals experience the presence and power of the Holy Spirit as we do? Some extremists may argue that we do not both have the Holy Spirit, that the experience of one or the other is not genuine in some way. However, I know that the Spirit which we felt that night as the Urshan Chorale ministered in song at SPS in St. Louis was real. And I know that all around that auditorium Oneness and Trinitarian Pentecostals alike got "in the Spirit."

Therefore, I dismiss as without any solid credibility those who are disingenuous enough to claim that other believers with the same experience of Spirit baptism and speaking in tongues, with the same healings, exorcisms, and miracles, with the same joy, are not genuine because they are in another group (Luke 9:49–50). Better to recognize that somehow the Holy Spirit has been able all these years to transcend the divide and work with and in both of us. Better still to follow the Spirit's example. But how can we do so?

There is a legitimate biblical and theological way of framing the importance of the shared presence of the Holy Spirit in our midst that transcends, to a degree, the differences between us. Admittedly, it does not dispel the differences; but, perhaps it can transcend the differences. In other words, our differences will not disappear, but they can be eclipsed by something that far outstrips them. What is that? It is our shared Pentecostal experience of Spirit baptism. Before proceeding, I probably need to include a qualifier. I am not for one moment suggesting that right doctrine is unimportant. Nor am I offering the slightest hint that our theology is irrelevant so long as we can share a kindred spirituality. Then what?

Some challenging words from John Wesley come to mind.

> I say of the heart. For neither does religion consist [*sic*] Orthodoxy, or right opinions; which, although they are not properly outward things, are not in the heart, but the understanding. A man may be orthodox in every point; he may not only espouse right opinions, but zealously defend them against all opposers; he may think justly concerning the incarnation of our Lord, concerning the ever-blessed Trinity, and every other doctrine contained in the oracles of God; he may assent to all the three creeds, — that called the Apostles', the Nicene, and the Athanasian; and yet it is possible he may have no religion at all, no more than a Jew, Turk, or pagan. He may be almost as orthodox — as the devil, (though, indeed, not altogether; for every man errs in something; whereas we can't well conceive him to hold any erroneous opinion,) and may, all the while be as great a stranger as he to the religion of the heart.[51]

---

51. John Wesley, "The Way to the Kingdom," *Standard Sermons*, I:6, accessible at http://wesley.nnu.edu/john-wesley/the-sermons-of-john-wesley-1872-edition/sermon-7-the-way-to-the-kingdom/. Thus, Harvey Cox's association of Pentecostals with "the decline in creed-bound Christianity, the

Wesley spent his life embroiled in theological debate, fighting for truth. He was by no means here minimizing the importance of correct doctrine or theology. Rather, he notes that having a right heart takes priority over correct theological principles. Of what does this consist according to Wesley? The next sentence explains: "This alone is religion, truly so called: This alone is in the sight of God of great price. The Apostle sums it all up in three particulars, 'righteousness, and peace, and joy in the Holy Ghost.'" (Rom 14:17)

I suggest that the experience of baptism with the Spirit which Oneness and Trinitarian Pentecostals share can and should establish a basis for fellowship and partnership in spite of our significant theological disagreements. If my appeal to our experience of the Spirit as a theological argument seems strange to anyone I would point out that I am following the Apostle Paul's lead in Galatians 3:2–5. Paul refutes the claims of the circumcision sect with "his argument from experience" in which "evidence of [the Spirit's] presence and power was unmistakable."[52] Since the Galatians had received the Spirit under Paul's preaching rather than subsequent legalistic interlopers, the question of God's confirmation of grace was settled.

Hence, I argue, the testimony of Scripture in Acts substantiates the potential of baptism with the Holy Spirit to overcome barriers between believers who have deep differences. Note particularly Acts 15:8–9: "So God, who knows the heart, acknowledged them by giving them the Holy Spirit, just as *He did* to us, and made no distinction between us and them, purifying their hearts by faith." In the chapter context, Jewish Christians were struggling with the status of Gentile Christians. There were deep seated, preexisting differences between Jews and Gentiles that had affected Jewish Christians and Gentile Christians. The turning point in the debate for favorable relations—that were not based on Gentile acquiescence to Jewish customs—was Peter's address. The heart of Peter's address was that God's gift of the Holy Spirit to both Jews and Gentiles eclipsed their other differences. Polhill aptly comments:

> God had proved his acceptance of Cornelius and the Gentiles at his home by granting them the gift of his Spirit. God only grants his Spirit to those he has accepted (cf. 10:44, 47; 11:17). The fact that they had received the Spirit

---

revival of faith [versus beliefs], and the birth of an Age of the Spirit," *Future of Faith*, 199, is correct in so far as it goes. However, Pentecostal reticence regarding creeds is not due to reluctance to commit to firm doctrinal standards; rather, Pentecostals are wary of human formulations of divine truth which run the risk of undermining scriptural simplicity and verity and displacing spiritual vitality—as I think Cox well understands despite a (not entirely misdirected) desire to exalt faith over belief, 207. The "'postdogmatic' Christian" label, Cox, *Future of Faith*, 222, is not necessarily a well-suited descriptor for typical Pentecostals. True enough, Pentecostals—including this Pentecostal—will agree that the "experience *of* the divine is displacing theories *about* it," Cox, *Future of Faith*, 20 (original italics); but Pentecostals are not willing to follow Cox in walking away from biblical truth and basic church teaching because it irks certain modern sensibilities, Cox, *Future of Faith*, 18.

52. George, *Galatians*, 214.

just as Peter and the Jewish Christians had was proof that God had accepted Cornelius and his fellow Gentiles on an equal footing (v. 9).[53]

In his Acts 11:17 Jerusalem report regarding the same event Peter had previously appealed to God's giving the Gentiles the same gift of the Spirit as he had unto the Jews. His language then was even stronger. Peter asserts that to reject those whom God had given the Spirit would be to "withstand" God. The word for "withstand" is κωλύω (kōlyō), and means to hinder, to prevent, to forbid. In short, Peter admitted that he was not one to oppose God's clear purpose. Hanging heavy in the air is an implied admonition to follow suit.

Trinitarian sisters and brothers, if Oneness Pentecostals have received the gift of the Holy Spirit, who are we to reject them? As Trinitarian Christians, we may, indeed do, reject elements of their *teaching* but we cannot reject *them*. If we do so, I fear that we will be found opposing God; that we ought not to do. Conversely, Oneness sisters and brothers, if Trinitarian Pentecostals have received the gift of the Holy Spirit, who are you to reject us? As Oneness Christians, you may, indeed do, reject elements of our *teaching* but you cannot reject *us*. If you do so, I fear that you will be found opposing God; that you ought not to do. God has chosen to baptize both of us in the Holy Spirit. That does not settle our theological disputes. But it should settle the matter of our mutual love and fellowship.

NAVIGATING THE THEOLOGICAL LANDSCAPE

Admittedly, navigating the theology of it is indescribably challenging. Since Karl Barth Trinitarian theology has been enjoying something of a revival. Kärkkäinen observes that for Barth the doctrine of the Trinity is "the structuring principle of Christian doctrine" and "the means of identifying the God of the Bible."[54] Indeed, Barth says, "The doctrine of the Trinity is basically what distinguishes the Christian doctrine of God as Christian . . . in contrast to all other possible doctrines of God."[55] No wonder Kärkkäinen concludes that for Barth "The doctrine of the Trinity is the only possible Christian answer to the question of who the self-revealing God of the Bible talks about."[56] Probably most Trinitarians, including Trinitarian Pentecostals, are inclined to agree. Yet it gets more complicated.

Barth could be innovative with his theology of the Trinity. Thus, Barth's use of "modes of being" to refer to the Father, Son, and Holy Spirit has led to suspicions of modalism.[57] And the body of his theological magnum opus is clearly Christocentric,

53. Polhill, *Acts*, 326.
54. Kärkkäinen, *Trinity and Religious Pluralism*, 14.
55. Barth, *Dogmatics*, I:1, 301.
56. Kärkkäinen, *Trinity and Religious Pluralism*, 14.
57. Barth, *Dogmatics*, I:1, 355. Higgins, et al, *Introduction to Theology*, 20, assert that it is essential to maintain that "the Bible teaches an ontological trinity (a trinity of being) and not just a modalist

even edging close to Christomonism. Kärkkäinen defends Barth against modalism, arguing that he gives room "for ontological distinctions in the triune God," but admits that Christocentrism is a recurring problem.[58] Barth's emphasis on God's sole revelation in Christ results in a breakdown of distinctions between Creator and Redeemer, God as immanent and God as incarnate, finally leading Kärkkäinen to assess his Trinitarian theology as "inadequate and internally inconsistent" displaying "the lack of a thoroughgoing Trinitarianism."[59] It's worth noting that the leading Trinitarian theologian of our age has some surprising affinities with both Oneness and Trinitarian Pentecostals—which ought to be a bit of an eye-opener for us all. Surely we should be humbly cautious lest we become fools who rush in where angels fear to tread.

There is an additional consideration which is critical. Christology per se, which is primarily the study of the ontology and person of Jesus Christ, including his relationship with the Father, is of central significance for Christian theology. Arguably, the primary purpose of Christian theology is to enable believers to answer, and to an extent, explain, or least interpret, the query of who Jesus is in his person (Matt 16:13–19). After all, "Christian faith is always and essentially faith in Christ."[60] Therefore, Kärkkäinen asserts that "no study comes closer to the core of Christian life and theology than Christology."[61] I agree. The really distinguishing mark of Christianity is its faith in Jesus Christ as Savior and Lord. The basic, and saving, Christian confession is that "Jesus is Lord" along with commitment to believing in his rising from the dead (Rom 10:9–10). Both Oneness and Trinitarian Pentecostals make that confession and that commitment. Shouldn't that mean something?

In the past two chapters we have discussed the two major theological controversies, sanctification and the Godhead, which resulted in three different wings of the Pentecostal movement: the Wesleyan-Holiness Trinitarian Pentecostals; the Baptistic/Reformed Trinitarian Pentecostals; and, the Oneness Pentecostals. They are firmly, even fiercely, opposed in certain areas. Yet there is a lot of overlap among the three, including shared doctrinal assumptions and dynamic spiritualities. The following chapters make no explicit attempt to continue sketching the lines of demarcation between these three streams of the Pentecostal movement, although drawing liberally here and there on each. Rather, the next section leaves behind the introductory approach of the first three chapters in Part One to begin a more direct engagement with essential features of Pentecostal theology which are the intended focus of this volume.

---

trinity (a trinity of revelation)."

58. Kärkkäinen, *Trinity and Religious Pluralism*, 15.
59. Kärkkäinen, *Trinity and Religious Pluralism*, 25–26.
60. Higgins, et al, *Introduction to Theology*, 6.
61. Kärkkäinen, *Christology*, 9.

PART TWO

A Description Not a Definition

4

An Unchanging Christ

AT THE HEART OF Pentecostal experience and testimony is affirmation of the ongoing applicability of Hebrews 13:8, "Jesus Christ is the same yesterday and today and forever" (cp. Malachi 3:6).[1] As will be seen, there are rich and far-reaching Christological, ecclesiological, and missiological implications of the Pentecostal understanding of this text. Reminiscent of the oft-recurring refrain of the book of Revelation (1:4, 8, 17, 2:8; 11:17; 16:5), Hebrews 13:8 describes Christ's participation in God's unchangeableness—that is, his divine eternity and immutability. It essentially equates Jesus with the fullness of the Godhead (cp. Col 2:9; John 8:58) and exhorts believers to enduring faith in Christ's unchangeableness (Heb 1:12).[2] This Christ portrayed in the NT is precisely the Christ Pentecostals expect to encounter today. Arguments that Christ no longer dramatically and miraculously saves, heals, and delivers are rejected out of hand as inconsistent with this guiding hermeneutical principle.[3] Cessationists emphasize changing times but Pentecostals emphasize an unchanging Lord.

---

1. Robeck, "Pentecostals and the Apostolic Faith," observes that "[Early Pentecostals] sought to emphasize the unchangeable character of God, as revealed in Jesus Christ, through frequent appeals to such biblical passages as Hebrews 13:8. Aimee Semple McPherson, like many of her day, sought to clarify that point by asking "Is Jesus Christ the Great I Am? or Is He the Great I Was?," 64. See also Aimee Semple McPherson, Divine Healing Sermons (no city: Aimee Semple McPherson, circa 1921), 11–22.

2. Adams, "Hebrews," 1295–99, 1392.

3. Pentecostals accept a wide range of gifts enumerated throughout the NT (e.g., Rom 12:6–8; Eph 4:7–13) but are best known for those in 1 Corinthians 12:1–11. Pentecostals do embrace the

AN INTERPRETATIVE PENTECOSTAL APPLICATION

Let's take a closer look at Hebrews 13:8. Adams points out that it functions as a bridge between verses 7 and 9 with implications for the following verses through its insistence that "Jesus Christ is the unchanging focus of the gospel message."[4] In times of changing leadership beset by challenging changes in the first century environment it was essential to maintain appropriate focus on Jesus. Grounded in the nature of Jesus Christ as the one who "shares the same unchangeableness as God himself" (Ps 102:27; Isa. 48:12), this exhortation assures believers, then and now, that "Though all else changes around us, Jesus does not change."[5] Given the central theme in Hebrews of Christ as our faithful high priest, 13:8 is a kind of "capsule summary of the entire book."[6] Various teachers were coming along offering often subtle, and sometimes not-so-subtle, changes to the original gospel message. Hebrews 13:8 instructs believers of all ages to hold fast to the gospel exactly as it was originally personified and proclaimed by Jesus and his apostles.

Not surprisingly, Hebrews 13:8 fuels Pentecostal primitivism and restorationism. A significant point is that Pentecostal desires to return to the NT model of Christianity do not arise out of idealistic or sentimental longings for a bygone age; rather, they arise out of commitment to the unchangeable nature of Jesus Christ. It is driven by Christology and directed by biblical hermeneutics. Notice a common Pentecostal interpretation and extension of this text. Just as no one should be allowed to change the message of the gospel, as in Judaizers wishing to return to an obsolete Levitical system, then neither should anyone be allowed to change the manner of the gospel's proclamation and demonstration in the power of the Holy Spirit. Is this an arbitrary application? Pentecostals do not think so.

First Corinthians 2:1–5 is a frequently cited text regarding the original—and as Pentecostals believe, ongoing—shape of apostolic ministry.[7]

> And I, brethren, when I came to you, did not come with excellence of speech or of wisdom declaring to you the testimony of God. For I determined not to know anything among you except Jesus Christ and Him crucified. I was with you in weakness, in fear, and in much trembling. And my speech and my preaching *were* not with persuasive words of human wisdom, but in

---

miraculous, Richie, "An Affirmative Pentecostal Theology of the Miraculous," http://pneumareview.com/an-affirmative-pentecostal-theology-of-the-miraculous/.

4. Adams, "Hebrews," 1391.

5. Adams, "Hebrews," 1392.

6. Adams, "Hebrews," 1392.

7. Conn's *A Balanced Church* argues that every healthy congregation needs the gifts of the Spirit (1 Cor 12:8–10), the fruit of the Spirit (Gal 5:22–25), and the ministry gifts (Eph 4:11–13) functioning together. Acceptance of the "fivefold ministries" of apostle, prophet, evangelist, pastor, and teacher is common among many Pentecostals and a primary distinctive of some. Cp. Black, *Apostolic Theology*, 657–58 and 664–70.

demonstration of the Spirit and of power, that your faith should not be in the wisdom of men but in the power of God.

Note first that Paul is summarizing his apostolic theology of ministry. Second, he describes the same Christological focus as Hebrews 13:8. Third, he confesses human inadequacies. Fourth, he relies on the power of God, not just for personal strength in discharging his ministerial vocation but in the Spirit's power to demonstrate the validity of the gospel. Fifth, Paul has found this approach effective for producing faith superior to other approaches in that it directs faith into God's power rather than into human ability or ingenuity. On the fourth observation, the connection of gospel proclamation and demonstration by the Spirit is not a peripheral subject; Paul often references it when describing his ministry (e.g., Rom 15:19; 1 Cor 4:20; 1 Thess 1:5).

Palma notes that Paul cites himself as an example of effective ministry through relying on the Holy Spirit.[8] Pentecostals believe that this example is still to be emulated today. God and Christ, and especially the crucifixion of Christ, are central to his message and ministry. The apostle's pneumatically enabled ministry was intentionally Christocentric and cruciform. I find these stated emphases interesting in light of frequent accusations against Pentecostals for allegedly taking focus off of Christ through their appropriation of pneumatology. In fact, it works quite the reverse (John 15:26–27).[9] Further, early Pentecostals (and many today) could appreciate Paul's aversion to persuasive eloquence and oratorical sophistry. Pentecostals can certainly appreciate Paul's emphasis on the Spirit's powerful demonstration. The word for "demonstration," ἀπόδειξις (*apodeixis*), indicates proof or attestation. Corroboration and substantiation of the gospel message of Jesus Christ depend not on human abilities but on the Holy Spirit's power and the manifestation of spiritual gifts (1 Cor 12:7).[10]

THEOLOGICAL SIGNIFICANCE OF SIGNS AND WONDERS

Pentecostal semiology exhibits both continuity and discontinuity with the historic Christian tradition. Pentecostals happily remind the broader Christian tradition that signs and wonders occurred not only in the Bible (e.g., Deut 4:30; Ps 135:9; Je 32:20; Luke 19:37; Acts 2:22, 43; 4:30; 2 Cor 12:12; Heb 2:4), but also throughout the history of both Eastern and Western churches, howbeit often on the fringes.[11] Pentecostals reject as biased and presumptuous modernistic tendencies to discount the miraculous out of hand, often pointing to "radical evangelicals" even before the birth of the global Pentecostal movement who experienced miracles, including divine healing, with

---

8. Palma, "1 Corinthians," 811.

9. Pentecostals can heartily affirm Neville's assertion in *A Theology Primer* that "The special and particular work of the Holy Spirit for Christians, however, is to witness to the Christ," 147.

10. Elsewhere in this epistle Paul qualifies this principle with emphasis on Christlike character (1 Cor 4:16–17; 11:1).

11. Burgess and McGee, "Signs and Wonders," 1063.

increased evangelistic fervor and conversions. Efforts to employ "apostolic methods" and "spiritual awakenings" were at times accompanied by Pentecostal "phenomena" or supernatural occurrences.[12] Can Pentecostals be blamed for viewing later attempts to downplay this history as disingenuous?

Yet undoubtedly the Pentecostal movement has experienced an unprecedented upsurge in miracles, signs, and wonders. Land notes that "Signs and wonders, even outbreaks of tongues, had occurred throughout history but never as part of such a large-scale restoration of apostolic faith and power."[13] Currently, much of Third World Christianity is Pentecostal in nature precisely through the supernatural or miraculous aspects of Pentecostal Christianity. Not surprisingly, Pentecostals connect effective evangelism and extraordinary missionary success to occurrences of such signs and wonders.[14] Although somewhat tempered over time, early Pentecostals insisted that charismatic occurrences among them were eschatological signs, or signs of God's coming reign.[15]

Land argues that signs and wonders constitute a foretaste of the kingdom.[16] Perhaps the underlying key thought of Land's classic text is: "The longing for the Lord to come, for the Holy Spirit and for the kingdom of God are part of the same thing: it is one passion."[17] For Land the Pentecostal revival signified that the "kingdom was breaking through from the future and the Spirit was being poured out" as part of an "already-not yet" eschatological tension of millenarian anticipation.[18] Everything about the Pentecostal experience, the witness, the fruit, the gifts, and filling with the Holy Spirit were all held together by "a single unifying passion which orders the affections and directs them to a single goal: the kingdom of God."[19] (A subsequent chapter will discuss affective transformation further.) And what was true in the early days still holds true today. "The message of millions of Pentecostals today is that the kingdom of God is breaking in, through the gospel ministry of words, power, and demonstration of the Holy Spirit."[20]

---

12. Burgess and McGee, "Signs and Wonders," 1066,

13. Land, *Pentecostal Spirituality*, 52.

14. Burgess and McGee, "Signs and Wonders," 1068. Nichols, *The Pentecostals*, suggests the policy of establishing indigenous churches has greatly contributed to Pentecostals' "warm reception" with "people in other lands," 68. However, he also notes the impact of "deliverance evangelism" emphasizing total well-being, including divine healing, as a key strategy for conversionary growth, 222.

15. Faupel, *The Everlasting Gospel*, 227, 307–08.

16. Land, *Pentecostal Spirituality*, 134, 173.

17. Land, *Pentecostal Spirituality*, 58.

18. Land, *Pentecostal Spirituality*, 73 (cp. 92). NT scholar Andrew Lincoln, *Paradise Now and Not Yet*, 187, 192, asserts that in Pauline theology the Holy Spirit binds together God's earthly people with the heavenly dimension of reality thus enabling them to begin experiencing the life of heaven in the present age even as it moves toward eschatological consummative fulfillment.

19. Land, *Pentecostal Spirituality*, 172.

20. Land, *Pentecostal Spirituality*, 173. Knight, *Anticipating Heaven Below*, 38, points out the necessity of maintaining the tension between the cross and Pentecost as, respectively, the content and power

The message of the gospel accompanied by signs and wonders accomplished by the Holy Spirit indicates not only that God's reign *will* come someday but that it *is* coming already.[21] Believers even now "have tasted the heavenly gift, and have become partakers of the Holy Spirit, and have tasted the good word of God and the powers of the age to come" (Heb 6:4–5). In Pauline language, what is even now already arriving by the Holy Spirit is an "earnest" or "deposit" guaranteeing the promised redemption which is still to come in full when Christ returns (2 Cor 1:22; 5:5; Eph 1:14). In the meanwhile, that is, presently, "The Spirit is the effective reigning power and sovereign agent of the kingdom whose king is Jesus."[22] Essential to Pentecostal theology is an understanding of *Jesus Christ as eternal and unchanging Lord powerfully present and active by the Holy Spirit.*

Pentecostal affirmation of spiritual experience and signs and wonders is not an immature infatuation with the sensational or spectacular. It is a responsive embrace to the presence of the crucified, risen, and ascended Savior, the Lord Jesus Christ, by means of God's gracious manifestation in his Holy Spirit. Acts 2:33 is a critical text. "Therefore being exalted to the right hand of God, and having received from the Father the promise of the Holy Spirit, He poured out this which you now see and hear." As the gift of the ascended Lord, Pentecost constitutes, by the Spirit, the continuing relationship of Jesus Christ with God's people till he comes again. Pentecostals encounter Jesus in their experience of the Spirit—and he is not a dead body which needs anointing for burial but a risen Lord alive with power (Mark 16:1).[23]

A long tradition of interpreters has connected the inauguration of God's sovereign reign with Jesus' resurrection and the Spirit's coming at Pentecost. For instance, Calvin took the fulfillment of Jesus' prophecy regarding the coming of the kingdom with power (Mark 9:1) to mean "the revelation of the heavenly glory which Christ began with the resurrection and then more fully offered when he sent the Holy Spirit and worked marvelous deeds of power."[24] Today Pentecostals such as Frank Macchia affirm the "Pentecost-Kingdom Connection" as well, asserting that the kingdom of God involves "new creation in the dynamic presence of Christ by the Spirit" with the signs and wonders that accompany gospel proclamation foreshadowing the kingdom.[25] The

---

of the gospel to avoid overemphasizing either the "already" or "not yet" dimension to the diminishment of the other and the detriment of both.

21. Luke shared with Jesus and first-century Pharisees a two-age eschatological understanding in which "this world" or age stands over by "that age" or "age to come"; but, for Luke (and Jesus) there was a significant difference: God's kingdom had already entered this present evil age through Jesus' ministry and the Spirit's presence. See Stein, *Luke*, 414–15.

22. Land, *Pentecostal Spirituality*, 51.

23. As Arrington says, "encounters with the Holy Spirit are miracles of God's grace that transform our lives profoundly, empowering us to be conformed more and more to the person and ministry of Jesus Christ," *Encountering the Holy Spirit*, 464. Note the twofold conformation.

24. John Calvin, *Commentarius in Harmoniam evangelicam*, Corpus Reformatum 73:483, cited by Beasley-Murray, *Jesus and the Kingdom of God*, 188.

25. Macchia, *Baptized with the Spirit*, 91–107 (95–96).

Messiah-Spirit Baptizer is the Inaugurator of the Kingdom (Matt 3:11).[26] Therefore, it is not surprising that Jesus' post-resurrection, pre-Pentecost promise of Spirit baptism is framed in kingdom language (Acts 1:1–8). The role of *Jesus Christ as eternal and unchanging Lord powerfully present and active by the Holy Spirit* aligns with the interplay between the kingdom and Pentecost in bringing Christ's righteous reign and glorious presence experientially into the lives of believers today.

It is tragically true that believers have at times been victims of charlatans and unscrupulous opportunists who exploit (sometimes naïve) openness to the miraculous for selfish advantage or financial gain. Both Jesus and Paul warned against such wolves preying on Christ's flock (Matt 7:15; Acts 20:29). Further, Jesus warned against the evils of being "sign seekers" (Matt 12: 38–40). Yet rather than dismiss or prohibit signs altogether Jesus gave them a greater sign than ever—his resurrection. Neither did he discontinue his own ministry of signs and wonders. Jesus' commonsense exhortation to examine the "fruit," or ethical conduct, of those who minister among us, coupled with exercising the spiritual charism or gift of discernment is applicable (Matt 7:15–20; 1 Cor 12:10). A sound charismology insists that charisma be married to character.[27]

ULTIMATE PNEUMATOLOGICAL EXEMPLAR

The ultimate example of Spirit-filled life and ministry is Jesus Christ himself. A particularly helpful window into the role of the Spirit in Christ's ministry is Apostle Peter's sermon at Cornelius' house in Acts 10:34–43. For starters, it has become a classic resource because of its climactic result in the Spirit's outpouring on the gathering, the so-called Gentile Pentecost (vv. 44–46).[28] Additionally, it provides one of the most succinct descriptive summaries of the Spirit's role in Christ's ministry in all apostolic

---

26. Macchia, *Baptized with the Spirit*, 99, 102.

27. An undisciplined penchant for signs and wonders coupled with a naively literal hermeneutic (e.g., Mark 16:17–18) can result in serious error. The practice of serpent-handling opposed by most Pentecostals but practiced by a few in southern Appalachia is a notorious example. Yet Kane, "Serpent Handlers," 212, observes that snake-handling was not "a gross aberration of southern religious life"; rather, its "roots lie deep in the religious heritage of the South." Serpent-handling at least partly spread through misunderstanding. E.g., some roughnecks once threw a huge timber rattler into a group of worshipers in which my grandfather was present, apparently intending to amuse themselves at the "holy rollers'" expense. However, my grandfather picked up the snake—which instantly went limp in his hand—wrapped it around his head turban style, walked outside and threw it down at the feet of the rowdy bunch. The snake immediately reawakened, crawling away into the underbrush. Apparently, the men were notably impressed. Some converted. Perhaps one might say, "So far, so good!" Unfortunately, as news of the incident spread some devotees erroneously argued the practice should be intentionally replicated in regular worship services.

28. I say "so-called" because some use this language to argue for an unrepeatable event—which is obviously inconsistent with Acts 19:1–7 and elsewhere. For me, "Gentile Pentecost" or "Ephesian Pentecost" rather signifies that Pentecost *is* repeatable. Else why would it keep being *repeated*?

preaching (v. 38). The apostle's pronouncement continues to exert singular shaping influence on Pentecostal Christology to this day.

Peter's sermon is in three parts. First, verses 34–35 declare God's impartiality toward all people, signifying God's willingness to accept Gentiles or those of non-Jewish ethnicities. Apart from this truth Peter's meeting with Gentiles would have been impossible. Second, verses 36–41 describes Jesus' personal career, essentially summarizing the Gospel of Luke, the prequel to Acts, with its focus on Jesus' identity as Lord and his life and ministry among the Israelites, especially his death and resurrection.[29] It is essential from the start to focus firmly on Jesus Christ as the only solid basis of redemption. Thirdly, verses 42–43 detail the apostolic mission to proclaim judgment and to offer forgiveness of sins through faith in Jesus' name in continuity with the previous witness of the prophets of Israel. This point establishes Peter's (and other apostles) credibility and responsibility in the ministry of the gospel. The sermon is remarkable overall for its consistent continuity with the religion of Israel coupled with openness and inclusiveness to others and denunciation of Jewish leadership's rejection of Jesus. However, its key feature is its central focus on the person and work of Jesus Christ.

In describing the core content of God's word concerning the person and work of Jesus, Peter focuses on Jesus' message of peace, his identity as Lord, his Spirit-anointed ministry, and his death and resurrection. These four points sum up what was essential for his Gentile audience (and everyone since) to hear in order to respond appropriately in faith to God's benevolent offer of forgiveness through Jesus. They require a closer look.

First, note that Jesus' preaching of peace identifies a key theme of the gospel. Perhaps it seemed especially appropriate to the Apostle of Christ, a Jew from the subservient state of Israel, as he broke new ground with a Roman military man and his family and their Gentile friends. In any case, peace is a decidedly relevant topic for this initial gospel proclamation. In similar terms, the prophet Isaiah had already identified peace as the goal (57:19) and later Paul taught about its accomplishment (Eph 2:14; Col 1:20). Peace here means reconciliation with God, and as a matter of due course, with others, "as offered to all people and made possible by the atoning death of Jesus Christ."[30] It implies much more than the cessation of enmity or hostility. The phrase for "preaching peace" (v. 36), εὐαγγελιζόμενος εἰρήνην (*euangellizomenos eirēnēn*), is literally "announcing [or proclaiming] the good news [or gospel] of peace."[31] Significantly, it not only links peace with the gospel but identifies the gospel as peace,

---

29. Pohil notes, *Acts,* 261: "This section is unique among the speeches of Acts in the amount of attention it gives to the ministry of Jesus. The other speeches of Peter emphasize the death and resurrection, as does this speech (vv. 39–40). Only the sermon in Cornelius' house, however, provides an outline of Jesus' earthly ministry (vv. 37–38)."

30. Arrington, "Acts of the Apostles," 587.

31. Unless otherwise indicated, throughout this volume I use the Society for Biblical Studies edition of the Greek New Testament.

thus indicating active participation in the abundant blessings of salvation.[32] With the removal ("forgiveness" v. 43) of sins harmonious relations are restored between a holy God and sinful human beings—and, undoubtedly, between estranged and hostile humans as a consequence.

Second, the significance of Peter's description of Jesus as "Lord of all" is twofold. First, it declares Jesus' sovereign deity. If not before, then at least since Thomas' profound confession (John 20:28), "Lord" had taken on its full significance for the disciples as a designation of Jesus as God.[33] But here, although it does not mean less than that, it means more. In his Pentecost Day sermon, Peter ascribed the title of Lord to Jesus as an indicator of God's approval (in spite of human opposition) and the outcome of his victory over death immediately after quoting David's messianic prophecy of Christ's triumph (Acts 2:36; Ps 110:1). Wrapped in the title of Lord is a description both of Jesus' person and work. He is the incarnate God who has overcome sin and death. Second, Peter describes the extent of Jesus' Lordship as unlimited. Jesus is not Lord in an exclusive sense but in an inclusive sense. He is Lord not only of Israel but also of Gentiles—of all nations and ethnicities. In short, Jesus Christ is the one and only truly universal Lord (cp. Rev 19:16). Peter describes Jesus as "Lord of all" at the beginning of his sermon even though his appeal to believe and receive forgiveness does not occur till its end. It is apparently a kind of up front assurance, or "pre-approved" guarantee in the language of modern commerce, that they would indeed be accepted.[34]

Third, let's turn to the Spirit-anointed ministry of Jesus. The anointing of Jesus with the Holy Spirit is often associated with the Spirit's manifest coming upon him at his baptism (Luke 3:21–22). Although Jesus was conceived by the Holy Spirit in the womb of the virgin, Mary (1:26–34), his baptism marked the beginning of a different phase in his relationship with the Holy Spirit. It is notable that Jesus' anointing for Spirit-filled ministry is immediately evident (4:1, 14, 18–19). Isaiah had long ago prophesied that the Spirit of the Lord would equip the Messiah with a special anointing for gospel service (61:1–3). At the beginning of his public ministry, Jesus specifically confirmed his receipt of the Spirit's anointing as prophesied by Isaiah centuries earlier (Luke 4:16–21). Isaiah's prophecy "announces the pattern of Jesus' total ministry."[35] It not only identifies Jesus as God's Anointed One, the Messiah or the Christ, it also describes the nature and substance of his gospel ministry.

Fourth, Jesus' death and resurrection are the clear climax of Peter's gospel sermon. He is not a biographer giving a historical account of a remarkable life, or even

---

32. The NT concept of peace builds on the OT concept of *shalom*. *Shalom* signifies overall wellbeing and a wholly satisfactory condition (Is 55:12; 60:17).

33. Borchert, *John 12–21*, 314–15.

34. Of course, it is possible that the Jewish Christian was preaching to himself. After all, it had taken a vision to get him to the scene (Acts 10:9–23).

35. Arrington, "Acts," 412.

of a remarkable martyr's death; he's a divinely commissioned witness proclaiming the way of salvation through faith in the death and resurrection of Jesus Christ (Matt 28:19; Acts 1:8). Peter was an eminently qualified witness as one of a select group who had seen Jesus alive after his crucifixion and burial (Luke 24:13–53; Acts 1:3–11). Significantly, Peter (v. 42), as did Paul when preaching to Gentiles in Athens (Acts 17:31), highlights Jesus' role as Judge (cp. 2 Tim 4:1; 1 Pet 4:5). Likely an "extra step" regarding final judgment was necessary for pagan hearers more so than for Jews already acquainted with that prominent Old Testament theme. Nevertheless, clearly Peter's main objective all along has been to announce, in sum, that, "All who believe in Jesus, both Jew and Gentile, will have their sins forgiven." (Cp. Acts 2:38–39)[36] More importantly, the announcement of forgiveness of sins through faith in Jesus appears to have been the divine climax as well for at that precise moment *God* (rather than the Athenians as in Paul's sermon, 17:32–33) interrupted Peter's sermon with a post-Pentecost Pentecostal outpouring of the Holy Spirit (v. 44)! Perhaps this was a kind of divine "Amen!" to the preaching?

THE SPIRIT-ANOINTED MESSIAH

The focus of this chapter is on *Jesus Christ as the eternal and unchanging Lord who is ever present with believers and active in their lives by the Holy Spirit's power*. Pentecostals agree with the early church that the Pentecostal experience "was 'like Jesus with them again,' though there was no one to see."[37] Lawson says it well: "The Holy Spirit is the agent who mediates to the Church in present experience the sense of the presence and power of God *as He is known in Jesus Christ*."[38] Again, Pentecostals heartily agree. What is distinctive about Pentecostals is the extent to which they expect to experience the reality of God's presence in their own lives today. Explication of this theme calls for special attention to the role of the Holy Spirit in Jesus' life and ministry. Accordingly, after having outlined Peter's overall sermon at Cornelius' household, I now return to its description of Jesus as the Spirit-anointed Messiah in verse 38.

In Acts 10 Peter offers a threefold focus of the Spirit's anointing of Jesus for ministry (v. 38). First, the Spirit's anointing enabled Jesus to do good deeds or works for the people. Second, the Spirit's anointing enabled Jesus to demonstrate sovereign victory over the devil and evil forces. Third, the miraculous ministry which was the outcome of the Spirit's anointing on Jesus clearly demonstrated in a discernible fashion God's approving presence with him, thus affirming visibly his messianic identity and

---

36. Arrington, "Acts,," 588. One wonders if the announcement of forgiveness was next in Paul's sermon but was forfeited due to the untimely interruption (Acts 17:32–33; cp. 13:38). If so, with allowances for context, and with the entirely different receptions by Cornelius' group and the Athenian intelligentsia aside, similarities between the concluding portion of the Petrine and Pauline sermons are striking.

37. Lawson, *Christian Doctrine*, 114.

38. Lawson, *Christian Doctrine*, 114. Italics are original.

salvific mission. In all of these ways and more, the enabling power of the Holy Spirit is present and active in the ministry of Jesus Christ. A simple attempt to explain how the Holy Spirit works in the ministry of Jesus leads naturally enough into a consideration of Spirit Christology.[39]

Peter's sermon in Acts 10:34–43 has been interpreted by some as depicting a minimalist Christology, that is, a "low" Christology which minimizes the status of Christ's divinity. Minimalists argue that Jesus' apparent need of the Spirit's anointing to perform his ministry coupled with a description of him as someone with whom God was present points to a special man of God, a great servant of God even—but no more (cp. Acts 4:30). Minimalists rejecting Christ's divinity, add to this general impression Peter's reference to "Jesus of Nazareth" (v. 38), an obvious emphasis on his humanity, and argue that this sermon represents an early Christology before subsequent, and inaccurate, claims to his deity became the norm. In this view Peter depicts a human Jesus with a special endowment of divine power. Thus (a minimalist Christology would say) he had divine power, but he was not a divine person. That conclusion would be premature and misguided, to say the least. Early in his sermon Peter had already declared that Jesus is *Lord of all* (v. 36). The rest of the sermon should be heard/read in that light.[40] Accordingly, a conclusion much more consistent with the text is that Peter's sermon affirms both the deity and humanity of Jesus Christ with an emphasis on Spirit Christology.

SPIRIT CHRISTOLOGY

In general terms, Christology is the study of Jesus Christ and Spirit Christology is the study of Jesus Christ in relation to the Holy Spirit. However, for our purposes we need a more definitive description.[41] As is so often the case with theological endeavors, Spirit Christology exists in multiple forms. Although Spirit Christology can be traced historically (if sporadically) from the time of the Apostolic Fathers (first and second centuries AD) to the present, it currently exists in one form as a revisionist effort by modernist theologians struggling with relating to the deity of Jesus. Unfortunately, for some of them the anointing of Jesus by the Spirit seems a possible way to sidestep his identity as God. Orthodox theologians have responded through development of a Trinitarian Spirit Christology which positively affirms Jesus' deity and relates it to the Holy Spirit constructively. For example, Clark Pinnock, popular among Pentecostals, portrays the Incarnation as the Son of God voluntarily emptying himself of divine attributes and abilities in order live in complete solidarity with humans in utter

---

39. Neville, *A Theology Primer,* puts it well: "From the appearance of the Spirit at Jesus' baptism through the Pentecost experience, Jesus was who he was because of the explicit witness of the Spirit," 147.

40. Peterson, *Acts of the Apostles*, 337.

41. In the following I draw on the exhaustive work of my colleague Odell Bryant, *Spirit Christology*, esp. 1–43.

dependence on the Holy Spirit (*kenosis* theory of Incarnation; see Pp 2:7).[42] Although Pentecostals have not typically attempted to construct specific models of Spirit Christology they have nevertheless used Spirit Christology in constructing in their own theology.[43]

Spirit Christology remains a fluid term defying precise definition, but a consensus assessment nevertheless suggests "Spirit Christology focuses on how the Spirit relates to Christ's identity and soteriological mission; specifically," and this is important for Pentecostal theology, "it elucidates Jesus' genuine humanity and the Spirit's agency in his life and ministry."[44] Finally, the Pentecostal take on Spirit Christology, as would be expected, is fairly straightforward, especially at the grassroots level. As Odell Bryant rightly notes, Pentecostals "readily recognize Christ's deity, and they accentuate the Spirit's anointing and empowerment of Jesus' genuine humanity for mission as a model for their own Spirit baptism."[45] For Pentecostals Spirit Christology is not primarily speculative theorizing about the two natures of Christ or intra-Trinitarian relations.[46] Perennially taking Jesus as their example in all things (John 13:15; 1 Cor 11:1; 1 Pet 2:21), the relationship between the Holy Spirit and Jesus in his life and ministry has implications for their own walk and work in the Spirit.

There are a number of questions crying for address. For one, what is the significance of Spirit Christology for Pentecostal theology? For another, what does it mean for Pentecostal faith and practice? Again, how does it impact Pentecostal spirituality and worship? And, is Spirit Christology a legitimate model for Pentecostal ministry? But, one of the main questions, providing the basis for all of these, comes first: Is it biblical?

LUKE-ACTS ACCOUNT[47]

Regarding the anointing of Jesus with the Spirit three episodes stand out as especially significant. The account of Luke's Gospel is particularly revealing: his baptism

---

42. Pinnock, *Flame of Love*, 85, 88, 100.

43. E.g., Thomas, "The Spirit in the Fourth Gospel: Narrative Explorations," 157–74; Sang-Ehil Han, "A Revisionist Spirit-Christology in Korean Culture," (unpublished PhD dissertation, Emory University, 2004); Yong, *The Spirit Poured Out on All Flesh*; Macchia, *Baptized in the Spirit*; S. D. L. Jenkins, "The Human Son of God and the Holy Spirit: Toward a Pentecostal Incarnational Spirit Christology," (unpublished PhD dissertation, Marquette University, 2004); and, Alfaro, *Divino Compañero*.

44. Bryant, *Spirit Christology*, 40. Note that "Christology and pneumatology are mutually conditioned and 'dependent' on each other," Kärkkäinen, *Spirit and Salvation*, 204.

45. Bryant, *Spirit Christology*, 41.

46. This observation neither diminishes such conversations in their place nor denies important voices of Pentecostal academics at that table, Kärkkäinen, *Spirit and Salvation*, 35–38.

47. For the sake of space and time I focus on the account of Luke-Acts as a canonical center for Pentecostalism's unique ethos. However, Spirit Christology is evident in all the Gospels and present everywhere in the NT. E.g., Matt 1:18–25; 3:11, 16; 4:1; 12:28; Mark 1:10, 12; John 1:33; Rom 1:4; 1 Cor 15:45.

(3:21–22), temptation (4:1–13), and synagogue sermon at Nazareth (4:14–30).[48] At his baptism the Spirit descends on Jesus as an objective, physical manifestation in the bodily form of a dove. Immediately Jesus was led by the Spirit into the desert to be tempted. While Matthew and Mark both connect the temptation with the Spirit's leading (Matt 4:1; Mark 1:12), only Luke describes Jesus as "full of the Holy Spirit" (4:1) and explains that he "returned in the power of the Spirit to Galilee" (4:14). Luke's emphasis on the Spirit-anointed Messiah shows clearly.

All four Evangelists record the descent of the Spirit on Jesus at his baptism but only Luke gives Jesus' self-understanding of the significance of the experience. Preaching his inaugural sermon from Isaiah 61:1–2 at a synagogue in Nazareth (Luke 4:18–19), Jesus announces that its prophecy was fulfilled in him then and there. In a word, Jesus understood the descent of the Holy Spirit upon him as the Messianic anointing for a charismatic, prophetic ministry of preaching, teaching, healing, and deliverance. In the course of Luke's Gospel, the Spirit's anointing, leading, and empowering become marks of Jesus' entire ministry. It is this pattern of Jesus' Spirit-anointed ministry which Peter's sermon at Cornelius' house summarizes in Luke's Acts sequel (10:38).

Luke's Gospel clearly portrays Jesus as the Spirit-anointed Messiah with a focus on the beneficial and productive consequences of that reality for his ministry. This portrait is entirely consistent with the Spirit Christology which so richly informs Pentecostal theology. Furthermore, Luke presents the pattern of Jesus' Spirit-anointed ministry as an example, even a model, for subsequent Spirit-anointed ministry. Just as the Third Gospel relates that Jesus executes his ministry in the power of the Holy Spirit, so its sequel, the Acts of the Apostles, records the life and ministry of the early church as it is empowered by the Holy Spirit to bear witness to the saving works of Jesus. Arrington says, "Jesus and His Spirit-filled ministry is the model for the Church," adding that, "the Spirit-anointed ministry of Jesus foreshadows and prepares for the worldwide mission of the Church."[49] Pentecostals believe the Spirit's anointing of Jesus is both precedent and pattern for the Spirit's anointing of believers today.

The book of Acts clearly indicates that "The ascended Christ was present with purpose and power in the life of the early church through the ministry of the Holy Spirit."[50] The same anointing Jesus received is poured out on his disciples at Pentecost (Acts 2), as the one who has received the Spirit becomes the giver of the Spirit (2:33). In Arrington's words, the disciples and the church "become heirs and successors to the Spirit-anointed ministry of Jesus, in that they become empowered to continue to do and teach what 'Jesus began to do and teach'" (1:1).[51] The Acts of the Apostles, or Acts of the Holy Spirit, if you will, records the continuation of Jesus' Spirit-anointed

---

48. The following draws on Arrington, *Spirit-Anointed Jesus* and Arrington, *Spirit-Anointed Church*.

49. Arrington, *Spirit-Anointed Church*, 17.

50. Smith, *Evangelical, Sacramental, & Pentecostal*, 10.

51. Arrington, *Spirit-Anointed Church*, 17.

ministry through Spirit-empowered witnesses (1:8). Arrington asserts that "Both the descent of the Spirit on Jesus and the outpouring of the Spirit at Pentecost are anointings for ministry."[52] Thus the ecclesiological and missiological implications of Spirit Christology come to the fore.[53]

Let's sum up a bit. First, an image of Jesus as the Spirit-anointed Messiah undergirds a Spirit Christology affirmative of his full deity and genuine humanity while accenting the significant role of the Holy Spirit in his life and ministry. Second, the role of the Holy Spirit in the life and ministry of Jesus places Pentecost into missiological perspective as empowerment for the church's ministry vocation. Third, a correlation of Jesus' anointing with the Spirit and Pentecost elucidates the nature of Spirit baptism as an experience of empowerment equipping individual believers as witnesses to Christ in words and in works.[54]

I think we can now safely say that much of the significance of Spirit Christology for Pentecostal theology lies in its potent implications for Christian mission and ministry. In describing "NT-based Spirit Christologies" in which "Jesus' earthly life with cures, exorcisms, and other forms of liberation play a prominent role," Kärkkäinen, goes so far as to say that "Intuitively, Pentecostal theology, with its focus on different roles of Jesus as Savior, Sanctifier, Healer, Baptizer-with-the-Spirit, and the Soon-Coming Eschatological King in the power of the Spirit, has also helped highlight the then and current ministry of Jesus."[55] In a word, this model helps explain why Pentecostals approach ministry as we do.

Additionally, Spirit Christology imbues Pentecostal faith and practice with an almost intoxicating, and certainly exhilarating, sense of God's manifest presence in Jesus through the Holy Spirit—thus profoundly impacting Pentecostal spirituality and worship. These topics of God's manifest presence and Pentecostal spirituality and worship will be taken up further in chapters five and six. Here, however, it is enough to assert that arguably Spirit Christology is quite biblical and, therefore, most certainly a legitimate model for Pentecostal ministry and mission.

In this chapter I have argued that a prevalent vision of *Jesus Christ as the eternal and unchanging Lord who is ever present and active with his church by the power of the*

---

52. Arrington, *Spirit-Anointed Jesus*, 94.

53. Ecclesiological and missiological categories embrace but also extend beyond traditional evangelism and witnessing categories to include ways in which the Luke-Acts narrative points to Spirit baptism as renewing social orders (e.g. Samaritans, Ethiopian eunuch, Gentiles) and dismantling false realities which foster inappropriate dualisms (e.g. males and females). See Stephenson, *Dismantling the Dualisms*, 89–90, 99, 195.

54. As Beth Moore, *Portraits of Devotion*, 318, says somewhat facetiously of the Day of Pentecost, the Holy Spirit "never comes just to show off" but "to show off and bring results"—especially saving lost souls (Acts 2:47).

55. Kärkkäinen, *Spirit and Salvation*, 376. I take up discussion of this "full gospel" dimension of Pentecostal theology in chapters 7 and 8. Further, Kärkkäinen's statement is an insightful comment on the nature of Pentecostal theology itself. It often "intuitively" arrives at significant theological truth (John 16:13).

Holy Spirit is paradigmatic for Pentecostal believers. I am persuaded that a reclamation of this prominent biblical perspective holds rich theological and missiological potential for the movement. The same ministry conducted by Jesus in the power of the Spirit is provided for and expected from the church today. Jesus has not changed. The Holy Spirit has not changed. God's Word has not changed. The gospel has not changed. The needs of humanity have not changed. The world has not changed (not really). Sin has not changed. Even Satan has not changed. The church should not change either. An unsaved world needs an undiminished church to bear unapologetic witness to its all-sufficient Savior and Lord in the undiluted power of the Holy Spirit.

5

Experiencing God's Presence in Worship

PENTECOSTAL THEOLOGY AND SPIRITUALITY affirm (and facilitate) experience of the presence of the God of the Bible in the church's life and worship today through personal encounter with the Holy Spirit.[1] An early Pentecostal writer said it this way: "[Jesus] has gone into the heavens but the executive agent of the Trinity is here."[2] In other words, during this post-Incarnation, pre-eschaton, Pentecost age believers experience God's presence through the Holy Spirit. This insight is not a departure from historic Christianity.[3] However, the Pentecostal emphasis is distinctive. Those who would define Pentecostal theology solely in terms of *intellectual* categories are mistaken. Rather, Pentecostals are intensely *relational*. They approach the worship of God as a mutual self-offering in freedom and love. As believers offer themselves to God in worship God offers God's own presence to worshipers.[4] Therefore, Pentecostals are all about encountering God's presence; and, authentic Pentecostal theology must be concerned with the same.[5]

1. As far back as 1993 I argued that Pentecostals are distinctive in their expectation of the demonstration of God's personal presence in their worship. See Richie, "Manifestation of the Spirit," 1–2.

2. Anonymous, *Latter Rain Evangel,* (Jan 1915), 4.

3. E.g., Lawson, *Christian Doctrine,* 111–12, 112–14.

4. Martin, *Spirit-Filled Worship,* 93.

5. Warrington, *Pentecostal Theology,* 20–27. Cp. Clark and Lederle: *What is Distinctive about Pentecostal Theology?* 36; Spittler, "Maintaining Distinctives," 134; and, Jacobsen, "Introduction: The History and Significance of Early Pentecostal Theology," 4.

AN INVITATION TO EXPERIENCE GOD

The religion of the Bible is an invitation to experience God. As the Psalmist David said, "Oh, taste and see that the Lord is good" (34:8a; cp. Heb 6:5; 1 Pet 2:3). The meaning is crystal clear. David plainly exhorts his readers to try experience. David desires that others "may experience what he has experienced, in order to know what he has known; the goodness of God."[6] God is not a theoretical hypothesis. God is a living being, a living person—or, more accurately, God is *the* living being, *the* living person. As we encounter God personally, experiencing God's presence for ourselves, God's goodness imparts itself to us and transforms our lives. No wonder C. S. Lewis (referencing Ps 34:8a) insists that abstract conceptions of God and reasoning about God require correction by spiritual experience.[7] Every experience of God is a kind of "tiny theophany" inspiring adoration of God.[8] In Pentecostal worship divine immanence and transcendence come together in definitive encounter with congregants.[9] Although often sternly criticized for emphasizing experience, Pentecostals are not off track here. Rather, this emphasis is an important and much-needed corrective for the theological endeavor, not to mention for congregational worship and individual Christian living. Pentecostal OT scholar Rickie Moore is right: "*Experience is vital to knowing the truth.*"[10]

For me, the value, and vitality, of experiencing God's presence was modeled in my grandmother's life. By "modeled" I do not mean that everyone's experience should be exactly like hers. Of course, authentic experience may be more or less sudden, more or less dramatic, and more or less intense.[11] Rather, "Grandma Richie" exemplified the great importance of experiencing God's presence. My grandparents were swept up in the early Pentecostal revival in the mountains of southeast Appalachia. Unable to read for herself, Grandma Richie memorized Scripture verses she heard read aloud in church services. She became so adept at this practice that if anyone misquoted a passage she could (and would!) correct them. One of her favorites, frequently quoted during testimony time, was Psalm 16:11: "Thou wilt shew me the path of life: In thy presence *is* fulness of joy; At thy right hand *there are* pleasures for evermore." (KJV) This verse became her explanation for what she experienced in worship. But what does it mean to experience God in this manner?

Psalm 16:11 is part of a group of prayers/songs which grew "from the soil of *confessing* the living God of revelation" "supported by it as by its *ground of faith and*

---

6. Lange, *Psalms*, 236.

7. Lewis, *Miracles*, 144–45, (11:14). Citation note: So many different editions of Lewis' works are available that it has become common to list both page numbers and chapter/paragraph format to facilitate access.

8. Lewis, *Letters to Malcolm*, 90 (17:13). Cp. Richie, "Manifestation of the Spirit," 11.

9. Martin, *Spirit-Filled Worship*, 84.

10. Moore, "A Pentecostal Approach to Scripture," 12. Italics are original.

11. Allen, *Spiritual Theology*, 37–39.

life" and taking the "form of *didactic testimonies.*"[12] These testimonies simultaneously edify and comfort along with prophetical discourse originating in personal experience from intimate communion with God. Therefore, Psalm 16:11 is a prophetic testimony of the praying believer's experience of the presence of the Lord as both a confession of present faith and a prophecy awaiting ultimate fulfillment. No wonder Pentecostals identify well with it.

Pentecostals testify of a present experience, not of a vague emotional thrill, but of a vital encounter with God's transforming and uplifting presence in vivid foretaste of joyful abiding eternally in God's presence.[13] Like the Psalms, Pentecostals relate experiencing God's presence to the Holy Spirit's agency (51:11) and render unto the Lord appropriately exuberant worship in response (95:2; 100:2) with firm assurance that the Spirit's presence reverberates throughout all their life (139:7). Here and hereafter God's own presence is the reward of righteousness (140:13). Experiencing God's presence through Spirit baptism is particularly direct and dramatic (Matt 3:11; Mark 1:8; Luke 3:16; John 1:33). True to the instincts of early Pentecostals, contemporary Pentecostal theology explicates an experience of God's presence as a simultaneously pneumatological and eschatological mode of being.

For many Pentecostals in the pews Psalm 16:11 suggests a fourfold setting, what we might call, the prophetic, the eschatological, the liturgical, and then the devotional. The prophetic affirms the obvious messianic import of Psalm 16:8–11 (cp. Acts 2:29–33). The eschatological involves all believers embracing the hope and promise of dwelling in God's presence for eternity. The liturgical involves experiencing God's presence in congregational praise and worship. The devotional involves experiencing God's presence in one's personal walk with God through a life of prayer, Scripture reading, and obedience. Overall emphasis is on "fullness of joy"— abundant joy undiminished and untarnished by the cares of this life or the sorrows of this world. Augustine describes it as such joy "that they should seek nothing further."[14] That remark reveals a great deal about the nature of ultimate fulfillment. Thus, Lewis' odd insight: "Joy is the serious business of Heaven."[15] As David so well knew, the joy of the Lord is more than uplifting; it is life-giving. Therefore, Pentecostals love to juxtapose the full, overflowing, and satisfying life of John 10:10 with the inexpressible, unexplainable joy of 1 Peter 1:8 as characteristic of their encounter with God. God is not parsimonious. Key to obtaining abundant, eternal life and indescribable, indispensable joy is experiencing God's generous presence.

---

12. Lange, *Psalms*, 126–27 (original italics).
13. Cross, *Answering the Call in the Spirit*, 14–16, 107.
14. Augustine, "Expositions on the Book of Psalms," 8:49.
15. Lewis, *Malcolm*, 93 (17:23).

THREE WAYS OF EXPERIENCING GOD'S PRESENCE

Canadian theologian Gordon Smith argues that according to the Book of Acts the NT church experienced God's presence in three ways: through the preaching of the Word, through participation in the sacraments, and through the immediacy of the Holy Spirit.[16] These grace-filled avenues into God's glorious presence are represented today by the Evangelical, Sacramental, and Pentecostal traditions. He argues, and I agree, that there is no need to choose between any of these, that all three are valid and that all three can and should be properly integrated into the life and worship of healthy congregations. The focus of this chapter is on the immediacy of the Holy Spirit. However, first a few brief comments about Word and Sacrament are in order.

Pentecostal theology easily affirms the importance of the preached Word. Most Pentecostals would agree that "the need of the hour is for preachers who know the Word and who deliver its eternal and unchanging truths under the anointing of the Holy Spirit."[17] Put thusly, the preaching of God's Word is not merely a human endeavor; it requires the agency of the Holy Spirit (1 Pet 1:12). Certainly, Pentecostals do believe we can encounter God through the preached Word. Pentecostal preaching should be instructive and inspiring, but these are not the main objectives. As Pentecostal pastor and OT theologian Lee Roy Martin puts it, "The goal of Pentecostal preaching is that God himself will come down in the midst of the congregation" in order that "the hearers may be transformed by the Holy Spirit."[18] Bare exhortation alone is insufficient. Preaching must involve an encounter with God because "transformation can only be accomplished by the presence and power of the Holy Spirit."[19] Encountering God the Holy Spirit through the preached Word can be a life-changing, life-giving experience.

Yes, Pentecostals are indeed evangelical in their emphasis on the preached Word. Arrington says Pentecostals are "people of the Book" as well as "people of the Spirit."[20] But for Pentecostals it is not an either/or option. The preaching of the Word falls short unless it ushers hearers into the presence of Scripture's Divine Author. Peter's Pentecost Day sermon (Acts 2:14–41) is a striking example of bold biblical proclamation in an environment of the Spirit's presence moving and working. In many ways, it serves as a model for today as well. There is no break in rhythm between the Spirit's moving and the preaching of the Word. The proclamation of the Word flows out of the Spirit's moving and then the Spirit's Word touches, and impacts, people's hearts (2:37). Pentecostal homiletics appropriately concerns itself with the craft of sermon preparation

---

16. Smith, *Evangelical, Sacramental, & Pentecostal*, 35.
17. Williams, "Spirit-filled Preaching is Relevant for the Twenty-First Century," 9.
18. Martin, "The Uniqueness of Spirit-Filled Preaching," 200, 201.
19. Martin, "The Uniqueness of Spirit-Filled Preaching,," 209. Not only in preaching but illuminating, transforming divine encounter is consistent with how—and why—Pentecostals read the Bible as well. See Davies, "What Does It Mean to Read the Bible as a Pentecostal?," 252, 255.
20. Arrington, *Christian Doctrine*, 1:25.

and delivery yet nonetheless invites hearers into a transforming encounter with God's presence as they respond in faith and obedience to the preached Word.

Pentecostals have somewhat of a checkered history on sacraments.[21] Doctrinally, Pentecostals have affirmed the ordinances of water baptism, the Lord's Supper (Communion), and, for some, foot washing, too. In practice, observance has been infrequent or irregular, especially at the Lord's Table.[22] Probably Pentecostal sacramental reticence has been in large part reactionary.[23] Frankly, to many Pentecostals some traditions have so focused on mechanical liturgies that they appeared coldly formal and dryly bereft of spiritual life. In this regard, Pentecostals often quoted Paul's warning against those who "having a form of godliness but denying its power" (2 Tim 3:5) are to be avoided. Certainly, that is applicable in some cases. However, it does not condemn sacraments *in toto*. Quite to the contrary, the rich revivalist tradition which has so prominently influenced Pentecostalism has significant examples of sacramental vitality.[24] The Wesleys, so central in Pentecostalism's rise, clearly considered regular participation in the Lord's Supper crucial for spiritual growth.[25] Fortunately, Pentecostal scholars such as Dan Tomberlin and Chris Green are retrieving and developing sacramental theology with valuable Pentecostal emphases.[26] Pentecostals can affirm an encounter with the Lord's presence during and through sacramental observance (Luke 24:31, 35). However, Pentecostals, unlike traditions with theologies of transubstantiation or consubstantiation, do not emphasize the material elements in and of themselves but relative to the presence and agency of the Holy Spirit as they signify redemption in the Lord Jesus Christ (John 6:63).[27]

---

21. Traditional Pentecostals prefer to speak of "church ordinances" rather than sacraments. They point out that the term "sacraments" is not in the Bible. Also "ordinances" emphasizes that the Lord Jesus ordained these observances. Finally, misunderstandings are avoided by avoiding terminology used by traditions with different understandings about the efficacious nature of these acts.

22. The congregation I now serve as pastor, New Harvest Church of God in Knoxville, TN, told me when I came that they had not observed Communion for several years prior to my arrival. We now have a monthly Communion Sunday, as well as other special times of observance.

23. Liturgical discontent appears to have contributed to the initial emergence of Pentecostalism in the early 1900s. Cp. Tucker, "North America," 616, and Bare, *They Call Me Pentecostal,* 64–66. Oddly, although Bare's denominational heritage (same as mine) affirms foot washing he only specifies baptism and communion.

24. Conkin, *Cane Ridge,* 64–65, 168–69.

25. Knight, *John Wesley,* Kindle location 1638.

26. See Tomberlin, *Pentecostal Sacraments,* and Green, *Toward a Pentecostal Theology of the Lord's Supper.* In a conversation over breakfast (2-7-2018), Dan Tomberlin explained to me that early Pentecostals and their heirs negatively reacted more so to rigidly fixed liturgies allowing little to no room for the free moving of the Holy Spirit than to sacraments (or even formal liturgies) in and of themselves. I agree. It has taken some time for us to realize the implications of that significant qualification. Today Pentecostals argue that "We Need the Lord's Supper," Morris, 26–27.

27. Transubstantiation argues for the changing of the elements of the bread and wine, when they are consecrated in the Eucharist, into the body and blood of Christ (doctrine of the Roman Catholic Church). Consubstantiation (or, similarly, sacramental union) is the doctrine that the substance of the body and blood of Christ coexist in and with the substance of the bread and wine of the Eucharist

One of the distinctive features of Pentecostal sacramental theology and practice is its use of bodily touch (the laying on of hands), anointing oil, and prayer cloths (Luke 4:40; Acts 19:11–12; Jas 5:14–15).[28] Of course, these practices are not replacements or substitutes for formal sacraments. However, conjunctions of the material and spiritual as well as of divine grace and presence in these "aids to faith" clearly indicate Incarnational and sacramental qualities.[29] Significantly, they are all natural/physical acts practiced in connection with prayer. Arguably, an environment of prayer is their defining element.[30] I will come back to this subject later. For now, note that prayer is most certainly a primary means of encountering God's presence in Pentecostal spirituality and theology. And note that even in areas of sacramental theology and spirituality Pentecostals offer creative and valuable insights and resources.

Now let's look at the immediacy of the Holy Spirit. Philosopher-theologian Robert Cummings Neville suggests one of the reasons Christological debates in the early church preceded pneumatological debates was because the Holy Spirit "seemed so obvious as the startling and self-authenticating presence of God in congregational and personal spiritual life."[31] The presence of the Holy Spirit was not assumed; it was experienced. Of course, this sense of the Spirit as God presence doubtless affirms the divinity and personality of the Holy Spirit. Furthermore, this perceptible awareness of the Spirit's presence models the NT norm for Christian churches. Pentecostals desire to recover this acute awareness of God's presence through the Holy Spirit from the sporadic ebb and flow of history as an enduring reality for contemporary believers. Pentecostals have been known to complain that too often God's children have gone to the Lord's house only to discover that their Heavenly Father did not seem to be "at home." Pentecostals lament the tragic contrast of so much of today's vacuous Christianity with the vibrant NT example.

The church in Acts experienced the Holy Spirit in Christian initiation (conversion), lived in an attitude of discerning dependence on the Holy Spirit's guidance, and received empowerment from the Spirit for its mission (Acts 13:4).[32] The NT church was keenly aware of—sensibly, perceptibly, aware of—the Spirit's presence in their midst, and made explicit efforts to be attentive and responsive to the Spirit. Thus, Smith well says, "The book of Acts describes an early Christian community that lived by a dynamic that can only be explained by virtue of the immediate presence of God

---

(associated with the pre-Protestant Lollard movment and with Lutherans). In this respect, Classical Pentecostals are closer to Calvin. Calvin agreed with Zwingli that the sacraments are symbolic but insisted on the participation of the Holy Spirit.

28. Tomberlin, *Pentecostal Sacraments*, 89–120. Pentecostal OT scholar Jacqui Grey argues that believers themselves are embodied signs of God's message and presence, "Embodiment and the Prophetic Message," 431, 434–38.

29. Thomas, "Anointed Cloths," 111.

30. Thomas, "Anointed Cloths,," 70.

31. Neville, *A Theology Primer*, 147; cp. Arrington, *Spirit-Anointed Church*, 31.

32. Smith, *Evangelical, Sacramental, & Pentecostal*, 28–30.

in their midst."[33] The reality of God's experienced presence through encounter with the Holy Spirit in Acts could hardly be clearer.

However, Smith makes a happy, if somewhat sudden and surprising, move. He notes a "true connection" between "the experience and expression of joy" and the presence of the Holy Spirit in the Luke-Acts narrative that transcends his earlier categorizations.[34] Tomberlin had earlier noted the prominence, at times paradoxically, of the theme of joy in Acts.[35] Two Scripture references stand out to me: Luke 10:21 and Acts 13:52. Luke 10:21 says Jesus "rejoiced greatly in the Holy Spirit" (NASB). Jesus is here under the power and influence of the Holy Spirit and his joy is inspired by the Holy Spirit.[36] In Acts 13:52 "the disciples were continually filled with joy and with the Holy Spirit." (NASB)[37] Acts 13:52 intentionally relates the disciples' joy with the Spirit's infilling in a manner that accents the daily reality of their charismatic experience of empowerment. Thus, the filling with the Spirit "should be an ongoing reality and the normal condition of Pentecostal believers."[38] Moreover, and especially significant, spiritual joy is its enduring accompaniment.

THE NATURE OF RELIGIOUS EXPERIENCE

So then, we have come full circle from our starting point with Psalm 16:11 to a place where experiencing God's presence in fullness of joy intersects in a life-giving encounter with Jesus Christ through the Holy Spirit. But what really do we mean when we speak of "spiritual experience" or "religious experience"? Generally, "experience" designates a particular instance of personally encountering or undergoing something. It signifies epistemic awareness of a happening or an occurrence. In a straightforward sense, spiritual or religious experiences are instances of being conscious of encountering God's presence and undergoing various attendant phenomena. John Wesley, who avidly affirmed the inner witness or testimony of the Holy Spirit with the human spirit (Rom 8:16), spoke of inward impressions on the soul and of believers feeling in themselves the mighty working of the Spirit of Christ. He described his own famous Aldersgate experience as having his heart "strangely

---

33. Smith, *Evangelical, Sacramental, & Pentecostal*, 29. The normative condition for first century Christians later became the purview of esoteric mystics, Lawson, *Christian Doctrine*, 233–35.

34. Smith, *Evangelical, Sacramental, & Pentecostal*, 36.

35. Tomberlin, *Pentecostal Sacraments*, 71–72. Tomberlin notes that for Pentecostals deep consecration in prayer, a sense of cleansing, and great joy can commingle with experiences of the Spirit such as falling down under God's power and speaking in tongues, 32.

36. Arrington, *Luke*, 451.

37. The New American Standard Bible (NASB) (La Habra, CA: Lockman Foundation, 1971) translation of these two verses is clearer that Jesus' experience of joy was related to the Holy Spirit rather than his human spirit, and that the disciples had an ongoing experience of filling with joy and with the Holy Spirit.

38. Arrington, *Acts*, 605.

warmed" (cp. Lu 24:32). Wesley further described faith and experience as spiritual senses comparable to the physical senses.[39]

In other words, Wesley believed one can sense that God is "*present* in numinous graces."[40] I am reminded of Paul Baloche's contemporary Christian song "Open the Eyes of My Heart" based on the words of the Apostle Paul (Eph 1:18).[41] Just as surely as one can see or hear or feel physically, one can also experience God. Pentecostals often say something like, "The Lord touched me!" or "The hand of the Lord came on me!" or "I felt the power of God!" (1 Kgs 18:46; Ezra 7:6; Isa 8:11; Acts 11:21) Another, and old, popular gospel song illustrates the constructive intensity of the spiritual potentially occurring in any given Pentecostal worship service. The lyrics of "Something Got a Hold of Me" read like a lay theology of the spiritual experience of divine presence with transforming power and joy.[42] Another, much more contemporary song, "A Soul on Fire," also speaks to the passion of profound spiritual experience in serving and worshiping God.[43]

Few deny that people have spiritual experiences. Many debate their validity. Terry Cross offers preliminary steps toward an affirmative theology of experience from a Pentecostal perspective.[44] While experiencing God is not the sole basis for theological reflection, too frequently experiences with God the Holy Spirit are allowed no basis. Using four doctrinal loci of traditional Christian theology, *finitum (non) capax infiniti* (the finite is (not) capable of holding the infinite), *Christus praesens* (the present Christ), *unio cum Christo* (union with Christ), and *internum testimonium Spiritus Sancti* (the internal witness of the Holy Spirit), Cross argues that each locus is deficient without an experiential dimension. Rather than creating an entirely new theology, he breathes life into existing Christian theological formulations by including reflection on human encounters with the Spirit. The question "What happens when the Holy Spirit meets the human spirit, when the infinite touches the finite?" is well worth exploring theologically.[45] When a believer sings "You ask me how I know he lives, he lives within my heart"[46] he or she is not avoiding the necessity of intellectual reflection but affirming the reality of personal experience.

---

39. Oden, *John Wesley's Scriptural Salvation,* has an excellent summary of Wesley on experience, 84–91.

40. Collins, *John Wesley,* 88. Italics are original.

41. Baloche insists that "Worshiping God rightly should open our eyes to God's amazing grace," *Worship Matters,* 146. This eye-opening experience is a work of the Holy Spirit, Baloche, *Worship Matters*, 32.

42. Written by A. P. Carter and sung by various artists. For lyrics, see: https://www.oldielyrics.com/lyrics/the_carter_family/something_got_a_hold_of_me.html.

43. Sung by "Third Day," http://www.thirdday.com/. See Gospel Music Association, "News: Third Day's 'Soul on Fire' Most Played Song of 2015, http://www.gospelmusic.org/news-third-days-soul-on-fire-most-played-song-of-2015/ (January 8, 2016). Retrieved May 30, 2019.

44. Cross, "The Divine-Human Encounter," 3–34.

45. Cross, "The Divine-Human Encounter," 9.

46. From the song, "He Lives" by Alfred H. Ackley, first published in *Triumphant Service Songs*, a hymnal published by the Rodeheaver Company, in 1933. Cross quotes it as an example of Christian reliance on experience.

Peter Althouse examines several typologies for understanding of the Pentecostal appeal to experience.[47] He concludes that the Pentecostal appeal to experience is primarily confessional but with important transformative and reconstructive aspects. More than anything else Pentecostals bear witness, or testify, of what they believe and undergo in their walk with the Lord. Yet there is clear intention to repeat the experience within the congregational setting for the sake of providing others with participatory opportunities. Thus, the Pentecostal worship service encourages and facilitates seeking such experiences as conversion and Spirit baptism. Pentecostal experience is not a vague, ambiguous experience common to all religions. It is specifically Christian with its own internal logic.[48] In that vein, these "experiences of the Spirit are transformative in that they create a deeper commitment to Christ through encounter with the divine."[49] At the root of all Pentecostal experience is personal encounter with God.

However, it would be a monumental mistake to assume that Pentecostals value experience to the exclusion of theology.[50] Peter Neumann demonstrates that "*both* theology and experience are deeply enmeshed and integral to Pentecostal identity."[51] In sum, Pentecostals' approach to experience includes three main features: a sense of divine immediacy in their experience of the Holy Spirit, a conceptual framework of Scripture, tradition, and reason, and, increasingly as the movement matures, awareness of reciprocity between their experience of divine immediacy and their interpretative conceptual framework. Awareness of this mediated nature of their experience coupled with the preservation of their sense of "the immediacy (or directness) of encounter with God" is essential for Pentecostal theological development in tune with its distinctive experiential emphasis.[52]

---

47. Althouse, "Understanding the Pentecostal Appeal to Experience," 399–411.

48. Simone Weil, a French philosopher, mystic, and social activist, explained in *Waiting for God*, 64–69, that in her conversion journey spiritual experience illuminated Christian doctrine which in turn gave experience form. This bilateral dynamic reminds of Pentecostals.

49. Althouse, "Understanding the Pentecostal Appeal to Experience," 411.

50. Just as it would be an error to assume that non-Pentecostal theology totally ignores the appeal to experience. See Neville, *A Theology Primer*, 16–18.

51. Neumann, *Pentecostal Experience*, 104. Hollenweger, *The Pentecostals* argued that Pentecostal "dogmatic theology" is an expression of Pentecostal "experience of life" (483–86). Unsatisfactory as an exhaustive description, Hollenweger rightly lifted up a distinctive characteristic of Pentecostal theologizing. See Stephenson, *Types of Pentecostal Theology*, 111–30.

52. Neumann, *Pentecostal Experience*, 161. Cartledge, *Mediation of the Spirit*, 87, employs the concept of *concursus*, often used in explicating the doctrine of divine providence, in articulating that divine and human agency coordinate in "pneumatological mediation." Cartledge, *Mediation of the Spirit*, 166, argues that the mediation of the Holy Spirit is both subjective genitive (the Spirit mediates the Trinity) and objective genitive (Christ, creation, and the church mediates the Holy Spirit). This insight is helpful for clarifying what we mean when we speak of "mediation" of the Holy Spirit. Pentecostals agree that it is the work of churches to facilitate encounter with God. However, it is the Holy Spirit who effects divine encounter.

Interestingly, Neumann complains about the ambiguity of Pentecostal definitions and articulations regarding the precise nature of experience.[53] Ambiguity can mean doubtfulness or uncertainty of meaning due to a lack of clarity or precision. However, it can also mean entertaining the possibility that a term or statement is unclear because it is capable of more than one meaning. In other words, it is multifaceted and multilayered. I am in agreement with Neumann in the first sense, which is, as I take it, his intention anyway. Pentecostal theology must clearly define what it means by the terms it uses, especially those very close to the core of its distinctive identity—such as experience.

Yet ambiguity in the second sense is unavoidable—but not necessarily undesirable. Spiritual experience is by definition (no pun intended) hard to pin down, hard to define. Rather than describing this characteristic of Pentecostal experience as ambiguous, especially in the sense of amorphous or vague, I prefer another, more appropriate, term. "Mystery" (μυστήριον, *mystērion*) is a concept with a rich biblical and theological heritage.[54] It applies here very well. Pentecostals may appreciate that it is used in contexts indicating the necessity of revelation from the Holy Spirit to those who embrace spiritual receptivity (e.g., 1 Cor 2:6–16). Thus, a biblical and theological understanding of mystery differs from common notions of that which is kept secret or remains unknown or unexplained or that which is obscure or puzzling. Rather, mystery is that which is only made known by divine revelation (Dan 2:18; Rom 11:25; 16:25; cp. Matt 13:11).[55] Even at that, the Bible repeatedly reminds us that there are definite limits to our understanding of God and God's ways (Job 5:9; 11:7; 36:26; Eccl 3:11; Rom 11:33).

There is a great deal in the Christian faith that is mysterious. The Godhead, Christ's two natures, the resurrection, just to name a few. The new birth, sanctification and the fruit of the Spirit, Spirit baptism and spiritual gifts, miracles—all partake of mystery. Perhaps believers today can sympathize with Nicodemus after all for not immediately comprehending that the moving of the Spirit is like the blowing of the wind—hard to trace but impossible to deny (John 3:8). The Holy Spirit is intangible and invisible yet incredibly powerful. As the early twentieth century Dutch theologian, Abraham Kuyper, said, "The Holy Spirit leaves no footprints in the sand."[56] In a word, the Holy Spirit is mysterious. But there is a caveat: Scripture reveals to us the character and nature of the Holy Spirit. Only thus do we avoid distortion and superstition.[57] The mysterious ways of the Spirit never contradict the biblical revelation of the

---

53. Neumann, *Pentecostal Experience*, 5–8, 100. Neumann nevertheless admits that contemporary Christian theology (as a whole) exhibits ambiguity on experience and adds that experience is a kind of "weasel word" for many theologians, 22, 23–24.

54. See Chase, "Mystery," 454–55. According to Chase, Augustine urged Christians to "to taste, enjoy and participate in the mysteries of God's essence," 454. Does not that sound a lot like experience?

55. Mystery is a particular prevalent theme in Ephesians. See 1:9; 3:3–9; 5:32; 6:19.

56. Cited in Sproul, *Mystery of the Holy Spirit*, 7.

57. Sproul, *Mystery of the Holy Spirit*, 7–8.

Spirit's character and nature. The Spirit can be enigmatic but is not inscrutable. It may be hard to understand the Spirit's *ways*, but we understand the *Way* (John. 14:6). The ways of the Spirit are always consistent with the way of Christ. As Pentecostals like to quip, "The Spirit and the Word agree."[58]

Spiritual experience is like that too. It cannot be neatly categorized and exhaustively analyzed. It defies classification. So then, while we assuredly seek to articulate it with as much precision as possible, a Pentecostal theology of experience must leave ample room for mystery. Yet all spiritual experience is subject to the principle of agreement or non-contradiction. Authentic spiritual experience will never contradict legitimate scriptural instruction; rather the experience of the Spirit affirms and confirms biblical verity (1 John. 3:24; 4:13). It cannot be otherwise because, as the Johannine corpus emphasizes, the Holy Spirit is the *Spirit of Truth* (John 14:7; 15:26; 16:13; 1 John 4:6).[59] Therefore, we assuredly know that we experience the presence of the God who sent his Son to be our Savior and Lord in the church's life and worship through personal encounter with the Holy Spirit in joyous and life-giving communion.

William Turner's fascinating study of Black Holiness-Pentecostalism within the United Church of America provides an insightful exemplification of the nature of spiritual or religious experience for many Pentecostals.

> Afro-Christian religion longed intensely for the Holy Ghost, who through his visitations gave rapture to the receiving soul. Religion, then, was the celebration of life. It made accessible the deeper meaning of this life and the life of the world to come. It was intense, emotional, and joyful. The highlight was the descent of the deity in the person of the Holy Ghost, in response to which the worshipers shouted, wept, fell out under the power, spoke ecstatically, and danced. This visitation, which came during preaching, singing, praying, or any one of the worshiping acts, was the high point for which there was always longing and expectation.[60]

Turner later explains that such openness to this kind of religious experience is supported by a worldview accepting the perforation of boundaries between the phenomenal and the noumenal which encourages a welcoming attitude toward experiencing the divine presence.[61] Furthermore, the experience of God's presence "is not subject to the criterion of positive knowledge in the sense that it can be disproved through

---

58. Arrington, *Christian Doctrine*, 1:77–81, who staunchly insists on the importance of experience and of the centrality of the Holy Spirit in biblical interpretation, nevertheless warns against either confusing one's own spirit, or some other spirit, with the Holy Spirit or on making experience the hermeneutical starting point.

59. For more on this topic see, Richie, "Approaching the Problem of Religious Truth in a Pluralistic World," 351–69.

60. Turner, *United Holy Church of America*, 119.

61. Turner, *United Holy Church of America*, 124–25.

arguments and constructions of those who refuse to believe."[62] Apparently, even though spiritual experience is certainly not above the need for assessment essential processes of evaluation are necessarily conducted from the perspective of discerning faith rather than recalcitrant skepticism. Let us pray that the "eyes of [our] heart" will be opened that we might understand the things of God (Eph 1:18).

A THEOLOGY OF WORSHIP

With the preceding in mind, we now turn to the topics of worship and prayer which are indicative of those specific acts in which Pentecostals focus their experience of encountering God's presence.[63] Before delving into the details, a general theological framework for Pentecostal worship may be helpful. Hollis Gause brilliantly identifies three integral elements of Pentecostal worship: *rapture, rapport,* and *proleptic.*[64] Rapture signifies the joyous ecstasy inherent in experiential worship. Rapport signifies the unifying love occurring between God and God's worshipers. Proleptic signifies the teleological dialectic between the historically accomplished redemption and its eschatological consummation. Grassroots Pentecostals would probably say something like, "We *feel* God as we worship, we are *filled* with God as we worship, and we have a *foretaste* of God's heavenly glory as we worship." Additionally, all worship is established on Christ's redemptive work and empowered by the Holy Spirit. Finally, authentic worship is in accordance with the Scriptures. Although Pentecostal worship, like a mighty river at times overflowing its banks, cannot be too tightly contained, a discerning eye will note these general features resurfacing repeatedly in the following—although with a good deal of variety.

Work well notes that "the decisive historical influence" on the Pentecostal movement is the original apostolic church (the NT church).[65] As such Pentecostal worship is centered on Christ, dominated by the Holy Spirit, and based on the Word. For Pentecostalism, "its founding experience was an eschatological restoration of the presence of the Spirit of the original apostolic church that was increasingly lost in later centuries. Its signs and wonders and distinctive liturgical forms reflect that conviction."[66] In short, Pentecostal worship is primitivistic in ideology, restorationist in objective, and eschatological in orientation.

Somewhat like certain recurrent theories of philosophy and art which are convinced of the superiority of the qualities of primitive or early cultures over those of

---

62. Turner, *United Holy Church of America*, 125.

63. As Martin concludes in *Spirit-Filled Worship,* biblically worship includes an allegiance to God expressed in a life of commitment, attitudes such as love and reverence, and actions expressing gratitude and devotion, 49.

64. As summarized by Alexander, "Singing Heavenly Music," 204–06.

65. Work, "Pentecostal and Charismatic Worship," 575.

66. Work, "Pentecostal and Charismatic Worship," 575.

contemporary cultures, Pentecostals are persuaded that the NT era represents the height of the Christian faith. However, for Pentecostals this superiority is not based on any idea that early and simple is inherently better than later and complex. Rather, Pentecostals are convinced that the pristine apostolic age represents Christianity in its purest and most powerful form because of its immediate proximity to Christ and his disciples. Therefore, Pentecostal worship endeavors to restore or bring back Christian worship to its former position or condition. On the one hand, this improvement may require removing the impairments of later accretions. On the other hand, and, perhaps most importantly, it requires reclaiming the original worship practices of the NT. Finally, Pentecostal worship not only harks back to ancient and original Christianity but also eyes the horizon of the future. Pentecostal worship functions as a foretaste of eternity inspiring enduring hope for the present until Christ returns.

Accordingly, for Pentecostals gathering to worship is much more than a weekly ritual. Harold Bare describes the importance Pentecostals place on gathering together in worship as "one of the great virtues of a walk in the Holy Spirit."[67] For Pentecostals, it seems "logical and inevitable" that those who are together in Christ and together in the Holy Spirit "should seek to assemble ourselves together constantly."[68] Indeed, it is a dramatic reenactment of the core values of their faith. Critical to that core is encountering God in worship. Sorge sums it up nicely: "If we have a heart which desires God, we naturally desire to come near to him. We want to be in his presence. So, one of the foremost priorities of believers is to congregate with other saints for the purpose of meeting with God."[69] Pentecostals understand that the church consists of the people of God as the body of Christ and the temple of the Holy Spirit. However, when the church gathers at a particular place and time it conducts itself as a worshiping community. These worship services are central to Pentecostal spirituality and theology.

Before focusing on the Pentecostal worship gathering, it is important to understand the relationship between "gathering" and "going" in Pentecostalism.[70] In short, going out in performance of evangelistic mission and ministries of mercy and gathering in for corporate worship are inseparable acts of dedicatory service to God. Thus, Land links Pentecostal spiritual practices through worship and witness in light of the coming eschaton.[71] Land insists that at the heart of the "worshiping, witnessing, forming, reflective whole" which is the Pentecostal community is its liturgical life or worship.[72] The Pentecostal experience of God's Spirit in worship informs and energizes Pentecostal witness in the world of God's saving grace in Christ. But also, Pentecostal witness in the world of God's saving grace in Christ informs and energizes the Pentecostal

---

67. Bare, *They Call Me Pentecostal*, 133.
68. Riggs, *The Spirit Himself*, 177.
69. Sorge, *Exploring Worship*, 29.
70. Work, "Pentecostal and Charismatic Worship," 579.
71. Land, *Pentecostal Spirituality*, 89.
72. Land, *Pentecostal Spirituality*, 23; cp. 47, 50, and 88.

experience of God's Spirit in worship. The "gathering" and the "going" of Pentecostal worship and witness flow out of and into each other in a continuing dynamic that is mutually empowering and sustaining. Now let's get back to corporate worship.

Although Pentecostals are often accused of being overly individualistic and subjective, the formative framework, the determinative setting, for Pentecostal experience is corporate, focusing on the gatherings of the community of faith or congregational assemblies.[73] For example, revival meetings and camp meetings as well as solemn assemblies for prayer and fasting have been well known highlights in Pentecostal worship history. In this light, it is helpful to distinguish between individual and personal experience in worship and prayer. "Individual" essentially describes a single human being as distinguished from a group. "Personal," although popularly used as a synonym for individual, or even for "private," can more precisely mean that which impacts a particular person whether or not he/she is part of a group.[74] That is to say, Pentecostals expect to have a personal experience of the Holy Spirit as participating members of their congregation rather than as isolated individuals.[75] Thus Work describes Pentecostal worship as "thoroughly social as well as thoroughly personal."[76] Nevertheless, corporate worship that suppresses individual expression is oppressive for Pentecostal worshipers.[77]

Pentecostals are not oblivious of the fact that the Day of Pentecost was a corporate experience (Acts 2:1–4). Therefore, corporate worship is the paradigmatic context for the Pentecostal experience.[78] This is the case even for "individual" experiences which occur away from congregational settings. The preaching of the Word and congregational worship and prayer serve to form and shape the pattern for Pentecostal experience. Jerome Boone describes community and worship as the key components which intersect to effect spiritual formation in the Pentecostal context.[79] My own bap-

---

73. Concerns over extreme subjectivism are of course legitimate. Cp. Lawson, *Christian Doctrine*, 107–08, 204–06, and 233–35. While abuses and extremes have and do occur, Pentecostals usually manage well through communal didactics and accountability. Scriptures often appealed to in the process include 1 Cor 14:32 and 1 John 4:1.

74. As Pannenberg, *Christian Spirituality*, 50, rightly notes, "a self-deceptive privatization of the Christian faith" is the real danger. Moore, "Canon and Charisma," 29–30, depicts Pentecostals as avoiding, on the one hand, "a Spirit-less Word" (rationalism), and on the other, "a Word-less Spirit" (subjectivism) effectively holding together "a canonical-charismatic revelatory paradigm."

75. Sorge, *Exploring Worship*, describes the inward aspect of worship where the worshiper is personally affected by the worship service, 107.

76. Work, "Pentecostal and Charismatic Worship," 576. Deiros and Wilson, "Hispanic Pentecostalism," compare Latin American Pentecostal congregations to a family in which individuals are recognized and accepted, 295.

77. Bare, *They Call Me Pentecostal*, 34–35 and 90–93. Yet Martin, *Spirit-Filled Worship*, explains that God's dealings with individuals are qualified by their participation in the covenant community, 81.

78. Gause, *Living in the Spirit*, observes that in Acts three is a pattern of the Holy Spirit coming during "situations of divine worship," 82.

79. Boone, "Community and Worship," 129–30.

tism in the Holy Spirit may serve as an illustration. I was slow to receive. For years I heard about Spirit baptism in sermons, songs, and testimonies. I saw many persons receive as a group of believers prayed with them in the "altar." I had prayed in the altar many times myself, but, although I often felt God's presence and was blessed, I did not receive my Spirit baptism. My wise pastor, Earl T. Golden, counseled me to continue praying at home. One morning I was up early before going to work, praying—and I received the baptism in the Holy Spirit! Was this an individual experience? No. Was it a personal experience? Yes. And, in a sense, although I was "alone with God," it was corporate. And I testified of it that very night in the midweek prayer service of the Church of God in Morristown, Tennessee.

Of course, both individual and corporate worship have their place. Isaiah chapter six certainly models individual worship while Psalm 100 exemplifies corporate worship. Yet I must immediately note that for Isaiah the temple background for his worship encounter certainly involves a definitive formative influence from his community of faith. Further, the Psalmist here points beyond the temple to address all the earth. It is not always easy to draw the lines between individual and corporate or to determine the precise extent of either. In my mind, the kind of extreme individualism that presents a problem in terms of spiritual experience is that which isolates itself from the community or sets itself in opposition to it as an antagonist. Too many so-called "prophetic" ministries have forgotten that the Hebrew prophets were so effective precisely because they challenged their community from within its borders, affirming its boundaries while calling it back to its own core values and best practices. Therefore, it is wise to maintain a delicate-but-determined mutual accountability between individual experience and communal authority.[80]

The importance of worship in Pentecostal spirituality and theology can hardly be overstated. Gause asserts that worship is essential to the satisfaction of God and to the fulfillment of human nature, and that it is vital to all of life.[81] The significance of worship as well as an enlightening insight into the nature of Pentecostal worship shows in the apt description by Miller and Yammori of worship as "the engine of Pentecostalism."[82] In other words, worship *moves* the Pentecostal *movement*. Thus, worship motivates Pentecostals. Pentecostals' experience of God's presence in worship overflows into all of their life and into the ministry and mission of the Pentecostal church as a whole. Martin likely expresses the view of most Pentecostals when he says, "worship is the highest occupation of the Church" and that "worship fulfills the ultimate purpose for which the people of God are redeemed."[83] This attitude places divine

---

80. Work, "Pentecostal and Charismatic Worship," rightly notes that although the Pentecostal "reputation for disorder" is partly deserved, Pentecostal leadership usually manages to "maintain communal order while encouraging congregational participation," 576.

81. Gause, "Biblical Worship," 139, 141, 151.

82. Miller and Yamamori, *Global Pentecostalism*, 23.

83. Martin, *Toward a Pentecostal Theology of Worship*, 1. In *Spirit-Filled Worship* Martin argues

worship at the top of Pentecostal priorities. It also suggests the impact of worship on Pentecostal faith and life.

Yet Martin bemoans that Pentecostal theologians have focused on doctrinal development while "taking for granted the context of Pentecostal theology, which is worship."[84] Unfortunately, Martin is right. However, I do not think neglect of the theology of worship by Pentecostals is due to any inherent incompatibilities between theology and spirituality. I have often participated in worship services in academic settings with scholarly colleagues in which God's manifest presence was certainly apparent and their enthusiastic responsiveness was abundantly evident. Of course, there are always (in any tradition, I suspect) those academics that become so cerebral they cease to be spiritual.[85] But in my observations, I have not found that typical of the Pentecostal theologians it is my privilege to know.

Rather, it appears that focus has been on doctrine with assumptions of its worship context. Yet Pentecostal doctrinal development apart from worship and spirituality is impotent—that is, void of spiritual power. Pentecostal theology without worship becomes empty and hollow. As "Crip" Stephenson convincingly argues, much of Christian theology, and especially Pentecostal theology, arises out of the church's liturgy and spirituality (viz., the practice of worship).[86] There is a reciprocating relationship between theology and spirituality, doctrine and worship, in which each is informed and influenced by the other. If this is so, and I am sure it is, then worship is not only the context of Pentecostal theology; worship is directly impactful on theology's content. It is worship as not only the *context* but also as essential to the *content* of Pentecostal theology that this section aims to address.

As Christians, Pentecostals concur with the broader tradition that worship involves believers' praise, adoration, love, reverence, thanksgiving, and obedience of discipleship, offered by the power of the Holy Spirit, to the living and true God in response to saving grace in the Lord Jesus Christ. Further, Pentecostal worship is characterized "by a profound sense of God's presence and blessings, with an emphasis on Christ as the center of devotion and an emphasis on the gifts of the Spirit."[87] Pentecostals also tend to be less structured, though appreciating planning and preparation,

---

theologically that worship is at the heart of biblical faith, pleasing to God, an expression of our love of God, and transformative for participants, 5–8.

84. Martin, *Toward a Pentecostal Theology of Worship*, 3.

85. Even Pannenberg, *Christian Spirituality*, 13, a German-born Lutheran academic theologian of the highest order, and certainly no enthusiast, admitted that studying doctrine apart from "the dynamic life of Christian faith" or in separation from its "experiential roots" becomes "little but the deadwood of an old tradition." He further argued, Pannenberg, *Christian Spirituality*, 13, that, although rare and unfamiliar, theology "can embody an emotional commitment exhibiting a recognizable brand of accepted Christian piety." Conversely, one encounters "substructures of theology" in Christian spirituality, Pannenberg, *Christian Spirituality*, 14.

86. Stephenson, *Types of Pentecostal Theology*, 111–30.

87. Arrington, *Christian Doctrine*, 3:201–02.

with emphasis on submission to the Spirit's leading and ministry to the worshippers' needs.[88] Note the following extractions: (1) Overarching emphasis on God's experienced presence; (2) Consistent emphasis on Christ's centrality; (3) Distinctive emphasis on the role of the Holy Spirit and on spiritual gifts; (4) Integration of order and freedom; and (5) Responsibility of worshippers. This entire chapter deals with experiencing God's presence and the previous chapter dealt with the centrality of Christ. Chapter Eight will deal more in depth with spiritual gifts although this section will consider the topic in this context. The following section addresses the Spirit's role in worship, liberty in worship, and believers' responsiveness in worship.

First, as to the Spirit's role in worship John 4:21–24 is crucial for any Pentecostal theology of worship.

> Jesus said to her, "Woman, believe Me, the hour is coming when you will neither on this mountain, nor in Jerusalem, worship the Father. You worship what you do not know; we know what we worship, for salvation is of the Jews. But the hour is coming, and now is, when the true worshipers will worship the Father in spirit and truth; for the Father is seeking such to worship Him. God *is* Spirit, and those who worship Him must worship in spirit and truth."

In dialogue with a Samaritan woman which included a comparative discussion of the nature of worship in their respective religions, Jesus dismissed the enduring essentiality of worship inexorably linked to place and ritual while affirming the distinctive and lasting significance of the Jewish understanding of the identity of God and of its salvation tradition. Jesus further informs regarding the pivotal significance for worship of his own eschatological arrival and messianic mission. He also accents God's nature as Father and as Spirit and explains that God initiates the worship encounter while identifying the nature of true worshipers and true worship as requiring it to be in spirit and in truth. Implicit is the admonition that worship which is not in spirit and in truth is false worship.

For Pentecostals correlation of God's being and nature as Spirit with the injunction that authentic, legitimate worship is in spirit and in truth is paramount. In sum, there are three primary implications. First, God's essential nature is spiritual. Second, the God whose essential nature is spiritual requires worship of a spiritual kind or in a spiritual manner. Third, worshiping the God whose essential nature is spiritual in a spiritual manner requires a spiritual nature.[89] While Jesus' assertion of God's being as Spirit is not in and of itself limited to the Holy Spirit, spiritual encounter between redeemed humans and their God nevertheless requires the agency of the Holy Spirit. Jesus reveals, and inaugurates in his own person, a new way of worshiping God which occurs in the realm of the spirit.[90]

---

88. Arrington, *Christian Doctrine*, 3:202.
89. Aker, "John," 26–27. Cp. Gause, "Biblical Worship," 145–48.
90. Marshall, *NT Theology*, 499.

The God who is life-giving Spirit is not limited to places or things—and neither is his worship thus restricted. But since Jesus came worship is restricted in another sense. It is restricted to the spiritual realm. Nevertheless, spiritual worship is accessible to all through Jesus Christ.[91] Therefore, real worship is impossible apart from the agency of the Holy Spirit connecting the regenerate, Spirit-filled heart and life with God who is Spirit (Rom 12:2; 2 Cor 3:17; Phil 3:3). The Holy Spirit is "a bridge of union and communion" between human beings and God.[92] This is true worship, worship in truth—real worship. The critical importance of worship in spirit and in truth is suggested in that the Greek text of John 4:24 is both emphatic and imperative. Even Christ "through the eternal Spirit offered Himself without spot to God" (Heb 9:14). How much more should we offer to God our sacrifices of praise and worship through that same Spirit (13:15; Rom 12:1–2 NASB)?

The Holy Spirit brings all of us together. As Telford Work well puts it, Pentecostal "Worshipers experience the eschatological presence of God and God's cloud of witnesses as the Spirit fuses temporal and spatial horizons."[93] The Spirit brings the God of eternity and the world of the Bible and all the saints throughout the ages into our worship encounter here and now in a remarkably real way. I have often heard Pentecostals insist in a given worship service that if our eyes were opened like those of Elisha's servant, we would see angels all around (2 Kgs 6:17). But even if we do not see them, we can still sense them so close. At times the spirit world can be present in an incredibly experiential way in Pentecostal worship services. And the Holy Spirit is the one who enables and energizes the entire worship encounter.

Second, as to liberty in worship 2 Corinthians 3:17–18 is a crucial text for any Pentecostal theology of worship. "Now the Lord is the Spirit; and where the Spirit of the Lord *is*, there *is* liberty. But we all, with unveiled face, beholding as in a mirror the glory of the Lord, are being transformed into the same image from glory to glory, just as by the Spirit of the Lord." Earlier in this chapter Paul contrasts the glory of the new covenant with the old covenant (vv. 7–1). The new covenant is more glorious because it is administered by the Spirit, life-giving, and ever enduring. Paul also contrasts the accessibility and openness of the covenants (vv. 12–18). In the former covenant God's glory was veiled because the people were not ready for the full revelation of glory. It is not so in Christ.[94] In Christ, the Spirit unveils God's full glory.

Pentecostal NT scholar Gordon Fee considers 2 Corinthians 3:16–18 one of the more significant Spirit passages in the Pauline corpus. He sums up its general theological thrust: "Thus, in the final analysis, the Spirit of the living God not only gives us the

91. Morris, *John*, 272. See esp. footnote # 62.
92. Gause, "Biblical Worship," 147.
93. Work, "Pentecostal and Charismatic Worship," 577.
94. In an inspiring reflection on the transfiguration of Christ (Luke 9:32), Beth Moore, *Portraits of Devotion*, 222, suggests Jesus progressively reveals his glory to his disciples that we may continually adjust our lives to an enlarged vision of the ever-greater reality of his divine glory.

life of God, but serves for us as God's presence and enables us to behold God's glory so that we are being transformed into his likeness. That is 'glory' indeed!"[95] Amen! Please note that the experience of God's presence in the Holy Spirit is a central idea. Although set in a thoroughly Christological context, this passage deals primarily with the work of the Holy Spirit, depicting the Spirit as the key to Paul's ministry and to the Corinthians' conversion as well as both his and their experience of God's presence.[96] As the one who applies Christ's work to the believer's life, the Spirit is the key to the eschatological experience of God's presence, and thus fulfills the presence of God motif in a thoroughgoing way.[97] The point of Paul's entire argument is that the role of the Spirit who is affirmed and emphasized by both Paul and his Corinthian readers is yet much more—not less!—than they have imagined. Significantly, the Spirit is the one who transforms us into the glory of God's own image and is "the key to our experience of the presence of God."[98]

Whenever anyone turns to Christ the Spirit removes the veil from their hearts, revealing the glory of Christ and ushering them into the experience of God's presence. According to Hernando, "In this presence. . .there is freedom, a freedom unknown to those who, without the Spirit, are bound by a covenant of letter, leading to condemnation and death."[99] To continue, "Believers in Christ have had the veil removed and now have access to the presence of God"—and furthermore, "The Spirit who effected that unveiling is now occupied in a marvelous work of spiritual transformation."[100] The entire process—conversion and unveiling, experiencing God's presence and the freedom it brings, and the work of transformation—belongs to the ministry of the Holy Spirit. Quite contrary to stereotypical caricatures, transformation is not suppression of human desire but liberation from the bondage of sin in order to become fully human.

Pentecostals emphasize the sovereign power, spontaneous presence, and personal experience of Christ in the Holy Spirit. Yet Pentecostals well realize that there are binding, hindering forces and systems in this world which threaten to smother the life out of them and to stifle their worship.[101] The Pentecostal understands him/herself to be caught in a constant battle, a spiritual conflict, between Satan, their implacable enemy, and their omnipotent Savior, Jesus. It is not an equal battle. Jesus is far superior (John 12:31; 14:30; 16:11). And the victory has already been won (Col 2:13–15). However, for a little while longer, in this present age, the battle still rages on, although believers are well armed and well armored (Eph 6:10–18). The indwelling Holy Spirit provides full assurance for a life of continuing victory (1 John. 4:4). Therefore,

---

95. Fee, *God's Empowering Presence*, 309–10.
96. Fee, *God's Empowering Presence*, 311.
97. Fee, *God's Empowering Presence*, 312–13.
98. Fee, *God's Empowering Presence*, 319.
99. Hernando, "2 Corinthians," 935.
100. Hernando, "2 Corinthians," 935.
101. Work, "Pentecostal and Charismatic Worship," 576.

Pentecostal worship can be both celebratory and combative. It celebrates "Victory in Jesus" (as the song says) even as it combats the forces of darkness.[102] Christian life and worship may be conceptualized as a spiritual realization and liturgical reenactment of the Exodus deliverance account. Pentecostals believe Jesus came to set them free and that the Holy Spirit, the Spirit of Liberty, supports and sustains their freedom in Christ (John. 8:36; 2 Cor 3:17; Gal 5:1). Therefore, Pentecostal worship instinctively emphasizes spiritual liberty.

However, Fee wants to limit the liberty of 2 Corinthians 3:17 to freedom *from* the old covenant in freedom *for* the new covenant.[103] Fee argues that all other kinds of freedom, which evolve from the first kind, are "at best ancillary" and "at worst distortions."[104] While his warning against abuse or distortion of freedom is apropos, a number of factors require us to modify, or at least carefully qualify, Fee's position. First, the Exodus account of deliverance or liberation from Egyptian slavery, which must be taken into consideration in any discussion of biblical freedom, and which lies in the background of Paul's discussion of the Mosaic covenant or dispensation, is a thoroughgoing liberty which is deep and wide, and arguably fundamental to any NT theology of liberty (Gal 6:16).[105] Second, Paul's co-equation of the Spirit and liberty transcend such restrictions to propose that the Spirit's presence is necessarily liberating in nature. Whatever binds and hinders or enslaves and oppresses is *ipso facto* overcome by the liberating presence of the Spirit of the Lord. Bondage cannot survive the Lord's presence. Third, the overall biblical treatment of liberty is all-encompassing in nature, that is, embraces and impacts all of life, both in the OT (e.g., Lev 25:10; Ps 119:45; Isa 61:1) and in the NT (e.g., Lu 4:18; Rom 8:21; Gal 5:13; Jas 2:12; 1 Pet 2:16). I argue that 2 Corinthians 3:17 should be considered against this background.

Accordingly, when Paul says, "Where the Spirit of the Lord is, there is liberty" he is expressing a general principle applicable in the context of his specific discussion of the old and new covenants but not limited to it.[106] It is tantamount to saying, "*Wherever* the Spirit of the Lord is, there is liberty." That includes the Corinthian situation but does not exclude broader contexts. Thus, for a notable example, Black Holiness-Pentecostals have long modeled an inclusive application of joyfully celebrating the Spirit's presence with intense passion for freedom in religious as well as socio-political

---

102. Although Pentecostal theodicy (doctrine of evil) recognizes, far more than most Christians today, the reality of actual evil entities which are implacably set in opposition to all righteousness, they also have a strong doctrine of human sin which directly addresses personal accountability and responsibility. See Arrington, *Christian Doctrine*, 2:78–81 and 2:119–23.

103. Fee, *God's Empowering Presence*, 313–14.

104. Hernando, "2 Corinthians," 313.

105. Beegle, "Exodus," 206.

106. Thus, in the fourth century Ambrosiaster, commenting on this verse, refers to "the law of the Spirit"; both he and Ambrose (also fourth century) connect it to freedom received by faith, *ACCS*, "1–2 Corinthians," 225.

forms.[107] Therefore, Pentecostals correctly assume that the freedom promised by the Liberating Spirit has a wider range of applications. One of these applications has special import for Pentecostal worship: the intricate interrelation of order and freedom.

Martin rightly observes that the "emphasis in Pentecostal worship has been on spontaneity and liberty rather than on liturgy and uniformity."[108] No doubt Pentecostals have been a bit reactionary regarding formal liturgy. Who can blame them? The traditionalists of formal liturgy constantly accused early Pentecostals of being "out of order" in their exuberant and pneumatic worship, often citing 1 Corinthians 14:40 for support.[109] Pentecostals today are more inclined to admit that an element of liturgical forms of worship likely existed in the NT. However, they still insist that these be brought under the authority of Scripture, which includes, among other things, openness to the edifying operation of spiritual gifts in worship.[110] Accordingly, the question today is "What is the proper relationship between order and freedom in Pentecostal worship?"[111]

First, this is neither a new question nor is it unique to contemporary Pentecostalism. Ever since Christianity's earliest origins churches have struggled with the dangers of degenerating into either formality or magic.[112] In formalism strict adherence to the external observance of traditional institutional forms takes priority over and eventually extinguishes the energy and vitality of the Spirit. In magic a desire to contact and have inward communion with, and perhaps to control, supernatural agents and forces, that is, the spirit world, especially the Holy Spirit, rebels against all authority and leads into flagrant fanaticism. Pharisaic concerns over ceremony and Sabbath observances at the expense of recognizing Jesus are examples of formalism (Matt 9:11; 12:12; 15:12). The desire of Simon Magus to obtain the baptism in the Holy Spirit only to exploit the power for personal gain exemplifies magic (Acts 8:9–25). Either way is worse than wrong.

---

107. Turner, *United Holy Church of America*, 16. Note that the experience of liberty in the Spirit can motivate courageous engagement of any form of oppression.

108. Martin, *Theology of Worship*, 4.

109. Work, "Pentecostal and Charismatic Worship," 578, rightly notes that in Pentecostal worship a leader and congregation are kept on the same track because all direct their exuberant worship toward God as the guiding and unifying purpose. Accordingly, worship expressions such as raising hands, applause, laughter, tears, shouts of acclamation, open displays of emotion, call and response during preaching, standing and moving individually and corporately during praise and prayer, all of which may be either directed or spontaneous, are considered movements of the Spirit so long as they are not disruptive. The frequent physicality of this worship is notable. Like ancient Docetic heretics (who rejected the literal Incarnation of Jesus Christ) much of contemporary Christianity appears uncomfortable with the physicality of creation and redemption. They are especially repulsed by physical expressions of worship which are quite common among Pentecostals. However, Pentecostal commitments to spirit-body correspondence encourage more holistic worship.

110. Gause, *Biblical Worship*, 142, footnote # 1.

111. Pentecostals recognize the importance of guarding against unbiblical and unhealthy worship practices, Martin, *Spirit-Filled Worship*, 4. The key is inviting the "fire" without inciting a "wildfire."

112. Lawson, *Christian Doctrine*, 115.

The disciplined and ordered life of the institutional church is not necessarily by nature inconsistent with, much less antagonistic to, the inward and personal walk with God. Yet there nevertheless exists a common, ongoing tension between institutional order and individual experience.[113] On the one hand, this deep and persistent tension is often behind the efforts of some institutional entities to use "order" as an excuse to control those inclined toward an element of (ideally) Spirit-inspired spontaneity in worship. On the other hand, some who are driven by a recalcitrant maverick attitude have and do use freedom in worship as a cloak to cover their disruption of authentic order. Although it is not new, the relation of order and freedom in worship is a particularly perplexing conundrum for Pentecostal theology. Everything is on the line. Without freedom for the Spirit to move the Pentecostal movement simply ceases to be.[114] However, unbridled enthusiasm inevitably undermines the authentic moving of the Spirit and inserts in its place mere emotionalism. Yet whenever institutionalization increases then fervor and freedom tend to go into demise. Historically this tension has been a problem for Pentecostals.[115] Pentecostal theology today must navigate these waters carefully.

Second, in context Paul's admonition on order (in 1 Cor 14:40) does indeed supply the insight needed for navigating what has been a quandary for many. Paul's succinct command to "Let all things be done decently and in order" is the fitting conclusion to a three-chapter discussion of spiritual gifts (12–14). Chapter Twelve first sets spiritual gifts in a Trinitarian context with Christological grounding and pneumatological focus before emphasizing their unity-in-diversity and benevolent purpose in the community of believers (vv. 1–7). Then it identifies representative spiritual gifts such as the word of wisdom, the word of knowledge, faith, gifts of healing, working of miracles, prophecy, discerning of spirits, speaking in tongues, and interpretation of tongues—still emphasizing their unity-in-diversity but in a more specific pneumatological mode (vv. 8–11). This chapter next utilizes the analogy of the human body for understanding the gifts at work in the one body of Christ with many members—still emphasizing unity-in-diversity—and adds gifts such as apostles, prophets, and teachers, helps or assistance, and government or administration (vv. 12–30). The last verse fittingly exhorts believers to desire the greater spiritual gifts but suggests "a more excellent way" (v. 31).

Chapter Thirteen, one of the most eloquent in all of Paul's writings and indeed in all the Bible, describes the kind of holy love which is the essential context and guiding motive for the appropriate operation of all spiritual gifts (vv. 1–7). It next explains that "Love never fails" (v. 8a) but spiritual gifts such as prophecy and tongues will cease in the eschaton when Jesus ushers in the age of absolute and ultimate perfection

---

113. Lawson, *Christian Doctrine*, 130, 233–35.
114. Martin, *Spirit-Filled Worship*, 199–200.
115. Blumhofer, *Restoring the Faith*, 3, 152, 169, 203, 217.

(vv. 8–12).[116] However, "faith, hope, and love" abide and endure in the present age although love is the greatest (v. 13).[117] This chapter is the all-important bridge between the preceding and the following instructions.

Chapter Fourteen begins with a comparison of prophecy and tongues that eventuates in the principle that understanding is essential for the purpose of spiritual gifts which is the edification the worshiping community to the glory of God (vv. 1–25). Paul encourages zeal for spiritual gifts with the objective of "edifying the church" (v. 12). Paul indicates that when spiritual gifts operate properly it causes a dramatic effect on unbelievers who come into a service: "Thus the secrets of his heart are revealed. And so falling down on his face, he will worship God and report that God is among you" (v. 25). Conversely, when spiritual gifts are abused they result in confusion (v. 33). Chapter Fourteen therefore concludes Paul's extended discussion of spiritual gifts with practical instructions for orderly worship in the ongoing operation of spiritual gifts (vv. 26–40).

Because it is rooted in the divine nature, Paul's admonition against confusion or disorder and exhortation to peace is universally applicable—as are the principles laid down throughout this section arising from it (v. 33). Notably, this verse is Paul's theological justification for his entire argument. Authentic Christian worship reflects the character and nature of God.[118] God is not confused or disorderly, therefore authentic Christian worship is not confused or disorderly. The word for "confusion" (KJV, NASB) or "disorder" (NKJV, NIV), ἀκαταστασία (*akatastasia*), can signify either confusion or disorder and can also be translated "disturbance" or "instability" but may be as strong as "insurrection" or "rebellion" in certain contexts.[119] Thus, it indicates the seriousness of the issue. In terms of contrast, this verse is linguistically and thematically linked to Paul's climactic exhortation to "Let all things be done decently and in order" a few verses later (v. 40). It "echoes its opposite."[120] "Decently" (KJV, NKJV) or "fitting" (NIV) or "properly" (NASB), from εὐσχημόνως (*euschēmonōs*), signifies

---

116. I read 1 Cor 13:8 and Josh 5:12 in the same light. Just as the manna ceased when Israel arrived in the Promised Land, because they no longer needed it but could then partake of Canaan's abundance, so tongues will cease when we enter the archetypical "Promised Land" with the Lord. At that point the need for journey-sustaining provisions will end in their final fulfillment via eschatological realization.

117. As David Cooper explains in a denominational magazine for Pentecostal laity as well as clergy, "Love is the first and most important principle of life and defines what it means to be 'spiritual,'" "First Things First," 13.

118. Fee, *First Corinthians*, 696–97. Oddly enough, Fee suggests that "God is not often thought of in terms of allowing spontaneity and joy," 698, specifically naming Pentecostal and Charismatic worshipers as culprits. Not to mention numerous other sections of Holy Scripture, he seems to have forgotten about the entire books of Psalms and Acts. One thinks of King David, the sweet psalmist of Israel, stripping off his royal robes to dance with all his might before the Lord in joyous, spontaneous worship—in spite of Michal's mockery (2 Sam 6:12–23). Also see above on the joy of the Holy Spirit in Acts.

119. NIV signifies New International Version of the Holy Bible (Grand Rapids, MI: Zondervan, 2011).

120. Fee, *First Corinthians*, 713.

that which is characterized by propriety in manners and conduct. "Order," from τάξις (*taxis*), signifies a condition of regular or proper arrangement, often sequential.

In short, Paul's instruction to "Let all things be done decently and in order" is in no way a prohibition against the operation of spiritual gifts in worship (or otherwise inhibition of spiritual liberty). Pentecostal NT scholar Anthony Palma rightly comments that Paul specifically avoids "an overreaction or misunderstanding by some who misinterpret him as proscribing tongues altogether in the assembly" (in v. 39).[121] Paul wants to regulate, not to eliminate, spiritual gifts, including speaking in tongues. Thus, Paul provides a means of regulation for their appropriate operation. Significantly, even though Paul is obviously trying hard to bring order to Corinthian worship, still "he wishes to emphasize the general ideas of diversity and spontaneity."[122] I therefore suggest we can draw from Paul's statement valuable resources for Pentecostal theology in the appropriate regulation of ecstatic experience and exuberant worship in congregational settings.[123]

Thus, I propose that biblical order will *direct but not restrict* and biblical freedom will *edify but not exalt*. The actual practice of Pentecostal worship requires management and guidance, according to biblical guidelines, and that fact requires those able to administer and supervise in wisdom, prudence, and patience. It does not require confinement or restraint (in the sense of being bound, although in the sense of reserve is appropriate). Pentecostal worship should benefit and build up individual believers and the congregation; it should not lead to becoming elevated in arrogance and pride. In the immediate or specific context of our discussion that means spiritual gifts should operate in the assembly with *both* freedom and order. More broadly, all Pentecostal worship should integrate freedom *and* order into every aspect of services. Accordingly, there is freedom for the Spirit to move in spontaneous, perhaps even surprising ways, yet chaos and confusion are quickly identified and halted as clearly out of order.[124]

Furthermore, and significantly, freedom in worship does not only apply in the type of worship encouraged but also in the participants involved. Work notes that for Pentecostals the empowering of the Holy Spirit "breaks down boundaries among ethnicities, the genders, social classes, and clergy and laity" thus enabling full congregational participation.[125] If a fresh wind of the sovereign Spirit chooses to blow upon someone, prohibitive human categories become forever passé (1 Cor 12:11). Acts 2:17–18 on the outpouring of the Holy Spirit on all people is an important text

---

121. Palma, *First Corinthians*, 888.

122. Palma, *First Corinthians*, 885.

123. Paul's description of his own heavenly encounter in 2 Cor 12:1–6 evidences his support of ecstatic experience. See Allen, *Spiritual Theology*, 143. Allen, *Spiritual Theology*, 149, 157–58, contrasts temporary ecstatic states with a more abiding sense of "habitual presence" while yet affirming the possibility and importance of ecstatic moments.

124. Martin, *Spirit-Filled Worship*, 122–23. As Work says, "The whole process is a harmonious interplay of spiritual gifts (1 Cor. 12–14) aimed at edifying the body of Christ," 578.

125. Work, "Pentecostal and Charismatic Worship," 576.

for Pentecostal theology. Note its inclusivity. The Spirit is poured out across gender, age, and class lines. Men and women, young and old, and even servants (slaves!) are free to prophesy by the Holy Spirit. Any so-called system of order that attempts to restrict ministry in worship to a certain class or group is biblically out of order. Pentecostals have ordained clergy, yet the laity is encouraged to participate in worship at an unprecedented level. Pentecostals frequently refer to this inclusive, open ministry and worship as "the prophethood of all believers."[126] Although Pentecostals have a rich heritage from early in our movement's history regarding laity, race, women, and marginalized individuals that did not last long. We have fallen far behind over the decades. Sadly, much needs to be done for us to catch up to our past. We had best better be about it! Specific, concrete action needs to be taken.[127]

Third, a proposal for integrating freedom and order is not an either/or proposition pneumatologically. In other words, it does not exclude the Holy Spirit in either case. Those who prioritize the Spirit's working in the operation of spiritual gifts and in exuberant worship may fear that any incorporation of structure will "quench the Spirit" (1 Thess 5:19). Those who prioritize the Spirit's working in liturgy may fear that any departure from "the proper order" inevitably leads to catastrophe (1 Chron 15:13). However, we have seen that Holy Spirit can be present and active in worship through *both* order *and* freedom.

The following example may be instructive. At times when I am preaching a message in tongues comes forth from someone in the congregation. My sermon is prepared in advance and delivered at a prearranged point in the service as part of the overall order of worship. Yet when a message in tongues comes forth, everything stops. Some Pentecostals call this a "divine interruption." Others argue that the service belongs to the Sovereign Spirit and nothing God does is an "interruption." Perhaps it is early in the sermon, usually it is later, perhaps even at its conclusion. In any case, we all stop. The order of worship is changed. Usually the Spirit will give someone the interpretation. Often spontaneous praise will erupt. Always I call for an expression of reverence in the Lord's presence. Depending on the nature of the message, we may then proceed in one of a number of ways. The message itself may call for a specific response. Or we may have a special time of prayer. Or I may just continue preaching, in which case the service may continue along the usual course but with an added element.[128] The same pattern is common in other congregational manifestations of the Spirit.

---

126. See Stronstad, *Charismatic Theology of Luke*, 65–66, 71, 92.

127. We can hope and pray that Kuhlin, "I Do Not Think I Could be a Christian on My Own," is correct in her assertion that "a broadly gender-equal expression of Pentecostalism" indeed "points to the movement's ability to adjust to different contexts," 482—and that it extends to other minorities as well. Perhaps we are moving toward what Jacqui Grey, "Embodiment and the Prophetic Message," calls "the imperative of inclusivity," 454?

128. Although Pentecostals do not have a formal order of worship we still conduct worship services according to a general pattern that begins with Scripture reading and prayer, and includes offertory, singing, preaching, and responsive prayer. On special occasions, including Communion Sundays,

In scenarios such as I just described, there is built into the order of the service an expectation (indeed, an anticipation) that the Spirit may move in ways not predetermined by the pastor or congregation. Yet Pentecostals believe the anointing of the Holy Spirit is on the preached Word just as it is on the message and interpretation of tongues.[129] The same is true of other aspects of the service and other spiritual gifts. However, planning the order of the service is no less important because it is open to the "surprises of the Spirit" as they are sometimes described. It is quite the contrary.

Martin gives helpful practical advice on planning and preparing for worship in a Pentecostal service.[130] It is obvious that Spirit-inspired spontaneity and careful planning and preparation (order) are not inconsistent for him. The following concluding paragraph is particularly telling.

> The Lord will honor your preparation. If you have prayed for God's favor and you have followed the leading of the Holy Spirit, God will manifest his presence and display his glory in the midst of the Church. People will be inspired, transformed, saved, healed, delivered, and filled with the Spirit.[131]

Amen! Amen?

---

baby dedications, water baptisms, and so on this model will vary a bit. At times special opportunities for testimonies are offered but they may be given spontaneously at other times, if the Spirit leads.

129. This anointing is key to identifying the call to preach and the performance of pulpit ministry, Welch, 'Women with the Good News', 67–71.

130. Martin, *Spirit-Filled Worship*, 203–11.

131. Martin, *Spirit-Filled Worship*, 211.

6

Experiencing God's Presence in Prayer

WE HAVE SEEN THAT Pentecostal theology and spirituality affirm (and facilitate) experience of the presence of the God of the Bible in the church's life and worship today through personal encounter with the Holy Spirit. We have further seen that worship and prayer are specific acts in which Pentecostals focus their experience of encountering God's presence. Having focused on the experience of God's presence in worship, we turn now to the topic of prayer and other spiritual practices. We are not now leaving theology. Rather, as Land correctly says, "Prayer is the primary theological activity of Pentecostals."[1] Yet prayer is also the "primary means of participation in worship and is a rehearsal for witness."[2] Accordingly, in prayer we find the integration of belief, affections or dispositions, and practices that lies at the core of Pentecostal identity and ministry.[3] Therefore, Pentecostal prayer may well be described as being first liturgical, then transformational, and finally missiological/vocational—but, prayer is always theological.[4] Prayer in this mode is enthusiastically active in Christ's service. It is not passive. It does not sit on the sidelines as a

---

1. Land, *Pentecostal Spirituality*, 165. Indeed, prayer is according to the relational nature of the Triune God. It is the quintessential enactment of perichoresis. Furthermore, humanly speaking, as respiration is to the body so prayer is to the soul. It is the very life of the believer.

2. Land, *Pentecostal Spirituality*, 164.

3. Land, *Pentecostal Spirituality*, 163.

4. Not surprisingly, Land, *Pentecostal Spirituality*, describes prayer as "the heart of true worship and witness," 166.

spectator. It moves. It does. It works. Not surprisingly, Doug Small describes prayer as worship at its center but as mission at its edge.[5]

Typical Pentecostal worship involves several components, including prayer and praise, music and singing, preaching and teaching, stewardship (tithes and offerings), spiritual gifts, testimonies, and ordinances/sacraments.[6] Pentecostal worship arises out of a conjunction of Pentecostal beliefs and practices which shape the Pentecostal spirituality which in turn shapes and sustains Pentecostal worship.[7] Nurturing Pentecostal spirituality are several spiritual practices, including uninhibited worship, tarrying in prayer, seasons of fasting, caring for one another, bearing witness to the world, testimonies, self-sacrifice, preaching the whole gospel, healing the sick, immersion in God's Word, and exercising spiritual gifts. All of these spiritual practices occur in the context of "a sense of urgency and longing in light of the soon return of Jesus."[8] Preeminent among these spiritual practices is prayer. Prayer informs and energizes all Pentecostal spirituality and theology.[9] Accordingly, I will turn now to a specific discussion of prayer which ever moves toward deeper understanding its role in encountering God's presence.

PRIORITY AND BASIC TENETS OF PRAYER

Green argues that it makes "sense to begin with our experience of God in prayer" as "the moment of divine encounter," as that time when "we find ourselves *communing* with God."[10] He is discussing various methods of understanding how we experience God, especially experiencing God as Trinity, and what theological inferences might arise, and how they might be best expressed. Rather than beginning with theological reformulations he chooses to begin with how we experience God in prayer, which, he argues, is unifying but still triadic—even for Oneness advocates (cp. Rom 8:26–27). Green says, "the shared experience of God in prayer is the crucible in which faithful theological language can be discerned."[11] In other words, since we most fully experi-

---

5. Small, Transforming Your Church into a House of Prayer, 28.

6. Bergunder, *South Indian Pentecostal Movement*, chapter 13 on "Church Life" surveys the ecclesiastical landscape of Indian Pentecostalism but also addresses social work, finances, worship and rites, organized events and festivals, pastoral care, and mission in a manner which is reflective of the worldwide Pentecostal movement's typical integration of theology and praxis in its worship.

7. Martin, *Spirit-Filled Worship*, 198–99.

8. Martin, *Spirit-Filled Worship*, 198.

9. E.g., congregations experiencing special seasons of the Spirit's outpoured presence frequently testify of an intense atmosphere of fervent prayer leading to dynamic worship and increased conversions, operation of spiritual gifts, and divine healings. E.g., see Arrington, *Encountering the Holy Spirit*, 458–62.

10. Green, "'In Your Presence is Fullness of Joy,'" 193. Italics are original.

11. Green, "'In Your Presence is Fullness of Joy,'" 198. Green hopes that first order (direct) experience of God's presence can transcend disagreements over second order (indirect) theological reflections for Oneness and Trinitarian Pentecostals, 188 (fn. 2) and 190 (fn. 11). My own proposal in Chapter 3 for revaluing relations between Trinitarian and Oneness Pentecostals focusing on the

ence the fullness of God's presence in prayer, prayer should shape all of our thought and talk about God and our walk with God. I am sure my grandfather would have agreed.

"Grandpa" Richie was not a theologian. He was not an academic at all. In fact, Grandpa was functionally illiterate until after his conversion to Christ and his baptism in the Spirit when he learned to read well enough to study his Bible. But Eli Richie was a man of prayer. Well known throughout southeastern Kentucky and southern Indiana, several miraculous healings, as well as some remarkable miracles involving natural phenomena, were attributed to his intercessory prayers. My father's father was best known, however, for daily climbing the mountain near his Perry County, Kentucky home to offer fervent prayer to the Lord. He could be heard praying all over the valley—and many who heard were converted, with some called into ministry.

Like other Pentecostals, Grandpa Richie took James 5:16b literally: "The effectual fervent prayer of a righteous man availeth much" (KJV). When he prayed, it changed the course of events. It made a difference in what happened in his and others' lives. As the saying goes, "Prayer changes things." But even more noteworthy than dramatic, miraculous answers to prayer was his experience of God in prayer. Through prayer he encountered God's presence. Through prayer God touched his life. Experiencing God's presence through prayer transformed his life. A notorious local sinner became best known and well-remembered as a man of prayer and faith and holiness. Grandpa Richie exemplifies the place of prayer in Pentecostal spirituality but his is not an isolated experience. As Pentecostal historian Mel Robeck notes, the famous Azusa Revival was birthed in a prayer meeting.[12] Notably, when Martin does an extended study of the components of a Pentecostal worship service, he begins with "powerful prayer."[13] Arguably, the place of prayer in Pentecostal spirituality and theology is unparalleled.[14]

Pentecostals generally affirm the same basic tenets of a biblical doctrine of prayer as the broader Christian tradition. Both the OT and the NT provide ample examples of individual and corporate prayer through petitions (supplications), intercessions, and thanksgivings (e.g., 1 Tim 2:1–8). From the OT onward prayer has been based on a high concept of God as one who thinks, wills, and feels and is omniscient, omnipotent, holy, and graciously benevolent and compassionate.[15] Throughout the Scriptures God is portrayed as a caring Creator involved in every situation of life—a trustworthy God who answers prayer.[16] Faithful and obedient Christians must constantly gauge their own prayer life by the pattern of God's Word.

---

import of Spirit baptism stresses sharing the most distinctively Pentecostal experience.

12. Robeck, *Azusa Street Mission & Revival*, 66–99.

13. Martin, *Spirit-Filled Worship*, 127–31.

14. Land, *Pentecostal Spirituality*, 165. Bare, in *They Call Me Pentecostal*, hints that the Pentecostal prayer emphasis is in need of rediscovery, 135.

15. Thomson, "Prayer," 412.

16. Walker, *Ministry of Worship*, 154, 171.

Jesus' doctrine of prayer insisted on the Fatherhood of God and the value of the individual before God.[17] Jesus further teaches that prayer is spiritual rather than formal (Matt 6:5–8), as exemplified in his own practice (John 17), and that the prayer of faith has unlimited potential (Mark 11:20–24). An inward disposition of love and forgiveness is essential to effective prayer (Matt 18:21–35), as is prayer in Jesus' name (John. 16:23–28). Prayer is often much concerned with the practical needs of this life. The Lord's Prayer or Model Prayer summarizes the salient features of Jesus' doctrine of prayer. Note:

> God, to whom we pray, is a Father who, dwelling in heaven, receives our adoration. The true aim of prayer is not the imposition of our wills upon God but the hallowing of his sacred name, the extension of his kingdom, our submission to his will. Only then does Christ direct us to petition the Father. Then the prayer ends, not with our needs or desires but with God, with whom it began, with his kingdom, his power, his glory.[18]

Similarly, the Pauline Epistles reveal a rich theology and prevalent practice of prayer. For Paul prayer and worship are intertwined (Eph 5:19–20; Col 3:16–17). Paul emphasizes intercessory prayer through the Spirit and through Christ (Rom 8:26–27, 34), indicating the Trinitarian nature of prayer. Paul further acknowledges the demanding, even "agonizing" nature of prayer (Rom 15:30; Col 4:12). The book of Acts emphasizes the corporate nature of prayer although James closely integrates corporate and individual prayer (5:13–18). Scripture is literally a great prayer book.

Over the centuries Christians have thought of prayer in terms of multiple metaphors.[19] The spirit of prayer may be thought of as a gift of God. Prayer can be soulful conversation or silent contemplation. Prayer can include expression of wonder, acknowledgment of finitude, and articulation of desire. Prayer is sharing in God's Trinitarian life. Prayer is an art. Prayer is raising one's mind and heart to God. Furthermore, prayer has a paradoxical nature. For example, it is both a joyous privilege and a serious duty.[20] Significantly, human psychology is not absent from the practice of prayer. Inevitably, prayer to God includes conscious and unconscious dynamics and ever inadequate images of the infinite and inexhaustible God—all of which are ultimately offered back to the living God in faith and humility.[21] In short, the Christian heritage of prayer is multifaceted and varied but ever profound.

---

17. Thomson, "Prayer," 413. As Richardson well says, "Christian prayer is possible only if we believe in the God whom Jesus called Father, not the clockmaker God of the deists, not the Absolute in whom all differences are reconciled, or the 'problem-solver' or Aladdin's Lamp of popular misconception," "Prayer, Theology of,"558.

18. Thomson, "Prayer," 413.

19. Dryer, "Prayer," 504.

20. Dryer, "Prayer," 504.

21. Ulanov, "Prayer, Psychology of," 506–07.

DISTINCTIVE CHARACTERISTICS OF PENTECOSTAL PRAYER

Several distinctive characteristics of Pentecostal prayer are noteworthy, including: praying in the Spirit, the role of the altar in prayer, tarrying prayer (or "praying through"), laying on of hands in prayer, use of anointed cloths in prayer, fasting in prayer, prayer as spiritual warfare, and concert prayer. During this section we will examine these characteristics for theological implications. Before delving into specific distinctive features of Pentecostal prayer, however, I pause for an important observation: prayer is the biblical presupposition for Pentecost. What does that mean?

Immediately prior to Pentecost, Luke reports that "These all continued with one accord in prayer and supplication, with the women and Mary the mother of Jesus, and with His brothers" (Acts 1:14). Immediately recognizable is the similarity to the Day of Pentecost itself when "they were all with one accord in one place" (2:1). The gatherings were similar. In fact Acts 2:1 appears to be a kind of continuation of Acts 1:14—with one important difference. At Pentecost the disciples were filled with the Spirit and spoke in other tongues. A reasonable inference is that unified prayer was an important antecedent for the advent of Pentecost. True, the Day of Pentecost would have come as a specified date on the religious calendar of festivals in any case. However, prayer prepared the disciples to receive personally what God had prepared for them—the Spirit of Pentecost. Not surprisingly, Pentecostals have found that prayer is especially critical to the reception and maintenance of the Spirit-filled life.[22] We therefore discuss specific features of prayer in the lives of Pentecostals with an understanding that without prayer there would be no Pentecostals at all.

Praying in the Spirit

Praying in the Spirit or praying in tongues is perhaps the most distinctive feature of the Pentecostal life of prayer.[23] It is rooted in a recurring pattern of NT prayer (1 Cor 14:2, 13–17; Eph 6:18; Jude 20). As Spirit-inspired speech it is admittedly mysterious, suspending, or rather transcending, human intellect without replacing human intelligibility and understanding, but especially edifying to the ones who thus pray through this particularly direct communication with God, whether practiced individually or corporately (1 Cor 14:2, 13–17).[24] Praying in the Spirit is an imperative

---

22. Unfortunately, I fear that many Pentecostals in the USA have not maintained their prayer emphasis with the same passionate faithfulness I have encountered among Pentecostal churches in Latin America, Asia, and Eastern Europe. Do we need to be reminded of the danger of allowing anything to steal the primary identity of our churches as God's "house of prayer" (Matt 21:13)?

23. I find it interesting that Land, *Pentecostal Spirituality*, chooses to discuss what it means to be "filled with the Spirit" in the context of praying in the Spirit which he describes as "Spirit-filled prayer," 167–69.

24. For Doolittle, "Praying in the Spirit," 14–15, the practice is "passionate and transforming communication with God" involving multiple benefits.

for Christians in a world fraught with spiritual conflict (Eph 6:18), and essential for strengthening the faith and stamina of believers unto eternal life (Jude 20).

Romans 8:26–27 is particularly explicative for a theology of praying in the Spirit.

> Likewise the Spirit also helps in our weaknesses. For we do not know what we should pray for as we ought, but the Spirit Himself makes intercession for us with groanings which cannot be uttered. Now He who searches the hearts knows what the mind of the Spirit *is,* because He makes intercession for the saints according to *the will of* God.

A number of observations are significant. First, note what is missing from this statement. It does not specifically mention speaking in tongues. However, Pentecostals believe that the phrase "groanings which cannot be uttered" is an implicit allusion to praying in tongues.[25] Coupled with Paul's explicit description elsewhere equating praying in the Spirit with praying in tongues (1 Cor 14:13–17), there is strong support that Romans 8:26–27, although broader implications are possible as well, intends to include speaking in tongues through prayer.[26] Fee wrestles mightily, and admirably, with this passage and this topic; but, he eventually concludes that, while dogmatism is impossible, the best interpretation for this passage is that Paul is talking about praying in the Spirit as praying in tongues.[27]

Second, significant pneumatological and cosmological nuances appear when we consider Romans 8:26–27 in context. This chapter began with in depth instruction on life in the Spirit, including righteous living by walking in the Spirit, being led by the Spirit, and the testimony of the Spirit (vv. 1–16). It then transitions, rather abruptly, into exhortations regarding suffering and glory (vv. 17–25) and ends with assurances regarding God's ultimate purpose and our incomparable victory in Christ (vv. 28–39). Paul's graphic description of praying in the Spirit as unutterable groaning flows directly out of the immediately preceding context (note Paul's "Likewise" in v. 26). Significantly, creation groans as with birth pangs in expectation of the eschaton, and believers, "who have the first fruits of the Spirit," groan in similar manner and with similar motive (vv. 23–25). In a sense, we might well describe praying in the Spirit as labor cries of the already redeemed as they await and anticipate the final redemption which is not yet realized.[28] Thus it connects the hope of the redeemed (vv. 24–25) with the assurance of redemption (vv. 28–30).

25. Augustine thinks it important to understand that the Spirit's intercessory groans do not signify the Spirit's need or distress but rather his moving us to pray with groaning, *ACCS: Romans,* 230–31.

26. In the fifth century, Philoxenus of Mabbug said, "the activity of the Spirit" prompts the "pure prayer" which brings to completion all the "good promptings" which are "stirred up in our soul as the result of the Spirit's promptings," *ACCS: Romans,* 232.

27. Fee, *God's Empowering Presence,* 575–86. Before coming to his conclusion, Fee carefully, and extensively, examines the immediate context of Rom 8:26, 27, Paul's discussion of praying in the Spirit in 1 Cor 14, and the challenging Greek of "groanings which cannot be uttered" or στεναγμοῖς ἀλαλήτοις (*stenagmois alalētois*).

28. Ironically, I once heard a harsh critic say that speaking in tongues sounded to him like baby gibberish. He further opined that this analogy implies the immaturity of tongues speakers. Biblically,

Third, Romans 8:26–27 has thematic connections with another passage to the church at Corinth: First Corinthians 2:6–16 (esp. vv. 10–13). Their resonation is especially evident in their shared epistemological assumption and shared pneumatological framework. The limitedness of human understanding contrasts with the Spirit's omniscience. Obviously, the Holy Spirit is able and willing to work in and through the receptive human spirit according to the divine purpose. Paul in Romans adds the idea that the Spirit helps believers overcome their weaknesses through intercessory prayer in strict accord with God's will as it can be known only by the Spirit of God.[29] Thus the Spirit's work in believers is not only revelatory but intercessory. The Spirit is actively and directly involved in a very particular manner in the prayer life of Christians.

This is where praying in the Spirit as praying in tongues comes into sharper focus. Pentecostals agree that the Spirit is active in the overall prayer life of a believer—not just speaking in tongues.[30] The Holy Spirit doubtless inspires and enables all authentic prayer. However, "devotional" tongues or the "prayer language" of the Spirit, as believers sometimes describe the practice of praying in the Spirit/tongues, is a specific manifestation of the Spirit's agency in prayer.[31] Why would the Holy Spirit choose to work in such a "strange" fashion? Note that for Paul accurate articulation in prayer is essential for its effectiveness.[32] And effectiveness in prayer is essential for the accomplishment of God's purpose in and through us. Praying in the Spirit helps overcome the epistemological and linguistic shortcomings of finite human beings in the accomplishment of the sovereign God's gracious and benevolent purpose. By using tongues speech in prayer, the Spirit expresses God's infinite and all-knowing will in intercessory form thus assuring its effective accomplishment.[33]

---

praying in tongues is more like the painful cries of an expectant mother bringing new life into the world.

29. In other words, Ambrosiaster says, "the Spirit given to us overflows with our prayers in order to make up for our inadequacy and lack of foresight by his actions and to ask God for the things which will be of benefit to us." See *ACCS: Romans*, 230.

30. Riggs, *The Spirit Himself*, 181, and Land, *Pentecostal Spirituality*, 167, 171. Morris observes that his grandmother, noted for praying until the room became "a most holy place," often began her prayers with praise and moved to petition followed by weeping and praying in the Spirit, "Divine Intimacy," 11.

31. Although Chrysostom relegates this practice to individuals having an exceptional prayer vocation, and, oddly enough, symbolized by the deaconate, that is, a kind of "spiritual man who has the gift of prayer," *ACCS: Romans*, 230, 231, there is no such exclusive limitation in Paul. Is this an instance of a tragic historical tendency to separate the spiritual gifts from the laity by restricting them to clergy? In any case, Pentecostal theology affirms praying in the Spirit as the potential privilege of every believer willing to receive it.

32. Yet Augustine observes that humans not only do not know future developments but cannot accurately distinguish between mere appearances and true reality, *ACCS, Romans*, 230.

33. Ambrosiaster argues that since the Spirit comes from God and by "his own nature" speaks what God speaks then the answer to the prayer is assured, *ACCS: Romans*, 230. Interestingly, Ambrosiaster considers the Spirit's groaning as a form of speech.

How is the believer benefited? Above all, praying in the Spirit is "intercourse and deep communion with God."[34] Accordingly, in addition to the obvious benefit of having prayers answered, the believer is personally and spiritually edified (built up, strengthened) by praying in tongues, experiencing communion with God's Spirit in an uplifting, formative manner, and learning to yield to the will to God (Would anyone deny that the tongue is a particularly sensitive area of surrendering to God? See Jas 3:8.). Praying in the Spirit often infuses the act of prayer, which can all-too-easily become routine or even rote, with an exciting dynamism potentially promoting more frequent pray*ing* and more faithful pray*ers*.[35] Nevertheless, it is critical to note that praying in the Spirit or in tongues is not a substitute or replacement for praying with understanding in one's native language. I would not call it a supplement, perhaps implying a minor addition, but more like a complement; together prayer with human understanding and prayer in the Spirit speaking divine mysteries complete each other in a well-integrated and effective prayer life. Paul explained that he practiced prayer both with his understanding, or in a known tongue, and in the Spirit, in other tongues (1 Cor 14:13–17). Thus, the understanding of a prayer and that of possible hearers can both be fruitful or productive for them and to God's glory.

For illustrative purposes, I will share from my experience, which may or may not be identical to, or even resemble, that of others.[36] I have had a recurring phenomenon regarding the role of understanding in prayer. While praying in my native English I have sometimes felt the frustration of realizing my sorely limited understanding and language were insufficient for the need at hand. I might then pray in tongues and experience a sense of "breaking through," if you will. However, I have occasionally had experiences when my understanding was not entirely disengaged when praying in tongues. When I am praying in the Spirit the image of a certain person or group or a strong sense of a certain need might come up in my mind in a persistent fashion. I am convinced that although I do not understand the specific words the Spirit is right then praying through me, that nevertheless the Spirit is helping me understand in a general sense how I am being guided through the prayer process. Significantly, the person or need is usually one which I have not previously been aware of as anything particularly pressing; however, it is not unusual to learn later that it was indeed a pressing matter.[37]

---

34. Land, *Pentecostal Spirituality*, 169.

35. Theodoret of Cyr (5th cent.) well said, that "By this grace we are encouraged to struggle, we are inflamed to pray more earnestly, and with ineffable sighings we implore God," *ACCS: Romans*, 232.

36. However, Doolittle, describes a similar experience, "Praying in the Spirit," 15.

37. I have also had this experience in reverse. Someone would call me, text me, or email me to let me know that the Spirit had laid me on their hearts in prayer in just this fashion. I have had it happen that either I had a need that they did not know about but I could confirm or that a need neither of us was aware of was soon confirmed by circumstances we could not have anticipated. In the latter case, the Spirit literally leads someone to pray about a pressing need before any humans involved have any (other) way of knowing anything about it.

Interestingly, Anglican NT scholar N. T. Wright similarly testifies of his personal experience of praying in tongues in a manner that may be informative. Admitting that he had never been very public in his practice of praying in tongues, he nevertheless adds, "But in pastoral ministry and various other contexts over the last thirty years it has been invaluable as a way of holding before God people and situations whose needs I had not yet understood sufficiently to put into words."[38] I daresay many could echo similar sentiments. Praying in tongues is not only personally beneficial but serves well as an effective aid in intercessory prayer too. It is particularly helpful when limitations of knowledge threaten to hinder prayer.

In sum, praying in the Spirit or praying in tongues has a valuable place in an overall, well-rounded life of committed, consistent prayer. Thereby the Holy Spirit helps make our prayers "honest and effective" as the Spirit "directs, empowers, and energizes" our prayers.[39] Not surprisingly, praying in the Spirit is a primary manner in which devotees may experientially encounter God's majestic and marvelous presence. Although it is most commonly an intensely personal practice, it can occur, often simultaneously and spontaneously, in corporate worship as well.

The Altar Service

The role of the altar in prayer is not entirely unique to Pentecostalism. It is shared by the broader revivalist movements and several wings of Evangelicalism. The "anxious bench" or "mourner's bench" popularized in the "new measures" for promoting revivals led by American pioneer evangelist Charles Finney served as precursors for altar terminology and spirituality.[40] However, Pentecostal interpretation and application are certainly distinctive—and particularly telling in terms of the movement's energetic ethos and inclusive instincts.[41] Pentecostals actually refer to a specific time in worship as the "altar service" and often have "altar workers" to help promote and stimulate altar experiences.[42] This terminology suggests the critical importance of the "altar call"

---

38. Wright, "The Word and the Wind," 143.

39. Martin, *Spirit-Filled Worship*, 114.

40. See Stamm, "Liturgy and Worship," 495–96 and Conkin, *America's Pentecost,* 168. Finney suspected that classic liturgical forms stifle the leadings of the Holy Spirit and thus preferred more heart oriented styles.

41. Although 19th century Blacks had been literally pulled from the altar when they dared pray with whites, the Azusa Revival scandalized the nation, and many Christians, when the races freely prayed together in the altar, Alexander, *Black Fire,* 28–29, 69, 119; cp. 83 and 125. The inclusion of women was also controversial, Alexander, *Black Fire,* 295.

42. Shepperd, "Worship," 1219–20. Arrington, *Encountering the Holy Spirit,* describes the "altar service" as a distinct part of the larger worship service, usually (but not always) after the sermon, in which worshipers are invited to the altar area (near the front of the sanctuary) for repentance, rededication, and prayer, 469.

and its associated practices. In fact, altar responses can be an important indicator of the effectiveness of a particular sermon or of a preacher's ministry.[43]

For Pentecostals the altar is a place to seek God, to offer one's self to God, to receive from God, and to meet with God.[44] In other words, the altar signifies consecration, provision, and communion. In the altar one commits and dedicates him/herself to God's service and worship. In the altar one receives gracious supply of their daily needs with eternity ever in mind. In the altar seekers enter into and continually deepen and strengthen an intimate and enduring relationship with God. In it all the altar is above all a place of divine encounter. This dramatic altar encounter is founded on its facilitation of focused prayer. It is often in the altar where conversions, healings, Spirit baptisms, occur.[45] In the altar one may hear God's "still small voice" regarding their specific calling and purpose in Christ or direction and guidance in life (1 Kgs 19:12 KJV). The use of anointed "prayer cloths," the anointing with oil of petitioners/supplicants, and the practice of the laying on of hands frequently occur in the altar.[46] Demonstrative occurrences such as being "slain" in the Spirit or falling out "under the power," dancing and shouting, weeping and/or laughing, and so on may well occur in altar encounters.[47]

If for Pentecostals the entire worship service is an opportunity for divine encounter, the altar service is doubtless the climactic moment in terms of encountering God's presence. Several years ago, a Catholic charismatic friend shared with me a fascinating comparison about the great Christian worship traditions. He explained that for "high church" or formal liturgical traditions the perceived climax of a given worship service is the Eucharist.[48] He further opined that for "low church" or more informal Protestant traditions, the perceived climax of a given worship service is the preached Word or

---

43. Alexander, *Black Fire*, 128.

44. Thus, Boone describes a Pentecostal altar service as "a time of deep receptivity to the Spirit of God" 141.

45. Abundant testimonies confirm this phenomenon, Arrington, *Encountering the Holy Spirit*, 454, 456.

46. Oddly enough, English (at least) struggles with an adequate term describing "one who prays." "Precant" is an odd and outdated word meaning "one who prays." "Petitioner" or "supplicant" often fills in but they are incomplete (only describing one engaged in certain kinds of praying). I often find myself using some form of "pray*er*" or "pray-er" but it can be confusing to distinguish between the practice (prayer) and the practitioner (pray*er*).

47. Although he had other issues, including leadership and race, Parham accused Seymour of practicing hypnotism in his altar services, Alexander, *Black Fire*, 139–40, due to a prevalence of spiritual manifestations.

48. "Eucharist" is from the Greek, εὐχαριστία (*eucharistia*), for "thanksgiving." It was often used in the early church, and hence in many historic traditions, to describe Holy Communion or the Lord's Supper.

sermon.[49] However, he added, for Pentecostals the perceived climax of a given worship service is the altar of prayer.[50]

For the most part, I agree with this descriptive assessment.[51] Further, I think it highlights important insights. Namely, it accents the sacramental focus of the liturgical traditions, the Word-centered nature of much of Protestantism, and, for our purposes, most importantly, what I might call the prayer-presence core of Pentecostalism. As stated in the previous chapter, Pentecostals also place great emphasis on the Word and are increasingly cognizant of the validity and value of sacramental emphases. However, I think it is still accurate to assert that Pentecostals generally perceive the altar of prayer to be the place and time that the highest and most intense point in the development of a worship service occurs as everything preceding it coalesces in fulfillment of God's purposeful goal for a particular worship gathering. Indeed, congregants are exhorted by their ministers to make a "family altar" at home and to make a "personal altar" as place of regular private prayer.[52] Arguably, the altar is the climactic moment in corporate worship and the critical component in personal discipleship.

Obviously, altar terminology and conceptualization are appropriations of ancient biblical traditions of sacrifice. The first specific mention of the term "altar" is the grateful sacrifice of Noah after surviving the deluge (Gen 8:20). However, the essential concept is certainly present as early as Abel's acceptable offering (Gen 4:4; Heb 11:4). Eventually, the altar became a clear focus of pre-national patriarchal and national Israelite religious devotion and expression. Early in the biblical narrative altar worship would be offered at any place where God was believed to have revealed God's Self; but, with the passing of time efforts to combat heathen abuses ("high places") led to exclusive temple offerings.[53] Jesus' references to the altar suggest the prominent role it still held in first century Judaism (e.g., Matt 5:23–24; 23:18–20; Lu 11:51). Paul famously utilized an Athenian altar as a point of contact for gospel proclamation in a religiously plural context (Acts 17:23). He also argues that participation in the OT altar sacrifices

---

49. In the 17th century "high church" came into vogue as a way of describing those with a *high* degree of commitment to the belief and practices of the established, state run church. By contrast, "low church" described those who had a *low* degree of commitment to the belief and practices of the established, state run church. Although increasingly unpopular today because of perceived negative connotations (at least for those in the "low" category) the terminology continues to be used by ecclesiologists and others.

50. With a sharp wit, he lamented that for many congregants the climax of any worship service seems to be exiting.

51. I would qualify by noting that although the altar service is *climactic* to Pentecostal worship the moving of the Holy Spirit throughout is *central* to Pentecostal worship. See Shepperd, "Worship," 1219. However, unlike Shepperd, I probably would not say that the service "stops" for the "moving" of the Holy Spirit. Rather, the service gets redirected according to the sovereign will of the Holy Spirit.

52. E.g., Pat and Karen Schatzline, "Rebuilding the Altar in Your Home," designated a specific room in their home to pray and seek God together, 23.

53. North, "Sacrifice," 208.

serves as a precedent for gospel support in the NT age (1 Cor 9:13) and as a precedent for union with Christ in the Lord's Supper (10:18).

Hebrews is at pains to demonstrate typological continuity between the OT altar and the NT faith even while arguing that the NT "altar" replaces, and in a sense, therefore, renders obsolete, the OT altar (7:13; 9:4). The reference to a "Christian altar" (as it has been termed) appears to be primarily a direct reference to Christ's sacrifice on the cross and only indirectly, that is, secondarily, a possible allusion to the Eucharist or Communion (13:10).[54] Fascinatingly, the book of Revelation is filled with references to the altar (6:9: 8:3, 5; 9:13; 11:1; 14:18; 16:7). At the least Revelation certainly evidences that altar imagery continued to capture the imagination of the early Christians, particularly in terms of comparison/contrast between earthly and heavenly realities.

Appropriating the Altar Tradition

For the purpose of our presentation of Pentecostal theology, the key question which comes to my mind is, "Have Pentecostal churches rightly appropriated the altar tradition in their time of focused prayer encounter?" Or, to put it another way, "Is the Pentecostal altar service merely a leftover from frontier revivals with at best limited, and perhaps questionable, application for Christian worship today?"[55] In response I insist both that the altar service is essential to Pentecostal spirituality and theology and that it is an appropriate practice.[56] I offer two supporting arguments for my position, the first biblical and the second historical.

Biblically, there is an enduring and profound association between the altar and prayer. This association with prayer is initially indicated in the patriarchs' repetitive practice of calling on the name of the Lord in the immediate aftermath of building altars (Gen 12:8; 13:4; 26:25). It is emphatically reaffirmed when the prophet Elijah repaired Israel's altar, called on the name of the Lord, and fire fell from heaven in dramatic testimony of YHWH's indisputable identity as the one true and living God (1 Kgs 18:1–39). Throughout the OT altar imagery and prayer are frequently linked (e.g., Pss 116:17; 141:2; Joel 1:13–14; 2:15–17). Close association between prayer and the altar continues in the NT as well (Luke 1:8–11; Rev 6:9–10; 8:3–4).[57] Accordingly, although of course Christians do not erect a literal altar used for offering animal

---

54. Ellingworth, *Epistle to the Hebrews*, 711–712.

55. Menzies, *Speaking in Tongues,* 120, asks: "Is it appropriate during our corporate gatherings...to call people to collectively seek God's empowering?" He answers with, "By all means, Yes!"

56. Please note that my concern here is not with whether or not we have a "mourner's bench" in the front of the sanctuary, although my congregation does, or with whether we conduct the altar service in this or that manner. Rather, I am concerned to assert the theological integrity of the Pentecostal practice of conducting altar services.

57. The association between the altar and prayer is evident in the Apocrypha as well. See Jdt 4:12 and 2 Macc 3:15.

sacrifices, the case for the altar as a place of prayer functioning as an aid to and incentive for consecration and transformation is biblically compelling (Rom 12:1–2).

Historically, we are also on solid ground. How often I have heard critics opine that Evangelicals and Pentecostals have unfortunately allowed an eighteenth-century revival technique to corrupt contemporary worship practices. But it just is not so! I mentioned above the influence of frontier revivalism and Finney's "new measures."[58] That is common knowledge. However, there is more to this topic. While as early as the second century of Christianity Ignatius of Antioch and Tertullian utilized altar imagery to describe the Eucharist, others such as Irenaeus and Clement of Alexandria asserted that the altar is specifically associated with offering unceasing, holy, and united prayer to God. In the third century Bishop Victorinus, commenting on Matthew 5:23, said, "By the testimony that our Lord bears to it, we perceive that the golden altar is called heaven" and also "Assuredly, our gifts are the prayers that we offer, and certainly our prayers ascend to heaven."[59] Clearly, very early on Christians affirmed a prayerful altar encounter. Indeed, throughout Christian history the altar variously represents themes such as refreshing, cleansing, active service, rekindling, transformation, consecration, and, above all, reverent and mysterious encounter with God.[60] Pentecostals shout "Amen!"

Let's put church furniture aside for a moment.[61] After all, the altar is not really a table, and not a bench either; it is the cross (as Luther well said).[62] When Pentecostals conduct an altar service focused on concentrated prayer they are not only drawing on a prominent theme in the biblical account but acting consistently with ancient Christian liturgy, spirituality, and theology.[63] I do not claim that early twentieth century Pentecostals or their immediate heirs did a patristic study and subsequently decided to have altar services. Neither do I claim that patristic churches would uncritically affirm (or not) everything that typically occurs in Pentecostal altar services. Rather, I

---

58. Revivalism is not limited to frontier history or rural areas. It has very contemporary and very urban occurrences as well. See award-winning religion reporter Steve Rabey's objective and balanced report, *Revival in Brownsville*. Although the theology of revivalism continues to be debated, with more than its fair share of defenders and detractors, 211–29, its significant impact on Christianity (especially Pentecostalism) in America (and the world) can hardly be denied, 41–61.

59. Bercot, *Early Christian Beliefs*, 14.

60. Oden, *Life in the Spirit*, 42, 90, 149, 166, 215, 256, 468.

61. Although a close study of the evolution of the use of tables, benches, communion rails, pulpits, and such, provides a fascinating look into fluctuating tensions between clergy and laity, with the former often trying to protect the altar from being "profaned" by the latter, and of conflicting Catholic-Protestant views on the relative prioritization of Word and Sacrament, White, "Spatial Setting," 806–10. Most Pentecostals would find the first scandalous and the second superfluous.

62. As cited in Oden, *Word of Life*, 306.

63. Whatever a specific tradition's application, the altar is the place where "the faithful are consecrated and sanctified to the service of God through the mediation of the Son, by the power of the Holy Spirit," Oden, *Living God*, 126. "Down on the praying ground" slaves in the American South forbidden freedom to worship and pray by fearful masters stole away to an altar deep in the woods, Turner, *United Holy Church*, 17.

am quite comfortable with the notion that the Holy Spirit guided those who follow his leading into an active prayer emphasis that is biblically, theologically, and historically valid. Therefore, Pentecostals today can confidently affirm and defend the altar service which typically climaxes their worship gatherings.

I have already noted that early in the biblical narrative altar worship would likely be offered at any place where God's self-revelation was believed to have occurred; but, with the passing of time heathen abuses led to the necessity of the exclusivity of temple offerings.[64] In combating persistent tendencies toward syncretistic idolatry, altar worship was eventually confined, though with limited success, to the purview of the priests within the temple environs. That is understandable, even laudable. Yet we can probably imagine that as the worship process became more limited it simultaneously became less characterized by liberty. Does that sound a bit like various Christian worship traditions today? On the one hand, we have rigid liturgical traditions dedicated to assuring that nothing amiss ever occurs. On the other hand, we have freedom loving traditions willing to risk occasional aberrations for the sake of what Harvey Cox calls "primal piety."[65] Not surprisingly, Cox identifies Pentecostals with an ever-surging desire for "the liberating Spirit."[66] Pentecostals are certainly freedom loving people. Do we have to wonder which side of the equation describes Pentecostals?

I may surprise readers by suggesting that the majority of Pentecostals I have known would perhaps most closely represent an integration of the "keep it straight" and "let go and let God" poles. As Land has well said, Pentecostals are pretty much equally concerned with an integration of orthodoxy (right belief), orthopathy (right affections/dispositions), and orthopraxy (right practices).[67] In the context of our development of altar spirituality and theology, I suggest that Pentecostals ought to note the need for guarded temple worship but never forget the freedom of journeying through the Promised Land building altars as they encounter God's amazing self-revelation. Perhaps this tension appears most prominently in Pentecostals' altar services.

Nowhere is the Pentecostal penchant for "wide open worship" more evident than in our altar services. Although not exclusively so, many of the practices—such as shouting and dancing, falling under the power, and, of course, the basis of the infamous and slanderous pejorative "holy roller," and so on, most frequently occur in particularly intense altar services.[68] Even a lot of Pentecostals themselves start to get uncomfortable at this point. Others remind that dramatic, life-changing conversions

64. North, "Sacrifice," 208.
65. Cox, *Fire from Heaven*, 82. Cox describes "primal speech," "primal piety," and "primal hope."
66. Cox, *Fire from Heaven*, 299.
67. Land, *Pentecostal Spirituality*, 31–34.

68. "Holy roller" has been used for churchgoers of the Holiness and Pentecostal traditions as a pejorative description denouncing outbursts of dancing, shaking, falling down, and various other boisterous activities occasionally occurring when worshipers are "in the Spirit." Although not heard much today, it was common in a previous generation. Much like Wesley's response to being called "Methodist," many Classical Pentecostals embraced it as a badge of honor.

and Spirit baptisms, healings, and the like are often attendant upon such altar services. Here is my take. Like Israel's early patriarchs, altar services are and ought to be based on a revelatory encounter with God appropriately expressed with freedom and passion. Like later temple worship, altar services should guard against abuse. Yes, the altar can be abused—and when it is then the Lord pronounces a stern word of judgment (1 Kgs 13:1–5; Lam 2:7; Ezek 6:1–7). Here sound theology and spiritual integrity require Pentecostals to exercise great pastoral insight and sensitivity. If they lean too far toward restraint, they run the risk of quenching the Spirit (1 Thess 5:19). If they lean too far toward unchecked expressionism, they run the risk of carnal chaos (1 Cor 14:33). Better to avoid extremes (Eccl 7:18 NIV). One must neither stifle freedom for order's sake nor disrupt order for freedom's sake.

Uneven Evolution of the Altar Context

Let's dig in a bit more deeply into the evolution of the context of altar worship in the Israelite faith in order to plumb possible implications for contemporary Pentecostal spirituality and theology. The process of its formation and growth is itself instructive.[69] We would do well to remember that building the temple was not God's idea. It was King David's dream. Moreover, God initially rejected the idea of dwelling in a fixed location, apparently preferring the mobility of the tabernacle. The Lord was clearly much more interested in building David a house (dynasty) than in David building God a house (temple). The Lord eventually acquiesces after registering disagreement and implementing some qualifications (2 Sam 7:1–29; 1 Chron 17:1–13). One is reminded of a similar process, ironically enough, when Israel demanded a king and God gave them Saul—David's troubled, and troublesome, predecessor (1 Sam 8:1–22).[70]

Bergen notes that God immediately corrected both his prophet, Nathan, and his king, David, regarding their premature assumptions on building a house (temple) for the Lord.[71] What David had in mind was completely consistent with the customary practices of other monarchs in the ancient Near East regarding their deities. But David's deity was different! Several factors are involved in YHWH's sharp response to David's temple-building plans but central to them all appears to have been God's determined desire to have a living dwelling rather than a dead structure. Apparently, the moving tabernacle made of the skins of (once) living animals, portrayed the dynamic and vital nature of God's living presence among the covenant people more to God's liking—although still inadequate—than a stationary, stiff "house of cedar." Ultimately

---

69. The following is consistent with Pentecostal biblical scholarship that post-exodus public worship became increasingly formalized and centralized, and that temple worship especially, despite significant benefits, presented its own difficulties as well, *Full Life Study Bible*, 680, 608–09.

70. There is a very important distinction between Israel's demand and David's dream: motive. Pre-monarchic Israel rejected God's reign. King David sought to honor God as his own Sovereign Lord.

71. Bergen, *1, 2 Samuel*, 336–341.

the divine purpose was, is, and will be fulfilled eschatologically in the living house of David through his messianic descendent, God's own Son (John 1:14), and in the indwelling Spirit of Pentecost (Eph 2:19–22).

Even though Israel's devout obviously adored the house where God's glorious presence was said to dwell (Ps 26:8), and Jesus treated it with reverence (Mark 11:17), God was ever at pains to remind of its shortcomings—primarily its implicit limitations on God's presence (Isa 66:1). To that point, Ezekiel, although himself a priest-prophet with close ties to the temple, nevertheless had an inaugural vision of the glory of God demonstrating exilic Israel's theological struggle to overcome an elite nationalist understanding of God to instead affirm YHWH as Lord of the whole world.[72] Its vivid imagery of wind, fire, living creatures, and chariot wheels "represents the basic characteristics of the divine nature."[73] Therein mobility and universality are essential to YHWH's nature. Significantly, the whole picture is an intense affirmation of God's ever-dynamic, incredibly versatile omnipresence.[74] Therefore, Lloyd Neve concludes that in the postexilic period God's presence came to be understood as manifest universally and continually as well as individually (Ezek 39:29; Ps 139:7).[75] Is it any wonder that in the NT early, often Jewish, Christians had to come to terms with the receding role of the temple in their faith and life (Acts 2:46; 3:1; 7:48; 21:26)? Rather, believers indwelled by the presence of the Spirit of God are the temple of the living God (1 Cor 3:16–17; 6:19; Eph 2:21).

In terms of a Pentecostal theology of worship, and especially a theology for the altar service and for the altar of prayer, I argue that the freedom and mobility of the patriarchs and of the tabernacle are especially instructive. I offer a few suggestive applications. First, a dynamic atmosphere is more conducive for the demonstration of God's living presence than a static format. Thus, dynamic vitality and versatility are great strengths for the Pentecostal movement. Secondly, a familial, and familiar, attitude is more evocative for human responsiveness to the divine presence than is a hierarchical, institutional structure. Doesn't this help explain in part the popular appeal of Pentecostal worship and prayer to the general public and to the marginalized (and contrariwise, frequent aversion among elitists)? Third, the Sovereign Lord nevertheless manages to make use of human institutions and traditions to accomplish God's purpose and to display God's glory in spite of added hurdles. This divine accommodation should warn Pentecostals against an arrogant dismissal of classic liturgical

---

72. Cooper, *Ezekiel*, 61–62.

73. Cooper, *Ezekiel*, 69. Not surprisingly, Ezekiel's inaugural vision has had a prominent place in Pentecostal spirituality and theology. E.g., it inspired popular Pentecostal evangelist, pastor, and denominational founder Aimee Semple McPhearson's signature emphasis on "The Foursquare Gospel," Robeck, "McPhearson," 857.

74. *Full Life Study Bible* asserts that "God is pictured on an ever-moving mobile throne that goes wherever the Spirit commands; imagery which symbolizes both God's sovereignty over all things and his presence throughout creation," 1181.

75. Neve, *Spirit of God in the OT*, 74.

traditions. Although the temple did not enjoy a daily display of the pillar of cloud or the pillar of fire (Ex 13:21–22), neither was it established without God's manifest presence being on glorious display (1 Kgs 8:10). Indeed, Riggs' classic text compares the inaugural outpouring of the Holy Spirit on 120 priests worshiping in unity at the temple with the advent of the Spirit at Pentecost on 120 Christians praying in one accord (2 Chr 5:13–14; Acts 2:1–4).[76] That may be a quite telling connection.

Certainly, God will visit his people with his presence and power wherever there is obedient openness, wherever there is welcoming willingness, to God's person.[77] Yet clearly divine manifestations resist restrictive rigidity in favor of dynamic freedom. I have heard Pentecostal preachers declare that the Spirit of God refuses to be "put in a box." That may be crudely expressed but it is biblically and theologically correct.[78] Regrettably, there appears to be an almost inevitable tendency in religious development and evolution to depart from initial democratization as increasing institutionalization occurs. Somehow this fossilization process has to be repeatedly reversed. Otherwise even the liveliest religious expression changes into mere lifeless remains with but bare traces of past glories. That is perhaps one reason why recurring revivals of the Christian religion have ever been necessary for its continuing vibrancy. It is indubitably one of the primary reasons for the rise and spread of the Pentecostal movement.

Finally, Wolfgang Vondey constructively relates encountering God around the altar theologically to the living out of the full gospel (see next chapter). He proposes that Pentecostal theology is a liturgical theology, a theology focused on the practices which glorify God in worship.[79] Therefore, Vondey says, "Pentecostal theology represents a liturgical tradition oriented around the altar."[80] Even earlier Dan Tomberlin had argued that with its orientation toward encountering the Holy Spirit, "the center and focus of Pentecostal worship is the altar."[81] As is already evident, I agree. Therefore, I appreciate Vondey's helpful plumbing of the multidirectional dynamic of the Pentecostal altar service. We certainly need to think about what leads to the altar (invitation/consecration), what occurs at the altar (formation/transformation), and what comes out of the altar (mission/vocation). The focus of the present section has

---

76. Riggs, *The Spirit Himself*, 171–72.

77. Both canonical (Neh. 9:12) and apocryphal literature (Wis 18:3) remind that the daily manifestation of the pillars was in part due to Israel's continuing need for guidance on their journey. Naturally, when they arrived in the Promised Land the twin pillars, like manna (Josh 5:12), ceased. Yet danger exists in forgetting the fire and its divine source (2 Esd 1:14; cp. Is. 63:10–11).

78. Interestingly, Gordon Fee, "Getting the Spirit Back into Spirituality," chimes in with, "I would make a general plea to church leaders to throw away the boxes in which they have kept the Spirit securely under their control," 43.

79. Vondey, *Pentecostal Theology*, 281–94. I take Vondey to be using "liturgical" in its general descriptive sense of worship rather than as a technical identification of certain historic forms of worship.

80. Vondey, *Pentecostal Theology*, 291.

81. Tomberlin, *Pentecostal Sacraments*, 19.

been on the engine of it all: focused prayerful encounter with the presence of the Holy Spirit around the altar.[82] This fusion point is paramount.

I do not think for a moment that the altar service is an incidental aspect of Pentecostal liturgy and spirituality. Neither do I think that it is an embarrassment to the movement biblically or theologically. Menzies rightly points out that the mighty wind and the tongues of fire present at Pentecost are dramatic signifiers of God's communicative presence; that is, they are theophanic displays.[83] Yet further note that fire is frequently associated with altar encounters (e.g., Gen 15:17; 22:6–7; Lev 1:7; 1 Kgs 18:30–39; Isa 6:6).[84] Perhaps we might suggest that inherent within the well-known imagery of the Day of Pentecost is a subtle pointer to the essentiality of an altar of prayer for the promotion of the Pentecostal experience. As Menzies well says, "Our churches desperately need to establish times when we come together for the purpose of prayer and to collectively seek all that God has for us."[85] The flames of Pentecost burn bright and are fanned ever higher in the altar service. Without it the fire dies out.

ATTENDANT FEATURES OF PENTECOSTAL PRAYER

I consider praying in the Spirit to be the most distinctive act of Pentecostal prayer and the altar service to be the most concentrated occurrence of various forms of Pentecostal prayer. The former is more private, the latter occurs in public settings. Practices such as tarrying prayer (or "praying through"), laying on of hands in prayer, using anointing oil and prayer cloths, fasting in prayer, prayer as spiritual warfare, and concert prayer tend to either operate out of that context or function in a supportive (not necessarily secondary) role. Some are described as distinctively Pentecostal only in their particular application.

Allow me to elucidate. Tarrying prayer or praying through is associated with extended periods of prayer in the altar (Luke 24:49). The laying on of hands, anointing with oil, and use of prayer cloths are most commonly integrated into the altar service (Acts 8:18; 28:8; 19:12; Jas 5:14). Fasting, obviously by no means exclusively Pentecostal in its origins or nature, still has had some rather unique applications by Pentecostals over the years but extends beyond public worship, including the altar

---

82. P. Douglas Small, Coordinator of Prayer Ministries for the Church of God (Cleveland, TN), rightly said, in a presentation on "Taking Prayer Seriously," AGREE 2019 prayer initiative, North Cleveland, Church of God (Cleveland, TN), January 9, 2019, we'll never appreciate prayer as we ought so long as we view "prayer as an engine which drives something else"—something implicitly more important. This valuable insight does not preclude the truth that the, literally, ultimate, aim of the Christian life, including prayer, is relationship with God or that prayer may indeed be a catalyst. It does, however, release the practice of prayer from all sorts of penultimate agendas.

83. Menzies, *Speaking in Tongues,* 165–68.

84. In certain cases, tongues of fire may symbolize a word of divine judgment (Isa 5:24; 30:27; 2 Esd 13:10).

85. Menzies, *Speaking in Tongues,* 120.

service (Acts 13:2–3). The same can be said of prayer as spiritual warfare—which is actually more characteristic of certain Charismatic groups than Classical Pentecostals but has become popular with many Pentecostals; it also has links with praying through, although praying through may be a contemporary exemplification of ancient prayers of lament as well (Ps 130; Dan 10:12–14, 20). Concert prayer simply describes congregational praying aloud all together and all at once, whether in the altar or not but often it is around the altar (Acts 1:14; 4:24). Each of these practices has theological significance for Pentecostals.

Steve Land sees tarrying prayer as a telltale mark of a truly Spirit-filled church. "A church that rejoices, waits, and yields in the Spirit, a church that loves the Word and will tarry as long as it takes to pray through to the will of God, the mind of Christ, and the leading of the Spirit, that church is Spirit-filled."[86] Indeed, what if one of the surest signs of the Spirit's presence is importunate, persistent prayer (Luke 11:5–13; 18:1–8)? Tarrying prayer or praying through involves extended periods of prayer by an individual or congregation. It arises out of biblical precedents such as wrestling intensely with God in prayer (Gen 32:22–32), seeking God earnestly and unceasingly (Ps 77:1–4), and waiting upon the Lord patiently (Isa 40:31). Pentecostals derive their applications particularly from Jesus' instructions for receiving the promise of the Spirit (Luke 24:49). Persistent, incessant prayer is completely contrary to the "quick fix" or "instant answer" mindset of much of modern/postmodern culture—including church subcultures. This is a case in which the process is as much or more important than the result. In tarrying prayer God works to form character that is conformable to Christ (Rom 8:29; 12:1–2). It may be agonizing, involving painful struggle through great inner conflict.[87] It is of course emotionally draining and physically tiring. Tarrying prayer requires patience and persistence. And it is transformative. Churches which do not provide ample opportunity for people to pray "as long as it takes" may rob seekers of innumerable heavenly treasures.

The laying on of hands, anointing with oil, and use of prayer cloths are most commonly integrated into the altar service (Acts 8:18; 28:8; 19:12; Jas 5:14). Like most Christian traditions, Pentecostals utilize the practice of laying on of hands in commissioning (ordaining, appointing); but, Pentecostals also follow the NT pattern of the laying on of hands in prayer for healing and for the impartation of Spirit baptism (as well as other needs).[88] The practice implies notions of conveyance in the sense that the Spirit of God chooses to work through believers to affirm others and to minister to their needs. Believers thus may be instruments of blessing to others but clearly the

---

86. Land, *Pentecostal Spirituality*, 165.

87. Martin suggests the Pentecostal practice of "praying through" bears profound similarities to Prayers of Lament. See Martin's Abbott Lecture, "Psalm 130: The Hopeful Cry of Lament," at PTS (February 21, 2018).

88. Williams, "Laying on of Hands," 834–36. Of course, commissioning is essentially intercessory prayer invoking the Spirit to empower and bless ministry, Oden, *Pastoral Theology*, 30.

source of the supply is always in God, not in human beings.[89] Thus any impartation of blessing is inseparable from the act of prayer.[90] Perhaps as much as anything else Pentecostals use touch to establish a sense of affinity, intimacy, and unity as believers identify with each other and agree together in prayer. In an increasingly digitalized, depersonalized culture, the Pentecostal emphasis on the laying on of hands in prayer is somehow reassuring and deeply satisfying. Amazingly, the practice can transcend culture, gender and race. Former slave Lucy Farrow, who was noted for being a woman of prayer and a leader in the Azusa Revival, reportedly laid hands on many people who received Spirit baptism or physical healing.[91]

Further, bodily touch (the laying on of hands) and material elements such as anointing oil and prayer cloths can take on a sacramental quality.[92] These practices are not replacements or substitutes for formal sacraments (water baptism, Lord's Supper, foot-washing) but indicate conjunctions of the material and spiritual as means of divine grace as tangible signs of divine presence.[93] In prayer they function as "aids to faith." The oil is a common biblical symbol for the Holy Spirit's presence and power (1 Sam 16:13).[94] Anointing a pray-er with oil amounts to a declaration in faith of the Spirit's presence and power to minister to a specific need. Prayer cloths represent a "point of contact." Or to put it better perhaps, they function as "mediating substances" through which the Holy Spirit works or, again, in other words, "as an extension of the Spirit's power through a mediating substance."[95] Thus Pentecostals frequently use prayer cloths to send forth prayers on behalf of someone not present in a given worship service. In each case the physicality or materiality of these items brings Incarnational and sacramental significance into the realm of prayer. Yet they are not "controlled" by an impersonal "mechanical" system—to which Pentecostals are intuitively averse; rather, they provide assistance for those who pray in faith. Finally, prayer cloths are not magical. They certainly are not amulets or charms. To the contrary, biblically they serve to expose and refute such erroneous and false superstition.[96] Prayer cloths direct

---

89. I have heard Pentecostals say that they wish to be a "channel" of God's blessings. However, Pentecostals are not at all using this term in an occult sense. They would see that as demonic and evil. Rather, they are speaking colloquially of a person God's Spirit can use to touch others.

90. Arrington, *Encountering the Holy Spirit,* 481. As of this writing in depth published theological reflections on impartation by Pentecostals are rare or non-existent. However, Billy Darrell Bewley has shared with me his current work on a Doctor of Philosophy dissertation for South African Theological Seminary on "A Critical Analysis of the Doctrine of Impartation in the Church of God Denomination" which intends to bring clarity and consistency to this significant topic.

91. Robeck, "Farrow," 632. In Farrow's person culture (slavery), race (African American), and gender (female) are transcended.

92. Tomberlin, *Pentecostal Sacraments,* 89–120.

93. Thomas, "Anointed Cloths," 111.

94. Powell, "Anointing with Oil," 318.

95. Thomas, "Anointed Cloths," 107.

96. Arrington, *Spirit-Anointed Church,* 301–05.

pray-ers to God through faith in Jesus Christ with full assurance of the Holy Spirit's presence and power in every situation.

Fasting, or temporarily abstaining from food for the sake of spiritual pursuits, by no means exclusively Pentecostal in its origins or nature, still has had some rather unique applications by Pentecostals over the years but extends beyond public worship, including the altar service (Acts 13:2–3). Fasting is an act of sacrifice but also a means of refocusing attention on the spiritual side of life rather than on the physical (which incessantly clamors for more than its fair share of time and energy). With a strong basis in Scripture, including the examples of Jesus and the Apostles, and historical Christian practice, it seems appropriate that Pentecostals emphasize fasting as an element of prayer.[97] Pentecostals affirm both the spiritual and practical aspects of fasting. Fasting can be a spiritual discipline and as well as a source of spiritual power. Fasting often accompanies seasons of revival (including dramatic conversions) and the operation of spiritual gifts and of healing. However, for Pentecostals fasting is usually a personal and voluntary matter. It is always to be conducted in humility and reverence. Martin observes that biblically fasting is associated with urgency in prayer, expressions of mourning, expressions of worship, as preparation for ministry, and humble dependence on God.[98] Significantly, fasting helps us draw near to God in order to experience "God's intimate presence."[99] Theologically, fasting is an essential component of Pentecostal spirituality—not simply in its doctrinal tenets but as a way of being with God in the world.[100] Above all, it has for its essential companion sincere prayer.[101]

Prayer as spiritual warfare is actually more characteristic of certain Charismatic groups than Classical Pentecostals but has become popular with many Pentecostals nevertheless. It has links with praying through, although praying through may be a contemporary exemplification of the ancient prayers of lament as well (Ps 130; Dan 10:12–14, 20). In its Charismatic forms spiritual warfare often involves complicated strategies based on extensive—and speculative—demonologies.[102] Most Pentecostals probably see spiritual warfare more straightforwardly as the "battle mode in prayer" during times of conflict and duress.[103] In other words, when one senses that they or their loved ones may be under spiritual attack, prayer effectively becomes a weapon against evil forces. This perspective is consistent with a strong NT tradition (2 Cor

---

97. Conn, "Fasting," 634.

98. Martin, *Fasting*, 80–95. Martin shares a powerful testimony of his own experiences in fasting and prayer, 169–70.

99. Martin, *Fasting*, 100.

100. Martin, *Fasting*, 147–50. Here Martin relates "the core" of Pentecostal spirituality and theology to the fivefold gospel, which the next chapter of this volume discusses.

101. Martin, *Fasting*, 99.

102. Richie, "Demonization, Discernment, and Deliverance," 171–84.

103. Schatzlines, "Rebuilding the Altar in Your Home," 22–23.

10:3–6; Eph 6:10–18). The prophet Daniel serves as a dramatic OT example (10:1–21). Spiritual warfare is usually associated with seasons of fasting and intense prayer. Many Pentecostals, often among the marginalized and disenfranchised of this world, and, naturally speaking, defenseless, find it attractive that they can wage "war" and win "battles" against oppressive evil in the spiritual realm through prayer.[104] And so it is.

Concert prayer, or simultaneously vocalized corporate prayer, simply describes everyone praying together aloud and all at once, whether in the altar or not; but, often it is around the altar (Acts 1:14; 4:24). Concert prayer has been disconcerting (no pun intended) to visitors in Pentecostals churches. As a pastor I have had non-Pentecostal visitors express discomfort when everyone began praying aloud together. Certain traditions will have a prayer leader speak aloud while others listen or pray silently. Those thus acclimated may be surprised to discover that often Pentecostals pray out loud and all at once. Partly behind this practice is belief in the power of agreement— that as everyone prays and believes God together it is effective (Matt 18:19–20). Land compares concert prayer to the musical presentation of an orchestra.[105] Thus concert prayer displays something of the underling unity of the overflowing Spirit which Pentecostals experience together in corporate prayer. Although Pentecostals are often accused of being extremely individualistic, Pentecostal experience is at its core corporate—as even concert prayer indicates. There is nothing quite like the sound of scores, hundreds, or thousands of voices lifted simultaneously to God in fervent, heartfelt prayer. At that moment, surely the church literally functions as a praying assembly.

In conclusion, I share an incident which for me illustrates something of the essential core of Pentecostal worship and prayer. About six or seven years ago our youngest granddaughter, Abigail, was only around nine or ten years old. As I crossed the Cumberland Mountains on my way into the Tennessee Valley finally nearing Knoxville after a long drive home from a season of ministering in Chicago my cell phone rang. My wife explained that Abigail wanted to talk to me about staying over and going out that night. Sue had already told her that likely I would be too tired, but she wanted to hear it from me. When Abigail came on the call she said, "I don't care what we do Papaw. I just want to spend time with you. I've missed you." Of course, I happily said yes—and enjoyed every moment. I once heard an atheist say that he could not understand an egotistical god who commanded everyone to constantly brag on him and then made them beg him for anything they wanted. I guess that was his crude (read rude) take on praise and prayer. I felt sorry for him. He had missed the whole point. Worship and prayer are above everything else about "spending time" with God.[106]

---

104. For a helpful discussion of this topic with both pastoral and theological insights, although heavily contextual, see Onyinah, *Spiritual Warfare*.

105. Land, *Pentecostal Spirituality*, 165.

106. *Full Life Study Bible* lists as first among reasons for praying as a means of fellowship and maintenance of our relationship with God and only secondarily as necessary for receiving God's blessings and power, 496. Similarly, first among blessings for worshipers is intimate communion with God and only afterwards other benefits, *Full Life Study Bible*, 682.

Worship and prayer are not about what you give or get. We are not talking about a cold transaction but a warm and loving relationship with our Lord and Savior. Worship and prayer involve a joyous encounter with the presence of God's Holy Spirit in delightful communion and loving union. As Small so well says, "The very heart of prayer is communion with God and enjoying God's presence."[107] Worship and prayer participate in a present reality that celebrates an assurance of ultimate redemption in anticipation of its full actualization. I am fully persuaded that Pentecostal theologies of worship and prayer must retain the exuberance and expressiveness that come naturally to holy love and ecstatic joy in authentic relationship.[108]

---

107. Small, *Transforming Your Church into a House of Prayer,* 39.
108. Morris, "Divine Intimacy," 10–11, puts it well.

7

A Full Gospel Biblical and Classical Framework

MANY PENTECOSTALS EMBRACE AN essentially Christocentric, pneumatologically charged paradigm known as "the fivefold gospel."[1] The fivefold gospel stresses the role of Jesus as Savior, Sanctifier, Holy Spirit Baptizer, Healer, and Soon Coming King. There is a restorationist ring to this paradigm which is often called the "full gospel."[2] It facilitates a vibrant Trinitarian and Incarnational integration of Logos/Spirit Christology.[3] Pentecostals confess faith in Jesus Christ as the eternal and unchanging Lord who is powerfully present and active by the Holy Spirit in all of one's personal life today and forever. The fivefold or full gospel paradigm sums up major motifs emphasized in Pentecostal spirituality and theology. Although the full gospel model is not anything like a full (yes, pun intended) explication of Pentecostal theology, it does provide a helpful entry point for summation and development. Since the denominating text for the contemporary Pentecostal movement includes fullness terminology it is no surprise that Pentecostals would appropriate it for their interpretation and application of gospel truth and experience (Acts 2:1–4).

1. Thomas, *Toward a Pentecostal Ecclesiology*, 4. Baptistic Pentecostals utilize a fourfold version collapsing salvation and sanctification into one. See chapter 2 for details.

2. Thomas, *Toward a Pentecostal Ecclesiology*, 412, 432. As Nichols notes in *The Pentecostals*, Pentecostals do not consider themselves to be starting anything new; rather, the full gospel is a restoration of original truth, 7–8.

3. Thomas, *Toward a Pentecostal Ecclesiology*, 519–20. Oneness Pentecostals interpret the full gospel in accordance with their theology. See chapter 2 for details.

It is precisely at this point that Pentecostals are often misunderstood. Land correctly observes that part of the problem is how to understand "the notion of being 'filled.'"[4] Other Christians can get the (mistaken) impression that Pentecostals are promoting a kind of two-tier system with "upper" and "lower" class believers. In such a model, lower class believers are "merely" (?!) born again but only upper or higher-class believers are "truly" (?!) Spirit baptized or Spirit-filled. Quite understandably, such an arrogant dichotomy would not bode well for building constructive, positive relations between Pentecostals and other Christians. Fortunately, it simply is not so. If I may, I will offer three suggestions. First, Pentecostals have greatly contributed to the misunderstanding by not always carefully and precisely explaining what we mean. Often, no one is to blame but us. Second, Pentecostals have indeed been misunderstood on this point because some other Christians who have not taken the time or made the effort to really hear what we do mean. It is high time for them to do that. Third, I think what we need is a *theology of fullness* which from the outset frames the conversation more accurately and sensitively. The following takes a few tentative steps in that direction. Therefore, before discussing specifics of the "full gospel" paradigm I would take a look at a biblical and theological approach to fullness. Even a brief, and therefore limited and selective, overview indicates that the recurring subject of filling and fullness so valued by Pentecostals is present with distinctive forms, shapes, and figures not only in prominent fashion but actually as a predominant feature both in Holy Scripture and in the historical development of Christian spirituality and theology.

A CENTRAL BIBLICAL THEME

My goal in this section is to identify the broad nature of descriptors such as "fill," "filled," and "full" in terms of divine-human encounters and relationship that it might inform a Pentecostal theology of fullness regarding Spirit baptism. God's initial imperative to humankind included a charge to fill the earth, apparently, at least superficially, in the sense of species productivity (Gen 1:28).[5] Instead they filled the earth with violence thus incurring divine judgment—doubtless indicating that God's idea of filling the earth had to do with a great deal more than mere reproduction (6:11, 13; cp. Isa 33:5).[6] Is it coincidental that several millennia later the Creator describes himself as the transcendent Lord who has "filled Zion with justice and righteousness" (Isa

---

4. Land, *Pentecostal Spirituality*, 167. Objectivization and quantification of the Spirit are especially problematic. It is *not* as if being filled with the Spirit involves a certain amount of substance occupying available space.

5. The Hebrew מלא (*mlʾ*), to make full or to fill, has a wide range of literal and figurative uses initiated by an underlying concrete meaning of completeness. Likewise, its Greek counterpart πληρόω (*plēroō*), to make full, to fill, basically meaning completeness or entirety, is used with some applicative latitude.

6. The filling of the land with wickedness continues to be a prominent concern (Lev 19:29; 2 Kgs 21:16; 24:4; Ez. 9:11; Ps 74:20; Je 16:18; 19:4).

33:5) while the original arch rebel was charged with being "filled with violence within" (Ezek 28:16; cp. Isa 14:21)? Yet the Lord still fills the earth with goodness and love (Pss 33:5; 119:64). Significantly, Paul describes the world of pagan idolatry as characteristically "filled with all unrighteousness, sexual immorality, wickedness, covetousness, maliciousness" and as "full of envy, murder, strife, deceit, evil-mindedness" (Rom 1:29). Like the OT, Paul assumes a point at which sin piles up until it reaches a kind of "full measure" or final limit precipitating inevitable judgment (1 Thess 2:16; cp. Gen 15:167; Dan 8:23).[7] In any case, after the deluge God immediately reaffirms the original mandate to fill up the earth (9:1). The motif of filling appears to be a consistent element of God's continuing purpose for humanity. Might the Great Commission mandate, as is called, to make disciples of all nations be considered an evangelistic application of this imperative to fill the world with righteous seed (Matt 28:18–20; cp. Isa 52:10)?

Fullness indicates a complete measure, with no lack, whether involving time, age (Gen 25:8; 35:29) or substance, a monetary amount (Gen 23:29; 43:21; Num 5:7). The Israelites were blessed to fill the land (pragmatic diminishment from the whole earth or missiological prefigurement?) with their own kind even during conditions of oppressive servitude (Ex 1:7; cp. Isa 27:6). But is it not ironic that Egyptian houses, including the palatial dwelling, were repeatedly full of pests during the judgment of plagues (Ex 8:21; 10:6)? Yet the Lord's ability to fill the empty stomachs of grumbling Israelites, who longed to be full of Egypt's bounty (16:3), during the wilderness wanderings demonstrated that he was indeed the Lord their God (16:8, 12). Here appears a not-so-subtle shift from the people acting as agents of filling to the Lord acting in that capacity, yet in both cases in negative situations. Perhaps implicit is an insinuation that when humans do not fulfill their obligations toward fullness then God fulfills his in a contrasting fashion? Notably, a great affirmation was that Caleb, obviously representing a minority in that day, followed the Lord fully (Num 14:24). Also, one might be described as full of the blessing of the Lord (Deut 33:23).

Perhaps by now it is beginning to be evident that fullness terminology is a favored figure of speech in Scripture for describing divine truth and spiritual experience. However, it is not until the tabernacle's construction that filling or fullness is related explicitly to filling with the Spirit.[8] The Lord informs Moses that he has filled Bezalel with the Spirit of God in order to equip him for the craftsmanship and vocational

---

7. Green, *Thessalonians*, 147. See also 2 Macc. and Matt 23:32.

8. Joseph (Gen 41:38) is a possible exception but the text involves an apparently unknowing pagan testimony, albeit to the presence of the true Spirit of God, and fullness terminology is at best implicit. The implication here, as with Daniel later (4:5; 5:11), again in a pagan setting and in a similar situation, appears to be that Joseph was recognized as "possessed by the Spirit"—which conceivably describes being filled with the Spirit. See Mathews, *Genesis*, 761. Interestingly, Joshua is described both as one in whom the Spirit dwells and one who is filled with the Spirit, further suggesting possible overlapping language (Num 27:18; Deut 34:9).

aptitude necessary for building the complex divine structure (Ex 31:1–5).[9] Later, the Lord reaffirms this filling with the Spirit, broadening it to include Oholiab (35:30–35). Further, Joshua's filling with the Spirit of wisdom for leadership continues a vocational theme but adds an idea of impartation through the laying on of Moses' hands (Deut 34:9). But perhaps the most dramatic occurrence of filling climaxes the tabernacle's completion as the glory of the Lord visibly filled the tabernacle (Ex 40:34–35).[10] Similar infillings of divine glory occasionally characterized the temple worship (1 Kgs 8:11; 2 Chr 5:13–14; 7:2); but, although he is ultimately optimistic Ezekiel warns against taking God's glory in the temple for granted (10:1–22; 43:1–5; 44:4; cp. Hab 2:16). The Lord ever remains at pains to remind that his omnipresent glory fills the whole earth (Num 14:21; Ps 72:19; Isa 6:3; Hab 2:14; cp. Jer 23:24).

The repetition of fullness terminology in the account of Elijah's battle with the prophets of Ba'al is instructive (1 Kgs 18:33–35), as is pronounced emphasis on the Lord's filling of the valley with water during Elisha's ministry (2 Kgs 3:16, 17, 20). Is the Lord, quite in contrast to worthless idols, particularly the God who is able to provide to the fullest? Certainly, post-exilic Israelites confessed that the Lord had filled their houses with all good things (Neh 9:25; cp. Job 22:18; Prov 3:10). Notably, worshipers' mouths were filled with praise for the Lord who had filled their mouths with abundance (Pss 71:8; 81:10; 126:2–3). Nevertheless, again, the fullness of divine provision must not be taken for granted (Hag 1:6; cp. Luke 15:16). Interestingly, Luke sees the coming of the messiah as issuing in full provision for the needy coupled with judgment resulting in deprivation for the rich (Luke 1:53). Paul even teaches Athenian pagans that God is responsible for their provisions and has filled their hearts with joy in testimony of his providential care (Acts 14:17). He describes his own financial support from the churches in terms of fullness (Phil 4:12, 18). But James reminds of Christians' ethical responsibilities to help fill the stomachs of the needy (2:16).

The Fourth Gospel describes the disciples' boat as filled with fish almost to the point of sinking when they followed Jesus' directions (5:7). It also clearly contrasts the fullness of Jesus' provision with any and all alternatives in the turning of water into wine (2:7) and, even more pointedly, in the feeding of the five thousand (6:12, 13, 26). Fullness and abundant provision are obviously related; yet implications that temporal, natural provision is a prelude to or reflection of eternal, spiritual provision appears ever present as well. In something of a counter mode, it does not seem like much of a stretch to suppose that Mary's anointing of Jesus' feet until the fragrance of the perfume filled all the house would further inspire full worship responses in others as well (John 12:3). God's generosity is not appropriately acknowledged with parsimonious responses.

---

9. This text figures into a Pentecostal line of reasoning which interprets Spirit baptism as vocational empowerment for missiological provision. E.g., Riggs, *The Spirit Himself*, 30–31, 80, 163 and Land, *Pentecostal Spirituality*, 168–69.

10. This event serves as a significant OT precedent for NT experience of Spirit baptism/infilling.

In both Testaments, various people are filled with certain emotions. During the exile itself the Jews had encountered enemies quite filled with rage against them (Esth 5:9). Jeremiah described himself as filled with indignation by the Lord (Jer 15:17; cp. Lam 3:15). Neighbors were filled with awe at the happenings surrounding the birth of John the Baptist as were those who witnessed the healing miracles of Jesus (Luke 1:65; 5:26). But the people of Nazareth were filled with wrath at the ministry of Jesus, as were some of the Pharisees (4:28; 6:11). Again, the disciples were filled with grief at Jesus pending departure (John 16:6). Antagonistic Sadducees were filled with jealousy at the success of the apostolic church (Acts 5:17), a reaction which develops into a pattern (13:45). By contrast, the disciples are filled with joy and with the Holy Spirit (13:52). The city of Ephesus however was filled with confusion in the riot which broke out around Paul's ministry (19:29). Obviously, emotion can pervade the psychic consciousness extending completely through people until they are essentially under its singular influence. Perhaps not surprisingly, Land suggests emotional fullness is analogous to being filled with the Spirit. "Thus, to be filled with the Spirit is to be decisively determined by and oriented to the things of the Spirit, to what the Spirit is saying and doing."[11]

By now our overview clearly suggests that the theme of filling is crucial for comprehending central biblical emphases. For a particularly significant example, filling is laced through and through with messianic overtones. Daniel envisions God's ultimate purpose as filling all the earth with the kingdom of God via the climactic messianic fulfillment of human history (2:35, 44). Haggai's descriptive prediction of the all-surpassing latter-day glory of the temple teems with rich messianic implications (2:6–9). Ironically, Jesus himself found it necessary to warn antagonists about filling up the measure of guilt and sin (Matt 23:32; cp. Gen 15:16; 1 Thess 2:16). In parabolic terms, failure to respond to the Lord's invitation is portrayed as tantamount to refusing to fill the house of one owed due respect and thus a culpable affront (Luke 14:23). An evident implication is that the Messiah conveys authentic fullness of life in contrast to all other incomplete, inadequate measures or means (John 10:10).

More to the point, the NT draws directly on the OT tradition of pneumatological filling as vocational endowment. Luke-Acts in particular stresses this theme.[12] To begin with, John the Baptist is filled with Holy Spirit even before birth in the context of his mission as the forerunner of the messiah (Luke 1:15). Then his mother Elizabeth

---

11. Land, *Pentecostal Spirituality*, 168. Gause, *Living in the Spirit*, 5, says "being filled with the Spirit is manner of life." His subsequent (2004 ed.) self-published edition adds "a quality of being" before "a manner of life" (8). By the way, I tend to reference Gause's original (1980) volume. When there is a specific reason for doing otherwise I identify it with "(2004 ed.)."

12. It appears in different forms in passages such as Matt 12:28 (cp. Luke 11:20). Although the present study focuses on the filling/fullness motif, the empowering ministry of the Holy Spirit is expressed variously in Luke: overshadowing Mary for Jesus' conception (1:35), coming on Simeon to prophesy (2:25–27), coming on or anointing Jesus for ministry (3:22; 4:18–19), and "clothing" the disciples for ministry (24:49).

and father Zechariah are filled with Spirit as well in the context of their mission of preparing the one who prepares the way for the Lord (Luke 1:41, 67). The child Jesus "grew and became strong in spirit, filled with wisdom; and the grace of God was upon Him" (2:40)—as had John the Baptist during his preparation for service (1:80).[13] The paradigmatic Pentecost event clearly depicts the Spirit's filling (baptism/outpouring) as empowerment for ministry (Acts 1:4–5, 8; 2:1–4, 33; cp. 2:42–47). Peter is filled with the Holy Spirit to preach (4:8), and the Jerusalem congregation is filled with the Holy Spirit after prayer in order to speak boldly (v. 31). In an odd but no less consistent reversal, Satan fills the heart of Ananias to lie about his offering (5:3). It seems Satan has his own agenda regarding fulness.

In Acts 2 an emphatic redundancy of the filling motif is telling indeed. From beginning to end Acts 2 is about being filled in one form or another! The Day of Pentecost fully comes, that is, it is completely fulfilled (v. 1), the house where the disciples were gathered is filled with the sound of a violent wind (v. 2), the disciples themselves are filled with the Holy Spirit (v. 4), then critics accuse the disciples of being filled with new wine (v. 13 NASB), the Messiah is described as filled with joy (v. 28), and onlookers in Jerusalem are filled with awe (v. 43 NIV). The filling theme immediately continues in the Acts. After the healing of the crippled beggar, people are filled with wonder and amazement (3:10). The apostles received a "backhanded" compliment from their opposition when they were charged with filling Jerusalem with the teaching of Christ (5:28). Stephen stands out as a man full of the Holy Spirit, wisdom, faith, grace, and power (6:3, 5, 8; 7:55). The conversion of Saul/Paul included the laying on of hands and praying for him to be filled with the Spirit (9:17). Tabitha is a woman full of good works (9:36). Barnabas was a good man full of faith and of the Holy Spirit (11:24). Spirit-filled Paul powerfully confronts Elymas the sorcerer who was (in stark contrast) "full of all deceit and all fraud" (13:9–10). Finally, it upset Paul to encounter Athens as a city full of idols (17:16). As a reminder, the theme of completeness runs consistently throughout all of these examples (either positively or negatively).

Neither does the filling motif vanish when we leave the narrative portions of the NT for the prose of the epistles. In the Pauline corpus, especially Ephesians, they become more concentrated, more compact, and more complex, too. Various threads are woven together almost seamlessly. But Christological basis and pneumatological accent remain intact and ever distinct. Paul's prayers abound on the one hand with affirmations of God's fullness and infinite plentitude (Eph 1:22–23), and on the other with petitions for believers to be filled through the Holy Spirit with the very same and with all its abundant fruits (Rom 15:13; Eph 3:17–19; Phil 1:9–11; Col 1:9–12).[14] Indeed,

---

13. Though both are possible, the context invites the translation and interpretation of "spirit" as "Spirit," Stein, *Luke*, 101–102.

14. In a somewhat enigmatic and much-debated statement in Col 1:24 Paul uses a filling metaphor to describe his own joining with Christ in suffering for the church. See Melick, *Philippians, Colossians, Philemon*, 239.

God's ultimate eschatological purpose in Christ is to "fill all things" (Eph 4:10)—or "to fill the whole universe" (NIV; cp. 1:23) while God's will for believers in the present anticipatory age is to "be filled with the Spirit" in overflowing joyous, grateful praise and worship (5:18–20; cp. 1 Tim 1:4; 1 Pet 1:8). Significant for our present purpose, note that believers' experience of fullness in the present age is directly linked to God's ultimate eschatological goals.

Interestingly, the Book of Revelation dramatically juxtaposes the fullness of God's wrath with the fullness of God's glory (15:7–8; cp. 8:5; 15:1; 21:9–10). One way or another, it seems all are destined for divine fullness—either through the fullness of divine judgment or the fullness of divine glory. The spectacular filling of heaven's temple with the smoke of God's glory is reminiscent of the tabernacle (Ex 40:34–35) and the temple (2 Chr 7:1–3) as well as notable prophetic experiences (Isa 6:1–4; Ezek 44:4). Thomas suggests that the filling of the heavenly temple with God's glory indicates "that God is fully present in majesty and glory to accomplish his purpose."[15] Indeed, John's hearers would "find themselves in the midst of the awesome presence of God."[16] Scripture's continuing theme of divine fullness culminates teleologically as enjoyment of the abundant, limitless presence of the true and living God in abiding, enduring glory.[17] From Genesis to Revelation and everywhere in between fullness is a central and critical theme in Scripture which is richly suggestive for understanding God's approach for accomplishing and completing redemption's wonderful purpose.

A CONTINUING HISTORICAL EMPHASIS

Ancient Christians often thought of the spiritual life as a kind of journey.[18] The language of journey or pilgrimage arises naturally enough out of the itinerant narratives of the Scriptures themselves. Not surprisingly, NT Christians often described themselves as pilgrims and sojourners (Heb 11:9, 13; 1 Pet 1:17; 2:11).[19] Further, Jesus described himself as the way and his disciples described themselves as followers of the way (John 14:6; Acts 9:2; 18:25). Irenaeus notably contrasted a developmental understanding of the Christian life with the heretical Gnostics' more static, achieved state of illumination. Clement of Alexandria and Origen viewed life in the Spirit, or the way of salvation, as different stages or levels in a dynamic (that is, non-static) process of spiritual development and growth in lifelong, ongoing transformation. Early

---

15. Thomas, *Apocalypse*, 464.

16. Thomas, *Apocalypse*, 464.

17. Macchia, *Baptized in the Spirit,* argues that Spirit baptism goes beyond individual human experience and the mission of the church to portend the eschatological filling of the new heavens and new earth with God's glorious presence, 85–88.

18. Sheldrake, "Journey, Spiritual," 388–90.

19. Jewish people during the Intertestamental period identified as sojourners as well (Wis 19:10; 1 Esd 5:7; 2 Esd 14:29).

Christian teaching highlighted perfection or union in this goal-oriented approach where "ultimately the end in view is fullness of life in God."[20] Throughout Christian history this theme of the experience of divine fullness is evident in connection to a progressive development of personal spirituality.

Origen eventually outlined a journey of three ascending stages. It included (*praxis*/beginners, *theoria*/proficients, and *theologia*/perfect) with a recovery of the divine image through an ever upward movement toward greater light. Gregory of Nyssa (c. 335–95) adapted this theme as a journey into greater darkness rather than light (apophatic understanding of God as never finally or completely known). Pseudo-Dionysius (late 5th/early 6th cent.) developed these earlier bases into an elaborate exposition of the "Three Ways" (also "Threefold Path" or "Triple Way").[21] Through a purgative, illuminative, and unitive process, believers were encouraged to ascend a spiritual mountain or ladder (cp. John of the Cross, 16th cent.). Benedict (6th cent.) described the spiritual journey in terms of twelve degrees of humility, which was developed further by Bernard of Clairvaux (12th cent.). Teresa of Avila (16th cent.) used the metaphor of progressively moving through the different rooms of an interior castle. Contemporary itineraries of the spiritual journey have been influenced by recent development theory in the human sciences, especially psychology, gleaning insights from the work of Carl Jung, Erik Erikson, James Fowler, and others.[22]

Margaret Miles affirms the value of the classic "ascent" model of the Christian spiritual journey primarily for emphases on dynamism and personal responsibility and activity vis-à-vis static, disconnected experiences.[23] However, there are serious criticisms as well. These include extreme separation of the natural and spiritual realms and the reality of overlap and integration along the so-called distinctive stages. The most serious for our purposes is the charge that "the notion of spiritual stages supports a hierarchy of spiritual and moral values."[24] In other words, are those on one level or stage of the faith journey necessarily *superior* to another? If the answer is affirmative it seems hard to escape the conclusion that others are by contrast *inferior*.

20. Sheldrake, "Journey, Spiritual," 388.
21. Tyler, "Triple Way," 626–27.
22. Sheldrake, "Journey, Spiritual," 389. See Tyler, "Triple Way," 627.
23. Sheldrake, "Journey, Spiritual," 389.
24. Sheldrake, "Journey, Spiritual," 389. Catholic theologian Karl Rahner objected that successive stages of spiritual growth are based on Neoplatonic anthropology and that the idea of increasing grace is problematic, Sheldrake, "Journey, Spiritual,," 389. However, Scripture itself *in some sense* affirms both spiritual growth and development and the increase of grace and virtues (e.g. Rom 5:20; 2 Pet 1:3–11; 1 John 2:12–14). Nevertheless, I understand Origen's three levels of the Christian life as (a) highly influential for what follows him, but (b) a decisive step away from earlier Christian practice which was more closely aligned with our Pentecostal model. Specifically, his three stages are built on the Hellenism of his time. He was following Clement's model (and Pantenaeus) of merging a catechetical school (Roman education) with the catechumenate. While the idea of stages or levels of progress goes back to the beginning, it was much more in alignment with a journey or pilgrimage. In sum, we follow "the way," not "the levels."

Readers will recall a similar accusation against Pentecostal theology introduced above in discussing Land's admission regarding problems with "the notion of being 'filled.'"[25] Thus this conversation about the classic model takes on special import for contemporary Pentecostals. It is essentially the same charge. Sheldrake suggests the problem may result from over individualization in the classic model. Yet Sheldrake is sure that the classic model retains spiritual wisdom for contemporary Christians.[26] Accordingly, what is needed is a corrective in terms of "a renewed emphasis on the collective understanding of discipleship in the New Testament."[27] Recovery of a more collective understanding by contemporary Christians of the spiritual journey can sustain appropriate solidarity among all believers. I have no doubt that Sheldrake is correct in advocating for a move toward a more community sensitive hermeneutic. Further, and fortunately, contemporary Pentecostal hermeneutics are increasingly cognizant of the need to include community dynamics.[28]

However, I suspect there is more to identifying different stages of spiritual life as inevitably hierarchical and, therefore, unacceptable than community versus individual. First, the "ascent" model, the model of "upward" mobility (spiritually speaking, not economically!), particularly when expressed as climbing a mountain or ladder into ever higher heights of spiritual and moral accomplishments, probably does have intrinsic, and objectionable, hierarchical elements. Perhaps this unfortunate impression could be greatly tempered by humbly remembering that when God's people went *up* to the mountain, even at that God came *down* to meet them (Ex 19:20; cp. Ex 34:5; Num 11:25; 12:5). Humility is in order. Let us not repeat Babel's fatal error (Gen 11:5).

Second, problems appear when critics incline toward discontinuity rather than continuity in the conception of what "stages" actually entail. Generally, a stage may be thought of as a single step or degree in a process. A stage is a particular phase, period, or position in a process of development or in a series. If one emphasizes particular steps, degrees, phases, periods, or positions in disconnect from the context of the process then a hierarchy becomes almost inevitable. However, if one emphasizes the process of the journey with stages or steps along the way then advancement without arrogance is reasonable and possible. All believers are, after all, at some point in the same process. When individuals or groups are on a journey they are not considered "better" or "worse" because they are earlier or later in the trip and, accordingly, farther or nearer to their destination. They are simply moving toward their goal commensurate with reasonable time and speed considered with the distance at stake and other possible variables such as varying embarkation points and times, more or less challenging road conditions, including weather, and so on (Although woe is upon those who delay or turn back—Luke 9:62; 17:32.). Thus, I agree with Tyler that the

---

25. Land, *Pentecostal Spirituality*, 167.
26. Land, *Pentecostal Spirituality*, 389–90.
27. Sheldrake, "Journey, Spiritual," 389.
28. E.g., Yong, *Spirit, Word, Community* and Archer, *A Pentecostal Hermeneutic*.

stages of spiritual development still have relevance and usefulness for contemporary Christians.[29] However, I add that the ascent model, a later development of an original patristic emphasis, is not the only way to view growth stages. I particularly insist, as should be already evident by now, that the metaphor of a journey (or pilgrimage) is much more appropriate as a descriptor and much less susceptible to problems attendant on the ascent model. Nevertheless, the onward journey assuredly has an upward orientation (Phil 3:13–14; Heb 12:22–24).

In a fascinating comparative analysis Pentecostal theologian Simon Chan argues that the Pentecostal "nexus of conversion, sanctification and Spirit-baptism bears strong *structural*, although not necessarily material, similarities to the traditional Three Ways."[30] Not surprisingly he thinks that Pentecostals can learn from the classical tradition (with appropriate revisioning). Chan prefers the model of a spiraling repetitive pattern rather than a linear pattern as it suggests more interaction and overlap between the progressive stages. Therefore, it is not at all intended as an evaluation of participants' spiritual maturity and/or superiority at any given time. Rather, it is an incentive and aid for growth and progress. Every Pentecostal pastor knows that "babes in Christ" often receive Spirit baptism. They also know that saints who have been baptized in the Spirit for years may struggle with life's challenges. In any case, the Three Ways describe "the progression that occurs in various stages of the spiritual life."[31] And that is important. As Allen argues, "Our conversion, which first turns us toward God, is not the terminus but merely the first state of the spiritual life."[32] Our conversion "leaves us with much to do" as it "sets before us the task" of moving toward the goal of loving God and neighbor as we ought.[33]

But what is the precise nature of said progress? "Ah, there's the rub" as they say. I recognize some difficulties with an ascent model which may come across as progressing to ever higher heights of spiritual accomplishments or feats. Ancient asceticism frequently fell into that very trap. Yet ascent has biblical and historical roots that cannot be casually dismissed. The mountaintop experiences of Moses, Elijah, and especially Jesus are noteworthy examples (Ex 24:17–18; 1 Kgs 19:8–9; Matt 5:1–2; Luke 6:12; 9:28–36). However, these encounters indicate a repetitious pattern rather than permanent arrival.[34] One does not dwell on the mountaintop. One visits it to gain strength and wisdom for the valley, and perhaps returns subsequently for further replenishment—but again temporarily, before descending back into the lower regions

---

29. Tyler, "Triple Way," 627.
30. Chan, *Pentecostal Theology*, 73. Italics are original.
31. Chan, *Pentecostal Theology*, 74.
32. Allen, *Spiritual Theology*, 8–9.
33. Allen, *Spiritual Theology*, 9. As McMahan assumes throughout *Deepening Commitments*, Church of God "Practical Commitments," specific practices for integrity formation in daily Christian living, revolve around love, especially loving our neighbor as our selves.
34. Maslow's *Religions, Values, and Peak-Experiences* is a fascinating study of such phenomena.

of daily life. A spiral metaphor of repetitive progress therefore seems an improvement. However, the spiral model obscures the idea of journey. It is hard to image the geometrical concept of a plane curve generated by a point moving around a fixed point while constantly receding from or approaching it as actually *going anywhere* definite. Admittedly, it does, or at least it may, but it is not an image that readily conveys journey (for me, anyway). I prefer to stick with the basic idea of a spiritual journey/pilgrimage. For me, as for Pentecostal theologian David Han, Spirit-filled life "undergirds the entire salvation journey until the believer's final union with Jesus Christ."[35]

How then to overcome the idea that linear progress does not allow for the all-too-evident realities of overlap and repetition (even reversal) in human spiritual experience? I suggest discarding an *idealistic* concept of journey for a *realistic* concept. In an ideal journey one may think of moving from point "A" to point "B" to point "C" and so on in a direct fashion. One merely marks out desired points on a compass and moves through them in a straight line. That is not how real journeys work at all! There are curves and hills and valleys and crossings and turns and delays for road construction or unexpected detours and all sorts of variables even in modern travels. Think of the wilderness "wanderings" of the Israelites. They did not at all travel in a straight line. Obviously, the Israelites did not use GPS (Global Positioning System) to determine the best or most direct or fastest route. They meandered. Theirs was a winding, indirect trip. It was circuitous at best and perhaps at times seemed aimless. It was not as if they did not know the way from where they were to where they wanted to be; but, there were issues and obstacles that had to be confronted along the way. However, they eventually entered Canaan. They made it to the Promised Land. They arrived somewhere definite. Then they started the struggle to inhabit the land. And that is a realistic portrait of the spiritual journey.[36]

CONTEMPORARY PENTECOSTAL ATTITUDES

We have seen that early Christian teaching highlighted perfection or union in a goal-oriented approach in which "ultimately the end in view is fullness of life in God."[37] In Christian history the experience of divine fullness is evident in connection to a progressive development of personal spirituality. Yet I am not here primarily interested in an apologetic for a classical understanding of spiritual discipline and development per se so much as in its applicability for Pentecostal ministry, spirituality, and theology. While by no means complete there are some interesting parallels. For example, the idea of progress involving a journey of distinct stages of development specifically stands out. Especially significant, the same charge is leveled against both classic Christianity and

35. Han, "Spirit-Filled Life," 6.

36. The example of Abraham's servant is worth emulating. He was careful what he said until he knew whether the Lord had made his journey successful (Gen 24:21).

37. Sheldrake, "Journey, Spiritual," 388.

contemporary Pentecostals: an elitist spiritual hierarchy is established which undermines the solidarity and unity of believers. In other words, it is said that it creates, as it were, different classes of Christians. So, is the charge legitimate? Without being disingenuous, I wish to answer firmly in the negative and then to offer a careful qualification.

I do not think for a moment that Pentecostalism necessarily or inevitably generates or sustains spiritual hierarchy. I say "necessarily or inevitably" because I do not deny that some Pentecostals (as with other groups) afflicted with sinful issues of arrogance and pride may portray themselves and the movement in just that light.[38] I know many humble Roman Catholics and Orthodox Christians; I have also met some who arrogantly thought everyone else is part of a "Johnny-come-lately" sect. I know many beautiful Baptists; I have also met some who thought nearly everyone else is (at least) quasi-cultish. I am sure readers get the point. But Pentecostalism in its essence, particularly as we discuss its appropriation of baptism and filling with the Spirit and its commitment to authentic Spirit-filled living, is not only not hierarchical it is a great leveler. Pentecostals as much or more than anyone else believe that Christ came for all who will believe and that the Holy Spirit is given to all who will receive. That kind of accessibility and universality is intrinsically counter to spiritual elitism. All who are baptized into Christ are therefore one in Christ (Gal 3:26–29). No, Pentecostalism does not create a hierarchy of different classes of Christians.

Now I offer a clarification. Does the deeply shared commonality of our *status* in the Lord indicate that there are no distinctions or variations in our *state* of discipleship and/or service? I do not think so. To employ just one example out of many possibilities, why does Scripture so frequently describe some as infants or children and others as adults (1 Cor 3:1–2; 14:20; Heb 5:12–14; 1 Pet 2:2; 1 John 2:12–14)? Of course, everyone admits that individual Christians may be, and are in fact, comparatively more or less mature. Maturity does not define one's status—that is, position in relation to others, or rank and station in Christ; but, it does affect their state—that is, personal condition, ability, capacity for service. Surely no one is going to seriously argue that all Christians are identical in every aspect of their spiritual life? Is anyone going to claim there is no difference here or there in this or that? Of course not! That would be absurd. All believers are one in Christ; yet, we are each an individual in our walk with our Lord.

So then, can we identify and develop a specific theological model that fits well with Pentecostal emphasis on being filled with the Spirit? Such a model already exists in Christian history in a stream that has had particular impact upon Pentecostals. The Wesleys preached and sang about "full salvation."[39] For John Wesley, "full salvation," including full pardon and full victory over sin's power (but not presence), involved a crisis-process dialectic. In other words, it involves both instantaneous experience and

---

38. Colkmire, "Young, Significant, Diverse, and Needy," 7, exhorts Pentecostals to humility, warning against prideful and wrongheaded attitudes that we are "chosen above others."

39. Oden, *John Wesley's Scriptural Salvation*, 324, 327, 330, 338.

developmental growth in maturity. As faith begins, salvation begins; as faith increases, holiness increases. Entire sanctification is attainable by those who receive it in faith and walk in its privilege daily. Nevertheless, entire sanctification or Christian perfection is defined in terms of the relational dynamic of perfect love—not a static state of sinlessness (1 John 2:5; 4:12, 17–18).

I do not here desire to redirect to a discussion of Wesley's doctrine of sanctification. Rather, I wish to appropriate the idea of "full salvation" as potentially fertile for a Pentecostal theology of fullness. Whether one agrees with Wesleyan sanctification or not the concept of "full salvation" deserves attention. However, this course requires extreme caution. It will not do for anyone now to assume that Pentecostals believe that those who have not yet experienced the Holy Spirit in a Day of Pentecost mode really are not "fully" saved after all. I do not think that was Wesley's original point and it is not the Pentecostal position either. Rather, even Christians—the converted, justified, regenerated—may to a greater or lesser extent experientially appropriate the benefits and blessings of Christ and his gospel of salvation (Rom 15:18–19, 29; cp. Col 2:2; 4:12; Heb 6:11; 10:22). Pentecostal altar workers often encourage seekers to receive "all God's got for you." That is the idea. It is not that those praying are somehow less than another. It is most certainly not that they really are not saved after all. It is about a life completely dedicated to living out the fullness of Christian salvation. Pentecostals join Paul in praying that all saints will come "to know the love of Christ which passes knowledge" and "be filled with all the fullness of God" (Eph 3:19).

I speak here of my own experience as one brought up as a Pentecostal Christian, and as a Pentecostal minister for nearly four decades. The Pentecostals I love and serve in the local church are not arrogant about their Pentecostal experience. Rather, they are humbled by it. It is an incredible thought that God who created the universe indwells and fills a mere human as a holy temple! Accordingly, they invite others to share it, not out of compulsion or pride, but out of Christian love and a sense of Christian mission. Without embarrassment or apology, I acknowledge that Pentecostals are "all the way" kind of people. As a pastor friend of mine is fond of saying, "If God tells you to dip seven times in the Jordan then six won't do!" (2 Kgs 5:10, 14)[40] My Grandpa Richie used to sing a repetitive chorus which had a line in it that went something like "Lord, I'm tryin' to make a hundred, 'cause ninety-nine and a half just won't do."[41] When Grandpa was lying in the hospital about to pass into the presence of the Lord his adult children gathered around his bedside. Grandpa sang that chorus one more time. Only he changed the lyrics slightly. He sang, "Lord, I'm glad you helped me

---

40. Bishop Rick Cottrell is pastor of the Church of God in Linden, Tennessee.

41. Originally written and sung by American gospel great Dorothy Love Coates (1928–2002), "99 and a Half Won't Do" has been recorded and/or adapted by numerous artists. Cp. McAllister, *The Musical Legacy of Dorothy Love Coates*.

make a hundred, 'cause ninety-nine and a half just wouldn't do." As he transitioned from this world to the next, he was singing in other tongues.[42] Hallelujah!

The real "push," if you will, by Pentecostals is not at *others* but *themselves*. They want to go all the way with their Lord. They refuse to settle for anything less. No halfway measures here! They are not about diminishing or denigrating others. They are challenging and encouraging themselves. Yes, they enthusiastically invite others to share the "Pentecostal blessing." Yes, they can at times be provocative (and, if hard pressed, combative!). But the essence of the Pentecostal experience and the impulse that arises out of it is not to "put down" anyone; rather, it is that Christ came to "pick up" everyone. If Pentecostals are to be faulted for behaving like they believe they have an experience worth sharing, then so be it; but it would be a total misunderstanding to suppose they do so out of any smug sense of superiority.

An interesting example in this regard is Carrie Judd Montgomery, an important early Pentecostal minister and leader. In a far-reaching study of Montgomery's life and work, Jennifer Miskov points out that her understanding of the Spirit's fullness emphasized a gradual process of receiving degrees of fuller measures of that which had already been given.[43] Connectivity to, and continuity with, the preceding is essential. Neither did the process of receiving the Spirit's limitless measures end with the distinct experience of Spirit baptism; it was a lifelong relationship of increasing intimacy with God.[44] Miskov concludes that Montgomery's paradigm was one of measures, not of stages, and involved encountering the Spirit in varying crises experiences, degrees, and measures throughout life.[45] In a word, "she saw the Spirit was without measure, and intimacy with God within the context of a relationship with Him, intimacy increased rather than stages to achieve."[46] Montgomery's position suggests the difficulty of categorizing individual Pentecostals even within the context of their own movement. More importantly for our present purposes, Montgomery exemplifies a general Pentecostal assumption that the fullness of the Spirit is not an achievement elevating one to an exalted position but is primarily about a deeper relationship with God.

It has been well said that "The Pentecostal experience is not a goal to be reached, not a place to stand, but a door through which to go into a greater fullness of life in the Spirit."[47] The Pentecostal experience is an edifying and positive emphasis. Let us note

---

42. As an interesting aside, in an analytic study of glossolalic singing in corporate contexts, Hinck, "Heavenly Harmony," 180, concludes that the practice is not chaotic or disorderly; rather, it represents "a humble recognition that one's own rationality is not the final arbiter of reality, that one is in need of community, and that one is part of the larger created order" which "can yield spectacularly beautiful results." Cp. 1 Cor 14:5.

43. Miskov, *Life on Wings*, 268.

44. Miskov, *Life on Wings*, 272.

45. Miskov, *Life on Wings*, 275.

46. Miskov, *Life on Wings*, 276.

47. Kärkkäinen, *Holy Spirit and Salvation*, 367.

a few summative observations arising out of the preceding but offered here for further considerate development.

1. First, the fullness of the Spirit is a fundamental biblical and historical theme for Christianity. Fullness is not an aberration and not peripheral; it is close to God's heart, and to the heart of the faith.

2. Second, the fullness of the Spirit is multifaceted for all of life. It encompasses the spiritual, practical, ethical, missiological, relational, and so on—all the dimensions of Christian life.

3. Third, the fullness of the Spirit is relevant for every believer today. There is no class of these and those; it is inclusive and welcoming to everyone.

4. Fourth, the fullness of the Spirit is about being completely under the influence of the Spirit. It does not entail being brought under the control of an alien intruder. It is fully and willingly yielding to the wisdom, power, and goodness of our resident Lord.

5. Fifth, the fullness of the Spirit is vital for growth and service. The calling and mission of Christ for Christians and churches cannot be carried out in human strength alone. The Holy Spirit enables and equips servant-witnesses of Christ in the world.

6. Sixth, the fullness of the Spirit is a foretaste of God's eternal purpose. All creation will be filled with God's glorious presence. There will be no place for sin and death, no place for darkness and sorrow. God's good Spirit will completely, perfectly, totally inhabit the cosmos, and all the Father's children, forever and ever with the Lord Jesus Christ.

Spirit baptism and the Spirit's fullness as understood and experienced by Pentecostals today is part of a unitary whole with overall redemptive purpose and experience. Pentecostal ministry, spirituality, and theology are based on a coherent and consistent vision of faith in Christ and the life it engenders in the Holy Spirit. Invitations to share in the fullness of life in God are amicable and appropriate.

8

A Full Gospel Theological and Pastoral Paradigm

As already noted, Pentecostals commonly describe the core essentials of their movement in terms of fivefold gospel commitment to Jesus Christ as Savior, Sanctifier, Spirit Baptizer, Healer, and Soon Coming King. John Sims calls this framework the "full-gospel heritage."[1] I readily concede that no single theological tradition fully captures the entire essence of Christianity. Such a claim would be both arrogant and ignorant.[2] The full gospel is truly fuller than anyone one group or movement can adequately embody. For example, the Mennonite heritage distinctively emphasizes "the standard of full gospel reform."[3] In it I recognize and admire a commitment refusing to settle for halfway measures. Thereby I am challenged to expand my own horizons.

---

1. Sims, *Our Pentecostal Heritage,* 61, 63. According to Cossey, "What is a Full Gospel Church?," 12, A. J. Tomlinson, an early leader in the Church of God (Cleveland, TN), identified the Pentecostal movement with "the preaching of a full gospel" as early as June 22, 1908. Cossey himself, "What is a Full Gospel Church?" 12–13, describes a full gospel church as one which believes in modern miracles, ongoing operation of spiritual gifts, the "second blessing" of Spirit baptism, the priority of the great commission, and the authority of Scripture.

2. Macchia, "Theology," 1124. As Yong says in his Preface to *Pentecostal Theology and N. T. Wright,* "even Pentecostals who proclaim a 'fivefold' or 'full' gospel often still are not as holistic as they might be," and yet it is "the full gospel that includes the charismatic and empowering work of the Holy Spirit that transforms even to the ends of the earth," xii.

3. Bender, "Mennonite Origins."

Yet I remain firmly convinced that the Pentecostal version of the full gospel offers a great deal that is needful and valuable today. As we proceed, it is important to remember Vondey's observation that "full gospel" is not a depiction of a set of doctrinal propositions, for example, an *ordo salutis,* so much as a narrative of how Pentecostals experience the gospel or, put another way, participate in the gospel.[4] In a word, the patterns in the full gospel "form a narrative framework for identifying the centrality of encountering Christ in several underlying experiences of the Holy Spirit."[5] In the following I will look at each of these five full gospel emphases one by one with an eye toward their place in the overall schema. I do not attempt a thorough explication of any; rather, I offer a theological description of Pentecostal applications.

SALVATION

When it comes to conversion Pentecostals generally affirm traditional Protestant/Evangelical conceptions of such matters as faith, repentance, justification (forgiveness, pardon), adoption, regeneration (new birth), and assurance (of forgiveness of sins and the gift of eternal life)—although clearly from a Wesleyan-Arminian rather than Calvinist/Reformed perspective.[6] Essentially, salvific conversion occurs by God's grace through faith in Jesus Christ as crucified and risen Lord and Savior (Rom 10:9; Eph 2:8–10; Titus 2:11–14).[7] Especially recently, there is coming to be more emphasis on pneumatological dynamics of justification which without denying Protestant Reformation views on forensic or transactional elements nevertheless accents the participatory and transformational (1 Cor 6:11; 1 Tim 3:16).[8] For Pentecostals conversion involves making peace with God (reconciliation) through faith in Jesus Christ and becoming a new creation by the Spirit's life-changing power (Rom 5:1; 2 Cor 5:17).

---

4. Vondey, "Pure Gospel or Full Gospel," 326, 330, 331. Vondey's article helpfully articulates how differing hermeneutical concerns foster differing paradigms, viz., the Lutheran "pure gospel" concern with doctrine and the Pentecostal "full gospel" concern with experience. Dayton, *Theological Roots,* while agreeing that the constellation forms the gestalt of Pentecostalism, describes "Full Gospel" as a fivefold doctrinal pattern with the terms "Latter Rain," "Apostolic," and "Pentecostal" indicating the coherent infrastructure of the message, 25–28.

5. Vondey, "Pure Gospel or Full Gospel," 329. Accordingly, while one observes that the Pentecostal full gospel paradigm is Christocentric it is certainly not Christomonist. Rather, it is a Christocentric-pneumatic orientation.

6. Sims, *Our Pentecostal Heritage,* 63, 68. As Black, *Apostolic Theology,* 715–31, exemplifies, Pentecostal groups attempting to acclimate to Calvinist themes such as perseverance of the saints and unconditional election do exist; but they are rare and, in my assessment, wrestle with theological inconsistencies.

7. Arrington, *Christian Doctrine,* 2:209–27.

8. Macchia, *Justified in the Spirit,* 14, 75, 86, 202, and Bernard, *Justification and the Holy Spirit,* 11–12, 112–15, 117, 121.

Yet for Pentecostals salvation is not limited to conversion—that is, to forgiveness and entry into a new relationship with God in Christ.[9]

For Pentecostals salvation is also freedom, recovery, and victory. Salvation is freedom from bondage, recovery from disaster, and victory over evil. In short, salvation is *deliverance* (Col 1:13; 1 Thess 1:10; 2 Tim 4:18). Therefore, Cheryl Johns and Jackie Johns rightly describe a Pentecostal soteriological model as inclusive of "both deliverance from sin and participation in the divine life."[10] For Pentecostal theologian Dale Coulter, divine life is liberating deliverance.[11] As Arrington notes, "The basic meaning of salvation is deliverance from a situation out of which a person cannot rescue himself or herself."[12] Thus the saving work of Christ delivers believers from the debilitating domination of "this present evil age" (Gal 1:4). Deliverance involves rescue from confinement or enslavement, danger or peril, deprivation or lack, evil entities and forces, violent destruction, and so on. Most of all, that is, in an ultimate sense, salvation is deliverance from the judgment of eternal damnation. In a very real sense salvation is emancipation from the binding, hindering restraints of this diabolical, sinful world order—thereby enabling the redeemed to serve God in joyful freedom with their authentic humanity.

Paradigmatic models which may serve as primary indicators of distinctive Pentecostal soteriological emphases include the exodus of Israel, the ministries of Jesus and of the apostles, and *Christus Victor* atonement theology. Historic Christianity has long drawn on the exodus tradition in its self-definition regarding the implications of the incarnation and atonement of Jesus Christ.[13] Similarly, African American spirituality and theology, immensely influential in the Pentecostal movement, draws from the liberative elements of the biblical narrative in an embrace of God as emancipator.[14] These historic trajectories are firmly rooted in Scripture. Pentecostal NT commentator James Shelton explains that Matthew's Gospel presents the ministry of Jesus in terms of the exodus deliverance as its fulfillment and as an indicator of the nature of God's saving acts.[15] Arrington delineates parallels in Acts between Moses and Jesus with Israel's deliverance prefiguring "God's mighty saving act from our bondage through Christ."[16] Pentecostal theologian Daniel Pecota stresses the nature of Christian salva-

---

9. Constantineanu and Scobie, *Pentecostal Theology in the 21st Century*, 5.

10. Johns and Johns, "Life in the New Creation," 173. Cp. Johns and Johns, "Life in the New Creation," 175–77.

11. Coulter, "Delivered by the Power of God," 447–67.

12. Arrington, *Christian Doctrine*, 2:160. In another vein, Pentecostals describe exorcism as specialized "deliverance ministry," McClung, "Exorcism," 624–28.

13. Kärkkäinen, *Spirit and Salvation*, 291.

14. Alexander, *Black Fire*, 39, 40. The exodus tradition is particularly prominent in this emphasis, portraying a God of freedom who befriends and defends the oppressed and sends his Son as liberator even as he calls forth obedience from his people. See Fields, *Black Theology*, 18, 31, 87–88.

15. Shelton, "Matthew," 139–40.

16. Arrington, *Spirit-Anointed Church*, 146.

tion as rooted in the experience of deliverance arising out of the exodus event and ongoing deliverance themes throughout Israel's subsequent salvation history.[17] Divine deliverance occurs in natural/physical, legal, or spiritual contexts but with emphasis on the spiritual. YHWH's deliverance or salvation of Israel out of the hands of the Egyptians is prototypical of Christian salvation and anticipates the mission of Jesus Christ to seek and to save or deliver the lost in setting rescued captives free (Luke 19:10; 4:16–19).

Predominant during patristic times, *Christus Victor* theology is a comfortable fit for contemporary Pentecostals.[18] *Christus Victor* emphasizes the nature of Christ's atonement as a ransom (Mark 10:45; 1 Tim 2:6). Christ's atonement effectively defeated the devil (Heb 2:24; Col 2:15; Rev 5:5). Death and Hell have been conquered (1 Cor 15:54–57; Rev 1:18). As promised by God, the seed of the woman (the Messiah) has crushed the head of the serpent (Satan) (Gen 3:15). For Pecota "Seeing the Atonement as the victory over all the forces of evil must always be a vital part of our victorious proclamation of the gospel."[19] Likewise Larry Hart underscores that "the concept of the atonement as a cosmic conflict and divine victory is central to the New Testament witness and the faith of the Church."[20] In the exodus event YHWH delivered Israel from Pharaoh and Egyptian bondage thus setting them on their journey toward the Promised Land flowing with milk and honey. At Calvary Christ delivered Christians from bondage to sin, death, and the devil thus setting them on their way to glory. Salvation is deliverance, rescue, from bitter servitude to evil and its attendant afflictions for the sake of freely serving the Lord and enjoying the abundance of divine blessings as heirs of eternal glory and joy.

What does salvation-as-deliverance mean for Pentecostal identity and ministry? Note a few brief observations. First, salvation has an *antagonistic element*. Life is a battle, often an intense conflict involving sustained struggle. Evil is real. Actual survival—here and hereafter—is on the line. Second, salvation has a *cosmic context*. Individual believers and communities of faith are integral parts of a larger, panoramic, even universal-sized scale of events and issues in which their own fates play a significant role in the ultimate outcome. Third, salvation has an *impossible scenario*. Hopeless against insurmountable odds, helpless in the face of inconceivable opposition, inadequate to the point of absurdity, unable to accomplish the effects necessary for their own existence and flourishing. Disaster, destruction, is inevitable—and usually, imminent. Finally, and most of all, salvation has an *omnicompetent champion*. The all-powerful, all-wise, all-good God dramatically and totally defeats all the forces of evil. God completely rescues and abundantly blesses those who believe, those who put their trust in God and obey God's will.

17. Pecota, "Saving Work of Christ," 325–29.
18. The classic study is Gustaf Aulén, *Christus Victor*.
19. Pecota, "Saving Work of Christ," 339.
20. Hart, *Truth Aflame*, 364.

Pentecostals believe the devil and his demons are malevolently bent on destroying them, and ultimately, through sin and death, on damning them, as part of evil's arrogant rebellion against the holy and righteous God, and that they are totally unable to rescue themselves or win victory. Pentecostals believe the good news of the gospel is that the benevolent and loving God has graciously accomplished their deliverance through their crucified and risen Lord and Savior Jesus Christ. Pentecostals believe that God empowers them by the Holy Spirit for divine mission and service until the destined consummation of God's purpose in the triumphant return of his Son Jesus Christ.

Given the preceding it should not be surprising that Pentecostalism has been credited with bringing about a remarkable renewal of interest in "spiritual warfare."[21] Spiritual warfare understands the Christian life as ongoing conflict between good and evil, the kingdom of God and the kingdom of Satan, and that malevolent beings bent on human ill must be withstood and overcome in faith, obedience, and prayer. The basic premise of spiritual warfare is certainly biblically correct (2 Cor 10:3–6; Eph 6:10–18). However, perhaps nowhere else is Pentecostal openness to the spirit world more prone to error or abuse. Intricately developed and highly speculative demonologies and strategies for dealing with them are by nature susceptible to excesses.[22] Moderation is in order. Gilbert's advice is well taken: focus should always be on the reality of God rather than on the demonic; inordinate power must not to be attributed to demons but neither should they be dismissed as harmless; and, the ethical dimensions of spiritual struggles and the allegiances they entail are best addressed only "with the supernatural help of the Holy Spirit."[23]

That being said, the life of faith does involve ongoing spiritual power encounters between good and evil with personal and/or individual and social and/or institutional consequences.[24] The ultimate demonstration of God's triumphant power in the resurrection of Jesus Christ and its unparalleled manifestation at Pentecost in the outpouring of the Holy Spirit empowers and equips believers for victorious service, positively, in Christian mission, and negatively, against all evil in whatever form it takes. Whether spiritual or physical, whether individual or social, all evil is overcome through active faith in Jesus by the power of Spirit. In addition to personal salvation and flourishing, the power of the Holy Spirit sustains resistance to oppression of other kinds, including economic and racial. Assuredly Pentecostal salvation-as-deliverance is both otherworldly and this-worldly. But this life is fixed on and framed by the life to come—by eternity, by Heaven and Hell—and not the other way around (Matt 12:32; Luke 18:30; Rev 20:11–15).

---

21. Gilbert, "Spiritual Warfare," 847.
22. Kraft, "Spiritual Warfare," 1095–96. Elaborate demonologies and so-called "mapping strategies" are more typical of Charismatics than of Classical Pentecostals.
23. Gilbert, "Spiritual Warfare," 850.
24. Hetzel, "Power," 696–700.

Finally, we should note resonance of Pentecostal salvation-as-deliverance theology with non-Western, Global South, Majority World Christians.[25] An African Yoruba chieftain once told me that he feared and resented Pentecostals more than any other Christians for this very reason. According to him, Yoruba belief in a complex cosmology of spirit entities makes its adherents vulnerable to Pentecostal beliefs and practices addressing those same realities from a Christian perspective. However, he defiantly argued that he viewed the result as more of a syncretistic mix than a clearly Christian religion. ("Even when they become Christian they are still Yoruba!") Nevertheless, research indicates that Pentecostal emphases on the Holy Spirit's power as experienced in Spirit baptism, speaking in tongues, spiritual gifts, and so on, have transformed notions of power among many traditional Africans, including Nigerians, the heartland of Yoruba religious devotion.[26] This is a repetitive phenomenon throughout the Global South. *Christians* in these areas often retain an enspirited worldview reminiscent of an indigenous tradition but transformed by *Pentecostals* into a deliberately biblical perspective. (One could say: "These Christians are not still Yoruba after all; rather, they are Pentecostal!")

SANCTIFICATION/HOLINESS

Chapter Two of this work examines in some depth the controversial nature of sanctification in the development of Pentecostal identity and ministry. But sanctification at its heart involves spiritual formation. Spiritual formation generally describes an intentional process of development and growth nurturing a life of holiness and human wholeness in the context of relationship with God and service to the church and the world.[27] While focusing on prayer, scripture reading, public worship, and other spiritual disciplines, spiritual formation also takes seriously insights from the human sciences, especially psychology, aimed at human integration. Spiritual formation is concerned with "the radical transformation of the self" with the goal of the spiritual formation journey always directed toward "self-awareness in relationship to God, and under the transformative power of grace."[28] Eschatologically, such transformation involves the exchange of the love and preoccupation of this temporal world order and its values for the abiding realities of the age to come.[29]

25. E.g., Muzorewa, *African Theology,* 85–86.

26. Hetzel, "Power," 698–99.

27. In the 4th century, Jerome's discussion of spiritual formation in Gal 4:19 describes believers as infants who are led "by diligent nourishment and study, up to the full maturity of Christ." *ACCS: Galatians,* 65.

28. E.g., Simmonds, "Formation, Spiritual," 310.

29. As both Origen (3rd cent.) and Theodoret of Cyr (5th cent.) argued from Rom 12:2, *ACCS: Romans,* 308–09. Lamar Vest, *Reflections,* 150, 152, who served as Presiding Bishop of the Church of God (Cleveland, TN), Chairman of the National Association of Evangelicals, President of the American Bible Society, President of Pentecostal Theological Seminary, and many other leadership roles, has

Notably, based on the Pauline usage of πνευματικός (*pneumatikos*) Gordon Fee argues compellingly that any biblical understanding of anything spiritual, including spiritual formation, must rely on the essential qualifying factor of the Holy Spirit's agency. His statement that "Spirituality without the Holy Spirit becomes a feeble human project" helpfully orients a Pentecostal ministerial theology of spiritual formation.[30] Spiritual formation is neither a faith-based self-help program nor a works-oriented spirituality. Life in the Spirit means that "the Spirit is both the 'locus' and the 'enabler' of our lives as believers."[31] Therefore, we might argue that spiritual formation entails an experiential process of "becoming more aware of the person and role of the Spirit in every aspect of Christian life."[32] Spiritual formation is not "spiritual" only because it addresses the spiritual side of humanity but because it arises out of the agency of God's Spirit.

Sanctification is not simply a doctrine or an experience (though it is both) but a description of Christ being formed in believers as they are transformed in accordance with God's will (Gal 4:19; Rom 12:1–2). Sanctification means that those who are converted (justified and regenerated) live holy lives according to God's calling in Christ for all believers (1 Thess 4:1–8). For most Pentecostals commitments to holiness and sanctification are fundamentally practical affirmations of the necessity of godly, righteous conduct rooted in Christ's atonement and in the work of the Holy Spirit (Luke 1:75; 1 Cor 1:30; 2 Thess 2:13; Heb 12:14). It is the privilege and responsibility of the redeemed to cooperate with God's grace through obedient faith for the actual accomplishment of God's holy will in their daily life (Phil 2:12–13). A holy life may be generally defined as wholehearted adherence to the great commandments of loving God and neighbor (Luke 10:27). Additionally, a holy life, a life that truly pleases God, includes social benevolence as well as personal purity (Jas 1:27).

The seriousness of holiness and sanctification can hardly be emphasized enough. God's grace and mercy toward sinners through the Lamb of God is the good news of the gospel. However, "the other end of the dialectic" expressed in the exclusion of those who reject Christ and rather embrace sinful lifestyles is also underscored.[33] Scripture is certain that nothing (or no one) that is unclean or impure (unholy) will dwell in the Lord's presence in eternity (Heb 12:14; Rev 21:27; 22:14–15). During the present age churches are warned against the eschatologically damnable consequences

---

expressed suspicion regarding his movement's traditional definitions of "worldliness." Admittedly, NT teachings (e.g., Rom 12:2; 1 John 2:15–17) on living distinctly from this present world order have been applied rigorously but somewhat indiscriminately. Land, "Pentecostal Spirituality," 486, well clarifies that the world as God's creation is good but the "interlocking systems and structures arrayed in rebellion against Christ the King" are not—nevertheless the mission of redemption "is here and now in *this* created, fallen, redeemed, and being-consummated world."

30. Fee, "Getting the Spirit Back into Spirituality," 42.
31. Fee, "Getting the Spirit Back into Spirituality,," 44.
32. Fee, "Getting the Spirit Back into Spirituality,," 44.
33. Thomas, *The Apocalypse*, 658.

of immorality and impurity (1 Cor 6:8-0). Much of Western culture winks at wickedness. The full gospel message of sanctification reminds both that God does not overlook sin and that God has amply provided for sin's remedy and cure. God's command to be holy in all we say or do arises out of God's own character (1 Pet 1:15-16). It is therefore unchanging, irrevocable.

However, in the Pentecostal tradition legalism has been a real and recurring problem.[34] Theologically it may be argued that the movement has exhibited a tendency toward Pelagianism (after a fourth/fifth century British monk who purportedly stressed the primacy of human ability and effort), perhaps inherited from more extreme elements in the Holiness tradition. Like many other youth overreactions to the mistake of many in assuming that somehow harshness equals holiness drove me away from the faith of my Holiness-Pentecostal parents. I vividly recall telling some folks "You are stricter than God!" I have heard it said that it is better to overshoot than undershoot. But I would point out that either way we miss the target. And "missing the mark" is what the Bible calls "sin" (ἁμαρτία or *hamartia*). Some sin by being too soft. Others sin by being too hard. Either way missing the mark of God's standard of living is still sin.[35]

My journey home to the faith of my fathers and mothers included acquiring an increasing appreciation for "true righteousness and holiness" (Eph 4:24). Here the standard is not some list of manmade rules; rather, it is God's own image and likeness as revealed in Christ reflected in us by the Spirit.[36] I have concluded that our general culture today, including a lot of church culture, appears to be more in danger from antinomianism than from legalism or Pelagianism. (Yet as stated above, we must assiduously avoid either error.) Antinomianism, from the Greek ἀντί (*anti*) "against" plus νόμος (*nomos*) "law"), theologically describes any position claiming that since we are saved by grace we can dispense with the moral demands of the law. The NT combats this aberration repeatedly (Rom 3:31; 6:14-15; 7:12; 1 Tim 1:8; Jas 2:8). The justifying grace of God received in conversion anticipates and initiates the sanctifying grace of God—but all is saving grace nonetheless (Eph 2:8-10; Titus 2:11-14). The gracious favor which forgives is the same gracious power which transforms. Sadly (but not surprisingly), holiness advocates often find it incredibly difficult to gain a fair hearing. Yet the burden of presenting holiness properly, that is, without the old baggage, in terms persuasive for these times, rests upon all today's preachers and teachers.[37]

---

34. I greatly appreciate when Bernard, *In Search of Holiness*, well says that "The Christian life is one of faith and liberty, not of legalism and drudgery," 27. For him, legalism is a failure to attain unto true holiness on several fronts, *Practical Holiness*, 61-63, which minimizes holiness in the life of believers, 63-64.

35. Thus Bernard, *Practical Holiness*, 131-32, insists that, "holiness people today should maintain their ground against the onslaught of worldliness and compromise." Bernard argues, *Practical Holiness*, 129-31, somewhat courageously and certainly correctly, that high moral standards in some non-Christian religions put many Christians in the West to shame—although he is quick to point out that their adherents are not justified by good behavior.

36. As Marius Victorinus said in the 4th cent., *ACCS: Ephesians*, 174.

37. Randy Howard and I co-wrote *Pentecostal Explorations of Holiness Today* with the objective of

Accordingly, we do well to hear the conclusion of Pentecostal theologian Jackie Johns that "membership in the family of God requires discipline and transforming encounters with God."[38] In sum, sanctification involves both specific transformational episodes and sustained formational processes. Redemption through Jesus Christ transforms the totality of human being and existence as the Holy Spirit works in individual hearts and lives refashioning them into the image and likeness of God (2 Cor 5:17; 2 Thess 2:13).[39] It is crucial to understand that whatever "training in righteousness" believers undergo is set within this redemptive context (2 Tim 3:16).[40] As Pentecostal NT scholar Karen Holley's study of John's Gospel and the First Epistle of John describes it, cleansing and sanctification is the work of the Father and of the Holy Spirit with the death of Jesus as the basis for the forgiveness and cleansing of human sin.[41] Thus, believers become what humans were originally created to be, and enjoy intimate communion and union with their Creator, Redeemer, and Sanctifier forever and ever.

As Wright so well says on creation and formation in God's image as Christians' *vocation*:

> The point about sin, therefore, is not just that it incurs moral guilt (though it does), but that it jeopardises the divine plan for creation. The point about redemption, therefore, is not just that it restores us to fellowship with God (though it does) but that it sets us on our feet again, and provides us with the Spirit, so that we can already, hear and now, be new-creation people: new creations in ourselves, and the means of new creation in the world.[42]

And that statement may say more all at once about the "what" and the "why" of holiness and sanctification than almost anything else one might hear or read all together.

SPIRIT BAPTISM

Without doubt Pentecostal teaching on the baptism with the Holy Spirit is the most distinctive and well-known marker of the movement. Pentecostals derive their doctrinal emphasis on Spirit baptism directly from the Scriptures (e.g., Matt 3:11; Mark 1:8; Luke 3:1:16; John 1:33; Acts 1:5). A joint statement on the "Essence of Pentecostalism" is worth quoting in its entirety.

---

assisting church leaders and pastors in the task of ably presenting holiness to their congregations and other listeners.

38. Johns, *Pedagogy of the Holy Spirit*, 153.
39. Johns, *Pedagogy of the Holy Spirit*, 98, 100.
40. Johns, *Pedagogy of the Holy Spirit*, 129–30.
41. Holley, "Johannine Theology of Sanctification," 238–48.
42. Wright, "The Word and the Wind," 145. Accordingly, we might say that between creation and new creation is formation which serves as a proleptic participation in the new creation.

> It is the personal and direct awareness and experiencing of the indwelling of the Holy Spirit by which the risen and glorified Christ is revealed and the believer is empowered to witness and worship with the abundance of life described in Acts and the Epistles. The Pentecostal experience is not a goal to be reached, not a place to stand, but a door through which to go into a greater fullness of life in the Spirit. It is an event which becomes a way of life in which often charismatic manifestations have a place. Characteristic of this way of life is a love of the Word of God, fervency in prayer and witness in the world and to the world, and a concern to live by the power of the Holy Spirit.[43]

I find this an apt description of basic Pentecostal identity. It is well set within the larger context of Christian faith without diminishing Pentecostal emphases. Additionally, it is consistent with the theology of fullness that this work has set forth in the preceding.

But to be more specific, Pentecostals believe in the baptism with the Holy Spirit as an experience subsequent to conversion which is signified by speaking in tongues (initial evidence); as an endowment of power for Christian mission and service, especially evangelism and witnessing; and, finally, as an entry point for the operation of spiritual gifts (charismata).[44] Chapters Nine through Twelve of this work look closely at Pentecostals' distinctive doctrines of subsequence and evidentiary tongues as well as the charismatic and vocational nature of Spirit baptism. The present section focuses on the underlying presupposition for those doctrines; namely, for Pentecostals Spirit baptism functions as a symbolic marker for the priority of personally experiencing the Holy Spirit as an active agent in believers' lives today.

In contemporary parlance, we might say that Spirit baptism terminology is a cultural signifier within Pentecostalism. What do I mean by "cultural signifier"? Barbara Wallraff explains.

> The idea is that the linguistic fine points we pay attention to — the accent we have, the vocabulary we use, the knowledge of traditional grammar we exhibit — say something about us. They hint at both the culture we come from and our place in that culture, and there's no getting away from this.[45]

The crucial substance of linguistic cultural signifiers is not found in their grammatical construction or phonetic precision but in the meaning which they convey within

---

43. Kärkkäinen, *Holy Spirit and Salvation*, 367 (quoting from "Essence of Pentecostalism" Statement by the Pentecostal Team at the International Dialogue between Roman Catholics and Pentecostals at Horgen, Switzerland, 1972).

44. Sims, *Our Pentecostal Heritage*, 105–06, 112–23.

45. Wallraff, "Walking the Walk = Talking the Talk." If "Christianity resembles a culture with its own distinctive language, practices, and systems of meaning," MacGregor, *Contemporary Theology*, 328 (on Lindbeck's theology of language), then the meaning-imparting power of cultural signifiers may be amplified.

the group.[46] Allowing for transposition, Spirit baptism functions comparably within Pentecostal circles.

In sum, Pentecostals believe the Holy Spirit still speaks and acts today just as in the Holy Bible. Thus, Pentecostals believe the Spirit still guides and leads believers. Spirit baptism is indicative of these emphases and their implications. In other words, Pentecostal teaching on baptism in the Holy Spirit amounts to an affirmation of the centrality of the Spirit's ongoing role in the lives of Christ's followers. It is unfortunate that many have become distracted by technical debates over subsequence and initial evidence to the point of missing the key importance of the Spirit in daily Christian life which is at the heart of Pentecostal belief and practice.[47] As shall be seen later, I am committed to the continuing relevance of the doctrines of subsequence and initial evidence, properly stated; however, it is critical to consider them in context as instruments or means. The Pentecostal doctrine of Spirit baptism and its attendant emphases are functional mechanisms which serve to affirm and validate the actual and active role of the Holy Spirit in the Christian way of life as Pentecostals understand it. The doctrinal flag of Spirit baptism safeguards the Day of Pentecost experience from fading into the background of Christian faith and life.

Therefore, the more crucial question is not, "Do you believe in Spirit baptism subsequent to conversion?" It is not, "Do you believe in speaking in tongues as the initial evidence of Spirit baptism?" Rather, it is, "Do you believe the Holy Spirit should be actively engaged in Christian lives today just as in the Bible?" For some Christians the answer to this question may be a simple "No." For others perhaps the answer is a qualified "Yes" or "No." For Pentecostals the answer is an emphatic and straightforward "Yes!" If we assume an affirmative response on this position, then we should see how Pentecostal doctrines of Spirit baptism and speaking in tongues function to encourage ardent expectation—and earnest aspiration! —of a definitive experience of the Holy Spirit modeled in the Day of Pentecost account.

However, if Spirit baptism is subsumed under conversion-initiation, as some non-Pentecostals are prone to do, or under ecclesiology, as others are prone to do, then emphasis on the direct, ongoing role of the Holy Spirit in individual believers is at best minimized. At the worst, it is outright marginalized. Eventually, it disappears altogether—as history shows. The phenomenal growth of Pentecostalism since the early twentieth century indicates that in Spirit baptism the movement has constructed an effective symbolic code capable of marking out or identifying and representing the Christian life as life in the Spirit and perpetuating it among adherents. I suggest that hundreds of millions of Pentecostal-type believers worldwide do not subscribe to an

---

46. An example is the word "cool." Literally, cool refers to a certain temperature. But then among youth it can also signify stylish or popular and finally that which is agreeable or acceptable. The relationship between signifier and signified is made meaningful in their group context. If one looks at signs in isolation, then misunderstanding inevitably occurs.

47. Hocken, *Pentecost and Parousia*, 131.

isolated experience; rather, they embrace a way of life that is initiated in and nourished by the Holy Spirit in the hearts of those who accept Jesus as their Spirit Baptizer.

Here Pentecostalism may need to interpret its own "tongue." However, the explanation is not cryptic after all. Many people have long asked of Pentecost, "Whatever could this mean?" (Acts 2:12) The Apostle Peter openly answered: "Therefore being exalted to the right hand of God, and having received from the Father the promise of the Holy Spirit, He poured out this which you now see and hear" (2:33). As Arrington declares, "All that is seen at Pentecost flows from the ascended Christ."[48] Pentecostals believe the exaltation of the crucified and risen Lord ushered in a new age of the Spirit which is now demonstrably present. Pentecost initiates it and encapsulates it.[49] The Pentecostal doctrine of Spirit baptism codifies it. Embedded in Pentecostals' doctrine of Spirit baptism is an entire mindset embracing life in the Holy Spirit as a present experiential reality.

Therefore, we may, indeed, we must, ask, "Is Pentecostalism's functional utilization of Spirit baptism for promoting a pneumatologically-enriched Christian faith and life a valid appropriation?" A spate of Pentecostal scholarship is ably demonstrating beyond any reasonable shadow of a doubt that the validity of the basic Pentecostal assumption that the Christian life has a pronounced pneumatic nature, and that this pneumatic Christianity has a continuing charismatic dimension, is a biblically, theologically, and historically defensible claim.[50] Furthermore, many non-Pentecostals, some of whom were former critics of Pentecostalism, now happily acknowledge positive contributions that the Pentecostal movement brings to Christianity today. Of course, not everyone agrees on everything (some never agree on anything); but, it is truly remarkable to find the broader Christian tradition affirming basic Pentecostal experience.[51] True enough, various traditions *frame* the experience according to presuppositions of their own denominational backgrounds but many of them nonetheless *claim* the experience for themselves. And that is good. That is very good.

DIVINE HEALING

Perhaps no other Pentecostal practice has generated quite the controversy with the general (both religious and secular) public as the commitment to divine healing.

---

48. Arrington, *Spirit-Anointed Church*, 85.

49. I find it fascinating that liberal Protestant theologian Harvey Cox, *Future of Faith*, 8–10, 199, makes a similar claim regarding Pentecostals albeit with different implications.

50. For just a few examples: Constantineanu and Scobie, *Pentecostal Theology in the 21st Century*; Chan, *Pentecostal Theology and the Christian Spiritual Tradition*; Mittelstadt, *Reading Luke-Acts in the Pentecostal Tradition*; and, Sims, *Our Pentecostal Heritage*.

51. Brand, *Perspectives on Spirit Baptism*, is an intriguing example. Catholic, Reformed, Wesleyan, Charismatic, and Pentecostal representatives each argued for distinctive understandings of Spirit baptism per se. However, there was remarkable agreement on experiencing the Holy Spirit, including the miraculous and spiritual gifts.

Sadly, much of the onus for that negative publicity falls squarely on the shoulders of Pentecostals themselves.[52] In misguided zeal to affirm the biblical doctrine of healing some have gone far beyond the Scriptures.[53] They made serious errors as they wrongly reasoned that if a sufferer was not healed, there must be a lack of faith or possibly hidden sin in their life. Some radicals further insisted that resorting to medical care—going to a physician or taking medicine—was a sign of a lack of faith and attached a stigma to professional healthcare. Many suffered needlessly. Some died. The public outcry was loud—and legitimate. There are far too many stories of adults and even children suffering and dying who almost surely could have lived longer, healthier lives with proper healthcare.[54]

According to Henry Knight much of the confusion and misunderstanding on divine healing arises from failure to properly place the doctrine of divine healing in the context of the theological poles of God's faithfulness and God's freedom.[55] I think Knight is right, and that his observation certainly includes erroneous views which place blame or deny medical means as well as normal human struggles when healing sometimes simply does not happen. Ideally, believers can approach circumstances of sickness with the certainty of faith even while acknowledging the sovereignty of God in and over all situations. As Ronald Kydd well says, "The healings flow from God, and God keeps his own good counsel. It is enough that we know that God looks with mercy on human pain."[56] And Pentecostals believe, and know, that God still heals. Thus, faith and wisdom are sustained together without injury to either. The blessings of healing are lifted high and made available without resorting to excessive claims.[57]

With the preceding in mind, let's press on to the basic contours of Pentecostal healing theology. Pentecostals stand squarely in the anti-gnostic tradition in affirming that creation and redemption are inclusive of materiality and physicality (which the ancient heresy of Gnosticism denies). Although many Christians throughout the ages have believed generally in divine healing, Pentecostals are direct heirs to the Holiness movement's distinctive emphasis on healing.[58] Accordingly, Pentecostals believe specifically that physical healing is a gracious provision of the atonement of Jesus Christ

---

52. Sims, *Our Pentecostal Heritage*, 83.

53. Roberts, *Divine Healing*, insisted that closer attention to Scriptures would have avoided many painful mistakes, 9–19.

54. Initially I planned to list a few cases where USA courts have challenged or charged parents who denied medical care to children because of faith healing. A search revealed so many, even, to my surprise, recent cases I decided against trying to select specific examples. Also, I do not wish to add further suffering to grieving families.

55. Knight, "God's Faithfulness and God's Freedom," 65–89. Cp. Sims, *Our Pentecostal Heritage*, 83.

56. Kydd, "Healing in the Christian Church," 698–711.

57. Roberts, *Divine Healing*, labors to give a balanced discussion. E.g., he lists many traditional considerations for receiving healing, such as prayer and faith and so on, but also lifts up recognizing medicine as a way God heals and observing natural laws for good health, 149–52 and 156.

58. Arrington, *Christian Doctrine*, 2:79–80.

which may be confidently claimed by faith. Biblically, they note clear connections of healing with the person and ministry of Jesus, including the atonement, and between healing and forgiveness/salvation (Matt 4:23; 8:16–17; 12:28). Pentecostals further note the prominent role of healing in the ministry of the NT church, especially in Acts, and a continuing connection of healing with forgiveness/salvation (Matt 10:1; Jas 5:13–16). Therefore, Pentecostals assert that Scripture teaches that the scope of salvation addresses both forgiveness of sins and healing for the whole person (Ps 103:2–3; 2 Pet 2:24).

Pentecostals do differ somewhat from their Holiness forbears on bodily healing. In addition to affirming that bodily healing is a provision of Christ's atonement Pentecostals further view healing as a manifestation of power bearing witness along with other signs and wonders to Christ's glorious gospel (Acts 4:30).[59] As is often the case, Pentecostals draw heavily on their historical roots but add their own distinctive theological twists. I will note two implications. First, the view that divine healing is a provision of the atonement calls attention to the soteriological foundation of God's compassion toward human sufferers. Second, the view that divine healing is a miraculous sign confirming the truth and validity of the gospel calls attention to the missiological aspect with implicative ecclesiological responsibilities. Let's look at these two suggestions successively.

First, a primary consideration is whether salvation is for the whole person. Pentecostals believe that salvation addresses the entire condition of the complete person in every area of life (Matt 9:22; Heb 7:25).[60] Just as sin has impacted the whole human person negatively and destructively, so salvation impacts the whole human person positively and therapeutically. In fact, we might go farther. For instance, Amos Yong argues for an expansive soteriological multidimensionality.[61] In this view the fivefold version of full gospel salvation is extensive in scope, including the personal, familial, ecclesial, material, social, cosmic, and eschatological realms of human existence. Therefore, salvation in Christ is far-reaching. It certainly is not limited to the spiritual only but includes the physical as well. Of course, divine healing as provided in the atonement does not imply mechanical or automatic reception of physical healing; it does however firmly ground healing in God's explicit redemptive purpose in Jesus Christ.

Second, it is critical to understand divine healing in the context of the church's ministry to hurting people and its overall gospel mission. Therefore, Pentecostal ecclesiology envisions the church as, among other things, a healing community.[62] The church proclaims the gospel message of salvation as forgiveness but as an intrinsic part of that very proclamation the church's demonstration of the gospel shows

---

59. Arrington, *Christian Doctrine*, 83–84.
60. Arrington, *Christian Doctrine*, 2:160–61.
61. Yong, *Spirit Poured Out on All Flesh*, 91–98.
62. Alexander, "The Pentecostal Healing Community," 183–206.

compassion for the sick. Care for the sick can include prayer for healing as well as medical care. Local Pentecostal congregations exist as diverse healing communities.[63] Wholeness (*shalom*) entails a holistic anthropology and soteriology with salvation/healing for spirit, soul, and body. Human affliction and suffering call for congregations to engage sincerely in believing prayer for healing and deliverance. Pentecostals believe that the church should offer help in the Lord for the whole person here and now as well as happiness with the Lord for all eternity.[64] Accordingly, not only forgiveness of sins and future blessedness but present healing and deliverance are intrinsic to the gospel and integral to the mission of the Church.

Having looked briefly at the basic contours of Pentecostal healing theology, it seems appropriate to draw out a few feasible theological applications. First, and foremost, divine healing is significant in relation to our doctrine of God (theology proper).[65] The God of Pentecostals is not far removed or unfeeling toward human affliction and suffering. Rather, God is compassionate and close at hand to call upon for help. Second, divine healing is significant in relation to the human person and other creatures, to all creation (anthropology and cosmology). God is not so otherworldly that material reality is outside the scope of divine concern. Rather, God's cares for the overall wellbeing of human beings and, by implication, the entire created order.

Third, divine healing is significant in relation to salvation (soteriology). The God of Pentecostals is not simply a judge seeking to pass sentence on sin. God is the Great Physician and the salvation of the Lord is therapeutic by definition and in application. Fourth, divine healing is significant in relation to eternity (eschatology). God is not inconsistent or irregular. Each specific instance of bodily healing is effectively an anticipatory witness to the bodily resurrection and to eternal enjoyment of wholeness in God's presence. And finally, divine healing is significant in relation to theology of nature (healthcare, medical science). God is not contradictory. Scriptural truth and scientific truth rightly understood and applied, both flow from the fount of the God of truth, offering strength and wisdom in life for all who truly love truth.

Before closing this topic, I would take note of a prevalent blind spot in Pentecostal healing faith and practice as it is sometimes implemented. Or perhaps I should say as it is all-too-often *not* implemented. Pentecostals typically enjoy testimonies extolling the blessings of divine healing. For example, I enjoy testifying about my son Joshua's instantaneous healing from crippled feet. As a toddler his physician diagnosed him with severe angle deformity. It would require surgery and braces. Even then running and playing or walking normally would be impossible. Yet God instantly and totally

---

63. Onyinah, "Pentecostal Healing Communities," 207–24.

64. This is all Christologically centered because, as Pope, "Why the Church Needs a Full Gospel," 272–84, has said, "the Church is the *Church* only because Jesus redeems, sanctifies, empowers, heals, and instills in us the hope for his return," 283 (italics are original).

65. I tend to agree with Pannenberg, *Introduction to Systematic Theology*, 8, 13, that our doctrine of God is of paramount importance for all theology.

healed him after an evangelist friend in a little country church revival prayed over him. An orthopedic specialist subsequently confirmed that his ankle bones were now normal. Josh never had surgery, never wore braces; but, he did play elementary school soccer and high school football. God can and does miraculously heal.

Yes, we love those kinds of testimonies. Yet not everyone is instantly healed. Admittedly, there are those who are not healed in this life at all. Authentic Pentecostal theology will be inclusive of the full range of actual life experiences. It must account for, include, and embrace those who are not yet healed.[66] It must reassure that in such cases God's sustaining grace and love are present and sufficient (2 Cor 12:9). As a pastor, I have seen the enduring, steady faith of those who were not healed immediately and completely nonetheless bear fruitful witness in remarkable manner.

Jerry Lynn grew up at New Harvest church into a tall and exceptionally strong man. Beginning when he was a young man of only thirty-eight years (in 1988) he had a series of debilitating strokes interspersed with critical heart attacks. Specialists eventually concluded that he suffered from a rare genetically transmitted blood disorder. For over two decades he wrestled almost daily with life and death. He was hospitalized frequently. The physicians repeatedly "gave up" on him, telling his wife Pat that there was nothing else that could be done, that she should prepare for the worst. Yet she never gave up. Somehow believing prayer pulled him through time and time again. His caregivers were always amazed. During all of this, Brother Jerry was a zealous witness of Jesus everywhere to everyone (literally). His unquestioning faith touched countless lives. He specifically instructed his wife and two daughters never to blame God for what happened to him. Rather, he wanted everyone to know that he knew and loved God. Before losing the power of speech and eventually becoming unable to attend services he loved to testify. He always said, "God is good!" His Lord finally (2010) took him home to glory. I preached on Jerry's favorite Bible verse at his funeral: "This *is* the day *which* the Lord hath made; We will rejoice and be glad in it" (Ps 118:24 KJV). It was a special blessing to catch just a glimpse of how his incredible faith had planted seeds of life in so many hearts. God does indeed work amazing miracles. But we should never limit God. God often works in ways beyond us.

CHRIST'S SECOND COMING

Eschatology is of inestimable significance for Pentecostal identity and ministry. Bill Faupel's now classic study of Pentecostal eschatology persuasively argues that "American Pentecostalism may be best understood as the emergence of a millenarian belief system that resulted from a paradigm-shift which took place within nineteenth-century Perfectionism."[67] His observation roots Pentecostal eschatology in its Holiness heritage. Perhaps more importantly, it also recognizes that eschatology was not

---

66. Clifton, "Dark Side of Prayer for Healing," 205–09.
67. Faupel, *Everlasting Gospel*, 18.

a peripheral factor in the rise of Pentecostalism but a singular driving force. Thus, early Pentecostals often summarized the distinctiveness of their movement's message as "the everlasting gospel" or "the gospel of the kingdom"—terms heavily laden with eschatological inferences.[68] However, as the young movement forged ahead in the face of disappointments and setbacks focus turned away from intense eschatological urgency toward growing and maintaining denominational organizations and their requisite structures. Interestingly, although it was not without a few extremes and missteps, Faupel concludes that "for Pentecostalism to remain a vital force in the twenty-first century, it must look to its origins as a source for theological and spiritual renewal.[69] If he is right, and I for one think he is, then Pentecostals must seriously (re)consider (and resuscitate?) their eschatology. And indeed, contemporary Pentecostal eschatology appears to be in something of a transitional phase.[70]

The basic contours of a typical Pentecostal eschatology are mostly straightforward (yet a bit convoluted for non-initiates). Pentecostals' efforts to ground their faith in the Scriptures above all notwithstanding, historical and cultural influences are clearly discernible.[71] Traditionally Pentecostals have adhered to a premillennial eschatology maintaining that the second coming of Christ will precede and prepare the way for a literal one-thousand-year reign of Christ on earth. For the most part that has meant belief in a pre-tribulation "rapture" (catching away) of the church to meet the Lord in the air (1 Thess 4:16–17), followed by seven years of unprecedented tribulation on earth (Matt 24:21) before the actual coming of Christ to earth (Heb 9:28), and then the millennium (Rev 20:1–6), itself followed by the judgment of the present age and establishment of the new creation (20:7–21:1), with eternal life for the righteous and eternal death (separation from the life of God, not annihilation of existence) for the wicked (Matt 25:46).

Pentecostals were closely associated with (classic) dispensationalists in the eschatological outlook outlined above. However, there were strong differences, especially with fundamentalist dispensationalists who denied healing, miracles, and spiritual gifts (cessationism), and vociferously denounced the Pentecostal movement. While Sims thinks the rift between Pentecostals and dispensationalists was "an unfortunate break," Charismatic theologian Peter Hocken goes so far as to blame dispensationalism for frustrating or sidelining "the heart of God's purpose" through the Pentecostal awakening.[72] In any case, the break likely served to free Pentecostals to develop their

---

68. Faupel, *Everlasting Gospel*, 42. Althouse, "Pentecostal Eschatology in Context," 205–31, argues that the whole full gospel paradigm has a thoroughgoing eschatological orientation.

69. Faupel, *Everlasting Gospel*, 309. Hocken, *Pentecost and Parousia*, 126–28, insists that a deeper significance of Spirit baptism lay in its associative eschatological implications.

70. As is evident throughout both Althouse, *Spirit of the Last Days,* and Althouse and Waddell, *Perspectives on Pentecostal Eschatologies*.

71. Sims, *Our Pentecostal Heritage*, 87–90.

72. Sims, *Our Pentecostal Heritage*, 90. See Hocken, *Pentecost and Parousia*, 131–32.

own views more consistently.[73] Let's look at one major option that is attractive to many Pentecostals today (including me).

Hollis Gause argues that a theology of *progressive revelation* better suits the ethos of Pentecostal eschatology.[74] Progressive revelation does not isolate and seal off biblical history as dispensationalism is prone to do. It does not engage in hermeneutical acrobatics regarding the church, Israel, and the kingdom of God as, again, dispensationalism does. Rather, progressive revelation describes an ongoing unfolding of divine disclosure throughout the biblical canon that retains a prophetic and predictive character without destroying its universal applicability while pointing to its climactic fulfillment in the eschaton.[75] A theology of progressive revelation respects the diversity-in-development of the Holy Scriptures without undercutting their overall advancement-in-continuity. Accordingly, progressive revelation does not deny miracles and charismatic gifts by relegating them to an earlier, no longer relevant age or dispensation (cessationism).

The general contours of an authentically Pentecostal eschatology are already largely in place.[76] Pentecostals view the outpouring of the Holy Spirit as sign of the end-times or "last days" that effectively places present day believers in a new age of the Spirit (Acts 2:17). Pentecostals compare the biblical Pentecost and its aftermath and the contemporary Pentecost to early or former rains and the latter rains prophesied by Joel to agrarian Israelites and identified by Peter on the Day of Pentecost (2:23, 28–32; cp. Acts 2:16–21). Therefore, Pentecostals believe the Holy Spirit enables Christians to experience in the present the power of the future and that the Spirit's present fullness is a foretaste of the coming kingdom of God (2 Cor 1:22; 5:5; Eph 1:14).[77] Thus the present age both participates in and anticipates the eschatological future through "the firstfruits of the Spirit" (Rom 8:23). This scenario signifies a "now-not yet" eschatology which receives God's future into the present even while reaching for its full completion in the eschaton. Thus, transformation is now underway through encounter with "the powers of the age to come" by the agency of the Holy Spirit (Heb 6:5).

Further, Pentecostal eschatology is an integral component of a powerful triad inseparably linking it with empowering pneumatology and an intense commitment to mission and service. More will be said about the missional purpose of Spirit baptism in a subsequent chapter. For now, it will suffice to state that the expectation, and Pentecostals argue, its actual realization, that Spirit baptism is an empowerment for vocational service, especially for evangelism and witness in these last days, has

---

73. Jessica Wilbanks, *When I Spoke in Tongues,* relates a poignant and at times painful story of the struggle of some Pentecostals to come to terms with fundamentalism of this sort.

74. Gause, *Revelation,* 18–21.

75. This idea of successive but closely related periods of time coming to their eventual fulfillment appears more compatible with how Paul uses the term "dispensation" (Eph 1:10).

76. Gause, *Revelation,* 84–86.

77. Gause, *Revelation,* 84–85.

generated a movement with unprecedented, almost unbelievable missional effectiveness (Luke 24:49; Acts 1:8).[78] The exalted Lord is pouring out the Holy Spirit upon the church in order to enable it to win lost souls prior to his imminent return.

Unfortunately, eschatology can be an area particularly prone to rampant and, often, harmful speculation. Pentecostalism has certainly seen more than its fair share of sensationalist eschatological speculators. Yet eschatology is a most important biblical theme which brings hope to many believers, including Pentecostals in particular. Eschatology instills life with transcendent meaning and directs and shapes existential purpose. The failsafe against embarrassing and misleading eschatologies is the grounding of prophetic understanding firmly in the Christian tradition biblically, historically, and theologically. Let's turn to that task now with aid from Kärkkäinen's excellent work on *Hope and Community*.

Kärkkäinen notes that eschatology, or human seeking to understand last things, persistently exhibits its presence everywhere, not only in Christianity but in other religions and even in non-theistic or secular forms.[79] Early Christians were particularly intense in their expectation of the imminent return of Jesus Christ; but, eschatological intensity waned, perhaps was even eclipsed, throughout the historical development of Christian thought.[80] More recently a wide range of disparate thinkers have sought to recover eschatology by essentially re-conceiving its core meaning and function.[81] Yet more reverent thinkers, recognizing the centrality of eschatology for the vast majority of Christians, currently are constructing balanced, mature eschatologies as well.[82] According to Kärkkäinen, it is essential to recognize that Christian eschatology distinctively offers meaningfulness to creation and hope for the future to its creatures, including and especially human beings.[83] Significantly, Christian eschatology has a uniquely transformative character.[84] Perhaps more than any other theological topic, in the study of eschatology it is important to integrate rational analysis with theological imagination and, above all else, with believing hope.[85] It is apparent that eschatology is amazingly persistent or resilient but also constantly changing shape and shifting its emphases.

---

78. Riggs, *The Spirit Himself*, 30–31, 80, 163 and Land, *Pentecostal Spirituality*, 168–69. Others are also beginning to emphasize, in their own fashion, missional empowerment through the Holy Spirit. E.g. see Leonard Allen, a prolific author out of the Stone-Campbell Restorationist movement, *Poured Out: The Spirit of God Empowering the Mission of God*. Allen, *Poured Out*, 15, insists that any diminishment of the sense of the Spirit's inbreaking presence and power "has big consequences for the church, and its mission," adding that to be filled with the Spirit is "to be lifted up out of apathy, defeat, and despair, and to become fruitful again."

79. Kärkkäinen, *Hope and Community*, 12–14. One can thus speak of "the (omni) presence of eschatology."

80. Kärkkäinen, *Hope and Community*, 9–11.

81. Kärkkäinen, *Hope and Community*, 11–12.

82. Kärkkäinen, *Hope and Community*, 13–15.

83. Kärkkäinen, *Hope and Community*, 16.

84. Kärkkäinen, *Hope and Community*, 20.

85. Kärkkäinen, *Hope and Community*, 20–22. Cp. Moltmann, *Theology of Hope*, 2, 16–22.

At this point one might ask a few hard questions. In which/whose eschatology ought we to ground our eschatology today? Or put another way, is eschatology a hopeless morass? Of course, it is not. Eschatology is complex, and can be confusing; but, is well worth the effort it takes to untangle.[86] Then, are abiding core eschatological assumptions discernible? I think so. If so, are they defensible? Yes. This brief tracing out of eschatological twists and turns aids in discerning the general shape of frequently shifting Christian eschatology (without real detail). With the general outline of Pentecostal eschatology in mind, as well as the shifting-but-persistent shape of Christian eschatology throughout church history, I offer a few proposals of my own.

Personally, I am strongly committed to five principles as essential considerations for a contemporary Pentecostal theology of last things.

- First, I am committed to divine sovereignty over the actual and ultimate eschatological outcome of history, that is, over the consummation (1 Tim 6:15). God is in charge.

- Second, I am committed to ecclesial synergy, or the role of the church in fulfilling its mission as it moves toward the eschaton (2 Pet 3:12). We have a work to do which must be done.

- Third, I am committed to the essentiality of eschatological imminence (Luke 12:40). Jesus may not come immediately but he will come momentarily.

- Fourth, I am committed to an eschatological reality inclusive of both materiality and spirituality (1 Cor 15:35–58). The cosmos and its creatures will be whole.

- Fifth, I am committed to the teleological and utilitarian nature of an eschatological transition to eternity (Ps 138:8; Isa 14:26–27). God will set all things right forever.

Admittedly, I have approached this chapter on a traditional Pentecostal emphasis on the full gospel in something of a non-traditional manner. Rather than attempt to defend it in a kind of point-by-point apologetic I have endeavored to elucidate a core reality behind it all—its ethos, its gestalt, if you will. Next, I will move on to consider specific crucial commitments without which I do not think the contemporary Pentecostal movement could have become what it is. Nor can it continue being so.

Pannenberg has offered significant contributions to contemporary eschatology as well, e.g., in his idea that the incarnational history of Jesus, especially his resurrection, is proleptic of his eschatological character. See Pannenberg, *Jesus—God and Man*, 53–66 (cp. 321, 402–03).

86. Frankly, even if one desired to dismiss eschatology altogether I seriously doubt whether it is humanly possible. Human nature appears so constituted as to require a constructive goal-oriented vision of an ideal future. In Paul's words, we are "saved by hope" (Rom 8:24–25). Interestingly, psychologist Adler, *Understanding Human Nature*, argues for the necessity of fictional finalism, teleology, and goal constructs for human health and wholeness, 15, 61, 134. Eschatological associations are easily drawn. Adler insists that "all the phenomena of our psychological existence may be described as preparations for some future situation," 15, and links universal human concerns for future preparedness for existence in an idyllic state through an intersection of psychology and religion, 77.

PART THREE

Crucial Commitments

9

The Doctrine of Subsequence

THE DOCTRINE OF SUBSEQUENCE is crucial to Pentecostal theology. It is not an overstatement that subsequence is to an extent decisive for determining the success or failure of the Classical Pentecostal movement as it has been articulated since the beginnings of the contemporary global revival. Pentecostals affirm that the *"baptism, or filling, with the Spirit is a distinct spiritual experience subsequent to conversion."*[1] Spirit baptism is a gift of God the Father through his Son Jesus Christ to believers enabling them to "walk in the truth of the gospel and in the power of the Spirit, giving loving service to Christ and to His church."[2] Pentecostals fully affirm the indwelling presence of the Holy Spirit in every convert due to regeneration (Rom 8:9; John 3:5, 6; Titus 3:5). Thus, Pentecostal ecumenist Harold Hunter rightly warns that Pentecostals "can never demean as inferior one who is not in the same circle."[3] Quite to

---

1. Arrington, *Christian Doctrine*, 3:51 (original italics). Catholic Charismatics view Spirit baptism as an experiential realization of an earlier sacramental impartation, Del Colle, "Spirit Baptism," 270, 276–79. Protestant Charismatics argue for Spirit baptism as a broader, multi-dimensional metaphor, Hart, "Spirit Baptism," 108, 167–68. For Pentecostals the crucial point remains essentially the same, Hunter, *Spirit Baptism*, 228–30.

2. Arrington, *Christian Doctrine*, 3:57. Pentecostals stress the gift nature of Spirit baptism—it is graciously endowed by God, not earned or merited. Faith, prayer, obedience, yielding, and confident expectation facilitate its reception, 85–95.

3. Hunter, *Spirit Baptism*, 231.

the contrary, Pentecostal subsequence affirms the inestimable value of all redemptive experience. Without it nothing else is even imaginable.

Yet Pentecostals do not see conversion (justification/regeneration) as a terminal point. It is not an *ending* but an *embarking*. There is more. As the Spirit was present in Jesus' life prior to the Spirit coming upon him at his baptism in Jordan as an empowerment for service (Luke 4:14), so it is with his disciples at Pentecost (Acts 1:8; 2:1–4). Pentecostals perceive a pattern of subsequence in the Book of Acts at (8:12, 15, 17; 9:9, 17; 10:44–48; 11:15, 17; 19:1–7).[4] From a pastoral perspective, the doctrine of subsequence incentivizes confessing Christians toward deeper spirituality and bolder ministry.[5] As Stanley Horton well says, being Spirit-filled is primarily about "a life wholly dedicated to God."[6] In the following we will plumb the depths of subsequence. Suffice to say here that subsequence is about much more than the timing of spiritual experience.

INTERRELATEDNESS OF REDEMPTIVE EXPERIENCES

The words "subsequent" or "subsequence" are not in the Bible. That is not to say they are unbiblical. Like "Trinity" and "Incarnation" subsequent and subsequence are shorthand or summary terms employed for describing an identifiable biblical concept. Important to bear in mind is that the term "subsequence" indicates a sequence of events or experiences by nature necessarily interrelated to that which precedes it. Thus, two errors are to be avoided. For Pentecostal theology, either to isolate Spirit baptism from or assimilate Spirit baptism into other redemptive experiences, such as regeneration or sanctification, is contrary to grammatical sense as well as to sound doctrine. However, speaking of Spirit baptism in terms of redemptive experience is not an insistence on it as a step in the order of salvation (*ordo salutis*) but recognition of its status as atonement provision—that is, it relates the work of the Holy Spirit to "the total experience of redemption."[7] More specifically, the Holy Spirit's "function in rela-

---

4. Didactic references in the Pauline corpus are marshaled to support these historical accounts (e.g., Gal 3:2; Eph 1:13–14); but Pentecostals agree with the weight of scholarship identifying Luke as both historian and theologian, Horton, "Spirit Baptism," 55–56. More recently, Menzies. "Subsequence in the Pauline Epistles," 342, has argued that although his language is different due to an emphasis on its "gift" nature, "Paul, like Luke, also highlights the need for each believer to experience a post-conversion infusion of spiritual power for ministry." Cp. 2 Tim 1:6; 1 Tim 4:14; Rom 1:11; and 1 Cor 12.

5. Even those who do not accept the doctrine of subsequence per se admit that it has been crucial to the movement, Del Colle, "A Catholic Perspective," 244. Nevertheless, Hocken, *Pentecost and Parousia*, 132–33, insists that endless debates about subsequence have become a distraction from "the fundamental significance of baptism in the Spirit."

6. Horton, *What the Bible Says*, 256–58. Nevertheless, Pearlman, *Knowing the Doctrines of the Bible*, describes Spirit baptism as "a baptism of power," which "is charismatic in character, judging from the descriptions of the results of the impartation," 312–13.

7. Gause, *Living in the Spirit*, 68.

tion to salvation" is as earnest, firstfruits, and seal (Eph 1:13–14).[8] Therefore, the gift of the Holy Spirit is the present foretaste and demonstrative assurance guaranteeing the full glory that is finally to come only eschatologically.

Hollis Gause points out four common bases unifying redemptive experiences.[9] First, all redemptive experiences are through the provision our Lord Jesus Christ. Second, All the benefits of divine grace are received by faith. Third, the Word of God is central to all redemptive experience. And, fourth, the personal agent for the realization and application of all redemptive benefits is the Holy Spirit. Accordingly, there is an underlying and overarching unity of all redemptive experiences, including justification, adoption, repentance, regeneration, sanctification, and, yes, Spirit baptism. Thus, Gause insists that "Pentecostal theology must unify its doctrines of salvation and baptism with the Holy Spirit."[10] His statement suggests Pentecostals have not always done this as well as we might have and challenges us to begin doing it better.

Ironically, I have observed a tendency by some Pentecostals to distance Spirit baptism from conversion as a defensive mechanism in response to two objections to their belief. First, Pentecostals have reacted to those who insist that Spirit baptism is merely another term for conversion. This position argues that everyone receives Spirit baptism when they are born again, and thus denies subsequence. Pentecostals argue that according to Acts (see below) Spirit baptism follows conversion and cannot therefore be correctly identified with conversion. Second, Pentecostals have responded against those who accuse them of making Spirit baptism as accompanied by speaking in tongues the litmus test of salvation. Of course, Pentecostal theology does not teach that only those who experience Spirit baptism and speaking in tongues are saved. Neither are Pentecostals comfortable with brushing aside Spirit baptism as optional or unimportant. Most Pentecostals would probably agree with Gause that "All of the prior experiences in redemption anticipate and are culminated in the baptism with the Holy Spirit."[11] Thus we affirm the inherent unity of soteriology and of pneumatology without collapsing either into the other.

Yet Gause asserts that Spirit baptism is a distinctive experience. As the pinnacle of a mountain is distinct from the path leading to it so Spirit baptism is distinct from redemptive experiences which anticipate it. As the pinnacle and the mountain are integral to each other so the prior redemptive experiences are "bound up in the life of the Spirit."[12] So then, Spirit baptism is distinguishable from regeneration, for example, or from sanctification, for another. Baptism with the Holy Spirit has its own special quality, content, purpose, and attractiveness. It is notable in and of itself as itself. Yet Spirit baptism never stands alone. Commitment to distinctions between regeneration

---

8. Gause, *Living in the Spirit*, 67.
9. Gause, *Living in the Spirit*, 12.
10. Gause, *Living in the Spirit*, 15 (2004 ed.).
11. Gause, *Living in the Spirit*, 5.
12. Gause, *Living in the Spirit*, 5.

and sanctification from each other and from Spirit baptism must never lead to fragmentation in our life in the Spirit. We must never forfeit the unity of redemptive provision and experience.[13] Concomitantly, we must never assume Spirit baptism is merely a synonym for Christian initiation or for conversion.

Spirit baptism doctrine rather reminds me of the delicate balance required in the doctrine of the Trinity. If we lean too far toward unity we are prone to deny the rich diversity and variety of the Triune God, "creating" a truncated Deity. If we lean too far toward plurality we run the risk of tri-theism—and thus a "Christian" version of ancient idolatry. Only by emphasizing both unity and diversity are we doing justice to the doctrine of the Trinity. Regarding Spirit baptism, if we isolate Spirit baptism from other redemptive experiences we destroy the soteriological foundation of the Christian life. If we assimilate Spirit baptism into other redemptive experiences, we (at best) diminish or perhaps (at worst) decimate the pneumatological vitality and energy of the Christian life and its missional effectiveness. Only by recognizing that Spirit baptism exists in unity with all redemptive experiences while nonetheless exhibiting its own distinctive contribution to Christian life and service are we able to do the doctrine and experience of Spirit baptism due justice.

Perhaps it will be helpful to note that the Pentecostal doctrine of subsequence articulates a logical distinction rather than a necessary temporal differentiation. To illustrate my point, I share a testimony about the experiences of my mother and one of my sisters in receiving Spirit baptism. My mother, God rest her soul, used to enjoy telling me about when as a teenage girl she had a powerful encounter with the Lord. In her words, she was "saved, sanctified, and filled with the Holy Ghost" all in one night's church service. She went up to the altar to receive Jesus as her Savior and it all kind of happened at once. As I young believer in my twenties who had not yet received the baptism in the Holy Spirit, I asked her to describe how she understood her experience. She explained that she felt like a little child, finding it easy to yield to God's Spirit. Many years later, her daughter and my sister, Sharon, a teenage girl at the time, too, was saved in a Sunday night revival service but received Spirit baptism on Tuesday—two nights later in the same series of revival services.

There was no contradiction between the two experiences of my mother and my sister. Due to the unity of redemptive experiences there was no reason Mom could not be converted and baptized in the Spirit in the same moment. Due to the distinctiveness of each redemptive experience there was no reason my sister could not (or should not) have a brief time lapse between her conversion and her Spirit baptism. The length of that time lapse may vary for individuals. However, whether it all happens in an instant or over a longer time span, the redemptive experiences are still unified but distinct.

Further, the Pentecostal doctrine of subsequence has a pastoral aspect to it. When one who understands him/herself to be a believer, that is, to have experienced conversion and to be living as a follower of Jesus Christ, reads the Bible it is conceivable

---

13. Gause, *Living in the Spirit*, 13.

that they may be struck with the intense spirituality of believers whose stories the Scriptures recount.[14] If the reader has not had a similar experience there are a number of possible conclusions they may reach. For example, they may conclude that such experiences are only for an elite few, that is, for exalted saints or special servants of God—kind of "super" Christians. This is the general view of traditional (e.g. Roman Catholic/Eastern Orthodox) hagiography which identifies "saints" by, among other things, the presence of the miraculous in their lives. Average or normal Christians are not to expect such experiences. Or for another instance, they may conclude that the biblical accounts are simply false. Such ones argue for the demythologization of the Bible. Supernatural elements in the Scriptures are assessed as mere myths held by naïve and superstitious ancestors. Therefore, miracles must be eliminated by people today who are more enlightened about such matters. Others may conclude that although such experiences were once common among believers as the Bible was being written, they no longer occur or are to be expected now that we have the complete Bible. This is the basic assumption of cessationism which I have already mentioned.

A Pentecostal might raise several objections to the preceding conclusions (or really, assumptions). The most basic objection would probably be that each of these arises from a distorted (that is, deficient) view of the Bible which is actually, at least to a large extent, driven by various self-serving agendas.[15] For example, arguably the hagiographical approach arose as a result of hierarchical and institutional developments of ecclesiology in post-patristic Christianity in which church administrators sought to gain control and consolidate their power. Additionally, one might argue that the outright rejection of the miraculous as myths results from post-Enlightenment philosophical and scientific reduction of reality to materialism—a move already seriously challenged by contemporary philosophy and science (e.g. postmodernism). In this case, scholars gained unprecedented supremacy over the "ignorant" masses. Cessationism, although existing beforehand, was embraced and propagated by Protestant reformers and many of their heirs as a defense against Catholic claims to the miraculous. Thus, the Holy Spirit could be confined to the text and then controlled by interpreters. Cessationism has subsequently been further influenced by modernism as well and prone to similar pitfalls. None of these options are acceptable for Pentecostals because of their commitment to the inspiration, integrity, and authority of the Holy Scriptures.

However, if when the reader of the Scriptures notices the intense spirituality of many of the believers whose stories it recounts, he/she may come to another conclusion. If they conclude that the Bible is both accurate and relevant, then they would not be blamed if they wonder why their own experience does not match that of their

14. Lewis, *Miracles,* 3, describes how philosophical presuppositions, e.g. naturalism, even experienced Bible scholars bring to the text can greatly influence their reading of Scripture's miraculous accounts.

15. Arrington, *Christian Doctrine,* 1:25, says "Convinced the Scriptures are God's Word, Pentecostals uphold the authority of the precious written Word and accept it as completely trustworthy for faith and conduct."

biblical counterparts. Two possible answers may come to them. First, they may suspect that their Christian experience is not authentic. Or second, they may suspect that it is incomplete. In the first case, they could become disillusioned. In the second, they could become stimulated. The Pentecostal doctrine of subsequence exhibits great pastoral sensitivity in that it assures those who have truly trusted Jesus as their Savior and Lord need not become disillusioned or discouraged because they notice an unacceptable difference in their own experience when held up to the mirror of God's Word. Further, the doctrine of subsequence instructs and encourages such believers to seek God further for the experience of Spirit baptism. While the Christian life is always a journey, and while a certain "holy dissatisfaction" with the status quo may remain, and that can and should be a good thing, upon reception of Spirit baptism one can sense they are on the right track—the biblical track—in their spirituality. But although theologically and pastorally sound, is the Pentecostal doctrine of subsequence biblically defensible?

BIBLICAL SUPPORT FOR SUBSEQUENCE

Three passages in Acts are of key significance for the Pentecostal doctrine of subsequence: 8:14–17, 10:44–46, and Acts 19:1–7. But before looking at these specific texts, let us note that Pentecostals also appeal to the biblical examples of Jesus and his disciples as precedents for the doctrine of subsequence.[16] The Holy Spirit was obviously present and active in Jesus' life before descending upon him at his baptism when he was empowered for ministry (Luke 4:14). Jesus himself therefore is seen as an example and precedent of subsequence. Similarly, Jesus' disciples were already believers (converts) before they received their specific impartation of the Spirit (Matt 16:16; Luke 10:20; John 15:3, 5). Of course, dissenters may argue that Jesus is a unique, nontransferable example while the disciples' example is inapplicable because much of it preceded the Day of Pentecost and even the death and resurrection of Christ. Yet Pentecostals have a valid point. After all, the NT does identify Jesus and his disciples as examples for believers with multiple applications (John 13:15; 1 Cor 11:1; 1 Pet 2:21). Therefore, a consistent pattern of subsequence should not be casually dismissed.

According to Acts 8:14–17 although the people of Samaria had already received salvation and been baptized in water through the ministry of Philip they had not yet received the Holy Spirit (baptism). Peter and John therefore laid hands on them in prayer that they might receive the Holy Spirit (baptism). Arrington notes that their reception of the Spirit as a "separate, subsequent experience. . .confronts us with the chronological separation" between their belief for salvation and their immersion in the Spirit.[17] Therefore, Pentecostals understand the experience of the Samaritan believers as a clear example of the doctrine of subsequence.

16. Arrington, *Christian Doctrine*, 3:58–60. Horton, "Spirit Baptism," 56–60.
17. Arrington, *Acts*, 158.

Non-Pentecostal interpreters do not deny the occurrence of subsequence in Acts 8:14–17. But they tend to struggle with making sense of it. For instance, Polhill, after admitting that various other passages in Acts do suggest an interval between salvation and Spirit baptism, acknowledges that "The current passage is the most difficult case of them all. Why was the receipt of the Spirit so disconnected from the Samaritans' baptism?"[18] He offers a few, if not convincing explanations, at least, possible considerations (such as racial tensions between Jews and Samaritans or the mother church at Jerusalem needed to affirm). However, I find the following comments fascinating:

> Obviously Acts presents no set pattern. The Spirit is connected with becoming a Christian. Sometimes the Spirit is connected with the laying on of hands, sometimes not. Sometimes coming of the Spirit precedes baptism. Sometimes it follows. The Spirit "blows where it wills" (John 3:8); the Spirit cannot be tied down to any manipulative human schema.[19]

Pentecostals agree. And that leaves ample room for subsequence. Although it appears that some (Polhill?) may adopt a rather extraordinary course of avoiding *any* pattern specifically to avoid paradigmatic implications of subsequence.

Pentecostals have been known to argue that the Spirit's falling on Cornelius and his household in Acts 10:44–46 indicates subsequence. However, accurate exegesis understands that Cornelius was a God-fearer (10:1). As such, Cornelius (and presumably, his household) worshiped the God of Judaism but had not been circumcised. He certainly had not been baptized in water as a Christian.[20] Therefore, while the account of Cornelius is of critical importance for understanding Spirit baptism accompanied by speaking in tongues as God's gift to both Jewish and Gentile converts it is not a specific example of subsequence. In fact, the Spirit fell on them as they responded favorably to Peter's preaching of the gospel (even prior to water baptism).[21] Yet neither does Cornelius' experience discount the doctrine of subsequence.[22] It is simply an example, as with my mother and sister, that the Holy Spirit can (and does) transcend our temporal chronology. Furthermore, this passage does support a kind of, if you will, general subsequence: that the experience of the Day of Pentecost is subsequently repeatable.[23]

---

18. Polhill, *Acts*, 218.

19. Polhill, *Acts*, 217–18.

20. Arrington, *Acts*, 177. Although Arrington argues elsewhere, *Christian Doctrine*, 3:60–61, that the Holy Spirit would have been active in Cornelius' life previously and that possibly he and his friends had already encountered the Christian influence of Philip the evangelist.

21. Arrington, *Acts*, 186. As stated in Chapter 3, some Oneness Pentecostals argue that Spirit baptism with the evidence of speaking in tongues is simultaneous with conversion and/or closely associated with water baptism. But then that position has its own problems, namely, in this context, the pattern of subsequence observable elsewhere in Acts.

22. Cp. Horton, "Spirit Baptism," 64.

23. Polhill, *Acts*, 264, somewhat inconsistently due to his earlier comments that the Holy Spirit transcends set patterns, argues that the unusual sequence of Spirit/water baptism in Acts 10:44–46 indicates it is "a unique and unrepeatable event." Cp. Polhill, *Acts*, 217–18.

If Acts 8:14–17 is a clear case of subsequence and Acts 10:44–46 is a clear case of simultaneity, then Acts 19:1–7 is more complicated than either. There is a great deal of disagreement about whether the twelve disciples Paul encountered at Ephesus were only disciples of John the Baptist or disciples of John the Baptist who had believed in Jesus but had not yet been baptized in the Holy Spirit. Based on exegetical and grammatical arguments, Arrington concludes that they were "the pre-Pentecostal kind of Christians—converted but not filled with the Spirit."[24] Accordingly, he describes their pneumatic experience as "the Spirit's anointing with power subsequent to the experience of salvation."[25] He further insists that the "outpouring of the Spirit at Ephesus shows that Spirit baptism is subsequent and distinct from conversion in the theology of both Luke and Paul" and that it "does not mark a conversion experience but an enduement of the Spirit's power for spreading the Gospel."[26] As Pentecostals and non-Pentecostals are often at odds regarding the relation, and possible tension, between Lukan and Pauline pneumatologies, this becomes an extremely important declaration.

Some solidly reputable Bible scholars do not agree that the Ephesian twelve were Christian disciples. For instance, Polhill tentatively suggests that "they were not at this point strictly Christian disciples but rather disciples of John the Baptist."[27] However, he readily admits that Luke might have found "a fine distinction between Baptist and Christian disciples strained" because for him "a true disciple of John, a *completed* disciple of John, *was* a Christian."[28] Nevertheless, Polhill continues his exegesis with the assumption that they were not Christians. Yet I argue that even if so, it does not appreciably change the interpretative outcome regarding Spirit baptism as a distinct, subsequent experience. Paul's question, "Did you receive the Holy Spirit when you believed?" (v. 2), which is capable of being translated either "when" or "after" but, in any case, indicates his presupposition that they may have believed but may not have received the baptism with the Holy Spirit. Otherwise the question is nonsensical. Furthermore, the process these twelve went through—hearing Paul's message, being re-baptized in water in the name of Jesus, having hands laid on them in prayer, and then the Spirit's coming on them with charismatic signs and wonders—nevertheless indicates a sequence of experiences even though they obviously took place in a single extended encounter. Therefore, in either case, whether disciples of John or of Jesus (or, in a sense, of both), Acts 19:1–7 does, I propose, exemplify subsequence in the reception of the Holy Spirit baptism or fullness with its charismatic dimensions.

Another passage is also particularly important for the Pentecostal doctrine of subsequence. Acts 9:17–18 is unique because it describes the experience of an

---

Polhill, *Acts*, 264.

24. Arrington, *Acts*, 298.
25. Arrington, *Acts*, 299.
26. Arrington, *Acts*, 300.
27. Polhill, *Acts*, 398–399.
28. Polhill, *Acts*, 399. Italics are original.

individual rather than of a group, and, if anything, even more interesting because that individual eventually became known as Apostle Paul. Horton observes that Paul's individual Spirit baptism refutes those who argue that Spirit baptism signifies incorporating different groups into the church.[29] Here we are given to understand that Saul/Paul was converted in his encounter with Jesus on the road to Damascus (9:1–9) but was physically healed and filled with the Spirit three days later under the ministry of Ananias. Therefore, Paul's own infilling with the Spirit serves as a clear example of subsequence.[30] Again, given the oft-repeated argument that Pauline pneumatology is exclusively soteriological, this is an incredibly important point.

Interestingly, and confusingly, Polhill admits that Ananias can greet the former persecutor as a Christian and that something of a conversion had taken place although Saul/Paul is specifically described as needing not only the recovery of his sight but the receipt of the Spirit.[31] Yet Polhill quite enigmatically declares that after the scene with Ananias in Judas' house, "Paul's recovery was now complete. More than that, his conversion was now complete."[32] Does Polhill mean to imply that Saul was somehow partially converted on Damascus Road and then fully converted under Ananias at Judas' residence? If so, that would be quite a long stretch to go just to get around subsequence. Much simpler, and a great deal sounder, is an interpretation that Saul was converted during his earlier encounter with the Lord Jesus Christ but had a subsequent encounter with the Holy Spirit in which he received his personal infilling.[33]

I find it disingenuous that some detractors of the doctrine of subsequence attempt to pass off whatever evidence contrary to their position arises as some sort of exception. For example, in Acts 8:14–17 it only applied because it was the first outreach to the Samaritans (the Samaritan Pentecost). Or in Acts 10:44–46 it was because it was the first outreach to Romans (the Gentile Pentecost). Or in Ephesians 19:1–7 the disciples of John the Baptist were not really Christians. Or Acts 9:17–18 does not apply because it is an individual experience depicted in an extended dramatization intended to substantiate the credibility of an infamous former antagonist. After a while one wants to ask, "How many 'exceptions' must occur before they are not really 'exceptions' anymore?" And this is not even to mention that the logic does not hold in any case.

Without turning too polemical, here are a few reasons why I find the *ethnic exceptions* argument unconvincing. The gist of this faulty argument usually goes something like: the apparent repetitions of Pentecost only occurred as the NT church's mission

---

29. Horton, *Spirit Baptism*, 62. To those who would further insist that Paul's status as an apostle involves yet another exception, I reply that their position dies the death of a thousand qualifications.

30. Arrington, *Acts*, 168–69.

31. Polhill, *Acts*, 238.

32. Polhill, *Acts.*, 238.

33. Ockham's Razor is a principle of problem-solving which argues that when presented with competing hypotheses the simplest solution, that is, the one with the fewest assumptions, is usually the right one.

moved into new people groups; therefore, they are not to be expected to occur again. In other words, although they were themselves "repetitions" they are labeled one-time, unrepeatable events. I offer two short interrogative responses and a more viable alternative. First, in the earliest years of the church's mission all movement was into uncharted territories (ethnically and geographically). How else would each repetition of Pentecost have occurred? Second, even if this were so, then would it not mean that every time contemporary Christian mission moved into contact with new people groups then similar repetitions of Pentecost would inevitably reoccur?

A much better explanation than non-paradigmatic ethnic exceptions is that the NT Pentecost-type events and experiences are *representative norms*. In this interpretative model the initial outpouring of the Holy Spirit at Pentecost as well as subsequent (!) outpourings at Samaria, Cornelius' house, Ephesus, and Damascus are prototypical indicators of the continuing availability of Spirit baptism as an established, expected standard for all groups and individuals in Christ regardless of their geographical and historical location or ethnic and racial identification (Acts 2:39; 11:17). Rather than one-time, non-repeatable events they are quite the opposite: affirming encouragements for ongoing occurrences. Thus, the essential elements of the events of the Day of Pentecost, as well as, if we will, of the Samaritan Pentecost, the Gentile Pentecost, and the Ephesian Pentecost, are not only repeatable, they are paradigmatic. And the biblical paradigms include experiences of pneumatic subsequence.

SPIRIT BAPTISM AS A BROAD METAPHOR

In reading this next section it would be well to keep in mind the preceding sections of this chapter as a foundational orientation for the present one. It suggests that without sacrificing any classic Pentecostal tenets it may be possible to expand the doctrine of the subsequence of the experience of Spirit baptism to be inclusive of a broad range of the Holy Spirit's activities in the Christian life. In a sense this task has already been accomplished quite effectively in Steve Land's *Pentecostal Spirituality*. Among other things, Land essentially synthesizes and revises traditional Wesleyan-Holiness and Pentecostal language of purity and power—that is, of sanctification and Spirit baptism—in ecumenical conversation with a wider range of theologians (most notably, Barth and Moltmann).[34] He effectively demonstrates that Pentecostal spirituality and pneumatology, while not less than previously conceived, has the potential to be more than has been conceived by Pentecostals themselves (as well as others). Accordingly, I would propose Land's work as a pioneering model for developing traditional Pentecostal theologies of Spirit baptism and subsequence in creative fashion.

Frank Macchia's *Baptized in the Spirit* frames (or reframes) the topic of Spirit baptism from a highly developed Pentecostal perspective. Macchia, in typical Pentecostal

---

34. Land, *Pentecostal Spirituality*, 181–220.

style, shares his own exciting testimony of being baptized in the Holy Spirit as a young student at Central Bible College (Springfield, MO). Although an accomplished theologian today, it is apparent that Spirit baptism is still much more to him than an interesting item for intellectual reflection. Some of the main themes he addresses include the nature of Spirit baptism as it involves experience; its function as a fluid metaphor surrounded by ambiguous imagery capable of encompassing numerous emphases; as both charismatic and soteriological in nature; and, as including a Pentecost/kingdom of God correlation in which the highest description possible of the substance of Spirit baptism is an eschatological gift that functions as an outpouring of divine love.[35] Significantly, Macchia maintains that the Holy Spirit's work cannot be compartmentalized or separated, chiding Pentecostals for being too narrow and consequently not developing a broader pneumatology.[36]

Amos Yong's *Renewing Christian Theology* also follows a trajectory which widens the scope of Spirit baptism without lessening its core categories as affirmed by Pentecostals. For Yong, Spirit baptism is "a scriptural trope that points to a more holistic understanding of the work of God in Christ to save, sanctify, and empower the people of God to participate in the cosmic history of salvation."[37] Thus baptism in the Spirit may be best described as multidimensional. Yong allows that Spirit baptism is a subsequent work of grace in terms of empowerment for witness to and service of Christ but argues that "it is also more than that, involving the full range of the saving work of God" (citing Gal 5:25).[38] Referencing the historical appropriations of differences between John Wesley and John Fletcher on the matter of Spirit baptism, Yong argues that Pentecostals can and should broaden our understanding of Spirit baptism as a metaphor capable of accounting for the range of human experiences of God's saving graces and the complexities of human encounters with God.[39]

What Land, Macchia, and Yong all have in common is that they do not present baptism with the Holy Spirit as an either/or option so much as a matter of both/and. So then, what does a broad approach to Spirit baptism mean for our present discussion of Spirit baptism and subsequence? Pentecostals and non-Pentecostals have contended for decades regarding the doctrine of the subsequence of Spirit baptism.[40] The biblical account itself is complex. Harold Hunter conducted an extensive study of subsequence in the NT, including the Pauline corpus, the Luke-Acts series, and the Johannine literature, as well patristic and historical sources. A Pentecostal himself, he concluded that "there is a specific work of the Holy Spirit which is charismatic in nature and not

---

35. Richie, "Review of Macchia, *Baptized in the Spirit*, 1.
36. Richie, "Review of Macchia, *Baptized in the Spirit*, 1.
37. Yong, *Renewing Christian Theology*, 93.
38. Yong, *Renewing Christian Theology*, 98. Cp. 101.
39. Yong, *Spirit Poured Out*, 105–06.
40. Macchia, "Theology, Pentecostal," 1129–31, outlines the most salient features of the still ongoing debate with their chief advocates and adversaries.

predetermined in action both initially and progressively."[41] Yet he is honest and transparent about pros and cons too, so to speak. Hunter breaks his conclusion down into nine extended elaborations. First, there is a distinct work of the Holy Spirit which is charismatic. This work is distinguishable from other acts of God or works of the Spirit.

Second, Spirit baptism is an appropriate term for describing the charismatic work of the Holy Spirit. However, there is enough biblical and historical diversity to discourage rigidity. Third, Spirit baptism is properly understood as the outworking of God's grace in a believer's life. Once again there is enough variety and vagueness to discourage dogmatic distinctions. Fourth, Pentecostals have (apparently) often misunderstood the intent of "one stage" emphasis on Christian initiation to imply exclusion of the ongoing charismatic work of the Holy Spirit. Its best proponents do not (at least, not any longer) make that assumption; but, often argue for a linear model of the Spirit's work. Fifth, the same is true of the actualization/appropriation schema of Spirit baptism theology. In other words, it can be so interpreted and applied as to encourage, or at least, to allow, charismatic or Pentecostal-type experiences of the Spirit which are understood as arising out of Christian initiation.

Seventh, the precise nature of Pentecostal pneumatology is admittedly a bit of a historical novelty. In other words, no major group has exhibited quite the same pneumatological constellation of beliefs and practices. Yet its essence has occurred in various forms throughout the course of Christian history. Eighth, the Pentecostal argument that Spirit baptism and sanctification are related but not inseparable stands up under exegetical and historical examination. And finally, ninth, the major problem with subsequence is an apparent generation of different "classes" or "levels" of Christians. Yet even here much depends on emphasizing the grace of God in all Christian experience as well as the graciousness of recipients and proponents of Spirit baptism toward others.[42]

Hunter's work accomplishes three much-needed tasks. First, it establishes the Pentecostal theology of subsequence as biblically and historically defensible and, therefore, feasible. Second, it establishes that dogmatic rigidity about the precise usage of specialized terminology is ill-advised and unwise by either proponents or opponents of subsequence. Third, and in either case, most importantly, it affirms the distinctive charismatic work of the Holy Spirit in contemporary believers' lives. These results suggest great progress. Attentive focus is no longer so much on whether Pentecostal experience reflects legitimate Christian spirituality. That vital point is increasingly assumed. Rather, contemporary theological energy has in the main shifted to the task of how to *interpret* Pentecostal experience within the context of established and accepted conceptual categories. Perhaps both Pentecostals and the larger Christian tradition will need to make appropriate *adjustments*.

Much is at stake for Pentecostal belief and practice. The continuing validity of individual experience and charismatic giftedness is essential to Pentecostal theology

---

41. Hunter, *Spirit Baptism*, 221.
42. Hunter, *Spirit Baptism*, 226–31.

and spirituality. Early in my adult Christian walk I attended a Baptist church for a couple of years. It was what I have since come to know as cessationist in orientation. The congregation was devout and welcoming. Overall my time there was beneficial for me. The pastor was a godly man who became a dear friend as well as a precious mentor and model of shepherding. Yet when I told him I had begun praying for Spirit baptism he sharply reproved me. As I recollect, he said, "We get all we're ever going to get in the new birth. There's nothing more. We grow in maturity, but we've already received all that we ever will." That idea was not encouraging. Neither was it convincing.

I understand the Aristotelian logic. Aristotle's "oak tree in the acorn" analogy comes to mind.[43] Here is potentiality and actuality. Then, there is creation itself. Arguably everything creaturely is inherent within us since the original divine act of creation *ex nihilo*. Then there is salvation. We "get everything we're going to get" in Christian initiation. This is really a rigidly materialistic argument. But does it hold well with *spiritual* realities? More specifically, does it hold with spiritual *experience*? No, it does not. Pentecostals do not deny that the same Spirit indwells all believers from their regenerative instance. Pentecostals understand that conversion is the beginning point and baseline of everything Christian for an individual. Yet Pentecostals do affirm that subsequent to conversion there may be a distinct experience of the Holy Spirit which is demonstratively charismatic in its features and missional in its effect. Not surprisingly, materialistic Aristotelian philosophical categories do not work well with spiritual experience.[44] But that does not mean that the spiritual experience is biblically or theologically unsound. Thus, I conclude that Pentecostals are completely correct in affirming and defending a distinct experience of Spirit baptism subsequent to conversion. Yet I gladly concede that the breadth and depth of Spirit baptism is doubtless greater than either Pentecostals or non-Pentecostals have understood.

In the final analysis, I affirm with Gause that baptism with the Spirit is "an initiating experience."[45] Spirit baptism initiates those who have been converted to Christ into a fresh encounter with the power of the Holy Spirit. It enhances their effectiveness in their worship of God, their witness of Christ, and their ongoing walk in the Spirit. Accordingly, the interrelatedness of redemptive experiences as unifying but distinct is preserved. The nature of Spirit baptism in relation to Christian initiation (properly speaking) and its function as initiation (experientially speaking) into a distinctive and purposeful encounter with the Holy Spirit is also protected. Therefore, every pastor who encourages members of his or her congregation to seek earnestly to be filled with the Holy Spirit following their conversion is not only biblically and theologically correct but he or she is also promoting a critical aspect of life in the Spirit offered as a promise to every believer (Acts 2:39).

---

43. Allen and Springsted, *Philosophy for Understanding Theology*, 90–91.

44. Recall that we saw in a previous chapter that religious or spiritual experience is an elusive but still valid concept.

45. Gause, *Living in the Spirit*, 63.

10

Purpose of Spirit Baptism

Perhaps before proceeding further it will be helpful to explain what Pentecostal theology does *not* claim for Spirit baptism. Pentecostals have long recognized that baptism in the Holy Spirit is neither a substitute for the process of discipleship nor a shortcut to spiritual maturity. This fact was emphasized, for instance, early in the movement's development by able expositor and prolific author Donald Gee. Gee, an English Pentecostal who, although lacking formal theological education, exerted great influence among early Pentecostals on an international scale through his intelligent, articulate, and evenhanded writings. Gee observes that a crisis experience of baptism with the Spirit does not automatically make one perfect; does not elevate recipients to such a supernatural level of living that their human finitude and frailties disappear; and, certainly does not eliminate the need for consistent walking in the Spirit.[1] In picturesque language, Gee says, "It was not all wings. They had to learn Pentecostal pedestrianism."[2] Gee based his observations on the NT account of Christians living after Pentecost and applied it to the lives of contemporary Pentecostals. In short, Spirit baptism is not an instant, automatic fix-all for everyone and everything. No one can be blamed for asking, "Okay, then what is it?"

---

1. Gee, *Now That You've Been Baptized in the Spirit*, 12–14. Parts of this compilation go back to 1930 and 1945.

2. Gee, *Now That You've Been Baptized in the Spirit*, 14.

As we explore the answer(s) to this question directly, I will first focus on the most prevalent definition of Spirit baptism among Classical Pentecostals as empowerment for service along with guidance into truth. Then, second, I will expand the discussion to include a few additional elements of Spirit baptism, especially the gifts of the Holy Spirit. Finally, I will identify the ethical and moral core of baptism with the Spirit, especially the role of love and of the fruit of the Spirit. This last step requires some attention to recurring controversies regarding moral failures among high-profile Pentecostals which have been all-too-common in the movement, especially among media personalities. Throughout this chapter the goal is to present Spirit baptism as Classical Pentecostals commonly understand it as well as to offer a bit of transparent assessment along the way.

EMPOWERMENT FOR SERVICE

The primary purpose of Spirit baptism may be summed up as empowerment for service and guidance into truth.[3] Pentecostal power is not for self-aggrandizement or self-exaltation. Jesus' pre-Ascension words, "But you shall receive power when the Holy Spirit has come upon you; and you shall be witnesses to Me in Jerusalem, and in all Judea and Samaria, and to the end of the earth" (Acts 1:8), suggest empowerment for *service*. Pentecost empowerment enables witnessing for Christ, including doing mighty works for Christ, and withstanding hostility and persecution for Christ's sake.[4] Jesus also said that when, "the Spirit of truth, has come, He will guide you into all truth" (John 16:13). The Spirit's truth is not esoteric, Gnostic-like elitism.[5] Spirit baptism guides believers into the knowledge of Jesus Christ (14:6; 15:26; 16:13–15). The Spirit teaches believers, imparting divine knowledge and wisdom for effective, faithful *service* to Christ (Acts 6:3; 1 John 2:27).[6] Thus, Pentecostal preachers have been heard to say, "Salvation is God's gift to the world. Spirit baptism is God's gift to the church."

Spirit baptism as empowerment for service signifies its missional and vocational nature. Several observations are enlightening. First, Pentecostal ecclesiology is primarily missional. Second, Pentecostal pneumatology is obviously vocational. Third, the Pentecostal doctrine of Spirit baptism integrates its missional ecclesiology and its vocational pneumatology. In short, the church exists to accomplish God's mission in Christ, the Holy Spirit provides effective power for fulfilling that task, and Spirit baptism endows believers with the Holy Spirit's power to perform their calling as witnesses to Christ. Although well known for bold, enthusiastic witnessing, Pentecostals

---

3. Arrington, *Christian Doctrine*, 3:69.
4. Arrington, *Christian Doctrine*, 3:70–75.
5. As is well known, Gnosticism insisted on salvation as special knowledge attained only by a few.
6. Stronstad, *Charismatic Theology of St. Luke*, argues that the NT emphasizes three dimensions of the Christian life—salvation, sanctification, service—and that the charismatic understanding of Spirit baptism applies to the third, 14, 98.

do not mean to imply that they themselves suddenly become irresistibly persuasive witnesses. Rather, the significatory works of God the Father bear clear witness to Jesus Christ his Son as the Spirit operates effectively through living human vessels (John 5:36–37; 8:18; 10:25; Heb 2:4). The Holy Spirit is the ultimate witness who testifies to Christ through many witnesses (John 15:26–27).

For Pentecostals, the existence of the church is firmly rooted in its divinely ordained mission in Christ as accomplished by the power of the Holy Spirit.[7] In other words, mission is the chief reason the church exists.[8] Thus, ecclesiology and missiology are inseparable. It is probably impossible to overstate the importance Pentecostal churches attach to mission. Pentecostal missiologists Julie Ma and Wonsuk Ma, affirming that ultimately mission belongs to God (*missio Dei*) further describe it as God's plan to restore fallen creation, including humanity, through God's invitation to humans to participate in the working out of that divine purpose.[9] Pentecostal missions are driven by a distinctive pneumatological orientation and by a sense of eschatological urgency. These motivators have resulted in a historically unprecedented and currently unparalleled emphasis on evangelism (the promulgation of the gospel). Pentecostals' evangelistic fervor and effectiveness is a direct result of their distinctive experience of Spirit baptism (Acts 1:8).

Pentecostals further believe that Christology and the Great Commission are closely connected (Matt 28:18–20; Mark 16:15–18; Luke 24:46–48; John 20:21). Chris Thomas explains that the mandate of the Great Commission "finds its grounding, being, and sustenance" in Christology.[10] Accordingly, Pentecostal missiology is remarkably evangelistic, pneumatological, eschatological, and Christological. In sum, Pentecostals believe that the church's mission is to proclaim the good news of the gospel of God's saving act in Jesus Christ by the power of the Holy Spirit in the light of Jesus' imminent return. Proclamation can and does include both words and deeds. Ecclesial mission is deep and diverse. Mission includes not only the evangelism of the

---

7. Richie, *Toward a Pentecostal Theology of Religions*, 29–30. As a member of the Tennessee State World Missions Board for the Church of God I see this emphasis in action constantly.

8. In an earlier section of this work on "A Theology of Worship" I discuss the church with the imagery of God's people, Christ's body, and the Spirit's temple. There are also colloquial images of the church. Some see the church as a "rescue ship" saving souls drowning in sin; others as a "classroom" where people are taught God's Word; still others as a "clinic" or "hospital" where they receive healing; and, yet others as a "family" where people connect with one another and build relationships while receiving inspiration and encouragement. An increasingly common image today is of a local church as a "team" with the pastor as a "life coach." Sadly, many appear to think of the church mainly as a "business" with the pastor as its "CEO." Obviously, other images could be listed with each highlighting (more or less) authentic aspects of what it means to be a church. For Pentecostals, I suggest one descriptive image could be of a church as a "toolshed" where believers acquire skills and tools for doing the work of Christian mission.

9. Ma and Ma, *Mission in the Spirit*, 6 (Cp., 286).

10. Thomas, "Christology and the Great Commission," 75.

unsaved but also the worship of God, edification of the saints, and social concern.[11] Yet in one way or another, the church is always witnessing to Jesus Christ.

For our present purposes, the place of Spirit baptism in the accomplishment of the church's evangelistic mission is of premium interest. This is where Pentecostal identity and Pentecostal ministry coalesce. As Colkmire says, "God raised up the Church of God to be a Spirit-clothed, holiness movement playing a significant role in the fulfillment of the Great Commission."[12] Indeed, there is a recurring biblical emphasis on the need for and provision of the Holy Spirit's empowerment to accomplish God's calling in Christ. Paul contrasted the inadequacies of human weakness with the effectiveness of the Holy Spirit's empowerment in his own apostolic calling (1 Cor 2:1–5). Not surprisingly, the Holy Spirit's empowerment for ministry is an oft recurring theme in Paul (Rom 15:19; 1 Cor 4:20; 1 Thess 1:5). Peter is audacious enough to apply it to none other than Jesus Christ (Acts 10:38). Indeed, Jesus himself clearly links his experience of and anointing with the Spirit's power with the effective launch of his public ministry (Luke 4:14–21).

In their application of the Holy Spirit's empowerment for Christian service Peter and Paul (and Jesus) were drawing on a deep, enduring scriptural tradition. As early as Joseph unique abilities and gifts in God's service are attributed to the Spirit of God (Gen 41:38). Much later but in a similar context, the same principle is reiterated in the ministry of Daniel (Dan 4:5; 5:11). During the Mosaic period Joshua is equipped and prepared for leadership by the Spirit (Num 27:18; Deut 34:9). Bezalel and Ohiliab are enabled by the Spirit of God for the craftsmanship and vocational aptitude necessary for building the Tent of Meeting (Ex 31:1–5). When Moses required the elders of Israel to join him in carrying the load of leadership, the Lord called them apart to receive an empowerment from the Spirit to enable them to accomplish their task (Num 11:16–18). Accordingly, a longstanding Pentecostal line of reasoning interprets Spirit baptism as vocational empowerment for missiological provision.[13] In other words, believers are baptized with the Holy Spirit for service to Christ.

Further, the purpose of Spirit baptism as guidance into truth signifies its illuminative and revelatory aspects in the service of Christian mission. As the "Spirit of truth" the Holy Spirit communicates the truth of Christ to believers (John 14:26; 15:26; 16:13–15). Acts consistently connects the post-Pentecost work of the Holy with exceptional spiritual wisdom and understanding (6:3; 7:10; 8:35; 9:22). Paul makes the same connection (1 Cor 1:5; 2:12; Rom 15:14). First John insists that the Holy Spirit's anointing is the actual Teacher (2:27). Pentecostals believe that the Holy Spirit illuminates the Scriptures and reveals God's ways through spiritual gifts and signs

---

11. Higgins, et al, *Introduction to Theology*, 175–76. The surprising scope of contemporary Pentecostal mission theology is evident in an entire *International Review of Mission* issue dedicated to the topic. See *International Review of Mission: Pentecostal Mission Theology* 107.1 (406): June 2018.

12. Colkmire, "Young, Significant, Diverse, and Needy," 7.

13. E.g., Riggs, *The Spirit Himself*, 30–31, 80, 163 and Land, *Pentecostal Spirituality*, 168–69.

(including dreams and visions, Acts 2:17). While surely all those born of the Spirit experience the Spirit's leading (Rom 8:14), Spirit baptism signifies an intensification of such spiritual verities.[14]

I well recall one of my first experiences of Spirit-inspired understanding. Although I was raised in a Christian home I neglected my youthful education. As an adult convert I began to almost devour the Scriptures. Yet I found myself becoming confused. Like the Ethiopian eunuch, I did not understand what I read (Acts 8:30–31). I spoke with my preacher father about it. He tried to explain some basic biblical truths to me; however, he mostly advised me to pray and ask the Holy Spirit to reveal God's Word to me. One week I had been studying the Exodus closely without understanding much about it. I decided to follow my father's advice. That night I prayed fervently for understanding. The next day on my job as I went about my usual business there was an unexpected moment of sharp clarity in which truth came to me suddenly. At once it seemed a light shone into my heart and mind. Glorious truths about Christ our Passover and the spiritual priesthood flooded my soul and have remained firmly rooted there ever since (1 Cor 5:7–8).

I certainly do not wish to intimate that my experience is a model for others. I can nevertheless share what I personally learned from this initial experience. First, the Holy Spirit can and will reveal divine truth to me—even to me. Second, believing, humble prayer is essential to spiritual revelation. Third, spiritual revelation is shaped by my authentic encounter with the Scripture. And perhaps most importantly, while God can, and does, speak in many ways, his ultimate Word is through his Son Jesus Christ (John 1:1; Heb 1:1). Over the years this pattern has been reaffirmed in my own life frequently with only minor variations. Yet I have also learned not to be too dogmatic about how the Holy Spirit reveals the things of God to anyone.

Pastor and missionary Ronnie Hepperly has done extensive mission work in places where people had never seen a Bible nor even a missionary. Yet he has had them tell him that someone in their village had had a dream or a vision indicating someone would come declaring unto them the way of salvation. Hepperly explains:

> Everywhere we go, we feel God has already prepared someone, like Acts 10: God prepared Cornelius through supernatural means, sending Peter to help him. The steps of a righteous man are ordered by the Lord (Psalm 37:23). We wind up in these countries and villages looking for people God has prepared to receive us.[15]

---

14. For more on Spirit baptism as intensification of existing moral and spiritual graces in the human, especially Christian, self, see McClymond, "Spirit Baptism as a Moral Source," 37–57.

15. Colkmire, "From the Woods to the World," 11.

I can only believe that this is the Holy Spirit at work through *praeparatio evangelica* (preparation for evangelism). Accordingly, missionaries are often Spirit-anointed facilitators and catalysts.[16]

Of course, it goes without saying that Pentecostals do not claim to have unlimited (or uninterrupted) access to divine omniscience. As Elisha learned, God reveals what God wisely choses to reveal—no more, no less (2 Kgs 4:25–27). Yet God does at times sovereignly elect to disclose deep mysteries (Deut 29:29; Dan 2:22; 1 Cor 1–16). Nevertheless, the Holy Spirit's impartation of spiritual wisdom and knowledge is no substitute for the careful study of Scripture (1 Cor 12:8; 2 Tim 2:15). Neither is either ever in competition with the other. A much-used Pentecostal slogan is "The Spirit and the Word agree!"

ADDITIONAL BENEFITS OF SPIRIT BAPTISM

Arrington adds, citing extensive scriptural support, that Spirit baptism results in greater: awareness of the presence of the Triune God; spiritual sensitivity; love of the Scriptures, openness to the gifts of the Spirit, consecration to God, measure of joy, and boldness in witnessing.[17] However, "these blessings in no way diminish what God does for us in regeneration and sanctification, before we receive the Pentecostal experience of being baptized in the Holy Spirit."[18] This last point is of paramount importance. It would be a miserable misunderstanding of Pentecostal theology to suggest that it in any way diminishes the importance of the new birth or holiness. Rather, the significance of Spirit baptism can only be properly appreciated in view of the inestimable value of the works of grace which precede it, that is, of regeneration and sanctification.

Significantly, the suggestion is not that those who have not yet experienced Spirit baptism do not have any awareness of the presence of God, spiritual sensitivity, love of the Scriptures, openness to the gifts of the Spirit, consecration to God, measure of joy, and boldness in witnessing. As a comparative adjective "greater" signifies an intensification of an existing state. Certainly, anyone who has been born of the Spirit through faith in Jesus would have some awareness of God's presence, spiritual sensitivity, love of the Bible, openness to spiritual gifts, consecration to God, as well as a measure of joy, and boldness in witnessing. Of course, the experience of these characteristics could vary for individuals. Spirit baptism significantly increases and intensifies these additional benefits in individual believers who receive it comparable to their existing experience beforehand. Spirit baptism often functions as a kind of amplification

---

16. As Ken Anderson, a leader in pioneer missions for the Church of God, said at the FIND Coalition, which focuses on UPGs (Unreached People Groups), a meeting at North Cleveland Church of God (Cleveland, TN) on January 9, 2019.

17. Arrington, *Christian Doctrine*, 3:78–84.

18. Arrington, *Christian Doctrine*, 84.

or augmentation of the Holy Spirit's presence and power which is already active in believers' lives.[19]

One item in the list of additional benefits requires further comment: openness to the gifts of the Spirit. There are several notable considerations. For one, there are very diverse definitions of giftedness. In today's culture one's natural abilities and talents may be described as one's gifts. That is not inaccurate; but, it is not what is meant by "spiritual" gifts" or gifts "of the Spirit." These originate in agency of the divine Spirit, not in the human spirit. As Pentecostals writers John Lombard and Jerald Daffe well say, although God has created human beings with astonishing capabilities and energies "when considering spiritual things, we realize the needs exceed our human capacities...We need spiritual gifts in addition to what *we* can contribute."[20] Spiritual gifts are not simply human abilities and energies identified and developed.

Even within the NT there are various lists of gifts. None of the lists are exhaustive and some are overlapping. Yet Paul's letters reflect the central importance of spiritual gifts in the life and ministry of the NT churches (Rom 12:6–8; 1 Cor 12–14; Eph 4:11–13; cp. 1 Thess 5:19–20; Gal 3:5). Romans 12:6–8 refers to a mix of gifts in a context of practical service: prophecy, service, teaching, exhortation, generosity in giving (stewardship), ruling (administration), and showing mercy. First Corinthians 12:8–10 describes a mix of gifts in a context of charismatic manifestations: a word or message of wisdom, a word or message of knowledge, faith, healings, working of miracles, prophecy, discerning of spirits, various kinds of tongues, and interpretation of tongues. Ephesians 4:11–13 describes a mix of gifts focusing on offices of ministry: apostles, prophets, evangelists, pastors and teachers.[21]

Non-Pentecostals accept the continuing validity of gifts listed in Romans 12:6–8 and Ephesians 4:11–13—though generally with reductive qualifications. For an example, some deny that prophecy in Romans 12:6–8 is anything other than a synonym for preaching. For another, some either deny the continuing validity of apostolic and prophetic ministries as described in Ephesians 4:11–13 or else redefine them as missionaries and preachers. Yet the real controversy, and perhaps the primary impulse for Arrington's "greater openness to the gifts of the Spirit" remark, is First Corinthians 12:8–10. While affirming all the gifts in all the NT lists, Pentecostals (and Charismatics) are distinctive in their insistence that these gifts of grace (*charismata*) listed in First Corinthians 12:8–10 are relevant and active today.

Interestingly, Lombard and Daffe ask a question which can supply further context for Arrington's assurance that Spirit baptism involves greater openness to the gifts

---

19. As I have heard Steve Land say so many times in the classroom or in conversation, we don't claim that we're better than anyone else because of Spirit baptism; but, we know that we are better than we were without Spirit baptism.

20. Lombard and Daffe, *Spiritual Gifts*, 124. Italics are original.

21. 1 Cor 12:28–29 has yet another, somewhat integrated, variation: apostles, prophets, teachers, miracles, healings, helps (assistance or service), governments (administration), and tongues and interpretation of tongues.

of the Spirit. "Are you open to his doing it? Do you desire for Him to operate the spiritual gifts in the Body?"[22] If Spirit baptism provides a gateway into the reception of the gifts of the Spirit, then an attitude of openness and ardent desire provides a gateway into their operation (1 Cor 14:1, 39). In other words, Spirit baptism often imparts spiritual gifts, but obedient openness activates gifts of the Holy Spirit in one's personal experience and service.

Yes, Pentecostals do highly value spiritual gifts as divine endowments necessary for the effective function of the church.[23] However, they also warn against misconceptions of the meaning and manner of the reception and operation of spiritual gifts.[24] Most Pentecostals wisely recognize that the sometimes sensational and spectacular nature of certain spiritual gifts may be (and have been) exploited by the unlearned or abused by the insincere. Accordingly, Pentecostals constantly guard against excess and exploitation (1 Cor 14:29; 1 John 4:1). Yet Pentecostals remain firmly convinced that *regulation rather than rejection* is the biblical pattern for the appropriate operation of spiritual gifts (1 Cor 12–14).

Perhaps surprisingly to some, Pentecostal charismology does not insist that spiritual gifts are limited exclusively to those who experience Spirit baptism.[25] Every regenerate believer is indwelled by the Holy Spirit and thus may be used by the Spirit, if only he/she willingly yields to the Spirit's sovereign promptings (1 Cor 12:7, 11). When I was a young Christian I heard of a tent revival near my White Pine, Tennessee home. Although I did not know anyone involved I decided to go, hoping for a spiritual benefit. However, during the service it quickly became apparent that two warring factions were present. The conflict became so intense that the leaders desperately turned to me as an unbiased visitor to arbitrate. I was caught completely off-guard. In a word, I was stunned. Furthermore, I had absolutely no idea what to say or do. I seriously considered fleeing the scene at a dead run. Yet as I breathed a quick word of prayer suddenly, in an instant, like a flash, I knew exactly what to do and say. And my frightened panic was immediately transformed into calm confidence. Although I had not yet preached a single sermon, I strode to the pulpit, read Scripture (1 Cor 14:33), and boldly spoke the words that had come unbidden into my mind. The result was instantaneous. Both groups were smitten with conviction. Someone did run that night, but it was not me. Everyone rushed to the altar in repentant prayer. The former combatants, people who had been having a public conflict right in the worship service, were literally weeping and hugging in brotherly love. In closing the service, the leadership openly expressed their shared conviction that a young man with a word from God had come to correct more mature believers.

---

22. Lombard and Daffe, *Spiritual Gifts*, 134.
23. Lombard and Daffe, *Spiritual Gifts*, 125–26.
24. Lombard and Daffe, *Spiritual Gifts*, 190–206.
25. Lombard and Daffe, *Spiritual Gifts*, 206.

At the time that this incident transpired I had not yet been baptized in the Holy Spirit. As a matter of fact, I was attending a non-Pentecostal church. To clarify, I had been attempting to distance myself from my Pentecostal roots in search of a what I thought would be a "more balanced and respectable" form of Christian expression. That did not work out so well for me.[26] Eventually I found it impossible to reconcile my hesitation about all things Pentecostal with my reading of Scripture. And I am so glad I did. But the point of this testimony is that the Holy Spirit nevertheless granted me what I now recognize as a form of the spiritual gift known as a word of wisdom (1 Cor 12:8). Pentecostals—of all people—must not attempt to place limits on the Holy Spirit!

Spirit baptism is not so much an introduction of anything new as an intensification or amplification of that which is already present through the indwelling Holy Spirit. Pentecostals utilize the Johannine analogy of "the well and the river" (John 4:13–15; 7:37–39). The living waters of Jesus Christ are the same in both cases but an increase in measure occurs. Yet baptism in the Spirit does indeed open a believer's inner spirit up in a special way fitting her/him for intensified service in Christ Jesus. In my case, the occasional impressions and insights of the Holy Spirit that I experienced after being born again but prior to being baptized in Holy Spirit became more consistent and more frequent. They also tended to become more intense—although the Holy Spirit often deals with me in gentle, subtle fashions.[27]

THE EVER-CRUCIAL ATTRIBUTE

With the amount of unembarrassed emphasis in the preceding on themes of power, revelation, and spiritual gifts it may come as a surprise to non-Pentecostal readers to learn that Pentecostals believe there is another attribute which takes precedence over everything else, effectively serving as an essential qualifier for all authentic demonstrations of the Holy Spirit: godly love. Gause argues that love is the essential personal attribute of the Spirit-filled life and that it is the bridge that connects and unites apostolic instructions on spiritual gifts.[28] First Corinthians 12–14 gives extensive regulations regarding the operation of spiritual gifts. However, "Love is the operating principle by which these regulations are fulfilled."[29] In Pentecostal theology, Spirit baptism does not, indeed cannot, stand apart from authentic expression of God's holy love. Accordingly, we may assert an essential relation of Spirit baptism with divine

---

26. I finally realized that in a spiritual sense I had become like Dave Loggins' 1974 hit song, "Please Come to Boston." See "Dave Loggins: Stories Behind the Songs" at https://daveloggginsmusic-com.webs.com/stories-behind-the-songs (accessed May 31, 2019). I was searching here and there for some special place but needed to come home to my real love (i.e. the Pentecostal movement).

27. Of course, people's "experiences of the reality of God" can and do vary from individual to individual and from setting to setting, Allen, *Spiritual Theology*, 51. Allen contrasts the diverse examples of Leo Tolstoy, T. S. Elliott, and Simone Weil.

28. Gause, *Living in the Spirit*, 125.

29. Gause, *Living in the Spirit*, 136.

love.³⁰ Furthermore, an essential and intimate relation between Spirit baptism and love is quite evident among the earliest Pentecostals, for example, and particularly, in perhaps its greatest leader, Pastor William Seymour.³¹

McClymond insists that Spirit baptism by nature involves an intensification of divine love.³² In this view, Pentecost includes an outpouring of divine love (Rom 5:5). God's impartation of God's self to believers by the Holy Spirit involves the gift of ἀγάπη (*agapē*) or divine love. Thus, God's grace enables ordinary human beings to live quite extraordinary lives. In contrast to the typical Protestant Reformed tradition's reaction against Roman Catholicism, Pentecostals do not so much stress ordinariness in and of itself as elevate ordinary people to enjoy extraordinary lives through union with God via Spirit baptism in divine love. "But this love is expressed in extraordinary fashion; through prayers for healing, deliverance, and divine intervention."³³ Divine love is not an add-on or afterthought in Pentecostal spirituality and theology; it is at the core of what it means to be baptized with the Spirit and for Spirit-filled living.

A couple of related questions come to mind. For example, how does an essential association of Spirit baptism with divine love inform our understanding, as delineated herein, of the nature of Spirit baptism? I once again recall the wisdom of Pastor Golden. After a few months of attending his congregation I requested a meeting. I was curious about his understanding of the Holy Spirit's role in the Christian life, especially regarding the relation of regeneration, sanctification, and Spirit baptism, so I asked him about these matters. He explained that in each of these experiences the Holy Spirit is working with a specific focus. Yet naturally as one yields more and more to the Spirit there is an overall increase in each work of grace. In the new birth the Spirit grants new life and a new nature. In sanctification the Spirit cleanses the heart and mind. In Spirit baptism the Spirit provides power for service. Yet there is an interconnected, cumulative impact on a believer's whole heart and life.³⁴ I found this a quite compelling explanation. I still do.

Second, if Spirit baptism takes up and extends the preceding work of the Holy Spirit in believers' lives, then why stop there? Indeed! Please recall the repeated "fillings" of NT believers after the Day of Pentecost (Acts 4:8, 31; 13:9, 52). As much as Pentecostals stress Spirit baptism they do not assume that God's Spirit stops there. Life in the Spirit is, or should be, ongoing and unending. An authentic Spirit-filled life involves commitment to the commandment to keep on being filled with the Holy Spirit (Eph 5:18). Spirit baptism is an initial experience of the Spirit's filling that incentivizes and sustains further encounters. This raises the relationship between Spirit baptism,

---

30. Arrington, *Christian Doctrine*, 3:97–98, 104–06; Lombard and Daffe, *Spiritual Gifts*, 214–18.
31. Alexander, "Baptism of Divine Love," 68–82.
32. McClymond, "Spirit Baptism as a Moral Source," 50–53.
33. McClymond, "Spirit Baptism as a Moral Source," 56.
34. This is termed in a classic Wesleyan-Pentecostal understanding, but its basic idea works with Baptistic Pentecostalism as well.

further infillings, and spiritual gifts with the fruit of the Spirit. Although the phrase "full of the Holy Spirit" appears to describe a consistent state of being, the first three tend to have something of an episodic nature—at least in the manner that they are appropriated experientially (Acts 6:3, 5; 7:55; 11:24). Fruit on the other hand signifies "planting" by the Holy Spirit in the human spirit followed by a process of intentional cultivation and gradual growth in Jesus' disciples. Yet clearly spiritual fruit and spiritual gifts are complementary in character.[35] Likely the state of being "full of the Holy Spirit" signifies a life consistently characterized by the overall work of the Holy Spirit as demonstrated in one's walk before God—that is, by the daily presence of both fruit and gifts (Gal 5:16, 25).[36]

Although not an exhaustive list, the fruit of the Spirit are love, joy, peace, longsuffering (or patience), kindness, goodness, faithfulness, gentleness, and self-control (Gal 5:22–23; cp. Rom 14:17; Phil 4:8; 2 Pet 1:5). Arrington explains that the fruit of the Spirit are devotional and ethical, not passive qualities but active aspects of the Christian life, and that they reflect what Christlike living should look like.[37] Love "embraces and includes" all the other fruit (1 Cor 13:4–7).[38] We may view the fruit of the Spirit and the gifts of the Spirit as counterparts, two sides of the same pneumatic coin, so to speak. In sum, spiritual fruit are the Holy Spirit's way of producing Christlike followers; spiritual gifts are the Holy Spirit's way of equipping Christlike servants.

Yet admittedly the Pentecostal movement has been plagued with notoriety because of prominent ministers whose scandalous careers challenge the ethical and moral core of the movement's self-understanding. For decades, cultural portraits of nefarious "Elmer Gantry" type ministers have caricatured Pentecostals.[39] Robert Duvall's poignant movie "The Apostle" dramatically exemplifies a minister running amuck. Unfortunately, it is not all fiction.[40] Tragically, several high-profile "televangelists" have repeatedly rocked the modern Pentecostal movement with scandals. Who can forget Jim and Tammy Bakker or Jimmy Swaggert? Is this the way Spirit-filled believers are expected to act? No! But then we painfully remember King David with Bathsheba (2 Sam 11:1–27). We recall with great sadness Cardinal Law and Roman Catholicism's recurring problems on the discipline of pedophilic priests. We hear of damaging reports about impropriety and misconduct allegations among Evangelicals such as Mark Driscoll at Mars Hill or Bill Hybels at Willow Creek. Celebrity scandals

35. Arrington, *Christian Doctrine*, 3:123–24.
36. Arrington, *Christian Doctrine*, 3:100.
37. Arrington, *Christian Doctrine*, 3:101–03.
38. Arrington, *Christian Doctrine*, 3:104.

39. Although Sinclair Lewis' title character in *Elmer Gantry* was not a Pentecostal there were characters in the novel loosely based on infamous Pentecostals with apparent indiscretions (viz., Aimee Semple McPhearson).

40. See Robert Ebert, "The Apostle," (January 30, 1998): https://www.rogerebert.com/reviews/the-apostle-1998. Occasionally, I reference items from pop culture (songs, movies), mostly for illustrative purposes but with theological implications.

aside, who does not know someone, perhaps in their own family or local church, who seems to be much better at "talking the walk" than "walking the talk"? Unfortunately, people do not always live up to our expectations or even to their own highest ideals. And a lot of people get hurt. It offers precious little comfort to know that Pentecostals are not alone in such sinful failures.

If anything, it may feel worse for us. Aren't Pentecostals supposed to have something more? Other communions aside, how do Pentecostals reconcile our lofty vision of the powerful purpose of Spirit baptism with such disastrously sinful shenanigans by some of our own most spectacular representatives? Is it all a sham? Are we self-deceived, unconscious hypocrites? Worse still, is the Holy Spirit's vaunted power impotent after all? God forbid! I am certainly no expert in this area; but, as a lifelong Pentecostal and long term (nearly 40 years) pastor and scholar I offer of few personal observations for the present context.

First, it only fair to note that most Pentecostal believers and ministers are faithful to the high standards of the Christian faith and of their ministerial vows.[41] Second, our attempts to respond to the ethical and moral crisis of contemporary believers and ministers should always have restoration uppermost in mind (Gal 6:1). Third, discipline is an essential element of genuine restoration (1 Cor 5:1–13). Fourth, and finally, we must inquire into what is at the root of the problem of moral failure among our constituency (2 Co 13:5). Let's elaborate on number four. While not the complete story, Harvey Cox may be onto something with his suggestion that the intense primal spirituality so intrinsic in Pentecostalism can be a double-edged sword.[42] On the one hand, it represents spiritual power that modernist Christianity has all-too-often forgotten—and dreadfully needs reminded of. On the other, raw, undisciplined spiritual power can at times exhibit a dark side, a dangerous antithesis to what Pentecostals believe the Holy Spirit's power and purpose is all about.

Even those who do not experience moral failure or public scandal can struggle with maintaining spiritual balance. A godly woman, Pastor Patty Yates recently shared with me something of her own spiritual journey.[43] She recalls when she herself was more prone to spiritual "highs and lows" that could sometimes result in starkly disconcerting emotional contrasts. Over the years she has come to appreciate more a certain steadiness of the Spirit. The enduring commitment and discipline now personified in her mature Christian walk are key to victory over the forces of fleshly propensities in a deeply spiritual people. And steadfastness—the quality of being resolutely firm and dutifully unwavering—is a highly esteemed biblical virtue (Ps 108:1; 1 Cor 15:58; 1 Pet

---

41. Most Pentecostals are more disappointed and embarrassed than anyone about the moral failures of some prominent spokespersons. Cp. Cox, *Fire from Heaven*, 274, 312.

42. Cox, *Fire from Heaven*, 276–79.

43. More than 20 years ago, Pastor Patty Yates planted New Life Church of God in Murfreesboro, TN.

5:9). Moreover, in Pentecostal parlance, a steadfast spirit can occur through spiritual renewal (Ps 51:10).

I have heard people speak of "the Elijah syndrome." We well recall that the great prophet's victory high on Mount Carmel was soon followed by despondency low under a broom tree—yet it was there where God met him yet again and led him to a better place (1 Kgs 18:20–19:18). Pentecostals can identify with the encouragement of James 5:17 that though Elijah was "a man with a nature like ours," or as the KJV so graphically puts it, "a man subject to like passions as we are," on different fronts. Although Elijah was as human as we are the Lord deigned to use him in a miraculous manner. It can also be stated in the converse. Although the Lord deigned to use Elijah in a miraculous manner, he was as human as we are.[44] Thus, Pentecostal commentator Timothy Cargal notes that James' assertion regarding Elijah's ministry is not primarily about human nature so much as "trust in God's goodness."[45] Pentecostals do well to pay close heed to both sides of this descriptive equation. Undoubtedly (to me), God has raised up Pentecostals, although not many of us are mighty and not many of us are noble (1 Cor 1:26–29), to bear witness that God is ready, willing, and able to use mortal human beings in miraculous manners. Yet Pentecostals do well to remember that we are but "earthen vessels" and that "the excellence of the power" is of God and God alone (2 Cor 4:7). Miraculous power, like anything else, is really about God's goodness not ours.

Pentecostal pastors frequently confront the struggle for equilibrium in the congregational context. Along with some Evangelical groups, Pentecostals are heirs to American revivalism.[46] The regular practice of conducting protracted services to promote spiritual revival in the congregation and community is part of this heritage. These services are often described as "revival meetings." They can be very effective at times. Yet pastors are often frustrated at a cycle often associated with such revivals. One is reminded of the Book of Judges. Some people repeatedly repent and serve the Lord with a fury for a short time before backsliding completely. The next revival they go through the same process again . . . and again . . . and again. A great American psychologist, Abraham Maslow was doubtless correct that the peak intensity of experience (religious and otherwise) is essential for self-actualization of human potentiality.[47] However, these "peaks" cannot, and perhaps ought not, be constantly maintained.

---

44. Tensions between perceptions of Elijah as an exceptional man of God vis-à-vis his common humanity are obvious in Bede's, *ACCS: James,* 62, comment: "But just in case you think that you could never measure up to someone as holy as Elijah, James adds that he was a man, just as we are, even if he was second to none in his virtue."

45. Cargal, "James," 1428.

46. Gause, *God, Prayer, Redemption, and Hope,* 81, caustically observes that the word "revival" has been so overused, and indiscriminately used, as to become practically meaningless. However, authentic revival is "a restoration of spiritual vigor and holiness of living" (81).

47. Maslow's *Religions, Values, and Peak-Experiences* is a fascinating study of such phenomena.

The human psyche is such that some occasional relief must be available. Consistency and steadfastness are essential for human emotional health and spiritual well-being.

Yet it would be a sorry solution to avoid religious experience because of potentially destabilizing intensity. Here "playing it safe" does not work well at all. Pentecostals do not find denying or avoiding the valid experience of Spirit baptism and its related phenomena an acceptable option. An ominous warning to the church of the Laodiceans has been oft-quoted by many Pentecostals: "I know your works, that you are neither cold nor hot. I could wish you were cold or hot. So then, because you are lukewarm, and neither cold nor hot, I will vomit you out of my mouth" (Rev 3:15–16). Pentecostals take this to mean that the Lord cannot tolerate mediocre commitment.[48] Rather, the Lord Jesus desires zealous servants. The incontestability that zeal is sometimes misguided does not negate the great value of real zeal (John 2:17; Rom 10:2; 12:8; 2 Cor 7:11; 9:2; Gal 4:17; Phil 3:6; Col 4:13).[49]

Rather, establishing spiritual equilibrium with genuine integrity lies in an apostolic assurance that "God has not given us a spirit of fear, but of power and of love and of a sound mind" (2 Tim 1:7). Pentecostal commentator Deborah Gill explains that Paul reassures his timid friend that the gift of the Holy Spirit overcomes fear and timidity with bravery and stability. She says, "God's Spirit overcomes cowardice, contributes clear thinking (especially in the face of false teachers), provides us power, and loads us with love."[50] I could not agree more. Therefore, I am sure that the inexhaustible resources of God the Holy Spirit are available for Spirit-baptized believers to serve Christ our Lord with balanced boldness, that is, with power and purity, and with intensity as well as with consistency.

In closing this section, I offer three conclusions. First, the heavenly power of the Holy Spirit imparted to believers through Spirit baptism is lofty and real. Second, human finitude and frailty remain even in the most exalted of saints. Third, an enduring, steadfast walk with the Lord, a life characterized by deep devotion and sound discipline, is critical to establishing and sustaining the spiritual equilibrium necessary for a consistent witness to Jesus Christ our Lord that glorifies God before all the angels and before all humankind.

In closing this chapter, I exhort every conscientious pastor to encourage members of his or her congregation to seek earnestly to be baptized with the Holy Spirit. The crossings of the Red Sea and of the Jordan River may serve as hortatory examples. Israelites fleeing from the Egyptians crossed the Red Sea on dry ground (Ex 14:21–22). It was a formative redemptive miracle for Israel. Paul compares it to Christian

---

48. Jenney, "Revelation," 1567–68, "Jesus finds their mediocre faith indigestible." Thomas, *Apocalypse,* says their lukewarm works and the state they reflect are "completely worthless" and "unpalatable" for Jesus, 188–89.

49. I do not agree that a sense of religious certainty inevitably leads to social intolerance and bigotry—although one must always guard against these sinful attitudes and the sinful actions which they spawn. See Cole, *Northern Evangelists,* 16.

50. Gill, "Pastorals," 1260–61.

baptism (1 Cor 10:1–2). Yet a subsequent generation of Israelites still needed a "repeat performance" at the Jordan River before facing the foreboding challenges of occupying Canaan (Josh 3:14–17). The Lord plainly explains that he performed the miracle so that their generation would know that just as he had been with the previous generation, so he would be with them (3:7, 9). Why did such an amazing initiation miracle in Israel's national identity need to be repeated? It was an encouraging sign of God's enabling power offering them tangible confirmation and validation of God's continuing presence.[51] Even so today those who have read and heard of God's mighty acts in previous generations still need to be baptized in the Holy Spirit for themselves.

In a word, each generation of God's people and every individual believer need God's power to do God's work in their day and time. Today's world needs more than enthusiastic churches. It needs congregations which seek and receive Spirit baptism, congregations where spiritual fruit is evident and spiritual gifts operate, and where "Spirit-empowered people go out to live as Christ's witnesses."[52] May we all receive a fresh anointing of the Holy Spirit (Ps 92:10). Amen!

---

51. Howard, *Joshua*, 123–124.
52. Colkmire, "Young, Significant, Diverse, and Needy," 7.

11

Examining Initial Evidence

PENTECOSTALS USE THE TERM "initial evidence" to describe their teaching on speaking in tongues as the first physically observable sign of Spirit baptism. Pentecostals, with a few variations, expect speaking in tongues (or glossolalia) to accompany reception of baptism with the Holy Spirit. "The doctrine of initial evidence is the chief doctrinal distinctive of classical Pentecostalism" according to Pentecostal historian Gary McGee.[1] For Vinson Syan, another Pentecostal historian, the movement's uniqueness encompasses other *charismata* but with special focus on divine healing and speaking in tongues.[2] From the perspective of a systematic theologian, Macchia insists Pentecostal distinctiveness cannot be reduced to tongues.[3] Furthermore, Warrington observes that while both North American and European Pentecostals affirm the validity of the contemporary practice of speaking in tongues, the specific doctrine of initial evidence itself is less common in Europe, including the United Kingdom, than in North America.[4] However, in these various conversations the emphatic importance of speaking in tongues for Pentecostals is not in dispute. In my view, there is great importance attached to other spiritual gifts and the significance of contemporary

1. McGee, "Initial Evidence," 790. A major difference between Pentecostals and Charismatics is the latter's use of an indefinite article when speaking about evidence of Spirit baptism and the former's use of a definite article.
2. Synan, "Classical Pentecostalism," 553.
3. Macchia, "Theology, Pentecostal," 1132.
4. Warrington, *Pentecostal Theology*, 120–22.

Pentecostalism certainly exceeds the practice of speaking in tongues; nevertheless, the functional value of the doctrine of initial evidence for promoting the Pentecostal experience of Spirit baptism is almost inestimable.

Contemporary Pentecostals recognize that initial evidence is the one Pentecostal doctrine that many other Christians find most problematic and that it requires further theological development.[5] That is understandable. Honestly. Yet there is another side to it too. Pentecostals can empathize with how Paul must have felt when Athenian philosophers told him, "You are bringing strange things to our ears" (Acts 17:20a). The gospel of the crucified and risen Savior doubtless sounded "strange" to those sophisticated Greeks. At times God's law came across as "a strange thing" even to the Israelites (Hos 8:12). I do not mean to cast aspersions on those who disagree with the doctrine of initial evidence. I only ask for a fair and honest hearing. Please do not allow the apparent "strangeness" of the doctrine itself to hinder a hearing. Whether one affirms or denies initial evidence the doctrine should be understood in its rightful context. In the following I will not so much try to convince anyone of initial evidence as try to understand where it is coming from, what it means, and, therefore, why it is of singular importance in Pentecostal theology and spirituality. The next chapter will deal with further theological development of speaking in tongues in general. This chapter focuses on initial evidence. After attention to the formative influence of its historical context, I examine the biblical basis of the doctrine of initial evidence before finally offering suggestions for theological clarity and development.

HISTORICAL PRECEDENTS AND DEVELOPMENT

Contemporary recovery of the lost importance of the evidentiary value of speaking in tongues can be traced generally to pre-twentieth century pietism and evangelicalism. It is especially apparent in the theology of Edward Irving, an eighteenth-century Scottish Presbyterian who insisted not only on the restoration of the *charismata* but also on the evidentiary nature of glossolalia as a sign of Pentecostal power with eschatological significance.[6] In addition to his theological studies, Irving formally studied science and linguistics with an eye toward eventual missionary service.[7] Similarities with early Pentecostals are hard to miss. Although leading a strong charismatic restorationist movement for a time, Irving's influence lagged after he lost his Presbyterian ordination due to his unorthodox ideas; thus, he did not leave a lasting impression. Most early Pentecostals seem to have been unaware of his thought or his movement.[8]

---

5. Chan, *Pentecostal Theology*, 40–41. Hunter admits that theological immaturity resulted in "inferior formulations" that are "not difficult to criticize" but in their essence these may stand up well under more careful investigation, *Spirit Baptism*, 221–22; 226.

6. McGee, "Initial Evidence," 784–85.

7. Bundy, "Irving," 803.

8. Bundy, "Irving," 803–04.

Yet there are indications Charles Parham, known by Pentecostals as the father of their initial evidence doctrine, may have been aware of Irving and his movement and that he may have drawn from them to an extent.[9]

If Parham did draw from Irving, several interesting questions arise. Why did the earlier movement toward some form of initial evidence doctrine fail with Irving but succeed later with Parham? What was different about the context that resulted in a different outcome? Was Irving too radical or too early? Did his unorthodoxy stymie his own movement? Was Scottish Presbyterianism ultimately unconducive to speaking in tongues as initial evidence? Whatever the answers to these and similar questions may be, we are left with a need to take a closer look at the environment out of which initial evidence arose with Pentecostals. The American Holiness movement stands out as a major contributor.

Both the Wesleyan and Keswickian branches of the Holiness movement were consistently interested in identifying the inward evidence and outward evidence of Spirit baptism.[10] Prominent Wesleyan theologian Larry Wood argues that the Pentecostal emphasis on evidence is an outcome of the Wesleyan emphasis on assurance.[11] The "fire-baptized" (from Matt 3:11) theology of late seventeenth-century radical Wesleyan-Holiness preacher Benjamin Hardin Irwin particularly pushed the issue of establishing evidence for a third work of grace (i.e., Spirit baptism after regeneration and sanctification) to the fore.[12] Irwin had been a lawyer so his quest for evidence appears in that light as well.[13] One might surmise that the legal interests of Irwin and the earlier scientific/linguistic interests of Irving provide fascinating backdrops for the doctrine of initial evidence. Both threads of thought would consider evidence a key need. Furthermore, evidence in this sense would have meant something like an indicator as to whether a belief or experience is true or valid. That is, speaking in tongues as initial evidence would function as an assurance, a kind of confidence-imparting declaration, that an experience of Spirit baptism was authentic. More generally, various synonyms for evidence come to mind: proof, confirmation, verification, corroboration, affirmation, or attestation. (See more on implications of this possibility below.) In any case, Irwin, like Irving, rose to temporary prominence but then lost any lasting personal influence. Irwin confessed to open sin and stepped out of his previous leadership role in the Holiness/proto-Pentecostal movements. Yet the Wesleyan-Holiness adaptation of spiritual power with observable evidence did not diminish. In fact, it increased significantly.

9. McGee, "Initial Evidence," 785.

10. McGee, "Initial Evidence," 785. Wesleyans emphasized a crisis-development model of sanctification while Keswickians stressed a positional-progressive model.

11. Wood, "Wesleyan Response," 167. If so, and there is much to commend this idea, then initial evidence could be understood as a positive declaration of confidence.

12. McGee, "Initial Evidence," 785.

13. Synan, "Irwin," 804.

As with Irving, in Irwin's case interesting questions arise—but from a different angle. He was successful beyond himself. Why and how did initial evidence doctrine take root and grow when its earliest proponents, such as Irwin (and Irving) were obviously troubled and, eventually, in one way or another discredited as leaders? Would not one expect the doctrine to fall into disrepute also? Is not the resilience of initial evidence itself remarkable? Does its recurring appearance indicate that as a doctrine its time had come? Further, could it be that even today the doctrine of initial evidence is larger than any individual or their movement? Does this possibility indicate that initial evidence has potential to extend beyond Pentecostalism per se? Yet (as already indicated) there was another individual whose influence in terms of initial evidence was unparalleled.

Historically speaking, the main person responsible for the surprising rise of the initial evidence doctrine was Charles Fox Parham.[14] A former Methodist minister, Parham's Bible school in Topeka, Kansas was the site of the original outbreak (1901) of Spirit baptism and speaking in tongues by Agnes Ozman which in turned fueled the subsequent Azusa Street Mission Revival and thereafter the global Pentecostal movement. Parham taught that speaking in tongues signified the outpouring of the Holy Spirit, verified reception of Spirit baptism, and provided end-time missionaries with linguistic expertise.[15] Parham's teaching on "missionary tongues" eventually failed in the face of realities on the mission field. However, support for tongues as a sign of the Spirit's outpouring and reception continued and grew. Nevertheless, Parham was controversial, and his early influence eventually waned and all but disappeared. In addition to his espousal of such unpalatable (for Pentecostals) doctrines as annihilationism and a feud with Seymour and consequent denouncement of the Azusa Revival, he was disgraced through a charge of sodomy.[16] Although charges were eventually dropped, and he always staunchly maintained his innocence, Parham's influence was permanently stifled for many Pentecostals. Nevertheless, the doctrine of initial evidence proved to be larger than any one person's influence. Accordingly, commitment to belief in speaking in tongues as the initial evidence of baptism with the Holy Spirit not only survived but thrived in the burgeoning Pentecostal movement.

Similar questions as those raised above regarding Irving and Irwin resurface with Parham. Only, if anything, they are more direct and challenging. How is it that a leader surrounded always by an aura of controversy could have had such a dramatic impact on the early Pentecostal movement? A hostile response might argue that questionable leadership jells well with the perceived lunacy of speaking in tongues itself. In other words, it suggests that the doctrine of initial evidence has been discredited along with

---

14. Goff, "Parham," 956.

15. McGee, "Initial Evidence," 785–86.

16. Although he had other issues, including leadership and race, Parham accused Seymour of practicing hypnotism in his altar services, Alexander, *Black Fire,* 139–40, due to a prevalence of spiritual manifestations.

leaders such as Irving, Irwin, and Parham. However, that is a rash assessment. On the contrary, it appears that the momentum toward a recovery of the spiritual practice of speaking in tongues, including the doctrine of initial evidence, was mighty enough to overcome embarrassment and humiliation. In this regard, it reminds of the early Christian movement during the NT age which could not be quelled although one of its original Twelve Apostles betrayed his Lord and another denied him. And yet we may remind that there were ten others among the original Twelve Apostles who were faithful and truthful witnesses to our Lord Jesus Christ.

The plain truth is that there were many men and women among the early Pentecostals who exhibited exemplary leadership. People such as William Seymour, Lucy Farrow, Jennie Evans Moore, Frank Bartleman, William Durham, Florence Crawford, A. J. Tomlinson, F. J. Lee, J. H. King, E. N. Bell, J. Roswell Flower and Alice Reynolds Flower, Andrew Urshan, G. T. Haywood, Charles H. Mason, and many others, exhibited enduring character and sacrificial commitment in the rise and development of various strands of Pentecostalism. Yet in a sense at least the Pentecostal argument that the movement had no single leader responsible for its existence and meteoric rise but is attributable to the Holy Spirit appears valid. True enough, several gifted leaders left their imprint on the movement. However, Pentecostalism had no Augustine or Aquinas, and no Martin Luther or John Calvin, it had no one comparable to John Wesley—no one who stood head and shoulders above all others as an originator. Pentecostals are not "Augustinians" or "Lutherans" and so on; we are "Pentecostals" because of *Pentecost*. Hence the survival of the doctrine of initial evidence in the face of all odds.

BIBLICAL INVESTIGATION AND ASSESSMENT

Pentecostals build their theology of initial evidence on a close association in Acts between Spirit baptism/infilling and glossolalia (speaking in tongues).[17] The context of this exegesis is an associative pattern between spiritual experience, inspired speech, and practical service deeply rooted in Holy Scripture (Num 11:16–17, 24–26; 1 Sam 10:6–7).[18] At the paradigmatic Pentecost event the Holy Spirit's coming was accompanied by speaking in tongues (2:1–4). This pattern was repeated in Peter's mission to the Gentiles (10:44–46) and Paul's ministry to disciples of the Baptist at Ephesus (19:1–7). When tongues are not specifically mentioned (Samaria) the presence of an observable sign is still indicated, which Pentecostals argue is likely tongues (8:18, 19). Pentecostals admit there is no indication of tongues when Paul received his Spirit baptism (9:17–19); however, he later affirmed that he frequently spoke in tongues (1 Cor 14:18). Significantly, speaking in tongues does not comprise Spirit baptism.

---

17. Arrington, *Christian Doctrine*, 3:62–63. Pentecostals note the significatory nature of Acts as consistent with evidential tongues, Richie, "From Suspicion to Synthesis," 262–63.

18. Stronstad, *Charismatic Theology of Luke*, 25.

Rather, this manifestation of Spirit-inspired speech shows "the relationship between the spiritual experience and practical service."[19]

Furthermore, deeply rooted in the revivalist tradition is a biblical hermeneutic which enables an acceptance of physical demonstrations or exercises as consequences and evidences of the Spirit's presence.[20] Arguably, the Pentecostal doctrine of initial evidence simply carries this revivalist, and actually quite Evangelical, heritage of evidentiary physicality forward by connecting it with their understanding of the relationship between Spirit baptism and speaking in tongues as presented in Scripture and informed by their own experience. When Evangelicals charge Pentecostals with error regarding physical demonstrations in manifestation of the Spirit's presence, including speaking in tongues, Pentecostals are often honestly astonished. They point to the signs of the Spirit in Evangelicalism's historical tradition. Will Evangelicals deny their own history in denouncing Pentecostals? Or will they embrace Pentecostals consistently with their own experiences?[21]

Having said that, Pentecostals have always argued that their position on speaking in tongues arises not out of any historical trajectory but out of the Bible itself. As indicated above, much of this biblical foundation is found in the book of Acts. Arguably, what is at stake in the debate over initial evidence is one's understanding of the nature of the book of Acts, especially its miraculous and spiritual manifestations, including but not exclusively, speaking in tongues. Thus, biblical interpreters must wrestle with the Lukan idea of evidentiary charismata, including glossolalia.

The Acts Prologue (1:1–5) significantly introduces the book with τεκμηριον (*tekmerion*) (v. 3), signifying, according to internationally and interdenominationally respected Bible scholar F. F. Bruce, "a compelling sign," and implying "proofs that carried certainty of conviction with them, as contrasted with those that were only probable or circumstantial."[22] Arguably, explicit references to the Holy Spirit and to Spirit baptism are suggestive. Applications beyond the interim between Jesus' resurrection and ascension to the Pentecost event and to the experience of the church appear quite possible. Accordingly, Luke's paradigmatic Prologue could imply an emphasis throughout Acts on evidentiary charismata as signs of "Jesus' enduring activity" through the Holy Spirit in his disciples (cp. Acts 2:33).[23] Indeed, Chrysostom

---

19. Arrington, *Christian Doctrine*, 3:65. Also, glossolalia is a form of praising God and of prayer, a sign to unbelievers, and a sign of the last days, 65–68. Further, it functions as one of the gifts of the Spirit bestowed for the edification of the church (1 Cor 12–14), 113–19; 150–62.

20. See Conkin, *Cane Ridge*, 21–22, 173, 178.

21. Pentecostals affirm that the Holy Spirit respects individual personality and temperament. Some people are by nature more reserved, others more expressive. That is as it should be. Yet many, like April, a typically quiet young mother from a non-Pentecostal background who received Spirit baptism, can be surprisingly demonstrative in their outbursts of joyful praise, Arrington, *Encountering the Holy Spirit*, 430. Pentecostals perceive such demonstrations to be legitimate responses to an overwhelming sense of the Holy Spirit's presence.

22. Bruce, *Acts of the Apostles*, 100, and Bowdle, ed., *Ellicott's Bible Commentary*, 856.

23. Bruce, *Acts of the Apostles*, 127. Lincoln, *Paradise Now-Not Yet*, 58, argues that "an interest in

argued from Acts 1:3 that continuing apostolic miracles in Acts provided "evidence" and "proof" of Christ's resurrection, and that this in effect "authorized" the Christian religion.[24] In other words, extraordinary demonstrations and manifestations of the Spirit's power have evidentiary value. This evidence includes (but is not limited to) speaking in tongues.

Admittedly, we may distinguish today between pre-scientific and scientific understandings of "evidence" or "proof." Nevertheless, an idea of reasonably persuasive witness to the certainty of a reality is clearly present. Is that level sufficiently robust for the Pentecostal argument? It is. Of course, it is *not* enough to substantiate the doctrine of initial evidence as Pentecostals understand it. It is enough, however, to frame Acts as a volume which assumes that miracles, signs, and wonders, including spiritual gifts, have evidential value (e.g. 3:16; 4:8–11; 5:12–16; 8:6–8; 9:42; 16:25–30; 17:31; 19:17–20; 28:1–10). And that conclusion goes a great distance toward a constructive conversation on the viability of initial evidence.

Even beyond the book of Acts the NT bears witness to the evidentiary value of spiritual gifts and other signs and wonders. For example, Hebrews 2:4 explains that the demonstration of "signs and wonders, with various miracles, and gifts of the Holy Spirit" is one of the ways God himself bears witness to the truth of the gospel and to the salvation it brings. These extraordinary happenings were regarded as supernatural manifestations serving as "evidence that authenticates the gospel" (cp. John 20:30–31and Rom 15:18–19).[25] Clearly, the NT presents signs and wonders and gifts of the Holy Spirit as, among other things, evidences signifying the reality and verity of the gospel of Jesus Christ. Biblically speaking, these extraordinary experiences are surely evidentiary or significative.

To be clear, I do not argue that the obvious evidential nature of miracles, signs, and wonders and spiritual gifts proves the doctrine of initial evidence. My point is that when the doctrine of initial evidence is properly placed within the context of the evidential nature of such extraordinary phenomena then it does not seem so "strange" after all (Hosea 8:12; Acts 17:20a). It fits right into the framework of other miraculous manifestations. This general backdrop of the significative qualities of spiritual gifts and manifestations is helpful for contextualizing the specificity of the doctrine of initial evidence in relation to baptism with the Holy Spirit. Therefore, instances of initial evidence in action (Acts 2, 8, 9, 10, and 19) exist in and exhibit clear continuity with the overall goal of extraordinary experiences to bear witness to the full gospel of Jesus Christ our Lord and Savior. The doctrine of initial evidence is not an oddity. It is not an exception. It stands in complete continuity and consistency with an overall presentation of biblical charismology and semiology.

---

the Spirit's visible manifestations" could have its "origins in the pentecostal beginnings of the church's life" and quotes extensively from Acts in support.

24. Chrysostom, *ACCS: NT: V: Acts*, 3–4.
25. Adams, "Hebrews," 1314.

THEOLOGICAL CLARITY AND DEVELOPMENT

British Pentecostal theologian Keith Warrington makes the surprising point that in Pauline theology speaking in tongues could function as a negative sign to unbelievers (1 Co 14:20–22).[26] In other words, speaking in tongues could signify to the uninitiate an incidence of group irrationality (mass hysteria!) resulting in liturgical confusion; and, it might even prompt an aversive reaction to the gospel. Clearly Paul is addressing uninterpreted tongues speech during a given worship service rather than tongues (whether as initial evidence or as interpreted) in the life of individual believers. Yet Warrington's observation raises a pertinent question: if tongues are given for a sign then who does the sign address? That is, who is the sign for? In terms of initial evidence, in practice the tongues testify to the believing recipient more so than anyone else. Only secondarily do observers in the community of faith share in the sign's impactful value. And unbelievers may have a negative response to the sign. Accordingly, it seems circumspect to affirm that the evidentiary value of speaking in tongues as a significator functions differently in different contexts and has differing results with different participants or observers. It may be that at times critics of speaking in tongues, especially initial evidence, often focus on one or the other aspects of the evidentiary impact of speaking in tongues without allowing for or realizing others that may be present. Of course, the same can apply in reverse for apologists who may be defending one aspect without acknowledging the critique of another. This observation is especially relevant because it is likely that defenders and detractors of initial evidence are speaking past one another at times. Although tongue-in-cheek, we might say that when people talk about tongues the gift of interpretation is needed all around.

Therefore, it is essential to be clear on *how* and *for whom* the Pentecostal tradition asserts that speaking in tongues functions as initial evidence of Spirit baptism. For the most part, in actual experience and practice tongues aid the individual *seeker* in obtaining assurance in their spiritual journey. His/her faith *community* accepts and affirms the seeker's experience in accordance with their shared beliefs and experiences. However, speaking in tongues does not function as a sign to *everyone* that someone is Spirit-filled. The universal sign of Christ's Spirit in one's life is the continuing, consistent presence of the fruit of the Spirit in one's Christian walk in daily life (Gal. 5:22–25; cp. Matt 7:15–20). However, this in no wise lessens an essential need for individual and congregational assurance regarding the Holy Spirit's specific agency in Spirit baptism; rather, it frames the environment in which Spirit baptism functionally occurs (1 Thess 1:5). After thinking about *who* is primarily involved in the witness of initial evidence, then we can consider *how* initial evidence functions as the distinctive indicator in the reception of Spirit baptism. Land describes evidentiary aspects of Spirit baptism in terms of a threefold distinction: "initial evidence," "essential evidence," and "ultimate

---

26. Warrington, *Pentecostal Theology*, 91–92.

evidence."[27] The essential evidence of Spirit baptism, without which it cannot be genuine, is love in manifestation of the character of God. The ultimate evidence, which is the goal in issuance of the experience, is a life of prayerful service to God in powerful witness of redemptive reality. The initial evidence is speaking in tongues. Thus, we can carefully qualify this evidential role of speaking in tongues, guarding against misrepresentations by either critics or proponents.

Still, and as Warrington observes, Pentecostals are struggling with whether to understand speaking in tongues as the evidence of or a sign of baptism with the Spirit.[28] Two ideas are competing for attention in this question. One is whether to use a definite or indefinite article (and what that decision implies). Another is whether to use the language of evidence or of sign (and what that decision implies). I offer a twofold observation. First, in keeping with Land's threefold distinction between initial, essential, and ultimate evidence we may well describe tongues as *the* evidence but not as the *only* evidence. Evidential tongues are experientially definitive but not exclusively decisive. And that qualification makes a great deal of difference. Speaking in tongues functions as a definite indicator that a seeker has received the experience of Spirit baptism only as a part of a continuing complex of decisive evidences. Speaking in tongues does not and cannot stand alone. Initial evidence is inoperable in isolation. Therefore, it is unconvincing on its own. Yet its role as the sign of commencement, the determinative beginning or starting point, as the port of entry, that is, as the *initium*, which is what Pentecostals claim for *initial* evidence anyway, is no less critically significant. The sound of the starter pistol firing is the critical signal to athletes that the race is underway. Yet it would be sheer folly to conclude that the race is over when its sound is heard. It would also be folly to attempt a race without a clear signal to begin. Any attempts to debunk the Pentecostal doctrine of initial evidence which do not take in to account its clear nature as *initium* lack credibility.

Above I mentioned that various synonyms for "evidence" include proof, confirmation, verification, corroboration, affirmation, or attestation. These terms may function as more or less equivalents to evidence. Each one can have its own nuance as well. I find the idea of "attestation" particularly intriguing in relation to initial evidence primarily because of its association with testimony. Throughout this volume I have repeatedly referenced the well-known Pentecostal penchant for testimony. As Paul Ricoeur, a French philosopher/theologian in the Protestant tradition, rightly argues, testimony is a kind of attestation.[29] Testimony as attestation exemplifies not "I believe-that" but "I believe-in"; or, in other words, it's "a kind of belief" but not that of modernistic rationalism. As such religious testimony is not synonymous with evidence in a court of law or a scientific laboratory—although even there, in a sense, testimony elucidates the evidence. Testimony is not the same as the "Just the facts, please" cliché

---

27. Land, "Nature and Evidence of Spiritual Fullness," 69–78.
28. Land, "Nature and Evidence of Spiritual Fullness," 123.
29. Ricoeur, *Oneself as Another*, 21.

by Joe Friday of "Dragnet" fame. It expresses more than bare facts; it attests to truth. This distinction does not mean that religious testimony is somehow less, as if it lowers the bar; but rather that it has a different, if anything a higher, purpose and therefore functions differently. Religious testimony involves a commitment of trust in the verity of the experience to which it attests. Auditors nevertheless assess the credibility of the testimony's attestation—especially if they are invited to place a level of personal commitment and trust in its verity as well. Yet it is the authenticity of the experience which is decisive rather than the results of working through a checklist of "pros and cons."

I argue that speaking in tongues as initial evidence functions for Pentecostals as an assuring testimony to their experience of Spirit baptism. If so, and if it is to be properly called "evidence" at all, then it should be understood as a specific kind of evidence. Recipients of Spirit baptism with the evidence of speaking in other tongues believe the Holy Spirit has testified through them of the experience. Therefore, they likewise testify. Theological discussion of initial evidence ought not waste time debunking ideas of evidence which are inapplicable in context. So, what difference does it make? Faith's testimony to what God is doing by the Holy Spirit is directed to the glory of God in Christ. It is not people-centered, not recipient-centered. Nor is it the cold hard facts of a court room or laboratory; but, the joyful assurance of a relationship rooted in loving trust. When a new convert testifies to being forgiven and born again the emphasis is not on that individual but on God. It is not "Look at me!" but "Look what God has done!" Often there is an insistent "Even in me!" or "In spite of me!" present in their testimony. Hallelujah! It is similar with initial evidence. The amazing generosity of God is on display. Initial evidence testifies in grateful worship to what God has done. As a key text on initial evidence clearly indicates (Acts 10:46).

Admittedly, there are diverse ways to express the idea of initial evidence. Historian/theologian Alan Anderson refers to initial evidence as "the doctrine of consequence" (a fitting counterpart to "the doctrine of subsequence").[30] Usually the doctrine of consequence indicates that the normative pattern of Spirit baptism includes speaking in tongues. Yet Anderson explains that some very early Pentecostals described speaking in tongues as "'usually' but 'not necessarily'" following Spirit baptism.[31] Additionally, some contemporary Pentecostal scholars, most notably Gordon Fee, describe "speaking in tongues as 'repeatable' but not 'normative.'"[32] I find said usage of these terms rather intriguing. "Repeatable" not only means to say words again (and again!) but also indicates acts are being performed or occurring again and again. For example, one can have a daily routine characterized by repetition. The necessity of one doing the same act every day at the same time in the same way may vary but the fact is that many people do just that for reasons they consider sufficiently satisfactory. Of course, "normative" means to establish a standard or norm of behavior. Furthermore,

30. Anderson, "Pentecostalism," 642.
31. Anderson, "Pentecostalism," 642.
32. Anderson, "Pentecostalism," 642–43.

it can have either descriptive or evaluative modes of meaning. As if that is not enough, normative has specialized meanings in philosophy, social sciences, and law (which are not necessary to get into here).

Surely it is not out of order to ask, "What do 'repeatable' and 'normative' mean in relation to the doctrine of initial evidence?" In practice, the statement that "speaking in tongues is repeatable but not normative" appears to indicate a position that speaking in tongues may, and quite often does, occur in connection with Spirit baptism but that it does not serve as a criterion for whether one has received the baptism with the Holy Spirit. On the surface that sounds like a sound, mediating position. But is it really? I am not so sure. Pentecostals have always understood that there would be exceptions to initial evidence. One of the most common examples at the congregational level involves a (hypothetical) recipient who is mute or has a speech impediment. Further, some quite prominent early Pentecostals (such as David Wesley Myland) testified to receiving an experience they described as the "beginning" of Spirit baptism with the "residue" (speaking in tongues) coming years later.[33] More than once when I was myself seeking Spirit baptism in an altar of prayer some dear old saint would tell me that they believed I had been *filled* with the Spirit but still needed to *yield* my tongue. They apparently understood that an intimate *connection* between Spirit baptism and speaking in tongues did not signify a rigid *identification* between them. Understood thus, initial evidence is a *gift of grace* not a *rule of law*. Initial evidence is geared for spiritual assurance and attestation rather than for legal proof or finished laboratory processes.

In sum, a carefully articulated doctrine of initial evidence is a valid and valuable teaching which may be enthusiastically defended. I suggest that developing Pentecostal theology of initial evidence would do well to elucidate the evidential value of speaking in tongues as assurance and attestation. I do not hesitate to affirm that speaking in tongues *ought* to occur with Spirit baptism. I will not presume upon the sovereignty of the Holy Spirit of God to insist that it *must* always occur in the manner that I personally experienced it or in the precise manner that my tribe explicates it. However, I am sure that as a clear, discernible sign of receiving Spirit baptism speaking in tongues serves quite well as a great aid for the promotion and reception of this priceless experience. I am further convinced that a diminished commitment to the doctrine of initial evidence results in a tragic dilution of opportune participation in the dynamic experience of baptism in the Holy Spirit as Pentecostals know it.

---

33. Jacobsen, "Myland's Vision of Spiritual Fulness": http://enrichmentjournal.ag.org/200803/200803_146_Myland.cfm. Admittedly, Myland was an exceptional character but he was certainly an influential leader too.

12

Significance of Glossolalia

THE SIGNIFICANCE OF SPEAKING in tongues is easily misunderstood—and not just by "outsiders" (i.e., noninitiates). Pentecostals themselves may wrestle with misleading examples and faulty assumptions in coming to grips with the significance of glossolalia in their own lives and in their churches. Pastor Sandra Kay Williams shares a stirring testimony to that effect.[1] Reflecting on 1 Corinthians 14:1, especially not only wishful desire for love but active pursuit of love, she probes the relation of love and spiritual gifts. Pastor Williams grew up in a Pentecostal church where the baptism in the Holy Spirit was paramount for young people. Youth sought Spirit baptism in children's church, at youth camps, in revivals, at camp meetings, and especially in lengthy Sunday night services where there was tarrying in the altar for no short amount of time.

Afterwards everyone wanted to know, "Did he/she speak in tongues?" Though maybe not intentionally, it made Sandra Kay think as a child of the church that speaking in tongues was the goal of every Church of God young person. She saw a lot of tongue talkers. Unfortunately, some of those same people would use their tongue to cut and murder others in the church. Thankfully, in time she learned First Corinthians 13:1 (ESV)[2]: "If I speak in the tongues of men and of angels, but have not love, I am a noisy

---

1. Rev. Sandra Kay Williams is Pastor of Prayer and Women's Ministries at North Cleveland Church of God and International Prayer Center (Cleveland, TN). She gave the above testimony when leading class devotions at PTS (September 4, 2018). I am grateful that she generously responded to my request for her speaking notes as a resource for this section.

2. English Standard Version of the Bible (Wheaton, IL: Crossway, 2001).

gong or a clanging cymbal." Today Pastor Williams insists that "As Pentecostals we must do theology in love, do ministry in love, do marriage in love, do family in love, we must do community, and seminary in love." She adds that, "The absence of love will make all the doing in vain." She further exhorts, "Let's desire spiritual gifts, but especially let us as Pentecostals be marked by love."

If Pentecostals sometimes struggle to understand the significance of speaking in tongues, how much more so non-Pentecostals? As stated in the previous chapter, Simon Chan doubtless is correct that initial evidence is the one Pentecostal doctrine that "the larger spiritual tradition" of Christianity finds most problematic and that it thus requires further theological development.[3] To a (slightly) lesser degree, this unease applies to other forms of glossolalia as well. Having said that, Pentecostal theologians are not slack in plumbing the depths of glossolalia. The following discusses several suggestive approaches to comprehending and presenting the significance of glossolalic utterances. My goal in this chapter is to express a more panoramic perspective on speaking in tongues. Hopefully this process will increase understanding for both Pentecostals and non-Pentecostals regarding glossolalic practice.

THEOLOGICAL RECONCEPTUALIZATION

Indicative of creative theological approaches to speaking in tongues is the work of Steve Land, Frank Macchia, and Tony Richie.[4] Land describes glossolalia as the language of the kingdom. The ability to form and utilize complex systems of communication is a most intriguing characteristic of human beings. The role of the brain in language is a subject of ongoing scientific research. Yet language is much more than a means of communication involving cerebral activity. Language has many social and cultural uses. It can signify group identity, social stratification, social grooming, and more. Arguably, tongues function as kingdom language in just such a multifaceted manner. As each nation or ethnic group is distinguished by its own language, so Pentecostal Christianity experiences glossolalia as an anticipatory expression of the eschatological Kingdom of God in Christ by the Holy Spirit. Accordingly, speaking in tongues may be viewed as both an identifier and expression of a distinctive spiritual culture.

Macchia describes glossolalia in terms of sacramental function and value in settings of Pentecostal worship. Most Pentecostals affirm that a sacrament or ordinance is an outward sign of an inward and spiritual grace that has been ordained by Christ and is experienced by believers through the agency of the Holy Spirit. These ordinances or sacraments involve physical or material (water, bread, wine) representations of spiritual participation in experiencing Christ's gracious presence by the Holy

---

3. Chan, *Pentecostal Theology*, 40–41. Hunter admits that theological immaturity resulted in "inferior formulations" that are "not difficult to criticize" but in their essence stand up well under more careful investigation, *Spirit Baptism*, 221–22; 226.

4. The following section draws on Richie, "Review of Robert W. Graves, ed. *Strangers to Fire*."

Spirit. Sacraments bear witness to Christ in continuity with his Incarnation—itself the ultimate exemplification of humanity and divinity. Thus, liturgical tongues are an outward, physical sign of God's presence as well as a means of grace. Speaking in tongues may thus represent an experience of divine presence and a means of spiritual grace for believing participants.

In my work I utilize the concept of tongues as transposition.[5] Speaking in tongues exemplifies the way much of Christian spirituality functions. Higher, heavenly treasures of the Holy Spirit are transposed into earthly, human vessels. Christian spirituality in general and particularly glossolalia has this strange and sometimes confusing mix of the divine and sublime with the human and humble. It is important to discern both aspects united in action, and to recognize that God has chosen to bestow the heights of spiritual experience on lowly beings fraught with human frailties. Pentecost is divine-human connection and expression with profound consequences.[6] In this case, speaking in tongues is an earthly expression of heavenly reality. Speaking in tongues is God's technique of translating the untranslatable into an experience which transcends human understanding without violating human identity, simultaneously capable of being contained in or transmitted through human vessels.

The preceding exemplifies the significance of speaking in tongues beyond that of an esoteric experience. The value of tongues in prayer and worship is great. However, when we ask ourselves "Why tongues?" then the broader dimensions of glossolalia begin to emerge. It is a sign (pardon the pun) of the health and strength of contemporary Pentecostal movements that they are identifying and explicating these dimensions. It would also be a good sign for non-Pentecostals to engage constructively in this process.

ECUMENICAL RENEWAL

An ancient and ongoing ecclesial tradition contrasts the significance of Pentecost tongues with those of Babel (Gen 11:1–9; Acts 2:1–4).[7] This exegetical and theological tradition includes luminaries such as Origen, Cyril of Jerusalem, Gregory of Nazianzen, Chrysostom, Augustine, Gregory the Great, and John Calvin. In this vein, Pentecost becomes the renewal or restoration of broken, fallen humanity as exemplified in the reversal of its confusion of languages at Babel. In a marvelous, mysterious manner the Holy Spirit moves to (re)unite humanity through making its divided tongues one. Hence not only Pentecost per se but tongues have ecumenical significance extending into contemporary Christian faith and life.

Modern exegetical scholarship affirms the Babel-Pentecost connection but adds several concomitant themes.[8] For example, Babel functions as a summative descrip-

---

5. This concept is drawn from the work of C. S. Lewis. See Richie, "Transposition and Tongues," 117–37.
6. Pinnock, *Flame of Love*, 172.
7. This section draws on Richie, "Epilogue," *Pentecostal Theology and Ecumenical Theology*.
8. Mathews, *Genesis*, 466–77.

tion of pre-historic humanity from creation to the tower. It is not an isolated event but has expansive significance. Further, the theme of reversal is emphasized both verbally and thematically throughout the Genesis account of Babel, setting up Pentecost as its own reversal of Babel. Again, Pentecost itself is the initiation of a unity and universality only completely realized eschatologically—as in its counterpart, Babel's rebellion (i.e., Babylon: Rev 5:9; 7:9; 13:7; 14:6; 17:15). The eschatological element is intriguing.[9] At the close of the age everyone will either be blessed in Pentecost's unity and universality or judged in Babel's rebellion. For the present purposes, the key aspect is that the Pentecost event—including and in some ways, especially, the tongues—have significance for ecumenism via the Holy Spirit's unifying mission in and through Christ's church.

In my mind, it is a sad commentary on the state of the churches that an experience intended to signify unity has rather become an emblem of division. Cessationists and continuationists have often become obstinate and intractable combatants in the tongues debate, unwilling to hear the other, much less speak to their concerns. Yet it is encouraging that much of the animus appears to be passing. As we begin to address together not whether tongues are biblical for today (which is indisputable) but how and why tongues are significant, then we can make better progress for the benefit of everyone.

Responding positively to the prayer of Jesus that all his disciples be one as the Father and the Son are one remains a pressing need today (John 17:20–23). Usually we pray to God for an answer to prayer. This is one prayer that we can help answer! We can answer the prayer of Jesus by tearing down the walls that divide believers and becoming one holy house unto the Lord (Eph 2:11–22). But this requires profound openness to the enabling power of the indwelling Holy Spirit (2:22). Glossolalia or speaking in tongues can be, ought to be, not only a sign of unity but a unifying force. All Christians, not just Pentecostals, can overcome the scandal of division in the body of Christ through the fullness of the Spirit.

ANTHROPOLOGICAL HOLISM

Even Clark Pinnock, a "Bapticostal" type theologian popular among many Pentecostals, has qualified speaking in tongues in a quite non-Pentecostal fashion. Pinnock thought that the significance of glossolalia had been exaggerated by Pentecostals with the odd result of diminishing the legitimacy of the gift as non-Pentecostals consequently refused to take it seriously enough.[10] For him tongues after Spirit baptism are "normal" but not "normative."[11] This appears to be another way to argue that tongues are not odd or out of order but should not be considered a criterion or sign as to whether anyone had received Spirit baptism. As in the preceding chapter's discussion

---

9. Here Hocken, *Pentecost and Parousia*, is especially helpful.

10. A "Bapticostal" is a colloquial description for a Charismatic Evangelical from the Baptist tradition with close ties to Pentecostalism.

11. Pinnock, *Flame of Love*, 172.

of Anderson's observations, Pinnock quotes Fee on this topic. Since we have already discussed that position there I will not reiterate.

What I wish to mention is that Pinnock takes pains to affirm the significance of glossolalia in other ways.[12] Though it is mysterious by nature speaking in tongues is a noble and edifying gift which builds up or strengthens believers (1 Cor 14:2, 4). Tongues express the inexpressible matters of God, transcending intellectual concepts or rational processes by reaching deeply into non-cognitive, subconscious being. Speaking in tongues involves surrender of control, submission or voluntary yielding to the will of the divine. It is particularly helpful in prayer. Recipients/practitioners are taken out of their comfort zone as this humble gift leads into a humbling state. Speaking in tongues, like other charisms, is given to help Christians be more fruitful in service of Christ. In short, for Pinnock glossolalia is the counterpart of, and therefore a cure for, inordinate human tendencies to over-rationalize their life and faith. Speaking in tongues opens and energizes an in-built, intuitive realm of the human spirit under the enabling, guiding impulse of the Holy Spirit.

As such, glossolalic utterance speaks to the nature of what it means to be human. *Cogito ergo sum*, a Latin philosophical proposition by René Descartes (1506–1650 AD), usually translated into English as "I think, therefore I am," is a strange tongue for Pentecostals. Pentecostals do not assume that human beings are only "thinking things." Intellect is an important part of what it means to be human; but, human beings are not reducible to reason. There is another side to us—a spiritual side, a profoundly mysterious side that is no less real. And spirituality is valuable. Arguably, the deep, inner workings of the human heart and soul are where humans encounter ultimate meaning and transcendent purpose in their earthly existence—and beyond. Speaking in tongues puts us in touch with this side of ourselves and with the *imago Dei* of the God who created us.[13]

Pentecostalism is not docetic or gnostic. Although speaking in tongues expresses the inner, spiritual nature of human being its means of expressing is a small fleshly organ—the tongue no less. To be human is to be embodied. Through the gift of speaking in tongues the Holy Spirit graciously brings together the inarticulate cry of the Spirit/spirit with the body without which it would be without voice. A Pentecostal theology of glossolalia is not an escapist descent into amorphous mysticism. It affirms the physical as an embodiment and expression of the Spirit/spirit. Accordingly, I suggest, speaking in tongues arises out of and gives credence and impetus to a theological anthropology in which the existence and nature of the human person is possible, much less intelligible, only via a holistic affinity between the divine self with

---

12. Pinnock, *Flame of Love*, 172–73.

13. As Stephenson, *Dismantling the Dualisms*, 192, says, any faithfully Pentecostal consideration of the image of God in humans should include that men and women equally bear the *Imago Dei* with men and women equally redeemed in the *Imago Christi* and equally transformed by the *Imago Spiritus*.

the entire human self. The entire human being cries out to be heard with language/speech/tongues that will not/cannot be silenced but which this world fails to hear or understand if it listens only with its cognitive faculties without utilizing its inherent, intuitive faculties. Therefore, Jesus says, if I may paraphrase, "Anyone with ears can hear what the Spirit is saying!" (cp. Rev 2:7, 11, 17, 29; 3:13, 22)

PHILOSOPHICAL RELEVANCE

Diogenes Allen notes that the nature of religious language is the most discussed topic in the philosophy of religion. This is not surprising when we contemplate that all thought and talk about God is permeated with mystery both because of the infinite inexhaustibleness of God's inherent nature and because of the inevitable limitations of finite human nature and speech.[14] Even the language of Scripture necessarily accommodates itself to limitations of human capacities. Yet the language of Scripture authentically communicates God's self-revelation and sets the parameters for all subsequent discourse about God.[15] Nevertheless, it is necessary to bear in mind that our distorted use of language can conceal the actual reality of Being (esp. God as Ultimate Reality).[16] What if we conceive of speaking in tongues as in some sense transcending the usual restrictions of human language?

Thus, speaking in tongues represents the profound mystery and complexity of language at an ultimate level. Speaking in tongues is not about the precise transmission of information. It is not about the logic of syntax. Speaking in tongues is language at a deeper, more instinctual level. It is the inarticulate, yes, inexpressible, but authentic and intimate cry of the innermost being to the Source and Sustainer of its existential identity. It is like the child of God crying out to the Heavenly Father (cp. Mark 14:36; Rom 8:15; Gal 4:6). Hindrances of human language are overcome, and transcended, through speaking in tongues, nurturing the loving relationship between God and his children incomparably, immeasurably, and—if not for tongues—inexpressibly.[17]

In the ongoing wake of postmodern and late modern philosophy the quest for certainty has itself become questionable in spite of the history of analytical philosophy's attempt to explicate and critique thought through an examination of language.[18] In the modern philosophical quest, the nature and function of language, especially

---

14. Allen, *Philosophy for Understanding Theology*, ix, xxiv, 57, 59. Arguably, recognition of this dynamic is an essential starting point for theology.

15. Allen, *Philosophy for Understanding Theology*, 16,110.

16. Allen, *Philosophy for Understanding Theology*, 193. However, here we need to distinguish between distortions due to limits inherent even in good talk about God and distorted God-talk—i.e. bad talk about God, talk that is false or perhaps blasphemous or idolatrous.

17. Philosophical implications are immense. E.g., Smith, *Thinking in Tongues*, 126, argues that a consideration of glossolalia in terms of phenomenology, hermeneutics, and speech-act theory contributes to "well-rounded philosophical engagement."

18. Allen, *Philosophy for Understanding Theology*, 211.

in the sense of the possible verification and/or falsification of truth claims, as well as the relation between experience and its expression, have been utilized to both defend and attack the dogmas of religion.[19] Yet language is simply not a neutral reality void of any cultural context; and, perhaps more importantly, there is more to reality than language can explicitly articulate even though language can creatively shape reality.[20] Significantly, the grammar of various language games (rules of play, so to speak) applies to the form of life to which it belongs.[21] Of course, the relation between language as speech and language as writing is complex and subtle. Desirable clarity and certainty are elusive.[22] At another level the use of language can be an investigation into what ought to be, in other words, not just descriptive communication but an ethical declaration in relation to the Other.[23] Yet our knowledge and values are inextricably linked to our sharing in the language of our community and in its activities—making it very much historically and culturally grounded.[24]

One of the most common questions I hear about speaking in tongues from non-practitioners is "Why would anyone want to speak in a language neither they nor their hearers can understand?" That question misunderstands the inexplicable nature of language itself. Apostle Paul specifically argues that language/tongues have an edifying effect on an individual although its content is a mystery (1 Cor 14:1–4). It is primarily for the edifying of the congregation that Paul so highly esteems interpretation and prophecy (1 Cor 14:5).[25] The world's religions seem to understand this transcendent feature of language better than most. Esoteric language is a common feature of religions. Recall Judaism's Hebrew, Roman Catholicism's Latin, Eastern Orthodoxy's Greek, Islam's Arabic, Hinduism's Sanskrit, and so on. See how what began as a traditional language of origin evolves until it takes on a mythical, and eventually, mystical character which evokes a sense of holiness and transcendence? Does it really seem all that implausible for speaking in tongues to signify holy and transcendent language with origins not in a human *ethnos* but in heavenly citizenship (Pp 3:20)?[26]

---

19. Allen, *Philosophy for Understanding Theology*, 213–14.

20. Allen, *Philosophy for Understanding Theology*, 217–19.

21. Allen, *Philosophy for Understanding Theology*, 222–23. E.g. an attempt to force religion to speak in a scientific tongue or science to speak in a religious tongue completely misunderstands the nature of both religion and science as well as religious and scientific language.

22. Allen, *Philosophy for Understanding Theology*, 227–28.

23. Allen, *Philosophy for Understanding Theology*, 232–33.

24. Allen, *Philosophy for Understanding Theology*, 244.

25. Thus, Moore, "Canon and Charisma," 28, eloquently argues that both "God's *dynamic* word" (prophetic) and "God's *enduring* word" (written) are necessary for the well-being of the faith community.

26. One might ask, "Is glossolalia special as an outbreak beyond the cultural bounds of language?" I would answer in the affirmative due to an understanding of God's reign as eternal and universal—and of the church as its ecclesiological anticipation.

LIBERATIONAL YEARNING

Maya Angelou's classic book, *I Know Why the Caged Bird Sings,* is a dramatized autobiography depicting the oppressive plight of Blacks, especially of Black women.[27] The title draws inspiration from the haunting poem of Paul Laurence Dunbar, "Sympathy," especially the third stanza:

> I know why the caged bird sings, ah me,
> When his wing is bruised and his bosom sore,
> When he beats his bars and would be free;
> It is not a carol of joy or glee,
> But a prayer that he sends from his heart's deep core,
> But a plea, that upward to Heaven he flings –
> I know why the caged bird sings.[28]

These profound words strike me as stirring witness to an irrepressible belief that neither pain nor bondage can effectively render mute the hopeful cry of the human heart to God above for the gift of bona fide freedom. I cannot but think of Romans 8:26–27, with its glossolalic association, in the wake of verses 18–25, with their eschatological affirmation of liberation from bondage. Is it too much of a stretch of the theological imagination to conceive of speaking in tongues as an ardent cry of anticipation and expectation, and of unquenchable, indestructible ambition and aspiration, for true, pure freedom such as can only find its fulfillment in and with God?

The final stanza of Angelou's own "Caged Bird," appears to express her personal take on that powerful metaphor.

> The caged bird sings
> with a fearful trill
> of things unknown
> but longed for still
> and his tune is heard
> on the distant hill
> for the caged bird
> sings of freedom.[29]

I do not mean to hijack Angelou's poignant words; but, for me they evoke a sense of intense yearning for the unknown and inexpressible freedom that can only be found beyond that which this world and this age have to offer. I cannot but think of the deep longing of Psalm 42 (especially vv. 1–2a and 7; cp. 1 Cor 2:10). Again, is it too much

---

27. Angelou, Maya. *I Know Why the Caged Bird Sings* (New York: Random House, 1969).
28. Dunbar, *Collected Poetry of Paul Laurence Dunbar*,102.
29. Angelou, *Poems of Maya Angelou*, 194.

to imagine speaking in tongues as a mysterious, inexpressible longing of the deepest, inmost being for the liberating presence of God? Obviously, I do not claim that either Angelou or Dunbar were talking about glossolalia. That is not the point at all. Rather, these precious human beings expressed a nightmare of suffering together with a dream of freedom from the crushing burden of oppression. Perhaps other, perhaps all, human beings, down deep, in one way or another, have that same longing. If so, is it incredible that the Creator of the little songbird would also give a spiritual song to the redeemed for much the same reason (1 Cor 14:15; cp. Ps 137:1–4)?

I remind that Pentecostalism has been especially popular among the disenfranchised and marginalized. Certainly, there are clear implications. Mainly, I suggest, the groanings of the Holy Spirit are like the cries of a mother during birth pangs (Rom 8:26). And the mother's name is freedom (Gal 4:26)! Her cries are heard. Her children are being born. Yet there are qualifications, too. Glossolalia is countercultural, yes; but, it is not anarchic. It does not rebuke righteous rule. It objects to oppression. It fights enslavement. Pentecostals do not typically speak so much in terms of human rights as they do of divine freedom. Deep within the human heart is a cry for freedom that resonates with the conviction of Pentecostal faith that the sovereign God offers freedom to all who believe. Speaking in tongues may be thought of as an irrepressible cry of yearning for God's gift of freedom not only in this world but in the next. Amen?

CREATIONAL RESONANCE

A look at the Genesis account of creation is informative regarding tongues speech. Pentecostals affirm God's immediate and direct creative activity, and weave together purposeful creation with redemption themes.[30] Note textually that God is the First Speaker and that God's First Speech is commanding and creative (1:3). "The divine word shatters the primal cosmic silence and signals the birth of a new cosmic order."[31] The deeper significance of the creative word is critical to Christian theology, especially Christology (Ps 33:6; Is 40:26; John 1:1–3; Col 1:16; Heb 1:2). There are clear implications for pneumatology as well (Gen 1:2; cp. Job 33:4; Ps 104:30; John 3:1–8). Note that the First Words follow closely upon the immediate, explicit agency of the Spirit of God (1:2). This pattern also occurs in the inaugural event of Jesus' baptism (Luke 3:21–22). Divine speech immediately follows the descent of the Holy Spirit in the form of a dove. Then and only then do God's spoken words identify and validate Jesus Christ as the Messiah. Not surprisingly, since Jesus' anointing is paradigmatic for that of his church, there is a repetition of this pattern on the Day of Pentecost (Acts 2:1–4).[32] The phenomena of wind and fire prepare the way for the activity of the Holy Spirit. Immediately upon the Spirit's action, speech—tongues—occurs which is

---

30. Munyon, "Creation," 215–16, 220–22.
31. Matthews, *Genesis*, 145.
32. Arrington, *Spirit-Anointed Church*, 73.

attributed to the Holy Spirit's enabling power. Holy Spirit-enabled tongues are a type of divine speech; and, they are the First Words of the Pentecost age. As such, they are creative. Speaking in tongues not only expresses reality it impacts reality.

It is not innovative or unusual to describe redemption in Christ in terms of new creation (2 Cor 5:17). God will eschatologically consummate the new creation already begun in Christ (Rev 21:5). But how might resonance between creation and Pentecost, between God's original word of creation and God's word of new creation inform our understanding of the significance of glossolalia? I offer two observations. First, glossolalia may be recognized as an intricately interwoven part of the overall tapestry of redemption. That is fair and straightforward. I emphasize it to put it into perspective. Speaking in tongues is not a peripheral practice. Second, and certainly subtler, tongues speech functions as participatory contribution to the ongoing creative work of the Holy Spirit in bringing to fulfillment the new creation in Christ Jesus.

I wish to inquire further into tongues speech as contribution to the Spirit's creative work in redemptive realization. Let's return to the glossolalic associations of Romans 8:26–27, especially its creation context. Presently the natural creation exists in a state of frustration that is nevertheless mingled with keen anticipation for the eschatological redemption portrayed as the adoption of the children of God (8:19–25). For Augustine, Paul's discussion of adoption is twofold: the present spiritual which is eventually completed by the future physical.[33] Present spiritual reconciliation and transformation has occurred for believers; but, the heavenly transformation of the physical awaits the resurrection of the body. I mostly agree with Augustine's basic point. However, what I want to lift out of this passage is recognition that redemption, whether in its spiritual or physical aspects, is yet an ongoing process in which the Holy Spirit continues to act in terms of creation. Is it significant that at this point Paul introduces the theme of Spirit-inspired prayer? I think it is. There is a tendency to limit this divine aid for our own prayer needs. Yet the context is the broader creation.

How does the process of Spirit-inspired prayer, that is, glossolalic prayer, impact the eschatological realization of God's redemptive purpose for the created order and its creatures? I have said that tongues speech may function as participatory contribution to the ongoing work of the Holy Spirit in bringing to ultimate fulfillment the new creation in Christ Jesus. Although it would obviously include other forms of tongues speech, it seems that praying in the Spirit especially links to the creative activity of the Holy Spirit in moving cosmological and historical processes toward their teleological destination in the ultimate and complete eschaton when God's redemptive purpose for creation and its creatures is finally fully realized. In other words, when God the Holy Spirit speaks through yielded believers via tongues the redemptive purposes of the Triune God for eternity are somehow furthered. We certainly do not comprehend the details of how this participatory co-creativity works. It is enough to know that divine

---

33. Augustine, *ACCS: Romans*, 227–28.

speech has the power to accomplish its purpose. We need only be grateful that God has graciously chosen to include the children of God in the performance of divine mission.

Of course, we can speculate. Perhaps events are realigned in accordance with opportunities for the proclamation of the gospel. Perhaps souls are brought under conviction and drawn to Christ. Perhaps hindrances are removed. Perhaps diabolical opposition is overcome. Surely, the tongues speaker is transformed. Most certainly, the Holy Spirit is working to accomplish the redemptive purpose of God in Jesus Christ to create and establish a new world.[34] And believers have the blessed privilege of being part of what God is doing. It goes without saying that praying in the Spirit is no substitute for proclaiming the gospel. However, if these two powerful forms of divine speech are consistently joined in efforts to reach a lost and dying world, who knows what might happen?

SUPERNATURAL NATURE

We have been talking about several complementary ways of comprehending the significance of glossolalia. Admittedly, "comprehending" the significance of speaking in tongues is an oxymoron. Better to speak of *experiencing* speaking in tongues with *appreciation* for the multifaceted nature of the practice. In some ways though it is just indescribable. One of the most difficult aspects of glossolalia to explicate is the relationship between the natural and the supernatural.[35] Acts 2:4 appears to blend or integrate its divine and human elements. Clearly the Holy Spirit is active, initiating and enabling, the experience of speaking in tongues. Yet it is also clear that the disciples were cooperating in obedient responsiveness in the experience of speaking in tongues. Divine-human synergy takes place. Paul's description of his own experience is similar. He does not refrain from saying, "I speak in tongues" or "my spirit prays"; and, his "I will pray/sing with the Spirit/spirit" combines both ideas (1 Cor 14:6, 14–15, 18). Yet his entire discussion of spiritual gifts, including prophecy and tongues, is set in the framework of authentic divine inspiration in the church vis-à-vis the false activity of idols among the pagans (1 Cor 12:1–11). The conclusion? Speaking in tongues is both divine and human, or supernatural and natural, in practice. Its origin is heaven (Acts 2:1). Its setting is worship on earth (1 Cor 12–14). So, in what

---

34 As Vesphew Benton Ellis (1917–1988), a Church of God minister and songwriter, put it in his joyous hymn, "I'm in a New World," in *Christian Joy* (Cleveland, TN: Tennessee Music and Printing Company, 1946):

"Now the Lord has been so good to me. He set my captive spirit free/Old things have passed away, all things are new today/He gave me life to pass on in, oh how I've changed since I found him/I'm in a new world since the Lord saved me."

35. See Richie, "Transposition and Tongues," 117–37. Interestingly, MacGregor, *Contemporary Theology*, 144, says, "The most important contribution" of Latin American Pentecostal pneumatology "is its shattering of the two-tiered Western Enlightenment universe that separates the natural realm from the spiritual realm."

sense is speaking in tongues *natural* and in what sense is it *supernatural*? And what significance does it have for our understanding of glossolalia?

The word "supernatural" does not occur in any of the major translations of the Bible. The Amplified Bible does use supernatural in bracketed definitional elaborations in several places, including its description of speaking in tongues as a supernatural sign (1 Cor 14:22).[36] Generally, "supernatural" indicates an experience or event which may be attributed to some force beyond scientific understanding or the laws of nature as currently understood. Conversely, "natural" indicates an experience or event which exists in nature or is caused by nature. Most Bible translations use words like "mighty deeds" or "wondrous works" (OT) and "miracles, signs, and wonders" (NT) to describe exceptional, spectacular phenomena that today we commonly designate as supernatural.[37]

Allow me to illustrate my use of the terms supernatural and natural. Several years ago, an elderly brother in our church who was terminally ill expressed a strong to desire to be in service with us one more time. Accordingly, his daughter Diane and her husband Jim Webb brought him to Sunday evening worship. We are ever grateful that the Lord blessed him in a special way that night. After the service he exited the building but was fatally stricken in the parking lot. Diane and I held him in our arms as he passed into the presence of our Lord. A small group had gathered around us. However, the ladies in our congregation kept the children inside during this time. When I was finally able to go inside again, Sister Michelle Ellis breathlessly told me of an astounding happening. My own granddaughter, Elizabeth, not quite 3-years-old at the time, did not know what was going on outside. Yet she suddenly looked up toward the ceiling of the church sanctuary in the exact direction where on the other side of the wall of the building we were with our dear brother. Then she asked, "Why are those two men in white flying up there? Where are they going with that man?" Later, when we questioned her, Elizabeth repeated the same words to us. Although some might scoff, they will not convince anyone who was there that night that she did not see the angels carrying our dear brother home to the Lord (Luke 16:22).

Like Paul, I do not know whether to call what Elizabeth saw a "vision" or not (2 Cor 12:1–3).[38] Perhaps like Elisha's servant the Lord opened her young eyes to see spiritual reality (2 Kgs 6:17). In any case, it illustrates the conjunction of the supernatural and natural which occurs in glossolalia too. She was a humble little child (Matt 18:4). She was not duplicitous. She was not in a trance. We believe the child really saw something that she was unaware of in any natural sense. It was a supernatural

---

36. The Amplified Bible (Grand Rapids, MI: Zondervan, 1987).

37. For more on this topic, see Grounds, "Miracle," 356–58; Young, "Supernatural, Supernaturalism," 507. Notably, Archer, "Pentecostal Hermeneutics," 131, asserts that "The essence of Pentecostalism is its persistent emphasis upon the supernatural within the community." This worldview is rooted in Scripture and affects all the Christian life, emphasizing "the omnipotent God breaking into the everyday life of the believer," Archer, "Pentecostal Hermeneutics," 137 (cp. 133, 144).

38. Lincoln, *Paradise Now Not Yet*, 85–86, argues that Paul's vision should be understood through the lens of Acts 2:17–21 as a charismatic manifestation of the Spirit not uncommon in the NT church.

revelation. Yet it requires faith to affirm it. Tongues speakers are generally well-aware of their surroundings. They willingly speak words from the Spirit that they do not know. They believe and trust God. It is supernatural *and* natural.

So then, speaking in tongues is supernatural in the sense that it has its origin in and is enabled by the Holy Spirit. Speaking in tongues is natural in the sense that it employs the faculties of human beings, inviting their free and knowing participation. One can hardly help but be reminded of the Incarnation of our Lord. The Divine Word became flesh, became human (John 1:14). Pentecost is also the coming together of the Divine and the human, the Holy Spirit and the disciples (Acts 2:4). Thus, the Incarnation and Pentecost exhibit a similar fusion of the supernatural and the natural. Speaking in tongues, or glossolalia, partakes in and reflects the Divine-Human union of the Incarnation and of Pentecost.

CONCLUSION

By now it should be evident to readers that I consider speaking in tongues to have huge significance in a myriad of ways. I do not pretend to have exhausted the possibilities in this chapter. Yet Warrington warns that there is a decrease of tongues and interpretation in Pentecostal churches today.[39] Later he adds, "Of great concern is the fact that speaking in tongues has waned in the lives of many Pentecostals."[40] How can this be so? In my opinion, there are probably several contributing factors. First, there may be a not altogether unexpected cooling of the early revival fires of the movement over time that affects the prioritization of spiritual experiences. This cause calls for fresh revival. Second, there appears to be a process of eventual dilution of the membership population of the movement, not by attrition but by addition, resulting in a majority constituency which is not dedicated to its original core values, including spiritual experiences. This cause calls for more effective discipleship.

Third, is a theological failure to adequately instill in members of the Pentecostal movement itself a sense of the huge significance of speaking in tongues. The diminishment of its significance inevitably leads to a diminishment of its occurrence. Tongues must not be reduced to a group identity badge or a personal blessing. Tongues must not come to be considered an esoteric practice rooted in quasi-cultish sectarian beginnings. There is much more going on here. It is my hope and prayer that this chapter will help remind of the almost inestimable biblical and theological significance of speaking in tongues. Paul said, "I wish you all spoke with tongues" (1 Cor 14:5a). He goes on to carefully qualify that statement in consideration of the need for congregational edification. But Paul does not retract his desire for all Christians to speak with tongues. Should we? No!

---

39. Warrington, *Pentecostal Theology*, 95.
40. Warrington, *Pentecostal Theology*, 122.

Bibliography

Adams, J. Wesley. "Hebrews." In *Full Life Bible Commentary to the New Testament: An International Commentary for Spirit-Filled Christians*, 1295–1399, eds. French L. Arrington & Roger Stronstad. Grand Rapids, MI: Zondervan, 1999.

Adewuja, J. Ayodeji. *Holiness in the Letters of Paul: The Necessary Response to the Gospel.* Eugene, OR: Cascade, 2016.

Adler, Alfred. *Understanding Human Nature.* Center City, MI: Hazeldon, 1998.

Aker, Benny C. "John." In *Full Life Bible Commentary to the New Testament: An International Commentary for Spirit-Filled Christians*, 1–118, eds. French L. Arrington & Roger Stronstad. Grand Rapids, MI: Zondervan, 1999.

Alexander, Estrelda Y. *Black Fire: One Hundred Years of African American Pentecostalism.* Downers Grove, IL: IVP Academic, 2011.

———. *Limited Liberty: The Legacy of Four Pentecostal Pioneer Women.* Cleveland, TN: Pilgrim, 2008.

——— and Amos Yong. *Afro-Pentecostalism: Black Pentecostal and Charismatic Christianity in History and Culture (Religion, Race, and Ethnicity).* New York, NY: New York University Press, 2011.

Alexander, Kimberly Ervin. "A Baptism of Divine Love: The Pentecostal Experience of Spirit Baptism." In *The Continuing Relevance of Wesleyan Theology: Essays in Honor of Laurence W. Wood*, 68–82. Ed. Nathan Crawford with Foreword by Stanley Hauerwas. Eugene, OR; Wipf & Stock, 2011.

———. "The Pentecostal Healing Community." In *Towards a Pentecostal Ecclesiology: The Church and the Fivefold Gospel*, 183–206. Ed. John Christopher Thomas. Cleveland, TN: CPT, 2010.

———. "'Singing Heavenly Music': R. Hollis Gause's Theology of Worship and Pentecostal Experience." In *Toward a Pentecostal Theology of Worship*, 201–20. Ed. Lee Roy Martin. Cleveland, TN: CPT, 2016.

Alfaro, Sammy. *Divino Compañero: Toward a Hispanic Pentecostal Christology;* Princeton Theological Monograph Series 147. Eugene, OR: Wipf and Stock, 2010.

Bibliography

Allen, Diogenes and Eric O. Springsted. *Philosophy for Understanding Theology*, Second Edition. Louisville, KY: Westminster John Knox, 1985, 2007.

———. *Spiritual Theology: The Theology of Yesterday for Spiritual Help Today*. Boston, MA: Cowley, 1997.

Allen, Leonard. *Poured Out: The Spirit of God Empowering the Mission of God*. Abilene, KA:Abilene Christian University Press, 2018.

Althouse, Peter. *Spirit of the Last Days: Pentecostal Eschatology in Conversation with Jürgen Moltmann*. New York, NY: T & T, 2003.

——— and Robby Waddell. "Christian Theology, the Logic of Critical Self-Description, and the Academic Disciplines: What Do Empirical Methodologies Offer Christian Theological Identity?" *Pneuma* 39:4 (2017) 425–29.

———. "Pentecostal Eschatology in Context: The Eschatological Orientation of the Full Gospel." In *Perspectives in Pentecostal Eschatologies: World Without End*, 205–31. Eds. Peter Althouse and Robby Waddell. Eugene, OR: Pickwick, 2010.

——— and Robby Waddell, eds. *Perspectives in Pentecostal Eschatologies: World Without End*. Eugene, OR: Pickwick, 2010.

———. "Toward a Theological Understanding of the Pentecostal Appeal to Experience." *Journal of Ecumenical Studies* 38:4 (2001) 399–411.

Álvarez, Daniel Orlando. *Mestizaje and Hibridez: Latin@ Identity in Pneumatological Perspective*. Cleveland, TN: CPT, 2016.

Anderson, Allan, *An Introduction to Global Pentecostalism: Global Charismatic Christianity*. Cambridge: Cambridge University Press, 2004.

———. "Pentecostalism." William A. Dryness and Veli-Matti Kärkkäinen eds., Juan Francisco Martinez and Simon Chan, assoc. eds., *Global Dictionary of Theology*, 641–48. Downers Grove, IL: IVP Academic 2008.

Angelou, Maya. *The Complete Collected Poems of Maya Angelou*. New York: Random House, 1994.

———. *I Know Why the Caged Bird Sings*. New York: Random House, 1969.

Archer, Kenneth J. *A Pentecostal Hermeneutic: Spirit, Scripture, and Community*. Cleveland, TN: CPT, 2009.

———. "Pentecostal Hermeneutics: Retrospect and Prospect." In Lee Roy Martin, ed., *Pentecostal Hermeneutics: A Reader*, 131–48. Leiden: Brill, 2013.

Archer, Melissa. *'I Was in the Spirit on the Lord's Day': A Pentecostal Engagement with Worship in the Apocalypse*. Cleveland, TN: CPT, 2015.

Armstrong, Chris. "Embrace Your Inner Pentecostal." *Christianity Today*, 50:9 (September 19, 2006). https://www.christianitytoday.com/ct/2006/september/40.86.html.

Arrington, French L., *Christian Doctrine: A Pentecostal Perspective: Volume One, Two, Three*. Cleveland, TN: Pathway, 1993.

———. *Encountering the Holy Spirit: Paths of Christian Growth and Service*. Cleveland, TN: Pathway, 2003.

———. *The Spirit-Anointed Church: A Study of the Acts of the Apostles*. Cleveland, TN: Pathway, 2008.

———. *The Spirit-Anointed Jesus: A Study of the Gospel of Luke*. Cleveland, TN: Pathway, 2008.

Augustine of Hippo. *Confessions,* Trans by R. S. Pine-Coffin. New York: Penguin, 1961.

BIBLIOGRAPHY

———. "Expositions on the Book of Psalms." In *Saint Augustin: Expositions on the Book of Psalms*. Philip Schaff, ed. Translated by A. C. Coxe. New York: Christian Literature Company, 1888.

Augustine, Daniela. *Pentecost, Hospitality, and Transfiguration: Toward a Spirit-Inspired Vision of Social Transformation*. Cleveland, TN: CPT, 2012.

Aulén, Gustav. *Christus Victor*. New York, NY: Macmillan, 1954.

Autero, Esa. "Reading the Epistles James with Socioeconomically Marginalized Immigrants in the Southern United States." *Pneuma* 39:4 (2017) 504–35.

Baker, Michael L. *Your and Your Church: An In-Depth Review of the Church of God*, 2nd Revised Edition. Cleveland, TN: Pathway, 2013..

Bare, Harold L. *They Call Me Pentecostal*. Cleveland, TN: Pathway, 1993.

Barth, Karl. *Church Dogmatics*, edited and translated by G. Bromiley and T. F. Torrence. Edinburgh: T & T Clark, 1956–75.

Barrett, David B. "The Worldwide Holy Spirit Renewal." In *The Century of the Holy Spirit: 100 Years of Pentecostal and Charismatic Renewal, 1901–2001*, 381–414. Ed. Vinson H. Synan. Nashville, TN: Thomas Nelson, 2001.

Basil the Great. *On the Holy Spirit*. Translated by David Anderson. Crestwood, NY: St Vladimir's Seminary Press, 1980.

Beasley-Murray, G. R. *Jesus and the Kingdom of God*. Grand Rapids: Eerdmans, 1986.

Bebbington, David W. *The Dominance of Evangelicalism: The Age of Spurgeon and Moody (History of Evangelicalism)*. Downers Grove, IL: IVP, 2005.

Beegle, Dewey M. "Exodus." In *Baker's Dictionary of Theology*, 206. Eds. Everett F. Harrison, Geoffry W. Bromiley, Carl F. H. Henry. Grand Rapids, MI: Baker, 1960, 1987.

Bender, Harold S. "Mennonite Origins and the Mennonites of Europe." (Accessed 4-11-2018). http://www.bibleviews.com/menno-heritage.html.

Bercot, David W. editor, *A Dictionary of Early Christian Beliefs*. Peabody, MA: Hendrickson, 1998.

Bergen, Robert D. *1, 2 Samuel: The New American Commentary Vol. 7*. Gen. ed. E. Ray Clendenen. Nashville: Broadman & Holman, 1996.

Bergunder, Michael. *The South Indian Pentecostal Movement in the Twentieth Century: Studies in the History of Christian Missions Series*. Gen. eds. R. E. Frykenberg and Brian Stanley. Grand Rapids, MI: Eerdmans, 2008.

Bernard, David K. *The Glory of God in the Face of Jesus Christ: Deification of Jesus in Early Christian Discourse*. Blandford Forum, Eng: Deo, 2016.

——— and Loretta A. Bernard. *In Search of Holiness: 25th Anniversary Edition Revised and Updated, Pentecostal Theology: Volume 3*. Hazelwood, MO: Word Aflame, 1981, 2006.

———. *Justification and the Holy Spirit: A Scholarly Investigation of a Classical Christian Doctrine from a Pentecostal Perspective*. Hazelwood, MO: Word Aflame, 2007.

———. *Practical Holiness: A Second Look, Pentecostal Theology: Volume IV*. Hazelwood, MO:Word Aflame, 1985.

———. *Oneness and Trinity: A.D. 100–300: The Doctrine of God in Ancient Christian Writings*. Hazelwood, MO: Word Aflame, 1992.

———. *The Oneness of God, Series in Pentecostal Theology vol. II*. Hazelwood, MO: Word Aflame, 1983.

———. *The Oneness View of Jesus Christ*. Hazelwood, MO: Word Aflame, 1994.

———. *The Trinitarian Controversy in the Fourth Century*. Hazelwood, MO: Word Aflame, 1993.

———. *Understanding the Articles of Faith: An Examination of United Pentecostal Beliefs.* Hazelwood, MO: Word Aflame, 1998.

Black, Jonathan. *Apostolic Theology: A Trinitarian Evangelical Pentecostal Introduction to Christian Doctrine.* Foreword by Warren Jones. UK: The Apostolic Church, 2016.

Blumhofer, Edith L. "Pentecostalism." In *The New Encyclopedia of Southern Culture: Volume 1: Religion*, 107–10. Gen. ed., Charles Reagan Wilson, vol. ed., Samuel S. Hill. Chapel Hill, NC: University of North Carolina Press, 2006.

———. *Restoring the Faith: The Assemblies of God, Pentecostalism, and American Culture.* Champagne, IL: University of Illinois Press, 1993.

Boone, R. Jerome. "Community and Worship: The Key Components of Pentecostal Christian Formation." *Journal of Pentecostal Theology* 8 (1996) 129–42.

Borchert, Gerald L. *John 12–21: The New American Commentary Vol 25B.* Gen. ed. E. Ray Clendenen. Nashville, TN: Broadman & Holman Publishers, 2002.

Brand, Chad Owen, ed. *Perspectives on Spirit Baptism: Five Views.* Nashville, TN: Broadman and Holman, 2004.

Bruce, F. F. *The Acts of the Apostles: Greek Text with Introduction and Commentary.* Grand Rapids: Eerdmans, 1952, 1990.

Bryant, Herschel Odell. *Spirit Christology: From the Patristic Period to the Rise of Twentieth Century Pentecostalism.* Cleveland, TN: CPT, 2014.

Bundy, David D. "Irving, Edward." In *New International Dictionary of Pentecostal andCharismatic Movements,* 803–04. Stanley M. Burgess, ed., assoc. ed., Eduard M. Van Der Maas. Grand Rapids: Zondervan, 2002.

Burgess, Stanley M., ed., *Christian Peoples of the Spirit: A Documentary History of Pentecostal Spirituality from the Early Church to the Present.* New York: New York University Press, 2011.

——— and G. B. McGee. "Signs and Wonders." In *New International Dictionary of Pentecostal and Charismatic Movements* 1063–68. Stanley M. Burgess, ed., assoc. ed., Eduard M. VanDer Maas, Grand Rapids: Zondervan, 2002.

Calvin, John. *Institutes of the Christian Religion: Volumes 1 and 2.* ed. John T. McNeill Philadelphia, PA: Westminster, 1960.

Cargal, Timothy B. "James." In *Full Life Bible Commentary to the New Testament: An International Commentary for Spirit-Filled Christians,* 1401–29. Eds. French L. Arrington & Roger Stronstad. Grand Rapids, MI: Zondervan, 1999.

Cartledge, Mark J. *Encountering the Spirit: The Charismatic Spirit, Traditions of Christian Spirituality.* Maryknoll, NY: Orbis, 2007.

———. *The Mediation of the Spirit: Interventions in Practical Theology.* Grand Rapids, MI: Eerdmans, 2015.

Chan, Simon. *Grassroots Asian Theology: Thinking the Faith from the Ground Up.* Downers Grove, IL: InterVarsity, 2014.

———. *Pentecostal Theology and the Christian Spiritual Tradition.* Eugene, OR: Wipf and Stock, 2011.

Chase, Steven. "Mystery." In *The New Westminster Dictionary of Christian Spirituality*, 454–55. Ed. Philip Sheldrake. Louisville, KY: John Knox, 2005.

Clack, Beverly. "Theaology and Theology: Mutually Exclusive or Creatively Interdependent?" *Feminist Theology* 7:21 (May 1999) 21–38.

Clark, Matthew S, et al., *What is Distinctive about Pentecostal Theology?* Pretoria: University of South Africa, 1989.

BIBLIOGRAPHY

Clayton, Allen L. "The Significance of William H. Durham for Pentecostal Historiography." *Pneuma* 1 (Fall 1979) 27–42.

Clifton, Shane. "The Dark Side of Prayer for Healing: Toward a Theology of Well-Being." *Pneuma* 36:2 (2014) 204–225.

Cole, Charles C., Jr. *The Social Ideas of the Northern Evangelists: 1826–1860.* New York: Octagon, 1966.

Colkmire, Lance. *Evangel* Interview with Ronnie Hepperly: "From the Woods to the World." *Church of God Evangel,* 108:7 (July 2018) 10–11.

———. "On My Mind: Young, Significant, Diverse, and Needy." *Church of God Evangel.* 108:7 (July 2018) 7.

Collins, Kenneth J. *John Wesley: A Theological Journey.* Nashville, TN: Abingdon, 2003.

Conkin, Paul K. *Cane Ridge: America's Pentecost.* Madison, WI: University of Wisconsin Press, 1990.

Conn, Charles W. "Fasting," In *New International Dictionary of Pentecostal and Charismatic Movements,* 633–35. Stanley M. Burgess, ed., assoc. ed., Eduard M. Van Der Maas. Grand Rapids: Zondervan, 2002.

Constantineanu, Corneliu and Christopher J. Scobie, eds. *Pentecostal Theology in the 21st Century: Identity, Beliefs, Praxis.* Eugene, OR: Cascade, 2018.

Cooper, David C. "First Things First: 1. Love God, 2. Love Others." *Church of God Evangel* 108:2 (February 2018) 12–13.

Cooper, Lamar Eugene. *Ezekiel* in *The New American Commentary, vol. 17.* Gen. ed. David S. Dockery. Nashville, TN: Broadman & Holman, 1994.

Cortez, Marc. *Theological Anthropology: A Guide for the Perplexed (Guides for the Perplexed).* New York: Bloomsbury T & T Clark, 2010.

Cossey, James E. "What is a Full Gospel Church." *Church of God Evangel* 108:5 (May2018)12–13.

Coulter, Dale. "Delivered by the Power of God: Toward a Pentecostal Understanding of Salvation." *International Journal of Systematic Theology* 10:4 (Oct 2008) 447–67.

Cox, Harvey. *Fire from Heaven: The Rise of Pentecostal Spirituality and the Reshaping of Religion in the Twenty-First Century.* New York: Addison-Wesley, 1995.

———. *The Future of Faith.* New York: HarperCollins, 2009.

Cross, Terry L. "The Divine-Human Encounter: Towards a Pentecostal Theology of Experience." *Pneuma: The Journal of the Society Pentecostal for Pentecostal Studies* 31:1 (2009) 3–34.

———. "'A Proposal to Break the Ice:' What Can Pentecostal Theology Offer Evangelical Theology?" *Journal of Pentecostal Theology* 11:2 (2002) 44–73.

Daniels, David. "They Had a Dream." *Christian History: The Rise of Pentecostalism* 58:17:2 (1998) 19–21.

Davies, Andrew. "What Does It Mean to Read the Bible as a Pentecostal?" In *Pentecostal Hermeneutics: A Reader,* 149–62. Lee Roy Martin, ed. Boston: Brill, 2013.

Davis, Derek Leigh. "Assembly, Religious." In *Lexham Theological Wordbook,* n. p. in digital edition. D. Mangum, D. R. Brown, R. Klippenstein, & R. Hurst (Eds.). Bellingham, WA: Lexham, 2014.

Dayton, Donald W. *The Theological Roots of Pentecostalism.* Grand Rapids, MI: Baker, 1987.

Deiros, Pablo A. and Everett A. Wilson. "Hispanic Pentecostalism in the Americas." In *The Century of the Holy Spirit: 100 Years of Pentecostal and Charismatic Renewal, 1901-2001,* 293–323. Synan, H. Vinson, ed. Nashville, TN: Thomas Nelson, 2001.

Del Colle, Ralph. "Spirit Baptism: A Catholic Perspective." In *Perspectives on Spirit Baptism: Five Views*, 241–89. Chad Owen Brand, ed. Nashville, TN: Broadman and Holman, 2004.

DiAngelo, Robin. *White Fragility: Why it is so Hard for White People to Talk about Race.* Boston, MA: Beacon, 2018.

Doolittle, Thomas J. "Praying in the Spirit: Passionate and Transforming Communication with God." *Church of God Evangel* 107:3 (March 2017) 14–15.

Dryer, Elizabeth. "Prayer." In *The New Westminster Dictionary of Christian Spirituality*, 504–06. Philip Sheldrake, ed. Louisville, KY: John Knox, 2005.

Dunbar, Paul Laurence. The Collected Poetry of Paul Laurence Dunbar. Joanne M. Braxton, ed. Charlottesville, Virginia: University of Virginia Press, 1993.

Edwards, James R. *The Gospel according to Mark.* Grand Rapids, MI: Eerdmans, 2002.

Edwards, Jonathan. *A Treatise Concerning Religions Affections, The Works of Jonathan Edwards, Volumes 1 & 2.* Peabody, Massachusetts: Hendrickson, 2011; 1834 British edition.

Ellicott, Charles John. *Ellicott's Bible Commentary in One Volume.* Donald N. Bowdle, ed. Grand Rapids: Zondervan, 1971, 1980.

Ellington, Scott A. "Reciprocal Reshaping of History and Experience in the Psalms: Intersections with Pentecostal Testimony." *Journal of Pentecostal Theology* 16:1 (2007) 18–31.

Ellingworth, Paul. *The Epistle to the Hebrews: A Commentary on the Greek Text.* Grand Rapids, MI; Eerdmans/Paternoster, 1993.

Ellis, Vesphew Benton. "I'm in a New World." In *Christian Joy.* Cleveland, TN: Tennessee Music and Printing Co., 1946.

Estrada III, Rodolfo Galvin. "Is a Contextualized Hermeneutic the Future of Pentecostal Readings? The Implications of a Pentecostal Hermeneutic for a Chicano/Latino Community." *Pneuma* 37:3 (2015) 341–55.

Everts, Janet Meyers and Jeffrey S. Lamp, eds. *Pentecostal Theology and the Theological Vision of N. T. Wright.* Cleveland, TN: CPT, 2015.

Faupel, D. William. *The Everlasting Gospel: The Significance of Eschatology in the Development of Pentecostal Thought, JPTSup 10.* Sheffield, England: Sheffield Academic, 1996.

Fauss, Oliver F. *Buy the Truth, and Sell it Not.* St. Louis, MO: Pentecostal, 1965.

Fee, Gordon D. *God's Empowering Presence: The Holy Spirit in the Letters of Paul.* Peabody, MA: Hendrickson, 1994.

———. *Gospel and Spirit: Issues in New Testament Hermeneutics.* Grand Rapids, MI: Baker, 1991.

———. "On Getting the Spirit Back into Spirituality." *Life in the Spirit: Spiritual Formation in Theological Perspective*, 36–44. Jeffrey P. Greenman and George Kalantzis, eds. Downers Grove, IL: InterVarsity, 2010.

———. *The New International Commentary on the New Testament: First Corinthians.* Grand Rapids, MI: Eerdmans, 1987, 1988.

———. *Paul, the Spirit, and the People of God.* Peabody, MA: Hendrickson, 1996, 6th printing, 2005.

Fields, Bruce. L. *Introducing Black Theology: Three Crucial Questions for the Evangelical Church.* Grand Rapids, MI: Baker Academic, 2001.

French, Talmadge. *Early Interracial Oneness Pentecostalism: G. T. Haywood and the Pentecostal Assemblies of the World.* Eugene, OR: Pickwick, 2014.

———. *Our God is One: The Story of the Oneness Pentecostals.* Indianapolis, IN: Voice and Vision, 1999.

Bibliography

Galli, Mark. "One Dangerous Religion." *Christian History: The Rise of Pentecostalism* 58:17:2 (1998) 8.

Gause, R. Hollis. *God, Prayer, Redemption, and Hope: Pastoral and Theological Reflections.* Cleveland, TN: Cherohala, 2016.

———. *Living in the Spirit: The Way of Salvation.* Cleveland, TN: Pathway, 1980.

———. *Living in the Spirit: The Way of Salvation.* Cleveland, TN: self-published ed. 2004.

———. "The Nature and Pattern of Biblical Worship." *Toward a Pentecostal Theology of Worship,* 139–51. Lee Roy Martin, ed. Cleveland, TN: CPT, 2016.

———. *Revelation: God's Stamp of Sovereignty on History.* Cleveland, TN: Pathway, 1983.

Gee, Donald. *Now That You've Been Baptized in the Spirit.* Springfield, MO: Gospel, 1972, 1978.

George, Timothy. *Galatians: The New American Commentary, Vol. 30.* Gen. ed., David S. Dockery. Nashville, TN: Broadman & Holman, 1994.

Gilbert, Pierre J. "Spiritual Warfare." In *Global Dictionary of Theology,* 847–51. William A. Dryness and Veli-Matti Kärkkäinen, eds., Juan Francisco Martinez and Simon Chan, assoc. eds. Downers Grove, IL: IVP Academic 2008.

Gill, Deborah Menken. "The Pastorals." In *Full Life Bible Commentary to the New Testament: An International Commentary for Spirit-Filled Christians,* 1219–83. French L. Arrington & Roger Stronstad, eds. Grand Rapids, MI: Zondervan, 1999.

Goff, James R. Jr. "Charles Fox Parham." In *New International Dictionary of Pentecostal and Charismatic Movements,* 955–57. Stanley M. Burgess, ed., Eduard M. Van Der Maas, Grand assoc. ed. Rapids: Zondervan, 2002.

———. "Peaceniks," *Christian History: The Rise of Pentecostalism* 58:17:2 (1998) 22–23.

González, Justo L. *A History of Christian Thought in One Volume.* Nashville: TN: Abingdon, 2014.

Green, Chris E. W. "'In Your Presence is Fullness of Joy': Experiencing God as Trinity." *Toward a Pentecostal Theology of Worship,* 187–99. Lee Roy Martin, ed. Cleveland, TN: CPT, 2016.

———. *Toward a Pentecostal Theology of the Lord's Supper: Foretasting the Kingdom.* Cleveland, TN: CPT, 2012.

Green, Gene L. *The Letters to the Thessalonians: The Pillar New Testament Commentary.* Gen. ed. D. A. Carson. Grand Rapids, MI: Eerdmans, 2002.

Grenz, Stanley J. and Denise Muir Kjesbo, *Women in the Church: A Biblical Theology of Women in Ministry.* Downers Grove, IL: InterVarsity, 1995.

Grey, Jacqueline. "Embodiment and the Prophetic Message in Isaiah's Memoir." 2017 Society for Pentecostal Studies Presidential Address. *Pneuma* 39:4 (2017) 431–56.

Grounds, Vernon C. "Miracle." In *Baker's Dictionary of Theology,* 356–58. Everett F. Harrison, Geoffry W. Bromiley, Carl F. H. Henry, eds. Grand Rapids, MI: Baker, 1960, 1987.

Han, David S. "Spirit-Filled Life." *Spirit* (Spring 2018) 6–7.

Hart, Larry D. "Spirit Baptism: A Charismatic Perspective." In *Perspectives on Spirit Baptism: Five Views,* 105–80. Chad Owen Brand, ed. Nashville, TN: Broadman and Holman, 2004.

———. *Truth Aflame: Theology for the Church in Renewal.* Grand Rapids, MI: Zondervan, 1999, 2005.

Haywood, G. T. *The Victim of the Flaming Sword.* Indianapolis, IN: Christ Temple, n. d.

Heltzel, Peter Goodwin. "Power." In *Global Dictionary of Theology,* 696–700. William A. Dryness and Veli-Matti Kärkkäinen, eds., Juan Francisco Martinez and Simon Chan, assoc. eds. Downers Grove, IL: IVP Academic 2008.

BIBLIOGRAPHY

Hernando, James. "Second Corinthians." In *Full Life Bible Commentary to the New Testament: An International Commentary for Spirit-Filled Christians*, 915–62. French L. Arrington & Roger Stronstad eds. Grand Rapids, MI: Zondervan, 1999.

Higgins, John R., et al., *An Introduction to Theology: A Classical Pentecostal Perspective.* Dubuque, Iowa: Kendall/Hunt, 1993.

Hinck, John. "Heavenly Harmony: An Audio Analysis of Corporate Singing in Tongues." *Pneuma* 40:1–2 (2018) 167–91.

Hocken, Peter. *Pentecost and Parousia: Charismatic Renewal, Christian Unity, and the Coming Glory.* Eugene, OR: Wipf & Stock, 2013.

Hollenweger, Walter J. "After Twenty Years' Research on Pentecostalism." *International Review of Mission* 75:297 (Jan 1986) 3–12.

———. *The Pentecostals: The Charismatic Movement in the Churches.* Minneapolis, MN: Augsburg, 1972.

———. *Pentecostalism: Origins and Developments Worldwide.* Peabody, MA: Hendrickson, 2005.

Holley, Karen Rembert. "A Johannine Theology of Sanctification: A Pentecostal Engagement." Unpublished PhD diss., Bangor University, 2015.

Holmes, M. W. *The Greek New Testament: SBL Edition.* Lexham: Society of Biblical Literature, 2011–2013.

Horton, Stanley M. "Spirit Baptism: A Pentecostal Perspective." In *Perspectives on Spirit Baptism: Five Views*, 47–104. Chad Owen Brand, ed. Nashville, TN: Broadman & Holman, 2004.

———. *What the Bible Says about the Holy Spirit.* Springfield, MO: Gospel, 1976.

Howard, David M., Jr. *New American Commentary Volume 5: Joshua*, Gen. ed., E. Ray Clendenen. Nashville, TN: Broadman & Holman Publishers, 1998.

Hunter, Harold D. *Spirit Baptism: A Pentecostal Alternative.* Eugene, OR: Wipf and Stock, 2009.

Jackson, Joseph E. *Reclaiming Our Heritage: The Search for Black History in the Church of God.* Cleveland, TN: Church of God Black Ministries, 1993.

Jacobsen, Douglas, G. "David Wesley Myland's Vision of Spiritual Fulness." *Enrichment Journal* (Summer 2008) http://enrichmentjournal.ag.org/200803/200803_146_Myland.cfm.

———. "Introduction: The History and Significance of Early Pentecostal Theology." *A Reader in Pentecostal Theology: Voices from the First Generation*, 1–18. Douglas G. Jacobsen, ed. Bloomington, IN: Indiana University Press, 2006.

Jenney, Timothy P. "Revelation." In *Full Life Bible Commentary to the New Testament: An International Commentary for Spirit-Filled Christians*, 1535–1629. French L.Arrington & Roger Stronstad, eds. Grand Rapids, MI: Zondervan, 1999.

Jenson, Robert W. *Theology in Outline: Can These Bones Live?* New York: Oxford, 2016.

Johns, Cheryl Bridges. "Cultivating a Heart for Holiness." *Engage Journal* 14:2 (Spring/Summer 2018) 32–37.

———. "A Letter to Young Christian Feminists (March 16, 2016) https://juniaproject.com/letter- young-christian-feminists/.

———. *Pentecostal Formation: A Pedagogy among the Oppressed*, JPTSup 2. Sheffield, England: Sheffield Academic, 1993, 1998.

——— and Jackie David Johns. "Life in the New Creation: Justification and Sanctification Revisited." In *Justified in Jesus Christ: Evangelicals and Catholics Dialogue*, 173–82. Steven Hoskins and David Fleischacher, eds. Bismarck, NC: University of Mary Press, 2017.

228

Bibliography

Johns, Jackie David. *The Pedagogy of the Holy Spirit: According to Early Church Tradition.* Cleveland, TN: CPM, 2012.

———. "Pentecostalism and the Postmodern Worldview." *Journal of Pentecostal Theology* 7 (1995) 73–96.

Jones, C. E. "Holiness Movement." In *New International Dictionary of Pentecostal and Charismatic Movements*, 726–29. Stanley M. Burgess, ed., Eduard M. Van Der Maas, assoc. ed. Grand Rapids: Zondervan, 2002.

Jones, Loyal. "Appalachian Religion." In *The New Encyclopedia of Southern Culture: Volume 1: Religion*, 21–24. Charles Reagan Wilson, gen. ed., Samuel S. Hill, vol. ed. Chapel Hill, NC: University of North Carolina Press, 2006.

Kane, Steven M. "Serpent Handlers." In *The New Encyclopedia of Southern Culture: Volume 1: Religion*, 211–12. Charles Reagan Wilson, gen. ed., Samuel S. Hill, vol. ed. Chapel Hill, NC: University of North Carolina Press, 2006.

Kärkkäinen, Veli-Matti. *Christ and Reconciliation: Constructive Christian Theology for the Pluralistic World: vol. 1.* Grand Rapids, MI: Eerdmans, 2013.

———. *Christology: A Global Introduction.* Grand Rapids, MI: Baker Academic, 2003.

———. *Creation and Humanity: Constructive Christian Theology for the Pluralistic World: vol. 3.* Grand Rapids, MI: Eerdmans, 2015.

———. *Holy Spirit and Salvation: The Sources of Christian Theology.* Louisville, KY: Westminster John Knox, 2010.

———. *Hope and Community: Constructive Christian Theology for the Pluralistic World: vol. 5.* Grand Rapids, MI: Eerdmans, 2017.

———. *Pneumatology: The Holy Spirit in Ecumenical, International, and Contextual Perspective.* Grand Rapids: Baker, 2002.

———. *Trinity and Religious Pluralism: The Doctrine of the Trinity in Christian Theology of Religions.* Burlington, VT: Ashgate, 2004.

———. *Trinity and Revelation: Constructive Christian Theology for the Pluralistic World: vol. 2.* Grand Rapids, MI: Eerdmans, 2014.

———. *Spirit and Salvation: Constructive Christian Theology for the Pluralistic World: vol. 4.* Grand Rapids, MI: Eerdmans, 2016.

Keener, Craig S. *Spirit Hermeneutics: Reading Scripture in Light of Pentecost.* Grand Rapids, MI: Eerdmans, 2016.

Knight, Henry H. III. *Anticipating Heaven Below: Optimism of Grace from Wesley to the Pentecostals.* Eugene, OR: Cascade, 2014.

———. "God's Faithfulness and God's Freedom: A Comparison of Contemporary Theologies of Healing." *Journal of Pentecostal Theology* 1:2 (1993) 65–89.

———. *John Wesley: Optimist of Grace.* Eugene, OR: Cascade, 2018.

Kauflin, Bob and Paul Baloche. *Worship Matters: Leading Others to Encounter the Greatness of God.* Wheaton, IL: Sovereign Grace/Crossway, 2008.

Kraft, Charles H. "Spiritual Warfare: A Neocharismatic Perspective." In *New International Dictionary of Pentecostal and Charismatic Movements*, 1091–96. Stanley M. Burgess, ed., Eduard M. Van Der Maas, assoc. ed. Grand Rapids: Zondervan, 2002.

Kuhlin, Julia. "'I Do Not Think I Could be a Christian on My Own': Lived Religion Among Swedish Pentecostal Women." *Pneuma* 39:4 (2017) 482–503.

Kydd, Ronald A.N. "Healing in the Christian Church." In *New International Dictionary of Pentecostal and Charismatic Movements*, 698–711. Stanley M. Burgess, ed., Eduard M. Van Der Maas, assoc. ed. Grand Rapids: Zondervan, 2002.

Land, Steven J. "The Nature and Evidence of Spiritual Fullness." In *Endued with Power: The Holy Spirit in the Church,* 55-82. Robert White, ed. Cleveland, TN: Pathway, 1995.

———. *Pentecostal Spirituality: A Passion for the Kingdom.* Cleveland, TN: CPT edition, 2010.

———. "Pentecostal Spirituality." *Christian Spirituality: Post-Reformation and Modern: Volume 18, World Spirituality: An Encyclopedic History of the Religious Quest,* 479-99. Louis Dupré and Don E. Salier with John Meyendorff, eds. New York: Crossroad, 1989.

Lange, John Peter, et al., *A Commentary on the Holy Scriptures: Psalms.* Bellingham, WA: Logos Bible Software, 2008.

Lawson, John. *Comprehensive Handbook of Christian Doctrine.* Englewood Cliffs, NJ: Prentice-Hall, 1967.

Lewis, C. S. *Letters to Malcolm: Chiefly on Prayer.* New York: Harvest, 1992 reprint of 1963 original.

———. *Miracles.* San Francisco, CA: HarperCollins, 1996 reprint of 1947 original.

Lewis, Sinclair. *Elmer Gantry.* New York: Harcourt, 1927.

Lombard, John A. Jr. and Jerald J. Daffe. *Spiritual Gifts: For Today? For Me?* Cleveland, TN: Pathway, 2008.

Lovett, Leonard. "Black Holiness Pentecostalism." In *New International Dictionary of Pentecostal and Charismatic Movements,* 419-28. Stanley M. Burgess, ed., Eduard M. Van Der Maas, assoc. ed. Grand Rapids: Zondervan, 2002.

———. "Black Theology." In *New International Dictionary of Pentecostal and Charismatic Movements,* 428-31. Stanley M. Burgess, ed., Eduard M. Van Der Maas, assoc. ed. Grand Rapids: Zondervan, 2002.

Ma Julie C. and Wonsuk Ma. *Mission in the Spirit: Towards a Pentecostal/Charismatic Missiology, Regnum Studies in Christian Mission.* Eugene, OR: Wipf & Stock, 2010.

Macchia, Frank D. *Baptized in the Spirit: A Global Pentecostal Theology.* Grand Rapids: Zondervan, 2006.

———. *Justified in the Spirit: Creation, Redemption, and the Triune God, Pentecostal Manifestos.* Grand Rapids: Eerdmans, 2010.

———. "Theology, Pentecostal." In *New International Dictionary of Pentecostal and Charismatic Movements,* 1120-40. Stanley M. Burgess, ed., Eduard M. Van Der Maas, assoc. ed. Grand Rapids: Zondervan, 2002.

MacGregor, Kirk R. *Contemporary Theology: An Introduction: Classical, Evangelical, Philosophical & Global Perspectives.* Grand Rapids: Zondervan, 2019.

Marshall, I. Howard. *New Testament Theology: Many Witnesses, One Gospel.* Downers Grove, IL: InterVarsity, 2004.

Martin, Lee Roy. *Biblical Hermeneutics: Essential Keys for Interpreting the Bible.* Miami, FL: Senda De Vida, 2011.

———. *Fasting: A Centre for Pentecostal Theology Short Introduction.* Cleveland, TN: CPT, 2014.

———. *Pentecostal Hermeneutics: A Reader.* Boston: Brill, 2013.

———. "The Uniqueness of Spirit-Filled Preaching." In *Spirit-Filled Preaching for the 21st Century,* 199-212. Mark L. Williams and Lee Roy Martin, eds. Cleveland, TN: Pathway, 2013.

———. *Spirit-Filled Worship.* Miami, FL: Senda de Vida, 2017.

——— ed. *Toward a Pentecostal Theology of Worship.* Cleveland, TN: CPT, 2016.

Maslow, Abraham. *Religions, Values, and Peak-Experiences.* Columbus, OH: Ohio State University Press, 1964.

Bibliography

Matthews, K. A. *Genesis 11:27–50:26: The New American Commentary, Vol. 1B*. Gen. ed. E. Ray Clendenen. Nashville: Broadman & Holman, 2005.

McAllister, Anita Bernadette. *The Musical Legacy of Dorothy Love Coates: African American Female Gospel Sing with Implications for Education and Theater Education*. Manhattan, KS: Kansas State University, 1995.

McClung, L. Grant. Jr. "Exorcism." In *New International Dictionary of Pentecostal and Charismatic Movements*, 624–28. Stanley M. Burgess, ed., Eduard M. Van Der Maas, assoc. ed. Grand Rapids: Zondervan, 2002.

McClymond, Michael J. "Spirit Baptism as a Moral Source in a Secular Age." *Pneuma* 40:1–2 (2018) 37–57.

McGee, Gary B. "Initial Evidence." In *New International Dictionary of Pentecostal and Charismatic Movements*, 684–91. Stanley M. Burgess, ed., Eduard M. VanDer Maas, assoc. ed. Grand Rapids: Zondervan, 2002.

McMahan, Oliver. *Deepening Commitments: Contemporary Applications of Biblical Commitments*. Cleveland, TN: Pathway, 2000.

Melick, Richard R. Jr. *Philippians, Colossians, Philemon* in *The New American Commentary, vol. 32*. Gen. ed. David S. Dockery. Nashville, TN: Broadman & Holman, 1991.

Menzies, Robert P. *Pentecost: This is Our Story*. Springfield, MO: Gospel, 2013.

———. *Speaking in Tongues: Jesus and the Apostolic Church as Models for the Church Today*. Cleveland, TN: CPT, 2016.

———. "Subsequence in the Pauline Epistles." *Pneuma* 39:3 (2017) 342–63.

Miller, Donald E. and Tetsunao Yamamori. *Global Pentecostalism: The New Face of Christian Social Engagement*. Berkley, CA: University of California Press, 2007.

Miller, John. *Is God a Trinity? 3rd ed.* Princeton, NJ: by author, 1922.

Miskov, Jennifer A. *Life on Wings: The Forgotten Life and Theology of Carrie Judd Montgomery (1858–1946)*. Cleveland, TN: CPT, 2012.

Mittelstadt, Martin William. *Reading Luke-Acts in the Pentecostal Tradition*. Cleveland, TN: CPT, 2010.

Moore, Beth. *Portraits of Devotion*. Nashville, TN: B & H, 1914.

Moore, Rickie D. "Canon and Charisma in the Book of Deuteronomy." In *Pentecostal Hermeneutics: A Reader*, 15–31. Lee Roy Martin, ed. Boston: Brill, 2013.

———. "Deuteronomy and the Fire of God: A Critical Charismatic Interpretation." In *Pentecostal Hermeneutics: A Reader*, 109–30. Lee Roy Martin, ed. Boston: Brill, 2013.

———. "A Pentecostal Approach to Scripture." In *Pentecostal Hermeneutics: A Reader*, 11–13. Lee Roy Martin, ed. Boston: Brill, 2013.

Morris, Leon. *The New International Commentary on the New Testament: The Gospel According to John*. Grand Rapids, MI: Eerdmans, 1971, reprinted 1987.

Morris, Russell A. "Divine Intimacy: Drawing Close to God through Prayer." *Church of God Evangel* (July 2015) 10–11.

———. We Need the Lord's Supper." *Church of God Evangel* 109:6 (June 2019) 26–27.

Munyon, Timothy. "The Creation of the Universe and Humankind." In *Systematic Theology: Revised Edition*, 215–53. Stanley M. Horton, ed. Springfield, MO: Gospel, 1994.

Muzorewa, Gwinyai H. *The Origins and Development of African Theology*. Eugene, OR: Wipf and Stock, 2000.

Neumann, Peter D. *Pentecostal Experience: An Ecumenical Encounter, Princeton Theological Monograph Series*. Eugene, OR: Pickwick, 2012.

Neve, Lloyd R. *The Spirit of God in the Old Testament, Centre for Pentecostal Theology Classics Series*. Cleveland, TN: CPT, 2011.

Neville, Robert Cummings. *A Theology Primer*. Albany, NY: State University of New York Press, 1991.

Newbigin, Lesslie. *The Gospel in a Pluralist Society*. Grand Rapids: Eerdmans, 1989.

Nichol, John Thomas. *The Pentecostals*. Plainfield, NJ: Logos, revised ed. 1971.

O' Brien, Peter T. *The Letter to the Ephesians*. In *The Pillar New Testament Commentary*. Gen. ed. D. A. Carson. Grand Rapids, MI: Eerdmans, 1999.

Oden, Thomas C. gen. ed. and Francis Martin, ed. *Ancient Christian Commentary on Scripture: New Testament V: Acts*. Downers Grove, IL: InterVarsity, 2006.

——— and Gerald Bray, ed. *Ancient Christian Commentary on Scripture: New Testament: VII: 1–2 Corinthians*. Downers Grove, IL: InterVarsity, 1999.

———gen. ed., and Mark J. Edwards, ed., *Ancient Christian Commentary on Scripture: New Testament: VIII: Galatians, Ephesians, Philippians*. Downers Grove, IL: InterVarsity, 1999.

——— and Gerald Bray, ed. *Ancient Christian Commentary on Scripture: New Testament: James, 1–2 Peter, 1–3 John, Jude*. Downers Grove, IL: InterVarsity, 2000.

——— and gen. ed. and Gerald Bray, ed. *Ancient Christian Commentary on Scripture: New Testament: VI: Romans*. Downers Grove, IL: InterVarsity, 1998.

———. *John Wesley's Scriptural Christianity: A Plain Exposition of His teaching on Christian Doctrine*. Grand Rapids, MI: Zondervan, 1994.

———. *Life in the Spirit: Systematic Theology: Volume Three*. Peabody, MA: Hendrickson, 1992, 2001.

———. *The Living God: Systematic Theology: Volume One*. Peabody, MA: Hendrickson, 1987, 2001.

———. *Pastoral Theology: Essentials of Ministry*. New York, NY: HarperCollins, 1983.

———. *Word of Life: Systematic Theology: Volume Two*. Peabody, MA: Hendrickson, 1989, 2001.

Oliverio, William L. *Theological Hermeneutics in the Classical Pentecostal Tradition: A Typological Account (Global Pentecostal and Charismatic Studies)*. Boston: Brill, 2014.

Onyinah, Opoku. "Pentecostal Healing Communities." In *Towards a Pentecostal Ecclesiology: The Church and the Fivefold Gospel*, 207–24. John Christopher Thomas, ed. Cleveland, TN: CPT, 2010.

———. *Spiritual Warfare: A Centre for Pentecostal Theology Short Introduction*. Cleveland, TN: CPT, 2012.

Palma, Anthony. "First Corinthians." In *Full Life Bible Commentary to the New Testament: An International Commentary for Spirit-Filled Christians*, 799–913. French L. Arrington & Roger Stronstad, eds. Grand Rapids, MI: Zondervan, 1999.

Pannenberg, Wolfhart. *Christian Spirituality*. Philadelphia, PA: Westminster, 1983.

———. *An Introduction to Systematic Theology*. Grand Rapids, MI: Eerdmans, 1991, reprint 1992.

———. *Jesus—God and Man, second edition*. Philadelphia, PA: Westminster 1968, 1977.

Parker, Christian. "Popular Religion." In *Global Dictionary of Theology*, 679–83. William A. Dryness and Veli-Matti Kärkkäinen, eds., Juan Francisco Martinez and Simon Chan, assoc. eds. Downers Grove, IL: IVP Academic 2008.

Patterson, John. *The Real Truth about Baptism in Jesus' Name*. Hazelwood, MO: Pentecostal, 1953.

Pearlman, Myer. *Knowing the Doctrines of the Bible*. Springfield, MO: Gospel, 1937, 5th ed. 1992.

Pecota, Daniel B. "The Saving Work of Christ." In *Systematic Theology: Revised Edition*, 325–74. Stanley M. Horton, ed. Springfield, MO: Gospel, 1994.

Peterson, David G. *The Acts of the Apostles*. Grand Rapids, MI: William B. Eerdmans, 2009.

Pinnock, Clark H. *Flame of Love: A Theology of the Holy Spirit*. Downers Grove, IL: InterVarsity, 1994.

———. "A Pilgrim on the Way." *Christianity Today* 42:2 (Feb 9, 1998). http://www.christianity today.com/ct/1998/february9/8t2043.html.

Polhill, John B. *Acts: The New American Commentary, Vol. 26*. Gen. ed. David S. Dockery (Nashville: Broadman & Holman, 1992.

Pope, Robert P. "Why the Church Needs a Full Gospel: A Review and Reaction to Pentecostal Ecclesiology." In *Towards a Pentecostal Ecclesiology: The Church and the Fivefold Gospel*, 272–84. John Christopher Thomas, ed. Cleveland, TN: CPT, 2010.

Reed, David A. *"In Jesus' Name': The History and Beliefs of Oneness Pentecostals (JSup 31)*. eds. John Christopher Thomas, Rickie Moore, Steven J. Land. UK: Deo, 2008.

———. "Oneness Pentecostalism." In *New International Dictionary of Pentecostal and Charismatic Movements*, 936–44. Stanley M. Burgess and Eduard M. Van Der Maas, eds. Grand Rapids: Zondervan, 2002.

North, C. R. "Sacrifice" In *A Theological Wordbook of the Bible*, 206–14. Alan Richardson, ed. New York: MacMillan, 1950, 1962.

Powell, Timothy. "Anointing with Oil." In *New International Dictionary of Pentecostal and Charismatic Movements*, 318. Stanley M. Burgess, ed., Eduard M. Van Der Maas, assoc. ed. Grand Rapids: Zondervan, 2002.

Rabey, Steve. *Revival in Brownsville: Pensacola, Pentecostalism, and the Power of American Revivalism*. Nashville, TN: Thomas Nelson, 1998.

Richie, Tony. "An Affirmative Pentecostal Theology of the Miraculous." *The Pneuma Review* (Spring 2015). http://pneumareview.com/an-affirmative-pentecostal-theology-of-the-miraculous/.

———. "Approaching the Problem of Religious Truth in a Pluralistic World: A Pentecostal-Charismatic Contribution." *Journal of Ecumenical Studies* 43:3 (Summer, 2008) 351–69.

———. "The Church of God Today: Part of the Body of Christ with Much to Learn but a Lot to Offer." *Engage Journal* 10:1 (Winter 2014) 29–31. http://www.cogengage.org/.

———. *Pentecostal Theology and Ecumenical Theology: Interpretations and Intersections* ed. Peter Hocken, Tony Richie, and Christopher A. Stephenson (Leiden, Netherlands: Brill, forthcoming 2019).

———. "Demonization, Discernment, and Deliverance in Interreligious Encounter,"*Loosing the Spirits: Interdisciplinary and Interreligio-cultural Mappings of a Spirit-Filled World*, eds. Veli-Matti Kärkkäinen, Kirsteen Kim, and Amos Yong (New York: Palgrave MacMillan, 2013) 171–84.

———. Review of *Strangers to Fire: When Tradition Trumps Scripture*, Robert W. Graves, ed. (Woodstock, GA; The Foundation for Pentecostal Scholarship, 2014), *The Pneuma Review* (Dec 2014). http://pneumareview.com/strangers-to-fire-when-tradition-trumps-scripture-reviewed-by-tony-richie/.

———. "From Suspicion to Synthesis: Toward a Shared Wesleyan and Pentecostal Theology of Spirituality," *The Continuing Relevance of Wesleyan Theology: Essays in Honor of Larry Wood*, ed. Nathan Crawford (Eugene, OR: Wipf & Stock, 2011) 252–68.

———. "The Grand Design of God in All Divine Operations: Jonathan Edwards' Distinctive Contribution to the Positive Significance of Non-Christian Religions," *From Northampton to Azusa: Pentecostals and the Theology of Jonathan Edwards,* eds. Amos Yong and Steven Studebaker (Bloomington, IN: Indiana University Press, forthcoming, 2019).

———. "Is Pentecostalism Dispensationalist? An Honest Answer to a Hard Question." (March 2007). http://www.christianzionism.org/articles/RichieT01.pdf.

———. "The Manifestation of the Spirit: Spiritual Gifts as the Continuation of the Theophanic Tradition in Contemporary Christianity." Unpublished paper presented to the 23rd Annual Meeting of the Society for Pentecostal Studies. Guadalajara, Mexico (Nov 11–13, 1993) 1–15.

——— and Randy Howard. *Pentecostal Explorations of Holiness Today: Words from Wesley.* Cleveland, TN: CPT, 2017.

———. "Pentecostalism's Wesleyan Roots and Fruits." *Seedbed* (March 14, 2014). http://seedbed.com/feed/pentecostalisms-wesleyan-roots-fruit/.

———. "Grundzüge der Pfingsttheologie. Einn ewiger und unveränderlicher Herr—machtvol gegenwärttig und wirkend durch den Heiligen Geust, from *Pentekostalismus: Pfingstkirchen als herausforderung in der* Ökumene, eds. Klaus Krämer and Klaus Vellguth. (Freiburg, Germany: Herder, 2019) 101–112.

———. Review of Frank D. Macchia, *Baptized in the Spirit: A Global Pentecostal Theology.* Grand Rapids: Zondervan, 2006. In *The Pneuma Review* (Dec 10, 2016). http://pneumareview.com/frank-macchia-baptized-in-the-spirit/.

———. *Speaking by the Spirit: A Pentecostal Model for Interreligious Dialogue,* Asbury Theological Seminary Series in World Christian Revitalization Movements. Gen ed., J. Stephen O'Malley, Pentecostal/charismatic Studies, William F. Faupel, ed. Lexington, KY: Emeth, 2011.

———. "Spiritual Transformation through Pentecostal Testimony." In *Knowing God in the Ordinary Practices of the Christian Life.* Eds., David Sang-Ehil Han and Jackie David Johns. Cleveland, TN: CPT, forthcoming.

———. *Toward a Pentecostal Theology of Religions: Encountering Cornelius Today.* Cleveland, TN: CPT, 2013.

———. "Transposition and Tongues: Pentecostalizing an Important Insight of C. S. Lewis." *Journal of Pentecostal Theology* 13:1 (October 2004) 117–37.

Richey, Russell E., ed. *Denominationalism.* Eugene, OR: Wipf and Stock, 1977.

Ricoeur, Paul. *Oneself as Another.* Translated by Kathleen Blamey. Chicago, IL: University of Chicago Press, 1992, 1994.

Riggs, Ralph M. *The Spirit Himself.* Springfield, MO: Gospel, 1949, 1977.

Riss, R. M. "Finished Work Controversy." In *New International Dictionary of Pentecostal and Charismatic Movements,* 638–39. Stanley M. Burgess, ed., Eduard M. Van Der Maas, assoc. ed. Grand Rapids: Zondervan, 2002.

Robeck, Cecil M. Jr. *Azusa Street Mission & Revival: The Birth of the Global Pentecostal Movement.* Nashville, TN: Thomas Nelson, 2006.

———. "Farrow, Lucy F." In *New International Dictionary of Pentecostal and Charismatic Movements,* 632–33. Stanley M. Burgess, ed., Eduard M. Van Der Maas, assoc. ed. Grand Rapids: Zondervan, 2002.

———. "McPhearson, Aimee Semple." In *New International Dictionary of Pentecostal and Charismatic Movements,* 856–59. Stanley M. Burgess, ed., Eduard M. Van Der Maas, assoc. ed. Grand Rapids: Zondervan, 2002.

———. "Pentecostals and the Apostolic Faith: Implications for Ecumenism." *Pneuma* 9:1 (Fall 1986) 61–84.

———. "Pentecostals and Christian Unity: Facing the Challenge." *Pneuma* 26:2 (2004) 307–38.

Roberts, Philemon. *Divine Healing*. Cleveland, TN: Daniels, 1982.

———. *God's Will for God's People*. Cleveland, TN: Pathway, 1958.

Roebuck, David G. "Loose the Women." In *Christian History: The Rise of Pentecostalism* 58:17:2 (1998) 38–39.

Saarinen, R. "Ecumenism." In *Global Dictionary of Theology*, 263–69. William A. Dryness and Veli-Matti Kärkkäinen, eds., Juan Francisco Martinez and Simon Chan, assoc. eds. Downers Grove, IL: IVP Academic 2008.

Schatzline, Pat and Karen. "Rebuilding the Altar in Your Home." *Church of God Evangel* 108:2 (Feb 2018) 21–23.

Shaw, R. Daniel. "Folk Religion." In *Global Dictionary of Theology*, 326–28. William A. Dryness and Veli-Matti Kärkkäinen, eds., Juan Francisco Martinez and Simon Chan, assoc. eds. Downers Grove, IL: IVP Academic 2008.

Sheldrake, Philip. "Journey, Spiritual." In *The New Westminster Dictionary of Christian Spirituality*, 388–90. Philip Sheldrake, ed. Louisville, KY: John Knox, 2005.

Shelton, James B. "Matthew." In *Full Life Bible Commentary to the New Testament: An International Commentary for Spirit-Filled Christians*, 119–53. French L. Arrington & Roger Stronstad, 119–53. Grand Rapids, MI: Zondervan, 1999.

Shepperd, J. W. "Worship." In *New International Dictionary of Pentecostal and Charismatic Movements*, 1217–20. Stanley M. Burgess, ed., Eduard M. Van Der Maas, assoc. ed. Grand Rapids: Zondervan, 2002.

Simmonds, Gemma. "Formations, Spiritual." In *The New Westminster Dictionary of Christian Spirituality*, 309–10. Philip Sheldrake, ed. Louisville, KY: John Knox, 2005.

Sims, John A. *Our Pentecostal Heritage: Reclaiming the Priority of the Holy Spirit*. Cleveland, TN: Pathway, 1995.

Small, Franklin. *Living Waters—A Sure Guide for Your Faith*. Winnipeg, Canada: Columbia, n. d.

Small, P. Douglas. *Transforming Your Church into a House of Prayer*. Cleveland, TN: Pathway, 2006.

Smith, Calvin L. *Pentecostal Power: Expressions, Impact and Faith of Latin American Pentecostalism (Global Pentecostal and Charismatic Studies)*. Boston: Brill 2001.

Smith, Gordon T. *Evangelical, Sacramental, & Pentecostal: Why the Church Should be All Three*. Downers Grove, IL: IVP Academic, 2017.

Smith, James K. A. *Thinking in Tongues: Pentecostal Contributions to Christian Philosophy*. Grand Rapids, MI: Eerdmans, 2010.

———. *Who's Afraid of Relativism: Community, Contingency, and Creaturehood (The Church and Postmodern Culture)*. Grand Rapids, MI: Baker Academic, 2014.

Howard A. Snyder, "Wesleyanism, Wesleyan Theology." In *Global Dictionary of Theology*, 929–36. William A. Dryness and Veli-Matti Kärkkäinen eds., Juan Francisco Martinez and Simon Chan, assoc. eds. Downers Grove, IL: IVP Academic 2008.

Solivan, Samuel. *The Spirit, Pathos and Liberation: Toward an Hispanic Pentecostal Theology*. Sheffield, England: Sheffield Academic, 1998.

Sorge, Bob. *Exploring Worship: A Practical Guide to Praise and Worship*. Foreword by Judson Cornwall. Grandview, MO: Oasis House, 1987.

Bibliography

Spittler, Russell P. "Maintaining Distinctives: The Future of Pentecostalism." In *Pentecostals from the Inside Out (Christianity Today Series)*, 121–34. Harold Smith, ed. Wheaton, IL: Victory, 1990.

———. "Robeck, Cecil Melvin, Jr." In *New International Dictionary of Pentecostal and Charismatic Movements*, 1023–24. Stanley M. Burgess, ed., Eduard M. Van Der Maas, assoc. ed. Grand Rapids: Zondervan, 2002.

Sproul, R. C. *The Mystery of the Holy Spirit.* Wheaton, IL: Tyndale House, 1990.

Stamm, M. W. and C. M. Hawn. "Liturgy and Worship." In *Global Dictionary of Theology*, 492–500. William A. Dryness and Veli-Matti Kärkkäinen eds., Juan Francisco Martinez and Simon Chan, assoc. eds. Downers Grove, IL: IVP Academic 2008.

Stamps, Donald C. gen. ed., J. and Wesley Adams, assoc. ed. *The Full Life Study Bible.* Grand Rapids, MI: Zondervan, 1992.

Stein, Robert H. *Luke: The New American Commentary, Vol. 24.* David S. Dockery, gen. ed. Nashville: Broadman & Holman, 1992.

Stephenson, Christopher A. *Types of Pentecostal Theology: Method, System, Spirit.* New York: Oxford University, 2013.

Stephenson, Lisa P. *Dismantling the Dualisms for American Pentecostal Women in Ministry (Global Pentecostal Charismatic Series).* Boston: Brill, 2011.

Stewart, Adam, Andrew K. Garbiel, and Kevin Shanahan. "Changing Clergy Belief and Practice in Canada's Largest Pentecostal Denomination." *Pneuma* 39:4 (2017) 457–81.

Strang, Stephen. "Nondenominational Pentecostal and Charismatic Churches." In *New International Dictionary of Pentecostal and Charismatic Movements*, 932–35. Stanley M. Burgess, Eduard M. Van Der Maas, assoc. ed. Grand Rapids: Zondervan, 2002.

Stronstad, Roger. *The Charismatic Theology of St. Luke: Trajectories from the Old Testament to Luke-Acts.* Grand Rapids, MI: Baker, 1984, 2012.

Studebaker, Steven M. *From Pentecost to the Triune God: A Pentecostal Trinitarian Theology, Pentecostal Manifesto Series.* James K. A. Smith and Amos Yong, eds. Grand Rapids, MI: Eerdmans, 2012.

Synan, H. Vinson. *The Century of the Holy Spirit: 100 Years of Pentecostal and Charismatic Renewal, 1901–2001.* Nashville, TN: Thomas Nelson, 2001.

———. "Classical Pentecostalism." In *New International Dictionary of Pentecostal and Charismatic Movements*, 552–55. Stanley M. Burgess, ed., Eduard M. Van Der Maas, assoc. ed. Grand Rapids: Zondervan, 2002.

———. "Evangelicalism." In *New International Dictionary of Pentecostal and Charismatic Movements*, 613–16. Stanley M. Burgess and Eduard M. Van Der Maas, eds. Grand Rapids: Zondervan, 2002.

———. *The Holiness-Pentecostal Movement in the United States.* Grand Rapids, MI: Eerdmans, 1997.

———. "Irwin, Benjamin Hardin." In *New International Dictionary of Pentecostal and Charismatic Movements*, 804–05. Stanley M. Burgess and Eduard M. Van Der Maas, eds. GrandRapids: Zondervan, 2002.

———. "Streams of Renewal at the End of the Century." In *The Century of the Holy Spirit: 100 Years of Pentecostal and Charismatic Renewal, 1901–2001*, 349–80. Synan, H. Vinson, ed. Nashville, TN: Thomas Nelson, 2001.

Theron, Jacques P. J. "Towards a Practical Theological Theory for the Healing Ministry in Pentecostal Churches." *Journal of Pentecostal Theology* 4 (1999) 49–64.

BIBLIOGRAPHY

Thomas, John Christopher. "According to John: Christology and the Great Commission." In *The Great Commission: The Solution. . .*, 53–76. Raymond F. Culpepper, ed. Cleveland, TN: Pathway, 2009.

———. *The Apocalypse: A Literary and Theological Commentary*. Cleveland, TN: CPT, 2012.

———. "Pentecostal Theology in the Twenty-First Century." *Pneuma* 20:1 (1998) 3–19.

———. "The Spirit in the Fourth Gospel: Narrative Explorations." In *The Spirit and the Mind: Essays in Informed Pentecostalism*, 157–74. Terry L. Cross and Emerson B. Powery, gen. eds. Lanham: University Press of America, 2000.

———. "Toward a Pentecostal Theology of Anointed Cloths." *Toward a Pentecostal Theology of Worship*, 89–112. Lee Roy Martin, ed. Cleveland, TN: CPT, 2016.

Thomson, James G. S. S. "Prayer." In *Baker's Dictionary of Theology*, 412–14. Everett F. Harrison, Geoffry W. Bromiley, Carl F. H. Henry. eds. Grand Rapids, MI: Baker, 1960, 1987.

Thorsen, Donald T. *The Wesleyan Quadrilateral: Scripture, Tradition, Reason, & Experience as a Model for Evangelical Theology*. Grand Rapids, MI: Zondervan, 1990.

Tomberlin, Daniel. *Pentecostal Sacraments: Encountering God at the Altar*. Cleveland, TN: Center for Pentecostal Leadership and Care, Pentecostal Theological Seminary, 2010.

Tomlinson, A. J. *The Last Great Conflict*. Cleveland, TN: White Wing, 1984.

Toon, Peter. "Fellowship." In *Evangelical Dictionary of Biblical Theology*, 255–56. Walter A. Elwell, ed. Grand Rapids, MI: Baker, 1996.

Tucker, Karen B. Westerfield. "North America." In *The Oxford History of Christian Worship*, 586–632. Geoffrey Wainwright and Karen B. Westerfield Tucker, eds. Oxford, UK/New York, NY: Oxford University Press 2006.

Turner, William C., Jr. *The United Holy Church of America: A Study in Black Holiness-Pentecostalism*. Piscataway, NJ: Gorgias, 2006.

Tyler, Peter. "Triple Way." In *The New Westminster Dictionary of Christian Spirituality*, 626–27. Philip Sheldrake, ed. Louisville, KY: John Knox, 2005.

Ulanov, Ann Belford. "Prayer, Psychology of." In *The New Westminster Dictionary of Christian Spirituality*, 506–07. Philip Sheldrake, ed. Louisville, KY: John Knox, 2005.

Urshan, Andrew D. *Almighty God in the Lord Jesus Christ*. Los Angeles, CA: by author, reprint 1919.

Van de Walle, Bernie A. *Rethinking Holiness: A Theological Introduction*. Grand Rapids, MI: Baker Academic, 2017.

Vest, Lamar. *Reflections on the Journey: Memoirs of Lamar Vest*. Cleveland, TN: PTS Press, 2018.

Villafañe, Eldin. *The Liberating Spirit: Toward an Hispanic-American Pentecostal Social Ethic*. Grand Rapids, MI: Eerdmans, 1993.

Vondey, Wolfgang. *Pentecostalism: A Guide for the Perplexed*. New York: Bloomsbury/T and T Clark, 2013.

———. *Pentecostal Theology: Living the Full Gospel, Systematic Pentecostal and Charismatic Theology Series*. Wolfgang Vondey and Daniela C. Augustine, eds. New York: Bloomsbury T&T Clark, 2017.

———. "Pure Gospel or Full Gospel: On the Principles of Lutheran and Pentecostal Theology." *Dialog: A Journal of Theology* 55:4 (Winter/December 2016) 324–33.

——— and Martin William Mittelstadt. *The Theology of Amos Yong and the New Face of Pentecostal Scholarship*. Boston: Brill, 2013.

Wacker, Grant. *Heaven Below: Early Pentecostals and American Culture*. London: Harvard University Press, 2001.

Waldvogel, Edith L. "The 'Overcoming Life': A Study in the Reformed Evangelical Contribution to Pentecostalism." *Pneuma* 1:1 (1979) 7–19.

Walker, Paul L. *The Ministry of Worship: An Exposition of Selected Psalms.* Cleveland, TN: Pathway, 1981.

Wallraff, Barbara. "Walking the Walk = Talking the Talk." *The Atlantic* (October 20, 2008). https://www.theatlantic.com/entertainment/archive/2008/10/walking-the-walk-talking-\the-talk/49609/.

Wariboko, Nimi and Amos Yong, eds. *Paul Tillich and Pentecostal Theology: Spiritual Presence & Spiritual Power.* Indianapolis, IN: University of Indiana Press, 2015.

Warrington, Keith. *Pentecostal Theology: A Theology of Encounter.* NY: T & T Clarke, 2008.

Weeks, Robert D. *Jehovah-Jesus—the Supreme God: Son of God, Son of Man,* ed. C. Haskell Yadon. Twin Falls, ID: by editor, 1952.

Weil, Simone. *Waiting for God.* New York: Harper & Row, 1973.

Welch, Kristen Dayle, *'Women with the Good News': The Rhetorical Heritage of Pentecostal Holiness Women Preachers.* Cleveland, TN: CPT, 2010.

Wesley, John. Complete Works of John Wesley. Rio, WI: Ages Software, Inc, 2202.

White, James F. "The Spatial Setting." In *The Oxford History of Christian Worship,* 793–816. Geoffrey Wainwright and Karen B. Westerfield Tucker, eds. Oxford, UK/New York, NY: Oxford University Press 2006.

Wilbanks, Jessica. *When I Spoke in Tongues: A Story of Faith and Its Loss.* Boston, MA: Beacon, 2018.

Williams, J. Rodman. "Laying on of Hands." In *New International Dictionary of Pentecostal and Charismatic Movements,* 834–36. Stanley M. Burgess, ed., Eduard M. Van Der Maas, assoc. ed. Grand Rapids: Zondervan, 2002.

Williams, Mark L. "Spirit-filled Preaching is Relevant for the Twenty-First Century." In *Spirit-Filled Preaching for the 21st Century,* 9–21. Mark L. Williams and Lee Roy Martin, eds. Cleveland, TN: Pathway, 2013.

Wise, Tim. *White Like Me: Reflections on Race from a Privileged Son.* Berkeley, CA: Soft Skull, 2011.

Wood, Laurence W. "A Wesleyan Response." In *Christian Spirituality: Five Views of Sanctification,* 162–67. Donald L. Alexander, ed. Downers Grove, IL: InterVarsity, 1988.

Work, Telford. "Pentecostal and Charismatic Worship." In *The Oxford History of Christian Worship,* 574–85. Geoffrey Wainwright and Karen B. Westerfield Tucker, eds. New York, NY: Oxford University Press 2006.

Yong, Amos. *The Future of Evangelical Theology: Soundings from the Asian American Diaspora.* Downers Grove, IL: IVP, 2014.

———. *The Hermeneutical Spirit: Theological Interpretation and Scriptural Imagination for the 21st Century.* Eugene, OR: Cascade, 2017.

———. *The Spirit Poured Out on All Flesh: Pentecostalism and the Possibility of Global Theology.* Grand Rapids, MI: Baker Academic, 2005.

———. *Renewing Christian Theology: Systematics for a Global Christianity.* Waco, TX: Baylor University Press, 2014.

———. *Spirit, Word, Community: Theological Hermeneutics in Trinitarian Perspective.* Eugene, OR: Wipf and Stock, 2002.

Young, Warren, C. "Supernatural, Supernaturalism," In *Baker's Dictionary of Theology,* 507. Everett F. Harrison, Geoffry W. Bromiley, Carl F. H. Henry, eds. Grand Rapids, MI: Baker, 1960, 1987.